# The People's Poet
## WILLIAM BARNES OF DORSET

It would be a great blessing if some genius would arise who had a talent of writing for the poor. He would be of more value than many poets living upon the banks of lakes…

Sydney Smith

It is [Barnes's] naturalness that strikes me most; he is like an embodiment… of the country, of Dorset, of rustic life and humanity.

Gerard Manley Hopkins

To read [Barnes] is to enter a friendly cottage where a family party is in full swing. One misses many of the allusions, one is not connected to the party by blood, yet one has no sense of intrusion. The party, like all unsophisticated gatherings, welcomes the entire human race.

E.M. Forster

# The People's Poet

## WILLIAM BARNES OF DORSET

ALAN CHEDZOY

*For Peter Day, in gratitude.*

BY THE SAME AUTHOR

Biography:
*William Barnes: A Life of the Dorset Poet*
*A Scandalous Woman: The Story of Caroline Norton*
*Sheridan's Nightingale: The Story of Elizabeth Linley*
*Seaside Sovereign: George III at Weymouth*
*Early Years* by Robert Young (Ed.)

Poetry:
*William Barnes: Poems Grave and Gay* (Ed.)

Language:
*A Bit of a Bumble: An Affectionate Look at the Dorset Dialect*

First published 2010

The History Press
The Mill, Brimscombe Port
Stroud, Gloucestershire, GL5 2QG
www.thehistorypress.co.uk

© Alan Chedzoy, 2010

The right of Alan Chedzoy to be identified as the Author
of this work has been asserted in accordance with the
Copyrights, Designs and Patents Act 1988.

British Library Cataloguing in Publication Data.
A catalogue record for this book is available from the British Library.

ISBN 978 0 7524 5538 9

Typesetting and origination by The History Press
Printed in Great Britain
Manufacturing managed by Jellyfish Print Solutions Ltd

# CONTENTS

# ACKNOWLEDGEMENTS

Literary research is a cooperative endeavour, and this book owes a great deal to the labours of others. It is over twenty years since the publication of my *William Barnes: A Life of the Dorset Poet*, and since that time there have appeared several important contributions to the study of the man and his achievements. Richard Bradbury's six-volume edition of the collected prose, in which he describes Barnes as 'this scandalously neglected voice of Dorset', has proved most helpful, as has Douglas Ashdown's recently published research into the Barnes family. Other new studies have considered Barnes's methods of poetic composition, his literary friendships, his sermons, his contribution to working-class education and even his favourite flowers.

As for the poems, in 1987 Christopher Ricks significantly re-evaluated them by including no fewer than twenty-three in his *New Oxford Book of Victorian Verse*, and since that time Andrew Motion has brought out two new anthologies of his poems within the space of a few years. The work goes on. Even as I write these acknowledgements, the post has delivered a new edition of Barnes's dialect version of a biblical text and, from Australia, the first draft of a comprehensive pronunciation guide to his poems. Such fresh interest calls for a new account of this extraordinarily original Victorian, whose art and teachings still offer significant challenges to the way we live now. This book, therefore, is not a reprint of my previous biography but an entirely new appraisal of the man and his work.

I would thank the following: the Trustees of the Dorset County Museum and the officers of the Sturminster Newton Museum Society, for permission to publish a number of illustrations.

Douglas Ashdown for advice on the Barnes family; Dr Frances Austin-Jones; Dr Katherine Barker for material on William Charles Macready at Sherborne; Richard Bradbury for his edition of collected prose; Dr Tom Burton of the University of Adelaide; Professor David Crystal for his advice on Barnes's philology; Warren Davis for permission to inspect the Old Rectory at Winterborne Came; the staff at the Dorset County Library; Professor Jean-Marc Gachelin of Rouen; Professor Robert Giddings for advice on Orwell and Wordsworth; Jonathan Harrison, Special Collections Librarian of St John's College, Cambridge; Andy Hutchings for his expert knowledge of the nineteenth-century railroads of Dorset; Helen Gibson for information on the Thomas Hardy collection at the DCM; Basil Greenslade and Dr Michael Irwin of the Thomas Hardy Society; Hugh Jacques, sometime County Archivist, Robin Ansell and their colleagues at the Dorset History Centre; Judy Lindsay, sometime Director of the DCM; Dr Jon Murden, the current Director of the DCM, and Dr Jenny Cripps, Curator; the staff of the London Library; Peter Loosmore and Steve Case of the Sturminster Newton Museum Society for advice on Robert Young; Professor Michael Millgate of Toronto for his knowledge of the movements of the young Thomas Hardy; Canon Hugh Mumford who has daringly embarked on a study of Barnes's sermons; Stephen Poulter for advice on Sir Frederick Treves; Dr C.S. Rodd for his unpublished edition of Barnes's *Song of Songs*; Furse Swann for information on the history of Cambridge University; Weymouth Library; the late Richard Wilding for his pamphlet on the Revd Osmond Fisher.

I have derived much pleasure, over many years, from conversations prompted by my readings of Barnes's poems in towns and villages throughout Dorset. Further stimulation has come from folk musicians, such as Bonny Sartin and the Yetties, and Tim Laycock of the New Scorpion Band, with their splendidly imaginative settings of the poems. Most especially, I remember with gratitude the late Fred Langford, sometime Editor of the *Dorset Yearbook*. Together with Douglas Ashdown and myself, Fred was a founder member of the William Barnes Society. Another great admirer of Barnes was our first President, the late Trevor Hearl, the most assiduous of all Barnes's biographers, whose splendid book on his career as a schoolmaster has proved invaluable to me. Whenever I telephoned Trevor to raise an obscure point about Barnes, he always seemed to know the answer. I have also profited greatly from discussions with members of the Society and thank: Alfred Barratt, Jill Bryant, Richard Burleigh, Brian Caddy and the late Tom Fox and his family of Oak Farm, Sturminster Newton, who taught me much about Barnes's early days.

In preparing the text for publication, I have been especially grateful to the following: Furse Swann for his meticulous proof-reading; Judith Stinton of the DCM for her knowledge of the Hardy and Barnes picture collections; George Wickham who has generously spent much time processing the illustrations; and my son, Robert, for technical advice.

What mistakes that appear here are entirely my own.

A.C.
*Weymouth, 2010*

# A NOTE ON THE TEXT

In early editions, some of William Barnes's dialect poems were published with an apparatus of textual markers ('diacritics') intended to indicate how certain words should be pronounced. Though a fervent admirer of Barnes, Sir Arthur Quiller-Couch advocated omitting such 'hieroglyphs', observing that, 'One should get rid of archaisms and superfluous difficulties, not add to them'. In his collected edition of the poems, Bernard Jones has left them out, and it his versions I chiefly quote here.

In the notes, therefore, to allow the reader easy access, I have referred to Jones as the source, but, so far as I have been able to trace them, I have also recorded the previously unpublished dates of the original printed versions, as they appeared in the *Dorset County Chronicle*. Often, however, there are differences between these earliest versions of the poems and the later ones as printed by Jones, because Barnes frequently revised his poems to move them more closely to standard English.

Furthermore, the date of the *Chronicle* publication does not necessarily indicate when the poem was written, because, as is explained here, after 1844 there was a gap of some twelve years in which Barnes published no dialect poems at all, though he must have been writing and storing them.

From his earliest days as a philologist, Barnes advocated the expulsion from the English language of foreign words, particularly those of Greek, Latin and French origin. Indeed, he took his Saxonising so far that the prose he wrote in later life was itself obscurely larded with Saxon expressions. For all that, he remained an early advocate of plain English. Consequently, in deference to his opinions, in writing this book I have tried to explain his often quite complex ideas in the simplest way possible. Nevertheless, he has often made me feel linguistically guilty, as at the present moment when, in looking this piece through, I find I have written the word 'deference'. Perhaps I should have said that I 'heeded' his views.

A.C.

# FORE-SAY

In the darkest time of the year, just four days after Christmas in 1869, an elderly woman sat down in a cheerless London basement to write a letter. She was a servant, one of over 1 million at that time, mostly women who had long ago left their homes in the country to work in great cities, drudging out their days in the service of others. Fatigued by the extra demands of the season, she now stole a few minutes of her employer's time to address a man who had given her a little solace amidst the bleakness of her life:

> Reverend Sir,
>
> I wish you most heartily a happy New Year, and hope you will excuse a poor Woman writing to you. I had to dust some Books the other day that came from a sale, and amongst them was your poems in the Dorset dialect. Sir, I shook hands with you in my heart, And I laughed and cried by turns. The old Home of my Youth and all my dear ones now mouldering in the earth came back to mind. How happy we used to be at Christmas time.
>
> And sometimes I sit down in the gloom of an underground London Kitchen and try to fancy I am on Beaminster Down, where I have spent many a happy hour years ago. But I try to think we must be content wherever the Lord has cast our lot, and not to hanker for the past. May God bless you and all yours, Is the true wish of an old Domestic Servant, who loves the very name of Dorsetshire. [1]

Eventually finding its way to an obscure hamlet outside Dorchester, her letter was dropped into a green postbox hanging within the verandah of a thatched cottage. It was the home of William Barnes.

Such expressions of love and reverence for him were not uncommon among working people. Few poets at any time could fill a hall as he did, with his neighbours, mostly work folk, coming to hear him read his verses. This was partly because in these poems they discerned an intimate knowledge of their own obscure lives. So it was with this old servant who, in turning his pages, would have glimpsed scenes of her own country Christmases past; of farm girls huddling and giggling their way across frozen bartons; of great backbrand branches dragged in to feed the fire; of neighbours round the hearth; of a grandmother shyly showing off her wedding shoes; of fiddle music and dancing; of games, jokes, forfeits and tale-telling; of old songs, and good healths pledged in ale and cider. And here too, she found an invitation to come home again:

## The Vrost

Come, run up hwome wi' us to-night,
Athirt the vield a -vroze so white,
Where vrosty sheades do lie below
The winter ricks a-tipped wi' snow,
An' lively birds, wi' waggen tails,
Do hop upon the icy rails,
An' rime do whiten all the tops
O' bush an' tree in hedge an' copse,
In winds a-cutten keen.
Come, maidens, come: the groun's a-vroze

Too hard to-night to spweil your clothes.
You got noo pools to waddle drough,
Nor clay a-pullen off your shoe:
An' we can trig ye at the zide,
To keep ye up if you do slide:
Zoo while there's neither wet nor mud,
'S the time to run an' warm your blood,
In winds a-cutten keen...[2]

('trig' – support you)

Especially comforting to many such as her was the language of the poems. This was because they were not written in the literary idiom that so delighted genteel readers, which common people found hard to understand, but in the homely talk of her own folk.

This led many urban readers, coming across his poems by chance, to suspect that they were probably the work of some 'peasant poet'; a ploughman, shepherd or carter perhaps. They were partly right. For Barnes was the child of a 'labourer in husbandry', and was rumoured to have started his working life collecting cow pats in a field.[3] But what might have surprised the curious was that the author of the *Poems of Rural Life* was no humble farmhand, but the Reverend William Barnes BD (Cantab), the Rector of Winterborne Came, and author of some forty books and pamphlets. Conscious of his elevated social status, the old servant's letter was, therefore, suitably deferential. Yet she had recognised certain signals in his use of dialect which gave her sufficient confidence to write to him. Despite his elevated social position, his dog collar and his book learning, she understood that they shared a culture which admitted of no class distinctions. She also sensed, correctly, that he was a man of great humanity and kindness of heart.

For three centuries after Shakespeare, the lives of the rural poor altered very little. Then came the 'Great Change'[4], brought about by agricultural collapse, proliferating enclosures, mechanisation and the coming of the railways. In the depression that followed the Napoleonic Wars, many small tenant farmers were evicted from their land and obliged to find work elsewhere. Within a few decades, the age-old culture of rural England, with its yearly round and folk traditions, was largely destroyed, and many members of the 'bold peasantry, their country's pride' were reduced to day labouring. Fortunately, William Barnes was at hand to record something of what had been lost. As Thomas Hardy wrote in 1886, he was 'probably the most interesting link between present and past forms of rural life that England possessed', becoming 'a complete repertory of forgotten manners, words, and sentiments' of the English rural community.[5]

Astonishingly, Barnes had made himself into a formidably philogical scholar, having taught himself to read over seventy languages. And it was this work that provided him with unexpected insights into the family speech that he had heard as a boy in the Blackmore Vale in north Dorset. From these studies, he now deduced that this same dialect had ancient origins and was probably the purest form of English. To say the least, this was an unorthodox conclusion. Until about the middle of the nineteenth century, the majority of working people were employed in agriculture and, like his parents, spoke regional dialects. Yet among many educated people at that time, such speech was despised. It was reckoned to be at best an unsuccessful attempt at standard English and at worst little better than the grunting of the beasts in the field. As for poetry, had not Matthew Arnold declared loftily that this was a matter of noble natures and a grand style? Little wonder then that the language of poetry was never that of the great mass of the English labouring class. Consequently, these people simply had no voice. Until William Barnes. Until he took their dialect, which hitherto had possessed no literature, and shaped it into art.

His story is an inspiring one. It tells of a luminous childhood, humble circumstances, early promise, courageous endeavour, profound learning, deep love, tragic loss, the threat of catastrophe, last minute rescue and contented neglect. Here are loyalty and aspiration, contempt and admiration, disappointment and achievement. And beneath it all flows the personality of a sweet-natured, modest genius.

A portrait of William Barnes by John Thorne, *c.* 1845. The book and scientific instruments signify that this schoolmaster is a man of learning. (Dorset County Museum)

Greeted with a patronising amusement by the middle-class readers of the provincial newspaper in which his poems first appeared, it took many years for their true worth to be understood, and many more until he was recognised to be 'an English classic'.[6] It is among other poets and writers that he has been most prized. Gerard Manley Hopkins understood him, Tennyson imitated him, Coventry Patmore praised him, William Allingham encouraged him, Francis Kilvert revered him and Thomas Hardy deferred to him. His more recent admirers have included Llewelyn Powys, E.M. Forster and Philip Larkin.

Separated from Victorian writers, as we now are by more than a century, it is at last becoming easier to determine which of them were truly great. Barnes was. Rising from provincial obscurity, he now emerges as a major figure, the only significant English poet to draw on the culture and language of thousands of the rural poor, a class of people otherwise neglected by the literary world. Because of this, his poems constitute an important contribution to the history of the English people. But this is not to say that their interest is merely antiquarian. Suffused by his own passionately held convictions, they continue to challenge our own contemporary assumptions. For us too, they pose the ultimate question of how to live.

Almost fifty poems are quoted here, whole or in part, so that readers new to Barnes may come to appreciate something of his appeal. He was a unique artist and a complete original. His achievement owed nothing to anybody else, though Thomas Hardy learned a great deal from him. When turning these pages, we may hear across the years faint voices from another, earlier land, which resonate beyond Dorset and even beyond England. Their talk goes out to those from all societies who sense their rural past, half recalling experiences buried deep in the folk memory. And here in these old poems they will glimpse once again scenes of haymakings, club walkings and apple-gatherings; of mowing, nutting, and evenings in the village. And here once more, those times come alive.

# 1

# GOING HOME:
# THE WAREHAM ROAD

## —— 1880s ——

One gloomy January afternoon, some sixteen years after the old servant had written her letter, two figures might have been observed trudging southwards out of Dorchester. They had come from the market, by way of High East Street and Fordington Green, where the tower of St George's stood out against the rain-swept sky. Here they took the Wareham Road and soon the Victorian villas fell behind them. Now they felt the full force of the weather. What few words they attempted to exchange were blown from their lips so they battled on silently, their heads bowed to the blast.[1]

The smaller of the two men was neatly bearded and fashionably dressed with a soberly cut coat and a hat, though this could not prevent the water trickling down his face. He was middle-aged, a one-time architectural assistant and now a successful novelist, come back to live in his home county after years of absence. About a mile out of the town, on the site of Mack's toll gate, stood his new house which was near completion. This was his destination. He was Thomas Hardy.[2]

The other man was much older, with a long white beard that emphasised his curiously outlandish appearance. For many years, William Barnes had paid a weekly visit to Dorchester market and he was now returning from one of these, with nothing better for protection than an antique hat and a piece of sacking over his shoulders. At a later time, Hardy wrote an affectionate memoir of his companion making just such a visit:

> Until within the last year or two there were few figures more familiar to the eye in the county town of Dorset on a market day than an aged clergyman, quaintly attired in caped cloak, knee-breeches, and buckled shoes, with a leather satchel slung over his shoulders, and a stout staff in his hand. He seemed unusually to prefer the middle of the street to the pavement, and to be thinking of matters which had nothing to do with the scene before him. He plodded along with a broad, firm tread, notwithstanding the slight stoop occasioned by his years. Every Saturday morning he might have been seen thus trudging up the narrow South Street, his shoes coated with mud or dust according to the state of the roads between his rural home and Dorchester, and a little grey dog at his heels, till he reached the four cross ways in the centre of the town. Halting here, opposite the public clock, he would pull his old-fashioned watch from its deep fob, and set it with great precision to London time. This, the invariable first act of his market visit, having been completed to his satisfaction, he turned round and methodically proceeded about his other business.[3]

Suddenly the weather got worse. Gusts of wind now blew more fiercely and the rain became incessant. There was no shelter. The road they had taken ran along the top of a ridge and there were few trees, only low hedges and a few bare thorns. Below, the fields dipped away. When the sleet and mist briefly cleared it was possible to glimpse a line of trees ahead, but these were too far off to be of immediate help. Fortunately, they were nearing the brick villa which was to be Hardy's new home. Work on it was not finished at this time, so the former field in which it stood was now a sea of mud, littered with tools, trenches, piles of bricks, upturned wheelbarrows and perhaps a workman's hut.

Barnes in old age, a
watercolour by John Leslie.
(Dorset County Museum)

Such rawness contrasted with the antiquity of the landscape around them, for the whole area was scattered with barrows and earthworks. Barnes was familiar with them all, for he had spent a lifetime learning the languages of the ancient peoples and excavating their burial sites. Farther back from the road lay the Romano-British cemetery on Fordington Hill, and 300yds to the east of Hardy's home stood the 'commanding tumulus called Conquer Barrow'.[4] By contrast, Max Gate was almost the last word in modernity, though still lacking bath facilities which the old Romans took for granted. Designed by Hardy himself, the builders were nominally his own father and brother, though the latter did most of the work. Here Hardy was later to plant thousands of Austrian pines for privacy and protection from the weather. Here too, beneath layers of mud and chalk, were found three Roman skeletons, folded for 1,500 years like little chickens into their egg-shaped graves.[5]

On coming to his gate, Hardy begged the old man to take shelter at his house but he only shook his head and went on alone. He had still half a mile to go to reach his home, the Rectory at Winterborne Came. There was a shorter route to it through the fields but because these were so wet, he kept to the road. There was no let up. Rain fell all over his little world; over Roman Dorchester and the village of Fordington; over the great hill fort of Maiden Castle, and over his son's rectory at Winterborne Monkton. His own parish church, and the little hamlet of Came, lay under a pall of cloud while water scudded in streams from the pilastered splendour of Came House, the home of his patron, Captain Dawson-Damer. Water deluged his little church at Whitcombe and laced across the ruined arch of his other 'church', standing in a field at Winterborne Farringdon. Farther off still, rain clouds loured over Came Wood and soused the tumuli on Bincombe Hill. Out in the Channel, drenched fishermen drew in their nets and turned their tossing boats towards Weymouth Harbour.

Completely drenched, the old man at last turned off the road into his own gate, which was always left unlatched. His little lawn had already been reduced to a swamp. As he crunched his way up the pebble path, conifers and pampas grass bowed their tops towards him under the force of the wind. Large drops fell from the manes of two stone lions, crouching 6ft apart on their plinths on either side of the path, their glistening heads turned to each other as if in eternal leonine conversation.

Beneath the cover of the verandah, he proceeded to stamp his boots and shake the water off. Anxious eyes were looking out for him. At his approach, the door was flung open and he was greeted by scolding, fussing women. Here was his spinster daughter, Laura Liebe, come to shush him in and help him off with his wet cape and shoes. Mary Cozzens, their cook, rushed off to fetch him hot tea, and pretty Rosanna Shepherd, the housemaid, settled him into his armchair in the dark little sitting room and pumped the bellows to get the fire roaring to warm his old legs.

It did no good. For many years he had tramped the roads of his parish in snow and rain, never minding the weather at all. His magnificent constitution had always pulled him through. But this time it was different. He soon found himself shivering and feverish. He was put to bed. The lamp was turned down.

His bedroom also served as his study. In summertime, he might look up from his desk to glance over his fruit garden, or inspect his apple and apricot trees, or watch the breezes waving the feathery heads of his asparagus. But this late winter afternoon, the room was dark. Behind his bedhead the wall was hung from ceiling to floor with a faded tapestry, while round the others ranged his books, his life's epitome. For this little room was his treasure-house; here were stored his grammars and glossaries, his dictionaries and lexicons. The mere sight of them set off half-forgotten phrases in his head, a silent chorus in the tongues of half mankind. Though his eyesight was weak and the room dark, even now from this bed he could still make out the spines of these old familiar friends. Though he could not read their titles by sight, he could still do so in memory. For many years past, even in his darkest days, these faded volumes had brought him company and comfort.

Warm and peaceful at last, he could hear the wind and rain beating on his window. Faint sounds came up from below: kitchen clatter, female voices, footsteps, doors opening and closing. Lying there, his thoughts ranged back over eighty years: to his children and grandchildren, some in Dorset and others far away in Florence; to his parishioners, working the fields of the Came estate; to a favourite pupil, whose face would float before him, though he might struggle to put a name to it. That boy was one of many now grown up and scattered all over the world. Then his thoughts drifted to St John's College, where Queen Victoria had once crossed the quadrangle in front of him. And long before that, to his impecunious clerking days in Dorchester with his friends, James Carey and Edward Fuller, and their studying together, their rowing parties, their jolly suppers and little concerts. Dorchester. The very name still had romance for him. It was there he had first glimpsed a youthful form stepping down from a coach at the King's Arms. That moment was followed by their long, long courtship and then their blissful years at Linden Lea. He remembered it still.

Most vivid of all were the recollections of his days as a boy, larking his summers away with Charlie Rabbets along the banks of the Stour. He could still glimpse them, even as he lay there dozing and dreaming.

Then he went to sleep.

# 2

# THE LITTLE ASTROLOGER OF BLACKMORE VALE

—— 1801-1818 ——

An exceptionally clever child born into the home of working people is at first an object of amusement and pride, but later one of embarrassment and increasing concern. For, as time goes by, a question presents itself ever more forcibly to his anxious parents: 'Yes, but how will he earn a living?'

This was the situation when the young William Barnes was living at home in a farm worker's cottage and scribbling little verses to amuse his brothers and sister. His hobby provoked a deal of good-humoured derision from the neighbours:

> To meake up rhymes, my mind wer zoo a-fire
> 'Twer idle work to try to keep me quiet,
> O' meaken rhymes my heart did never tire;
> Though I should never be a gainer by it.
> 'You meake up rhyme!' vo'k said, 'why who would buy it?
> Could you write fine enough to please a squire?
> An' rhyme's what plain vo'k woudden much require;
> You'd vind your rhymes would earn but scanty diet,
> An' if I'd any cure vor it, I'm sure I'd try it'.[1]

His parents were quick to reinforce the message. What was the use of their son daydreaming about becoming a writer? Poetry, to their minds, was an esoteric affair, somehow connected with Latin and learning and other mysteries far beyond the reach of a mere farm boy. Besides, there was no future in it. Though living far from the literary world, even John and Grace Barnes had heard about famous poets almost starving to death in a place named Grub Street:

> An' father too, in learnen noo great crammer,
> Zaid rhymen were a treade but few got fat in:
> That men wi' neames a-ringen wi' a clamour
> Did live in holes not fit to put a cat in,
> An' sleep on locks o' straw, or bits o' matten;
> An' mother zaid she'd sooner hear me stammer
> Than gauk about a-gabblen rhymes an' Latin.
> I'd better crack my noddle wi' her patten,
> She used to zay, or crack en' wi' a hammer,
> Than vill en up wi' rhymes, an silly stuff o' grammar.

('gauk about' – look round gaping; 'patten' – overshoe with wooden sole)

In later life, William Barnes would repeat the sad history of a Blackmore farming family, in which the children were encouraged to aspire to things beyond their station. One day an old-fashioned farmer observed his nieces walking by to their piano lessons. Shocked by the sight, he involuntarily shouted out, 'Moosic and it be milken toime! Zummat will come o' that!' Sure enough, it did. Their father was later obliged to sell up his farm.[2] A popular jingle summarised the inevitable result of such presumptuous behaviour:

> Man with his tally-ho
> Wife's squalling pian-o
> Girl with her satin-oh!
> Boy with his Latin-oh
> Is splash, dash and must end in ruin-oh.[3]

Not that the barely literate John Barnes, William's father, could ever have afforded a piano and satin dresses for his wife and daughter, but the mere notion of his son going in for book learning was evidently enough to alarm him.

In the last decade of the eighteenth century, the Barneses lived up a long, straight drove road, set among common land and small fields in the hamlet of Bagber. It was situated in a loop of waters where the tiny River Lydden meets the Stour. Their home was about a mile and a half west of Sturminster Newton, the 'capital' of the Blackmore Vale in Dorset. Here, John Barnes rented Rushay, a property so small that his son described it as a mere 'farmling'. Perhaps because it offered more room to a growing family, in later years they moved nearby to Golden Gate, which may originally have been an inn. 'Barnes's Oak' still grows in the hedgerow nearby. Sometime after 1816, they moved yet again to a property still known as Barnes's Orchard. There is little sign of them left in these sites. In the late nineteenth century, the aged Sturminster poet Robert Young took a visitor across the fields to look for the cottage where 'the honest old labourer' John Barnes lived, 'but alas, the only remains were a few old bricks, there were scarce a vestige of the garden to be seen, a withered tree covered with moss and lichen, from which my companion plucked a morsel'.[4]

John Barnes continued to work that patch of ground for years, long after William and two other sons had left the Vale. He was a quiet man, one of thousands of rural drudges worn down by repeated setbacks and never-ending labour. His portrait, painted by the Blackmore artist John Thorne in 1838, suggests diffidence and apprehension, as if he were expecting that at any moment life would deliver him yet another blow.

In the 1801 census, John Barnes described himself as a 'labourer in husbandry'; that is to say he worked his own bit of land and for the rest of the time hired himself out to local farmers. The family had once been property owners, with farms in various places as far away as Hampshire. But John's parents, who had their own farm in Manston, near Sturminster, had died of smallpox within a few months of each other in 1776, leaving their five children to the care of a relative who had lost the estate through bad management. In later days, John may still have owned a freehold house and land elsewhere but, if so, he did not live in it and it probably brought in very little extra income. The grim reality was that, like many another small tenant farmers at that time, he was perilously close to becoming a mere journeyman. Things might have been worse for him had he not had the support of his sister and brother-in-law, Anne and Charles Rabbetts (or Roberts), the tenants of Pentridge Farm, just a mile or so away on the banks of the Stour at Hinton St Mary.

In May 1789, at Lydlinch Church, John Barnes had married Grace Scott of Fifehead Neville. He was twenty-seven and she was twenty-nine. If the Barneses had been reduced to comparative poverty, the Scotts had tasted actual destitution. Grace came from a one-parent family. Her father had died when she was three and her mother would most likely have had to labour in the fields or work as a servant to support her three daughters.[5] Grace was barely literate – she could only make her mark on the marriage register – but her granddaughter recorded that she was 'a woman of refined tastes with an inherent love of art and poetry… a slight, graceful figure with delicate features… [who] recited to [her son William] passages of poems which she had learned'.[6] This artistic trait created a special link with the boy, for as he grew older he too revealed similar leanings. He became his 'mother's pride'.

Grace had already given birth to one son, christened William, in 1791, but he died on 2 October 1800. In accordance with a common custom at that time, when her next baby was born five months later, he was given the same name as his deceased brother. At his birth on 22 February 1801, 'our' William had four surviving siblings. John was the eldest, though his exact age is unknown; then came Charles who was eight, James who was six, and Anne or Ann, who was three. The Barneses last child, Henry, was born four years after William in November 1805.[7]

Home was a poor, thatched cottage, probably with just two rooms and a flagstone floor. From out of a patchwork of little fields, studded with oak and enclosed by thick elm hedges, a rutted track led up to their door. The rhythm of their life was determined by the seasons. In the short, dark days of winter, John Barnes might have little to do but to stay at home, feeding his animals in the barn and fetching in root crops and wood for the fire. Soon after it was dark, they went to bed. Summer days were very different. In the morning, he would be up with the sun and out into the cowlease with his three-legged stool and two milking pails hanging from a yoke. Having milked for himself he would be off, trudging miles across the Vale, to take what work was on offer, whether milking, hedging, haymaking or harvesting.

It was the hearth that illuminated the earliest memories of William Barnes. This was his mother's domain, where family life gathered. In winter, the room was full of dark recesses, save where the firelight fringed her hair with gold. As an infant, he would be plumped down on damp flagstones, back a bit from the fire, and here he would prattle and listen to the kindling crackle and spit. Here too he played with his sister, Anne, and here his older brothers fetched in bundles of 'fuzz' (furze) to make the flames roar. His mother was always coming and going, carrying in buckets of water from the well, filling her stock-pot hanging from its hook, or turning her salt-box over to dry out the other side. From time to time she would insert her long spade, or 'peel', into the bread oven and triumphantly lift out a loaf. She was always there. His mother was his whole existence.

When John Barnes stamped in from work on those winter evenings, she would stir up the fire to make a cheerful blaze for him and set one of the older boys to help him unlace his gaiters and boots. Come perhaps from a day of timber-felling in driving rain, exhausted, wet and chilled to the bone, he would slump in the settle, spread his legs and hold his hands up to the heat. William would watch, fascinated, as his father's clothes steamed gently. On summer evenings John came in much later, announced by the jingling of horses' chains. Having unharnessed and seen to his beasts, he would enter hot and sweaty from the hayfield. If he were not too tired, after supper he might take a little stroll outside with Grace while the light still lasted. They would walk arm in arm round their little orchard and sit for a bit outside on the bench to watch the sun go down, while young John or James would be sent to the cider-house to fill a can for father.

*Above left:* Sketch of a boy, thought to be a self-portrait by Barnes. (Dorset County Museum)

*Above right:* A Blackmore cottage. (Sturminster Newton Museum Society)

The stock-pot and the bread-oven were Grace's entire means of cookery. Her family's diet was perforce very plain, both because of their lack of elaborate cooking facilities and also because they were too poor to eat meat often. For though Blackmore people boasted that an acre and a quarter of its thick clay was sufficient to feed a Devonshire ox for a year, the same measure of land could barely support a farm worker and his family.[8] And as for many other country people, it was the success of the recent harvest that determined how well the Barneses ate. Bread was their staple of life, 'supplemented by tiny quantities of butter, cheese, bacon and tea; fresh meat was a luxury rarely seen at the table of the poorest labourers'.[9] Many farm workers subsisted almost entirely on a diet of potatoes and tea.[10] Things were probably better than this for the Barneses, however, because there was sometimes a rabbit or hare for the pot. Besides, John Barnes's little farm still provided the greater part of their diet and he also retained his commoner's rights, which entitled him to graze his pigs and geese, to collect firewood and to gather mushrooms, herbs and medicinal 'simples' from Bagber Common.

With the coming of warmer spring days, the life of the growing boy expanded into a vista of shimmering grasses and blue skies. When the weather allowed, Grace Barnes would take her young children out into the meadows and along the banks of the Stour. Here in May, marsh marigolds clogged the river, followed in summer by yellow flag irises and 'clotes' (water lilies). These banks became the childhood playground for William and his brothers and cousins. When tired of paddling and splashing, he would lie overlooking the stream, dreaming the afternoon away, watching great castles of reflected cumulous drifting across the surface. In the meadow, he noticed, almost without noticing, purple loosestrife, marsh orchids, lady smock and ragged robin. Above the stream, clouds of gnats dipped and flicked. Water-boatmen trod the tenuous skin while pond-skaters pursued their mysterious lives. Flitting from one lily pad to another came the brightly coloured dragonflies: ruddy darters, emperors and banded demoiselles. Below the surface shoals of small fish, minnows, trout and grayling nosed their way upstream. Sometimes the boy might glimpse a water vole, an otter, a grey heron or even the flash of kingfisher blue.

A Blackmore river scene, where Barnes played as a child. (Private collection)

All these things were stored in his memory, only to resurface years later in his poetry:

> No city primness train'd our feet
> To strut in childhood through the street,
> But freedom let them loose to tread
> The yellow cowslip's downcast head;
> Or climb above the twining hop
> And ivy to the elm-tree's top;
> Where southern airs of blue-sky'd day
> Breathe'd o'er the daisy and the may.
> I knew you young, and love you now,
> O shining grass, and shady bough.
>
> Or in the grassy drove by ranks
> Of white-stemm'd ashes, or by banks
> Of narrow lanes, in winding round
> The hedgy sides of shelving ground;
> Where low-shot light struck in to end
> Again in some cool-shaded bend,
> Where we might see through darkleav'd boughs
> The evening light on green hill-brows.
> I knew you young, and love you now,
> O shining grass, and shady bough.[11]

As he grew older and more adventurous, William's roving took him further downriver. He always remembered the time when he steered his 'fleet' on the Stour. It consisted of himself in a large tub and the cat towed behind in a wooden bowl, 'her back arched and her tail extended in the agonies of terror'. Sometimes his wanderings would take him across the meadows to the little footbridges and the weir at Newton. Here, near the six-arched bridge which joined Newton to Stur, stood an ancient flour mill. It was a noisy place. Even when far off, the boy could hear the constant clatter from the water wheel and the roaring of the weir, accompanied by heavy thumpings from the brick-built fulling mill next door. Here, great hammers beat at woollen fabric, impacting it into heavy duty 'swanskin' cloth.

Wandering the higher meadows and looking towards the south and east of the Vale, he could glimpse a circle of blue hills, the last ridges of the bare chalk country of the Dorset ridgeway. He soon learned to name them: 'Hambledon, Bulbarrow, Nettlecomb-Tout, Dogbury, High Stoy and Bubb Down'.[12] These hills remained unclimbed for the time being, but already they provided the framework of his days. Blackmore was his own world, entire unto itself.

Grace Barnes was quick to notice that her son had started to reveal unusual talents and that he seemed to share her delight in artistic things. When quite young he liked to draw, though the only materials he had were a piece of chalk and the flagstone floor. Barnes never forgot the occasion when she led him by the hand 'through the pleasant country lanes to where some figures in molten lead, representing the seasons, stood on the parapet of an old bridge near her old home in Fifehead. Another of his recollections was of his mother holding him up in her arms to see a statue [a stone boy] on the pillared gate of an old disused manor-house'.[13]

The Barneses were Anglicans and very pious. From his earliest years, William would be carried or walked across the fields with his family to worship at St Mary's, the parish church of Sturminster Newton Castle, as it was then called. His birth was registered there in the parish records on 29 March 1801. As he grew older, the church organist, Tom Spinney, noted his flair for music and set about coaching him in singing and the violin. This link between the Barnes family and St Mary's was maintained over many years. Long after William left home, John Barnes was still a faithful worshipper there, sitting in the (now demolished) lower gallery in his old brown coat.[14]

The mile-and-a-half walk across the fields to attend church now became a regular feature of the boy's childhood. He also went to Stur for his education. He remembered that, 'After sitting awhile on the low form of a Dame school, at the feet of a good Mrs Humphries, I went through a common course of schooling in a boys' school at Sturminster Newton'.[15] His walk there took him along the track across the fields used by cowherds when driving their cattle to market. The building which served as his school was a three-storey house in Tanyard Lane, adjacent to St Mary's Church.[16] Here, he quickly made friends. The master, Tommy Mullet, soon perceived the boy's talents and took extra pains with him. From Mullet, Barnes gained three things: a habit of application, a good grounding of elementary knowledge and a lifelong interest in mathematics. And perhaps surprisingly for an exceptionally bright child, Barnes seems to have been popular with the other pupils. One old lady who had been his classmate told his daughter that at school he had been called 'little Willie Barnes' and that 'all the scholars, both boys and girls, would willingly, if necessary, have fought and protected him'.[17]

Nevertheless, like many another shy but gifted children, Barnes had to earn this popularity with a talent that his classmates could readily understand. In his case it was magic. At the age of seven or eight he became friends with a local 'witch' or 'wizard' named Jemmy Jenkins who kept a library of magic and astrology. From Jenkins he learned 'tricks' which he demonstrated to his school friends, who were no doubt awed by his display of recondite lore. They began to call him 'the little astrologer'. His parents had differing views about this. Grace was superstitious but her husband was not. John Barnes did not hold with the practices of his neighbours, some of whom, when a horse or cow or even a family member took sick, would send to Shepton Mallet for the advice of the 'cunning man'.[18]

As the boy grew older, Grace became progressively anxious about him, and went to the local 'witches' for reassurance. She was convinced that an imaginative child like this, with such a quick, fanciful nature, delicate physique and tapering, sensitive fingers, would never be able to tolerate a life of manual labour on a farm. So she confided these worries to the wise women of the village, one of whom, after examining his 'psychic' hand, pronounced that the boy was born with a silver spoon in his mouth. Another declared, 'Never you mind what he looks like, he'll get his living by learning-books and such like'.[19]

Of all William's boyhood friends, his cousin, Charlie Rabbets, was the closest. Charlie's home, Pentridge Farm, was a lively, welcoming place with numerous cousins to play with. Uncle Charles was an affable man and his Aunt Anne a motherly woman. Another Barnes aunt, Jenny, lived with them as a sort of family servant. She too was kindly but hot-tempered. When in one of her tantrums, she was given to slamming doors, kicking the cat and flinging milk pails about.[20] Signs of these coming tempests were cues for the boys to race off across the summer meadows, to swim in the Stour or climb trees to gather birds' eggs or nuts. Sometimes they would braid horsehairs to make fishing lines, cut ash-twigs for whistles, or skin eels to make whips for their tops.

By the age of ten the boy was set on becoming an artist. For a few pence he would draw portraits of his friends and relatives in pen and ink. He even painted an inn sign for the Black Horse at Sturminster and walked six miles to exhibit it at Shroton Fair. But though proud of his attainments, his mother still could not see how they might lead to any gainful employment. There was not much call for artists in the Vale.

Her worries were allayed to some extent by a Sturminster solicitor named Thomas Henry Dashwood, a man celebrated locally for his benevolent nature. Robert Young recalled that, 'numberless were this good man's deeds, many... the boys and girls that he clothed'.[21] Dashwood's offices at Vine House were adjacent to the church and school and close to the leather-making quarter of the town. In Barnes's day the street was called Tanyard's Lane, but this was later changed to Penny Lane, so-called after a certain John Penny who met his death after felling a tree on Dashwood's premises. In 1814 or 1815, Dashwood needed a new engrossing clerk; that is, one whose job it was to copy out deeds. There was an increasing amount of such work required at this time because of the many enclosures of common land that were taking place.

There are two accounts of how William Barnes came to be taken on by Dashwood. According to Lucy Baxter, the solicitor called at the school one day to enquire whether there was a pupil capable of copying documents in a clerkly hand. Mullet did not hesitate to recommend William. So the boy was asked to take a quill and paper and demonstrate his skill. As a result, he was appointed on the spot.

An alternative version was offered by Frank Lemon, who was a clerk at the same office from 1897 until 1906. He wrote, 'While crossing a field [Mr Dashwood] saw a boy who had been sent to clear the meadow of cow dung. Instead, he had turned his wheelbarrow on its side and was sitting on it, sketching a cow. Mr Dashwood admired the drawing, became interested in the artist… and took him into his office'. Every morning from then onwards, William would make his way across the fields to sit at his desk in Vine House, copying out deeds. 'Later, when [Dashwood] and his wife were looking through the office one evening they found the shelf under Barnes's desk full of Greek and Latin books'.[22]

Stur, in William Barnes's time, was a small manufacturing town set among miles of fields. Its chief industry was cloth-making, and its most celebrated product was the 'swanskin' which, before oilskin was invented, offered mariners some degree of water resistance in their garments. So effective was this cloth that swanskin was exported as far away as North America and particularly prized by the fishermen in the Newfoundland trade. Robert Young remembered that in the early years of the nineteenth century, 'the spinners and weavers were kept well employed' and 'the racks on which the [swanskin] cloth was fixed covered one or two fields'.[23] Most of the work was done in people's own homes. The town's inhabitants included fifty-three male weavers, and 295 women spinners. Apart from cloth-making, there was also Mitchel's soap and candle works, a patten factory (pattens were overshoes, essential to people living in the muddy country who wished to keep their shoes clean), and people employed in the manufacture of both 'ring' and 'sugarloaf' buttons. These, together with the cattle market and all the trades necessary to service and supply the local farmers, were the principal occupations in Stur.[24]

The young solicitor's clerk would have soon become familiar with the sight of some of the town's more eccentric characters. There was old Mr Thomas, who got fidgety when he could not find supplies in his tiny, dirty shop and would bustle about muttering, 'Butter me and sugar me and then I shall be good'. Another well-known resident was Billy Sweet's toad, a creature he called Marier (Maria). Billy was an enthusiastic gardener and employed his toad to eat slugs and other vermin. Not liking to leave his pet alone when he went to the ale-house in the evenings, he would frequently carry her along in his pocket. Sitting round the table with his cronies, he would eventually take out Marier and invite them all to admire her beautiful eyes.

Parts of Stur were filthy. Near to a manure heap, beside an old stable, pigs would congregate to feast on the refuse thrown out from the local cider-house. Predictably, the pigs were often tipsy. Stur was also a violent and cruel place. There was bull baiting, badger baiting, pigeon shooting, cock fighting and cudgel fighting. Drunkenness was rife and would lead to frequent affrays in the ale-houses. The streets could be menacing at times to those especially vulnerable. One well-known inhabitant was a half-witted old woman named Gimmer Nan, who mumbled to herself when she walked through the streets and who was frequently surrounded by groups of idle boys calling out, 'Which way did the bull run, Nan?' At this she would cackle and call out, 'Over the bridge, over the bridge', and they would all roar with laughter and ask her again.

Young William may have witnessed a public whipping that took place in the town. The victim was a quiet, inoffensive man but his wife was a known 'tartar' and in the end he could take no more of her scolding. So he ran away, leaving her a charge on the rates. Having been arrested in Poole, where he had been working as a cooper, he was hauled back to Stur and the local magistrates ordered him to be flogged. Robert Young remembered:

> It was a painful and degrading spectacle to witness, the poor man stripped to the waist, his hands fastened to a frame fixed to a wagon his outstretched arms unable to move, his naked back streaming with blood under the lash, while many among the crowd of witnesses were women fainting and screaming was [sic] carried from the scene.[25]

William Barnes cannot have failed to observe the grossness of this society, its ignorance and cruelty. Even in his moments of leisure in Vine House, when from beneath his desk he discreetly pulled out his Latin grammar or Greek lexicon, he was still assailed by pitiful bleatings and odours from the market and tan yard to remind him of the brutality of life. Yet he seems to have been untouched by these experiences, and in his later writings, Stur never featured at all. This was because his whole emotional and imaginative existence was still bound up in his home life in Bagber, in the familiar fields and orchards by the Stour, in the neighbours, their jokes and tricks and sayings, and in his family and all their usages and ways. It must have seemed to him that things would go on like this forever.

They did not. In quick succession there now came a series of events which were to bring this life to an end. The first was the financial failure in 1813 of his uncle, Charles Rabbets, who had worked Pentridge Farm for over thirty years. At that time, landowners were seeking to enclose as much acreage as possible for their own use. Higher profits were to be made from bigger farms. Accordingly, many tenant farmers were either given notice to quit or their rent was put up so much that they could no longer pay. Furthermore, now that the war with France was nearly over, there was a resumption of agricultural imports from the Continent. Both these tendencies were bringing about a recession in English farming. The small man just could not compete. Why exactly Rabbets had to leave Pentridge is not known; perhaps his landlord, Lord Rivers, had raised his rent. Whatever the reason, the eviction and subsequent sale of the farm were deeply painful to all concerned. Barnes never forgot it:

*Left:* Vine House, Sturminster Newton, where Barnes first went to work for the solicitor Thomas Dashwood. (Private collection)

*Below:* The White Hart in Barnes's town, Sturminster Newton, in the nineteenth century. (Sturminster Newton Museum Society)

A sale of… an uncle's stock, and which I saw when a boy, made on my mind a strong impression. My uncle was a farmer in the West of England, but became insolvent from the depression of the agricultural interest after the end of the French war. My aunt had a numerous family, and her long exercised solicitude as a mother, and her continual struggles against misfortune had nearly brought her with sorrow to the grave; she was calm, and it was only when one of her daughters passed her, that a tear rolled down her sallow cheek.

 The young men were in that severe and reckless mood in which men are usually thrown when assailed by misfortune which they can still resist.

 The girls were bewildered and scarcely knew what happened around them; then were driven away the cows under which the weeping milkmaid had so often sung the simple songs of the country; then went the wagon in which the merry haymakers had so many times ridden to the feast of harvest-home, and in short, then everything that was dear from familiarity was taken away, and my uncle as he looked on the fields he had so long cultivated with hope, and of which he had taken the produce in grateful joy, sighed and dropped a tear.[26]

Later he put his feelings into verse:

Pentridge! – oh! my heart's a -zwellen
Vull o'jay wi vo'k a-tellen
Any news o' thik wold pleace,
An' the boughy hedges round it,
An' the river that do bound it,
Wi' his dark but glis'nen feace.
Vor there's noo land, on either hand,
To me lik' Pentridge by the river.

Be there any leaves to quiver
On the aspen by the river?
Doo he sheade the water still,
Where the rushes be a-growen,
Where the sullen Stour's a-flowen
Drough the meads vrom mill to mill?
Vor if a tree were dear to me,
Oh! 'twer thik aspen by the river.

Bleaded grass is now a-shooten
Where the vloor wer woonce our vooten,
While the hall were still in pleace.
Stwones be looser in the wallen;
Hollow trees be nearer vallen;
Ev'ry thing ha' chang'd its feace.
But still the neame do bide the seame –
'Tis Pentridge – Pentridge by the river.[27]

('jay' – joy; 'thik wold' – that old; 'drough' – through; 'vooten' – footing; 'wallen' – walls)

Saddened as he was by the sale, the boy also sensed that there was something profoundly wrong about it. It should not have happened. For his uncle and aunt were the salt of the earth, kind to their work-folk, contented with their lot and generous. Moreover, they were hard-working and independent. People more useful to the country would be difficult to find. Yet despite their constant labour, they had failed. Why was it? He was too young at that time to understand the causes of this catastrophe, but he pondered the matter for years to come. Meanwhile, with a heavy heart, he resumed his daily walk through the fields to Dashwood's office, to copy out yet more deeds of enclosure.

Victory was in the air the following year. In March 1814 Lord Wellington captured Bordeaux and the allied armies entered Paris. In April, Napoleon abdicated and was sent into exile in Elba. Surely, thought English people, he had been conquered at last. Wellington's triumphant return called for national celebrations. In London, 1,700 guests attended a masquerade at Burlington House. Lord Byron appeared as a monk and his mistress, Lady Caroline Lamb, sported green pantaloons.

Celebrations in Stur were more homely. They were held in Gough's Close, a field running down to the river. The thirteen-year-old William Barnes learned that the 'respectable inhabitants' had combined to treat the poor with a dinner of beef pudding and strong beer. There was a band, dancing on the grass and sports, including sack-racing, grinning through horse collars and chasing a pig with a greased tail. As a finale, an effigy of Bonaparte, 'the arch enemy of England', was paraded round the field, then hanged, shot and finally burnt.[28]

Shortly afterwards came the break-up of his family. His elder brothers, John and James, now left home for good. The failure of Charles Rabbetts was only one of many signs that there was just not enough land in England to support the burgeoning population and farm work was getting scarce. So the brothers went off to get jobs as seamen. They probably took ships from Poole, following the swanskin trade, and perhaps they later found work as fishermen in the Newfoundland cod waters.

Even more grievous to the boy was the death of his mother. Grace Barnes was fifty-six when she was buried, on 21 January 1816. It was a good age at that time for a working woman who had given birth to seven children.[29] Her illness is not recorded; perhaps she was simply worn out. The effect upon her delicate, sensitive son cannot be overstated. Hers is a persistent presence in the poems he wrote in later years. In his inner ear, he could always hear her homely expressions and country sayings, her little laugh and the cadences and inflections of her voice.

No one had understood him as his mother did, and now there was little to keep him at home. In the evenings, John Barnes would often go out into the fields without a word and return to sit in gloomy silence before the embers. Sister Anne kept house for their father, but there were signs that she would soon be off and married. As for Henry, aged eleven when his mother died, he shared none of William's scholarly interests and already seemed destined for life as a farm labourer. Theirs was a largely illiterate household. Coming home in the evenings from Dashwood's office, William found little solace there other than in his Latin grammar.

In 1817 Thomas Dashwood died. Though his business continued, William Barnes's services were no longer required. What was he to do? There was no other suitable employment in the Blackmore Vale for the bookish son of a labouring man. For a time he worked for a Mr George Score, though in what capacity is not known. It now seemed that his mother's worst fears might be realised and he would have to take up farm work. The only other possibility was to roam beyond the rim of blue hills and enter a far country in order to find employment, and perhaps the company of more congenial people. Should he try this? He understood the risks involved. Living among strangers, without work or money, he might well starve.

# 3

# LOVE AND LITERATURE: DORCHESTER

—— 1818-1822 ——

Neither the sweating carter, reining back his team where the road slopes steeply down from the Bow outside St Peter's, nor Mr Thomas Hardy, master mason from Higher Bockhampton in town with his cart for a load of Broadmayne bricks, nor Reverend Richman hurrying in for mattins, would have given much attention that morning to a shabby youth who was pausing to ask the way to a certain lawyer's office. Nor, had they done so, could they possibly have guessed that some seventy years later, a statue of him would stand on that same spot.

Having been directed, William Barnes, aged seventeen, resumed his walk up High West Street to start his first day in a new job. Once again he had found work as an engrossing clerk, this time with Thomas Coombs, a Dorchester solicitor. How he had got the post is not known. Perhaps he had just turned up on the off-chance of getting work, or perhaps he had written around to lawyers' offices in the town, hoping that a combination of Dashwood's good reference and his own beautiful copperplate might recommend him. Evidently, it did.

Barnes had arrived in the town with only a few shillings in his pocket. Fortunately, his new employer turned out to be a kindly man and may have already arranged for his new clerk to board above Mr Hazard's pastry shop. The rooms were to be shared with another of Coombs's clerks, and Barnes was to pay half the rent of seven guineas a quarter, which probably included an evening meal, and perhaps leftovers from the shop to furnish his lunch the following day. Such a sum must have alarmed the youth from Stur, whose earnings were probably not much more than 8 or 9s a week. Happily, he found a reassuring companion in his new flatmate, William Gilbert Carey from Wiltshire, who proved to be very welcoming and lively, with the same studious interests as himself. At their first meeting, Barnes sensed that he had found a friend.

Dorchester was much busier than Sturminster. The pastry shop was at the junction of Trinity Street and High West Street, and Coombs's office further up at Top O'Town. When walking up to work in the mornings, Barnes was obliged to dodge shopkeepers putting out trestle tables and to duck his head to avoid blinds pulled down over frontages. At busier places, the line of carriers' carts along the pavement's edge provided an obstructive wall, while their horses, hobbled to posts with their forelegs to the pavement, would occasionally nip passers-by. So much rush and bustle! So many people! And yet in one way it resembled Stur, for the place had an agricultural feel. Here, pigs were penned in recesses set back from the road, flocks of sheep bleated their way down the street, and the ironmonger's, cooper's, saddler's, wheelwright's and chemist all displayed items for farm and field.[1]

Farther up High West Street, things were quieter. Here stood old-fashioned houses, superior to any in Stur, with their iron balconies and 'antique air'.[2] He could peep in at their front doors, right through into back gardens, some bright with geraniums.[3] Exploring a little further, he discovered the town's elegant 'walks', lined with limes and chestnuts, and the water-meadows running down to the river. Dorchester was the county town and the company so much more genteel than any he had previously known. Carey had told him that the gentry kept their houses, went to concerts and sent their children to school here. Here too were barracks, with officers in scarlet tunics, a theatre and crowded coaches from London pulling up with a swish at the King's Arms, just across from where he was lodging. It was all so much grander and busier than at home. He was rather overawed.

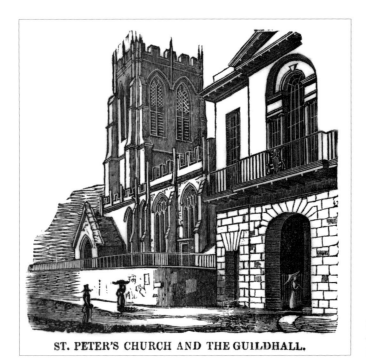

**ST. PETER'S CHURCH AND THE GUILDHALL.**

St Peter's Church, Dorchester, engraving by William Barnes. (Dorset County Museum)

So began his new life. For long hours each day he copied out deeds but, when there was nothing else to do, he busied himself with his studies. Mr Coombs did not object; in fact, he positively encouraged him. Pure love of learning was Barnes's chief motivation, but it was not entirely unmixed with social ambition. He later noted:

> I was not unfaithful to my desk work, but I daily spent a share of my spare time on the study of those higher branches of learning, Latin and Greek and others, which I had not reached at school, but with my strong love of learning, and wit, I felt that I was not in my right or most mind-fitting way of life... It was always from my early days, in my mind that I would try to rise to a higher standing than that to which my late father had fallen, though my choice of learning was not, as may be, the most likely way to reach it.[4]

This suggests that like many other dreamy, bookish children of working people, and conscious of the family tradition that his family had once owned extensive estates, young Barnes carried with him the sense that his present condition did not attest his true social status. He remembered too his mother's gentle, artistic nature, so much more refined than that of the other cottage women of Bagber. Like her, he was fastidious and could not bear coarse company, wilful ignorance and lewd talk. Was it not possible, then, that his innate gentility was inherited? From all of which, it might have been expected that he was stand-offish and gave himself airs. On the contrary, his genial good manners, high spirits and ready laugh made him popular with people of all classes.

Fortunately, the county town afforded a much greater choice of suitable companions than he had found in Stur, and it was not long before he had made good friends with several young men like himself. They tended to be an earnest set, devoted to private study and self-improvement. After work he and Carey would read the classic authors together. And when the longer, warmer days came on, he would stroll along the banks of the Frome, practising French conversation with a new friend, Edward Fuller. This town offered many novel and delightful experiences; music, for example. Friends were treated to duets, with Fuller on violin and William on the flute. Soon, this ensemble was enlarged by the recruitment of the Zillwoods, brother and sister, who supplied a second violin and a 'Forte-piano'.[5]

Always a pious Anglican, in Dorchester Barnes attended St Peter's. Almost next door at Holy Trinity, the rector, the Revd Henry John Richman, was an unusually erudite clergyman. At the age of eight he had been elected to a scholarship at Winchester College where the headmaster was Dr Thomas Warton, the sometime Poet Laureate and friend of Dr Johnson. Warton's *History of English Poetry* (three volumes, 1774-81) had revealed an interest in primitivism, but despite this flirtation with the doctrine of the natural goodness of man, under his rule the college became noted for bullying and brutal punishment. How the timid little Henry Richman survived such harsh discipline is a matter for wonder. At Winchester, he was made to endure such torments as being led by the nose round the classroom with a pair of tongs, and having a frog or toad held beneath his nose.[6] Despite, or perhaps because of, this, when he became headmaster of Dorchester Grammar School, a post he occupied for twenty-five years, he was noted for his gentle, humane rule. In this he deeply influenced William Barnes.

What then could be more natural than that an earnest youth such as Barnes should attract the notice of Richman? Discovering his interest in the classics, the rector was soon giving him private lessons and getting him interested in archaeology. He also allowed him access to his own considerable private library. They were not exactly friends – the divisions of age, education and social class were too great for that – but in Richman and Coombs, as with Dashwood in Stur, Barnes had once again succeeded in finding patrons. For him, these men provided not only encouragement but patterns of scholarship and gentility.

There being no public libraries at that time, access to Richman's collection provided the impetus to what was to be Barnes's lifelong programme of self-education. He was free to browse here, and one glance along the shelves became for him a voyage of intellectual discovery. What took his fancy most? Languages, probably; grammars and dictionaries in a variety of tongues. Throughout his life, his linguistic interest and facility was intellectually paramount. There is no record of his reading novels. They had barely come into fashion then and, anyway, it is most unlikely that this morally fastidious youth would have approved of the sexual amorality of Tom Jones or the sniggering indecency of Tristram Shandy, even if, as is unlikely, Richman had them on his shelves. The essays of Addison, Steele and Johnson would have been more Richman's kind of thing, in the form of back numbers of the *Spectator*, the *Rambler* and the *Idler*.

As for poetry, we would expect to find Milton and the Augustans in the library of any cultivated clergyman at the beginning of the nineteenth century. And so, it was here at Richman's that the labourer's son probably looked through the pages of *Paradise Lost* for the first time and discovered the works of Pope, Collins and Gray. Because of Richman's connection with Warton, we may be sure that the works of Samuel Johnson were prominent in his collection, and it was in turning the pages of his poem 'London' that Barnes would have found a line to give him cause for thought: 'SLOW RISES WORTH, BY POVERTY DEPREST'.

That first summer after his arrival in Dorchester was a carefree time, packed with new friends and new pursuits. Though his day job was repetitive and unchallenging, it at least enabled him to take a certain pride in the beautifully written documents he produced. We may also suppose that Coombs was quick to discern unusual abilities in his new clerk and was soon ready to trust him with work of greater responsibility, such as composing, though not signing, letters. Then there were his studies with Carey and Richman, his private reading, his music-making with the Zillwoods and his churchgoing. Nor was life all earnest endeavour. After office hours, he might go strolling the banks of the Frome with his friends. Somehow, he even acquired a boat of his own, though he had very little money. More necessary was a decent suit (and top hat?) for work. Despite this, it was still one of Bob Cratchit's threadbare forebears who walked up High West Street each morning.

Then he fell in love. One morning in March 1818 he was on his way to work when a Magnet coach drew up 'with a great dash and clatter of the hoofs of steaming horses' and a portly woman with two young girls got down. The younger miss was wearing a sky-blue 'spencer' or jacket, and had 'blue eyes and wavy brown hair'. He was smitten immediately. Involuntarily he muttered to himself 'that shall be my wife'.[7] On making enquiries, he learned that she was Julia Miles, daughter of James Camford Miles, an excise officer lately appointed to the Dorset area.

Cupid engraving for 'Orra: A Lapland Tale', 1822. (Dorset County Museum)

There then commenced a little comedy of 'accidental' meetings on street corners and in shop doorways, of stolen glances, hat raisings, timid bows and blushing acknowledgements. Barnes's admiration quickly became apparent to the girl, and she signalled that his attentions flattered and pleased her. Soon their encounters became more serious, all beating hearts and lingering looks. When her parents got wind of their dalliance and forbade their meetings, the young lovers were obliged to be more discreet, restricted as they were to snatched moments and whispered confidences. It was disobedient but all very innocent.

Julia's youth was the ostensible ground of her father's objection, for she was still only fourteen or fifteen. But, smarting with indignation, Barnes chose to believe otherwise. He was convinced that Miles's dismissal of his interest was both snobbish and mercenary; it was because he was not a gentleman and had no money. If the latter reason were true, it was not unreasonable. Miles had two daughters and eight sons to provide for, and though a number of the boys had been endowed with impressive names such as Julius and Octavius, they were mostly an idle lot, spending their time with their father chasing smugglers along the Dorset coast. Consequently, Miles was hard pressed and would not countenance Julia's connection with an impecunious clerk. Nor could he possibly afford a marriage settlement for the girl. What he hoped for her was that when she was old enough, she would marry a man who could keep her in some style. Miles's apparent motivation came as a shock to Barnes. He had never troubled himself about his own lack of money, nor understood how seriously others might regard it. But because of his involvement with Julia, for the first time in his life he became painfully aware of his straightened circumstances.

In order to avoid the custom officer's notice, the lovers now took to doing a bit of smuggling themselves and passed notes to each other on the sly. One from Barnes, in 1820, reveals that Julia had been forbidden to talk to him:

> Miss Miles: There being no possibility of my having an oral communication with you, I have presumed to trouble you with a Letter, to request that you will grant me the happiness of conducting you and your Sister to the concert tomorrow Evening. Intreating your pardon on my presumption, I remain Yours devotedly William Barnes.[8]

Because Julia was not allowed to receive letters from him at home, he was instructed to address them to her friend's house:

> Miss Julia Miles at Miss Frampton's, Dorchester: If Miss Snook should take an excursion in the Boat this Evening perhaps you will go with her, should that be the case, I hope to meet you in Churchill's walks about 1/2 past 6 o'clock.

Julia's attachment to Barnes was now a topic of sentimental gossip for her circle of young ladies, including her sister and her friends, the Misses Snook, Frampton and Groves. They probably found it all rather 'romantic', to quote a word then coming into fashion.

As time went by, the situation became increasingly frustrating for the pair. Barnes's feelings were particularly stung by the sense that Miles seemed not to appreciate his true worth. Yet he still hoped that the revenue officer must eventually come to understand that he was no mere inky copyist, but an exceptional young man with a faithful heart and a delicate sensibility. He felt his academic attainments were surely witness to his true gentility; after all, he was fluent in Latin and Greek.

Miles remained unimpressed, so Barnes resolved to demonstrate his merits not only to his prospective father-in-law but to the whole town. In 1820, G. Clark of Dorchester published a booklet of ten of his *Poetical Pieces*.[9] Each poem plays out an imaginary resolution to his own love affair. Julia defies her mother to marry Cyprian; the poet grieves for Eliza from whom he must part; Emily's love has faded; the poet remembers Anna in their old familiar haunts, and so on. All their Dorchester acquaintances would have recognised the references.

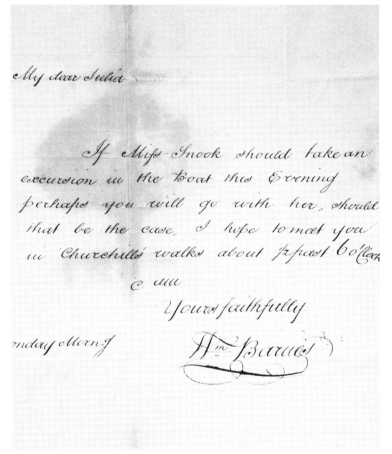

A love letter sent to Julia from Barnes while he was in Mere. (Dorset County Museum)

What especially caused trouble was a piece entitled 'Destiny'. This poem, grandly garnished with an epigraph from Pope's *Essay on Man*, recounts the story of Julia choosing between admirers. When she decides, her father refuses her lover because of his poverty:

> Her fortunate stars had to Julia given,
> Of lovers a numerous train,
> Who for twelve months, or more, had incessantly striven
> To win her fair hand – but in vain.
> They were all youths of merit, although they were poor,
> And to one she'd nigh given her heart,
> But her father he lik'd the pecuniary ore,
> Insomuch that in one of his passions he swore,
> That Julia should ne'er again enter his door,
> If to him, she her hand should impart.[10]

Despite her father's response, Julia still cannot help rhapsodising about her young man:

> He is rather genteel, his complexion is light,
> His eyes are rather dark, and his hair black as night,
> And I certainly think that his love should require,
> Were it not for my father's restriction.

Here, Barnes hoped, was his passport to the would-be genteel world of the Mileses, for he had demonstrated that he too could write polite literature. Despite his lack of formal education, he had mastered all the tricks of the Augustans. He could turn a rhyme, shape a stanza, quote Pope and assume the pastoral style then fashionable. Surely, he thought, he had triumphantly vindicated himself. Now at last, Miles would have to admit that this clever young man was indeed a gentleman, and well worthy to be his son-in-law.

Miles did no such thing. In fact, he was furious. For Barnes had gravely miscalculated the effect of his book. In writing 'Destiny', he seems to have let his resentment run away with him without anticipating the consequences. He had identified the Mileses with a money-grabbing character who loved the 'pecuniary ore'. Naively, he had not anticipated that this phrase would make them the laughing stock of Dorchester. But it did and they were incensed. Whereas before they had simply been 'not at home' when he called, Miles now took to deliberately ignoring him in the street.

Unsurprisingly, both the lovers became unwell, suffering from various unnamed illnesses. As time went on, Miles showed no sign of relenting but simply changed the nature of his objections to the match. When Julia was nearly seventeen, he could no longer argue that she was too young to be married. Nor, after such a lengthy courtship, could he still maintain that Barnes was a mere trifler with his daughter's affection. Nor could he go on pretending to have doubts about his ability or education, but the young man's poverty continued to prove an insuperable barrier.

So Barnes was put to considering how he might improve his fortunes. He had to find a way to become more prosperous if he was to gain Miles's approval. But how was he to do so? He and Julia revolved many schemes between them. Without another job to go to, he dared not resign his post with Coombs, though it would never pay enough to satisfy Miles. What he needed was a part-time occupation which would bring in extra income. Then at last he hit upon a scheme which might enable him to do just that, and even lead to his entering a much more lucrative and prestigious profession than that of a solicitor's clerk.

These hopes sprang from his revived ambition to become a successful engraver. In his spare time, he began to make woodcuts and to offer them around to prospective purchasers: 'I had from a love of arts early tried my graver on wood, quickened moreover by Bewick's works; and it was a daydream of my youth that I might follow art as my way of life'.[11] Soon, he became more ambitious and tried his hand at etching copperplate and even silver. In 1822 a local bookseller, James Criswick, proposed to republish a guidebook, *Walks round Dorchester*, which had first come out two years before and asked Barnes to furnish him with wood engravings. He duly obliged with illustrations of Lulworth Castle, Milton Abbey, Cerne Abbey, the Roman Amphitheatre (Maumbury Ring), Bindon Abbey, Corfe Castle, the Arched Rock at Lulworth (Durdle Door) and Poundbury Camp.[12]

That November, unnamed friends (Fuller? Carey? Richman?) wrote to R. Ackerman, the London engraver, enclosing a selection of his drawings and engravings, to enquire whether there might be a job there for Barnes. In reply, Ackerman's agent, H. Walton, detected 'a considerable display of talent' in the work but considered that the artist needed to be matured under 'some eminent Master', i.e. he needed training. Walton had sent the items on to Edward Scriven, another engraver, for a further opinion and he too recognised a 'marked talent' in the work, but thought that it was impossible for the young man to commence engraving at once with a tolerable salary.[13] What Barnes needed, he opined, was to learn the craft by means of an apprenticeship. This, of course, was impossible. Barnes could never have financed his way through such a course. Nevertheless, he continued to work at his engravings with vague hopes that the enterprise would lead somewhere.

There was one immediate reward for his 'hobby', however, for the money he earned from Criswick paid for another project, the publication of his poem 'Orra: A Lapland Tale'.[14] This was an ambitiously lengthy affair of sixty-five stanzas, appended with earnest notes on the habits of the Scandinavian Wagtail, the various tribes and traditions of Laplanders, and their national instrument, the 'harpu'. The title page displays two epigraphs, a quotation from Virgil's *Georgics* and a loose translation of it by Dryden, evoking a scene in which 'perpetual night is found / In silence brooding on the unhappy ground', that poet's notion of an arctic landscape.

Included were five woodcuts 'engraved by the author', intended as advertisements. They depict: the arctic waste, a harp (or 'harpu'), a man sailing in a boat, a Cupid firing a bow and a young woman, apparently in profound agitation, gazing down at the sea. At the back of the book a notice solicited orders: 'The author of this poem having taught himself the arts of Copper & Wood Engraving and Drawing. Likenesses taken in Pencil, at from 7s.6d to 19s.6d each; and correct drawings made of Antiquities, Architecture, Curiosities, &c.' The accompanying sketch presented two women gazing into a mirror.

All of which raises the question of what on earth a Dorchester clerk was doing in bringing out a poem set in Lapland. He had never been to Lapland, nor was ever likely to go there. One would think that the place was as remote from his interests as it was possible. Predictably, it was in Richman's library that it had its origin, because there Barnes discovered a remarkable book, *Travels through Sweden, Finland, and Lapland, and to the North Cape*. The author was Giuseppi Acerbi (1773-1848), who had journeyed from his native Italy in search of wildly picturesque northern scenes and rugged native peoples. This account of his travels was handsomely produced and illustrated by seventeen engravings, depicting barren landscapes, mountainous seas and fierce bears. One especially vivid print displays a dog train and sled, making its way on the ice field between gloomy rocks and dark conifers. Perhaps Richman allowed Barnes to take the book back to his own lodgings, where he might pore over the engravings by the light of a candle. And even as Hazard's baking odours wafted up the stairs, his imagination was caught and hauled across the frozen waste of continued rejection. For, somehow, he sensed that these scenes epitomised his personal situation.

In 'Orra', Barnes conceived Lapland to be a place of chilly innocence, inhabited by Rousseauistic, noble savages, or 'simple sons' like himself. These people have no desire for wealth:

> No riches covet they – and they have none.
> Nor are they less content than those who lead
> A life of luxury and splendor here,[15]

Assuming the voice of the poet, he professed to despise the idle rich who regard poetry at best as a toy:

> There are who scorn the Muse's soothing power,
> And deem the rhyming art an idle thing
> To please the wealthy in a tedious hour.

This suggests that the very notion of worldly riches now rankled with him. In this poem, a life of 'coveting' is presented as a demeaning affair, bringing nothing but tedium and discontent. It is no doubt partly as a form of self-defence that Barnes affects a moral superiority to the rich, but it was not simply because he had little money himself that he pretended to despise it. Throughout his entire life, he maintained a low opinion of money making as an end in itself. But in 'Orra' especially, the sentiment is fuelled by bitter indignation at being rejected on account of his poverty.

Perhaps to deflect a charge of merely dramatising his own situation, he reversed the genders here and presented the story from the woman's point of view. The plot of 'Orra' is simply told. Young Lawo, a mountain Lapp, is first seen rowing his little boat up river to the settlement of the maritime Lapps where his true love, Orra, lives with her father. She has already given Lawo her promise that she will never marry anyone else. Even as he pulls up his boat he hears, from within the tribal tent, Orra singing at a feast. At once, Lawo enters to announce he has left his own tribe and has now come to declare his suit. He offers Orra's father a ceremonial cup with which to seal the engagement but the man refuses it. In fact, he has already made a bargain with another suitor and both tribes at that moment are sitting together to celebrate the betrothal. Orra, her father declares, will never be his bride. It might be James Miles speaking.

Sadly, Lawo is the type that gives up easily. On hearing the news, he turns on his heel and sails away, never to return. Which leaves poor, faithful Orra abandoned, just as Barnes dreaded that he might be. Dauntless, she now pursues her lover in a little boat and lands on a rocky shore where she takes refuge in a cave. While she sleeps, her boat is washed out to sea and she is confronted with the choice of throwing herself from a height to retrieve it, thereby risking being dashed to pieces, or starving to death on the rock. In this extremity Barnes leaves her.

In 'Orra' are to be heard faint echoes of poems Barnes read in Richman's library; of *Paradise Lost*:

> Far sweeter than the sweetest lay
> That e'er the many-tongued bird
> Chants in the woods on a summer's day.

Of Pope's 'Pastorals':

> Where flocks around the verdant mountains feed,
> And yellow corn enbrowns the fading year.

Of Samuel Johnson:

> For youth and beauty are not wanting there;
> Nor is ingenuous passion deemed a crime.

And of Thomas Gray's 'Elegy in a Country Churchyard':

> But leaves the land to winter and to night.

Far from detracting from his achievement, however, such echoes reveal just how much poetry he had absorbed. True, 'Orra' is largely an amalgam of other people's sentiments and styles. But Barnes felt that if this sort of thing was what was meant by writing well, he had demonstrated that he too could do it. And with the two little books of verse he had published, he had proved that he really could write literature. One anonymous admirer had recently hailed him as the 'Poet Laureate' of Dorchester?

Emotional matters were more difficult. Somehow, his reading of Acerbi's book had got mixed up with his personal situation and he had made the story of Orra a test bench for one possible ending to his (very chaste) affair with Julia. In the poem he had imagined just how it would be if, while he remained faithful, she grew tired of their prolonged courting and accepted her father's advice to find a wealthier suitor:

For ORRA loved her sire full well,
And love she knew to him was due;
But then she felt a nameless spell
That bound her to her lover too.

In the poem, James Miles is even given his own lines to speak:

'Youth' said the venerable man,
I cannot take the proffered wine,
'Thy suit alas! is vain, nor can
The maid thou askest e'er be thine'.

If this should prove true then, like Lawo, he too would become a 'weary wretch... doomed to prove the anguish of the ever-aching breast'. In 'Orra', he anticipated a final rejection. Yet in the very act of publishing it, he was making yet another attempt to alter that decision by demonstrating his talents, and therefore proving his worthiness as a prospective husband for Julia. Miles was unmoved.

The lovers' relationship had now become more open, for though Miles did not approve of it, she had grown into a forceful Miss with a mind of her own. And there were still good times. They continued to meet for 'happy walks and meetings' and 'boating excursions on the Frome', but there was now an element of pathos about them. In one of his most poignant sketches written at this time, Barnes described such an occasion:

## The Aquatic Excursion

The Glittering waters smoothly flow,
The moon is shining bright,
My love is come that I may row
Her up the stream tonight...

... Soft gliding we have sailed a mile,
And Julia sitting at the stern,
Looks on me with a winning smile
And gently asks me to return.
I turn the boat, the stream is wide
And we are sailing with the tide
And throwing down the oars to rest
I sit me down by Julia's side
And press her to my breast.
She slyly turns the rudder round
And in the bed of reeds we ride
And Julia she begins to chide
'Away', says she, 'away and guide
The boat, or else 'twill run aground.'
I take the oar, on flies the boat
The boat strikes up the foam
As o'er the glittering waves we float
And we again reach home. [16]

By 1822, they had been courting for four years and were still no nearer to getting married. Barnes now became even more despondent and apprehensive that Julia would eventually break things off. To calm his fears, she agreed to a secret betrothal, though this guaranteed nothing at all. And in their hearts they both knew that things could not go on like this for much longer.

# 4

# TEACHING HIMSELF: MERE

## —— 1823-1828 ——

It was Barnes's friend, William Gilbert Carey, who made the suggestion that changed his life. As Barnes's confidant, he had long lived with the story of his friend's love life and well understood that it was poverty that was the chief obstacle to his marrying Julia Miles. Almost nightly, gazing down on sleeping Dorchester from the windows above the pastry shop, the two young men discussed the matter, while Barnes's mood swung from hope to despair.

Carey had been educated in a small private school in Mere, Wiltshire, and towards the end of 1822 he received news that Mr Robertson, his old schoolmaster, had died. Apparently, there was no one to succeed him. This set Carey thinking. Why should Barnes not go to Mere and take Robertson's place? As he talked about it, the plan seemed to accrue advantages, and Barnes's other friends also warmed to the idea. There was nothing to stand in his way. In those days, no formal qualifications were required of a schoolmaster, and no significant financial investment. Anyone might start up a school. At Mere, Barnes could combine the roles of professional and businessman. Moreover, his temperament and interests were ideally suited to the profession. He was a scholar, could read Latin and Greek and, at twenty-one, he was far better educated than most country schoolmasters. Parents would surely pay handsomely for the extra tuition he could offer. Most importantly, a successful private schoolmaster running his own establishment could earn considerably more than a clerk, so Barnes, at last, would be able to afford a wife.

Barnes himself was doubtful. Constitutionally modest and diffident, he was painfully aware of his limitations. The only early education he had ever had was in a small parish school and he was not a university man. Not having enjoyed the sort of private education which Carey now proposed that he should offer others, he feared the parents would find him out. Moreover, such a scheme involved a considerable risk, requiring him to exchange his only sure source of income for a very doubtful enterprise. He would also have to leave his circle of friends in Dorchester to go to a place where he knew nobody. Worst of all was the prospect of a prolonged separation from Julia, who might at last give in to her father and accept a wealthier suitor.

On the other hand, he had to admit that the scheme had advantages and seemed to offer the only hope that he might eventually marry his sweetheart. His friends agreed. Carey, Fuller and the Revd Richman all encouraged him to go to Mere. Still he hesitated. What turned the scale, however, was the fervent advocacy of the plan by Julia herself. She reminded him that her own brother, Frederick, already conducted a similar small private school and was making a commercial success of it. And when Barnes wistfully pleaded against their separation, she put courage in him. Yes, she said, she too dreaded their parting but he must grasp this opportunity. Not only might it eventually make it possible for them to marry, but it pointed the way for him to become a successful professional man, respected for his scholarship; a gentleman even. And suspecting, perhaps, that he was still not entirely sure of her, she announced that if Barnes went to Mere, in order that she might become better fitted as a schoolmaster's wife, she would take on pupils herself. He decided to go.

About twelve miles from Barnes's old home at Sturminster, Mere was situated at the northern edge of the Blackmore Vale. It was not easy for him to get there from Dorchester because, then as now, the main roads in the West Country tended to run from east to west rather than north to south. Not that he could have afforded a stagecoach fare, even if he sat on top. In later days when travelling to and fro, he generally rode on a fish cart, which was a cheap, if smelly, mode of transport. So it was probably on some such a vehicle that he first jolted his way into the cobbled town in the New Year of 1823.

One look round was sufficient to make his heart sink. Mere was a drab little place. The three principal thoroughfares of small grey houses, Salisbury Street, Boar Street and Castle Street, all met at the market square, around which were grouped the White Hart, the Angel and the Old George (sometimes known as the Talbot). That was it. There was no more. Around the town, the level fields stretched far away, broken only by the mound of Castle Hill to the west, and chalk downs to the north.

On enquiry, he learned that Mr Robertson's school had been conducted in the Old Cross Loft which was the upper room of the Market House. This proved to be an ancient gabled building in the square. Arched apertures, protected by massive wooden doors, gave onto the street. On market days, these were thrown open so that wooden stalls might be pushed out onto the flagstones, radiating from the building like the spokes of a wheel.[1]

The Old Cross Loft was a bare room furnished with rough benches. A ladder in the alcove by the great east window enabled access so that the town clock might be wound.[2] The loft must have been quite large because Barnes later wrote to tell Julia that, 'Whenever the comedians visit Mere, my room is generally their theatre'. This then had been Robertson's school. But when Barnes made enquiries, he was taken aback to discover that it had ceased to exist. There was no school.

*Above:* The Market House, Mere, where Barnes kept his first school. (Private collection)

*Left:* The Old Cross Loft, above the Market House, Mere. (Private collection)

Now began the most testing time of his life. He was only twenty-two and thrown entirely on his own resources. First he found lodgings, most likely in Salisbury Street, and then went about the business of recruiting pupils. Quite how he did this is not known, but he must have begun by calling upon those parents who had previously sent their sons to Robertson. He was not suited to canvassing, for his was a retiring nature. But he was now obliged to tramp the streets, calling on shopkeepers and farmers, trying to drum up custom. Perforce he braved indifference, patronising smirks and curt rebuffs, yet he stuck to his task grimly.

He had picked a bad time. Agriculture was still in recession after the Napoleonic Wars and many tenant farmers simply did not have the means to educate their sons. Nor was the local linen industry in good shape. There had been a time when there was such a demand for linen goods that the local flax had to be supplemented by supplies from Ireland and Hamburg. The weaving sheds of Mere had been crowded with men, while hundreds of women worked at looms in their cottages. The town was celebrated for its cloth, especially dowlas, cheesecloth and tow. But by the time Barnes arrived, the linen industry was in general decline throughout the West Country. In 1826 half the weavers in Mere were laid off. As a result the town was 'very much burdened with the poor', reported one observer.[3]

What counted most in Barnes's favour, however, was not the quality of the education he offered but the position of his school in the market square. Though only a small place with a population of about 2,500, Mere stood at the intersection of two important routes and this square was the centre of its economic life. Here was the stopping place on the turnpike road between London, Taunton and Exeter, and also for cross-country traffic between Bath, Blandford and Salisbury. Smart coachmen would pull up with a fine clatter to let down their passengers at the Talbot, while groaning wagons laden high with goods rumbled to a halt outside the humbler taverns so that sweating carters might refresh themselves. There were always comings and goings here, and upon this traffic the economy of the town depended. Barnes's school was therefore surrounded by little shops and businesses, and it was these small tradesmen and proprietors who were his chief patrons. For it did not take long for them to work out that in patronising him, they could save on expenses. If they sent their boys to Mr Barnes, they would be spared travel costs and boarding fees.

Meanwhile, in the first months of the year back in Dorchester, Julia anxiously awaited news of him. January came and went, as did February and March, and it was not until April that she got a letter:

Mere 9th April 1823

My Dear Girl

It is not without resistance to the feelings of my heart that I have refrained so long from writing to you, but I was unwilling to deceive you with false hope, much less would I vex, with ill-founded doubts, a heart of sensibility as I believe yours to be, and one which I hope is sufficiently attached to me to feel hurt at any calamity which may fall upon me.

At present I have every reason to hope for success in my new profession. I have ten pupils which I am satisfied with, as a beginning; for, as there has not been a school of any consequence here lately the greater number of boys are sent to Schools out of the Town, from which their friends will not of course take them without giving some sort of notice – I know of 10 or 12 boys whose friends intend to send them to me in the next quarter, and I have little doubt of having, after a reasonable time, a good school.[4]

Yet despite this modest success, Barnes still yearned for the wider cultural life of Dorchester and the company of his friends there. The buildings of Mere, he informed Julia, were 'very mean' and 'the Society much inferior to Dorchester, there being very few well-informed Young Men in the place', so that he could not hope 'for an acquaintance equal to Mr Fuller'. Above all, he missed her. With something like a sigh he described his solitary walks to the south of the town, from whence he could look out over 'an immense plain' and, on a good day, see to within eight miles of Dorchester.

Much of what we know of him in these years derives from these old love letters. They were not very frequent, because postage rates were so high. Though Dorchester and Mere were less than fifty miles apart, it still cost 8*d* to send a single sheet between them, which would have been a significant sum to Barnes. To get round this, people often entrusted their letters to friends who happened to be travelling in the desired direction, depending on an informal passing from hand to hand thereafter. But travellers between Mere and Dorchester were probably few and far between and missives conveyed by this method were not always sure to find their destinations. Nevertheless, a number of letters between Barnes and Julia have survived.

She replied immediately on 16 April. Aware when writing to a schoolmaster of her inadequacies in spelling and grammar, ('excuse all imperfections'), she kept her dignity and distance by a formality of tone. For fear of compromising herself, she addressed her absent lover merely as 'Dear Barnes' and signed herself 'your Sincere Friend'. A girl of eighteen, she was still not sure of the appropriate way to express herself to this young man who was by no means certain to be her future husband. Dorchester gossip was her main topic. 'About a fortnight ago,' she told him, 'Mr Boniface was maried [sic]', while her brother Frederick's school was doing very well with twenty boarders. Fearing perhaps that her news might strike him as trivial, she included a solemn little homily: 'We should ever remember that patience is required of everything we undertake'.

Nevertheless, she had something to tell him which presaged a great change in their prospects:

> On Tuesday I went for a little ride out of town with my Father and as we was returning in the Evening he began a Conversation which I have long wish'd to hear him begin, it was as you must suppose Concerning us, he told me plainly he had no objection to you in the leaste [sic] – but on the contrary you was a person he much respected – but then he told me I must Remember that when you first walk'd with me I was but a meer Child, and it was his deuty [sic] as an affectionate Father to make objections – but still he wish'd me to understand that he would not be an obstacle in the way if I had placed my affections, by no means...

She then recounted the history of the painful relations between her father and him in past years, but ended with the news for which they had both been waiting:

> ... he thought your Intentions were Honourable – but at the same time you had not openly avou'd them to him and he should by no means give his consent to any thing untill [sic] you had, I then reminded him you had written twice and come twice to the house with the intention to speak with him on the subject he said he was aware of that – but still whenever he met you in the street you always passed him with such contempt that he certainly did not like it but he thought if he had but half an hours Conversation with you that would set you to rights and you would be very good friends...

Barnes now gathered rightly that he was an accepted suitor. From that time onwards, whenever he had the opportunity to visit Dorchester, he was accepted as one of the family in the Miles household. Julia's news had at last dissipated the dread he had felt since arriving in Mere, that at any moment he might receive a letter from her breaking off the match.

Success with Julia, however, still depended on his making a go of the school. On 28 April 1823 he placed an advertisement in the *Salisbury and Winchester Journal* which gives some idea of the curriculum that he could offer. The list also indicates just how much self-education he himself had undertaken since his years as a pupil in Sturminster's school for the children of the poor:

MERE WILTS

> W. Barnes respectfully informs the inhabitants of Mere, and its vicinity that he has opened a School in a commodious Room over the Market Place, in that Town, where he teaches Reading, plain and ornamental Penmanship, Geography. Arithmetic and English Grammar, at Three Guineas per annum; and if required, Drawing, Music and Latin at Three Guineas each per annum.[5]

Concluding, he assured parents of his continued 'unremitting exertion' in discharging his duties to his pupils.

The offer of Latin tuition tactfully signalled that his was a middle-class establishment and the schoolmaster a man of superior abilities. Yet many of the cash-strapped parents of Mere would have had more practical skills in mind. What they required was that their lads should be taught to read and write proficiently, and to keep accounts. And also, perhaps, that they might learn to speak without too much of the local dialect so that they might be distinguished from their prospective employees, the labourers' children who filled the free places at Mr Glover's parish school.

What Barnes was anxiously testing was whether there were enough local parents to pay his fees. Recruitment was slow and there were others trawling for the same pupils. In May he wrote to tell Julia that he now had twelve pupils, though 'a Schoolmaster has come here to oppose me'. In July he wrote again, expressing 'the anxiety' he felt concerning the fortunes of his school. It was necessary, he said, for him to be very active in order to counteract a rival who was 'using every means to procure the Children of the Neighbourhood'. He decided to postpone his longed-for summer holiday visit to Dorchester because these weeks were the prime recruiting time for the forthcoming academic year. His efforts paid off. By August he had obtained twenty-four pupils.

Getting paid was quite another matter. So unworldly was Barnes that he never imagined that parents might try to cheat him. But they did. His bills were retrospective; parents were expected to settle after they had received his services. But when, after he had delivered accounts, he still received no payment, he was obliged to go round knocking on their doors to remind them. Then some would complain that they could not find the money at that time, or plead that they could afford only part of his fee, or argue that their boys had been taken out of school for haymaking and that therefore they should not have to pay for lost days. Others would simply procrastinate from one week to the next in order to avoid paying altogether. By the end of the year he complained to Julia that though his school was 'somewhat increased', he had difficulty in getting his bills settled because of the 'depressed state of agriculture or from the peculiar poverty of Mere'. The financial anxieties induced by such problems never allowed him to feel secure at the Market House School.

Come Christmas and the lovers were briefly reunited in Dorchester, but in January 1824 he had to return to Mere with no improvement in their situation. His was now a life of damp, dirty days; of rowdy boys stamping snow off their boots on the steps up to his cold classroom; of the whirring and striking of the clock in the loft; of the great roar from the street on market days, when he had to shout to make himself heard; of late-paying parents avoiding his eyes in the streets; and long dark evenings peering at pages by the light of a taper. In her artless and occasional letters, Julia retailed the tittle-tattle of Dorchester life: Miss Hazard had returned to London; Miss Forrest desired to be remembered; the Dorchester races had been a success. But Dorchester was of diminishing concern to him. More hopeful was the information that Julia had now started to take pupils and, very endearing, her sweet little enquiry concerning the collars he wore. If he sported the fashionable kind, she said, she would use a little of her spare time to make him more.

A letter in November brought sad news. Julia wrote to say that there had been a great storm in Dorset, so fierce that the promenade at Weymouth had been entirely destroyed. Worse still, it had toppled a stack of chimneys on the house of Barnes's Dorchester patron, the Revd Richman, and both he and his wife had been killed in their bed.

The emotional lives of this pair now revolved entirely around the few days each year when they could be together in Dorchester during the Christmas and summer holidays. But in April 1825, Julia wrote with news that threatened to separate them for good. Her father, James Miles, had now been ordered by his superiors in the excise office to leave the town in order to take up a new post in Nailsea. Along with the rest of her family, she would have to follow him. As far as she could say at the time of writing, the Mileses would leave Dorchester at the end of the summer. Barnes was desolate. In his romantic reveries, it was always in Dorchester that he pictured Julia and himself together, for this was the town where he had first seen her getting down from a coach. Replying, he told her that 'the rambles at Frome, the Excursions on the water and the stolen meetings in the Walks with many other incidents are so fresh on my memory that I should not be able to see Dorchester without pain if you were absent'.[6] On reflection, however, he realised things might have been worse. After all, Nailsea was in the West Country, only seven miles from Bristol and twenty from Bath. It was no farther from Mere than Dorchester, so that they could still spend their holidays together. Had her father been sent to the other end of the country, they would never have been able to see each other again.

As it turned out, though most of the Miles family left Dorchester by the following June, Julia stayed on a little longer. This was partly in order to finish a term's teaching, but also, no doubt, so that she might spend a few days with Barnes. This summer holiday took on a particular poignancy for them both because they believed they were saying farewell to Dorchester, the town where they had first met and which was consequently so dear to them.

Another cause for alarm was that Julia was now repeatedly unwell. Quite what was wrong with her is not clear, but she suffered several such setbacks during the next few years. She comforted herself, however, with the thought that when she enjoyed the clean air of Nailsea Heath, she would soon be much better. She was in for a shock. Having expected to find a salubrious country village, she discovered that it was the site of the largest glassworks in the country. In September she wrote:

> Nailsea which from my Sisters description I had every reason to believe was the very place I should have chosen for my residence even through life turns out to be a most miserable smoky place our house which is not one of the most commodious in the world stands directly opposite the Glass works and in wet weather the smoke which issues out of the Chimneys in large clouds descends on our house which renders wet weather doubly dreary...

But a month later she was able to admit that though, for a time, she had been an invalid and quite unable to write, she was now much better. That Christmas was the first they spent together in Nailsea.

Meanwhile, Barnes was struggling on with his school. Sometimes he had a few more pupils, sometimes a few less. On average it was about twenty boys of all ages who came chattering up to the Old Cross Loft each morning. When he began teaching, Barnes had no pedagogic skills or experience other than the recollection of his own schooldays in Sturminster. How could one teach boys of many different ages and abilities all at the same time? How did one go about explaining the elements of English grammar, or the principles of long division? He was obliged to answer these and a hundred other questions daily in his classroom. He learnt his profession by practising it, by teaching himself. On one matter, however, he had a settled view from the start. In an era when flogging was rife in public schools, he never used any form of corporal punishment. Throughout his long career as a teacher, his manner to his pupils was always gentle and considerate. Despite this, he never seems to have had any disciplinary problems.

His was a lonely life. During his early years in Mere he had few friends because his social position was anomalous. Too refined to mix with the labouring classes and too erudite for the company of most tradesmen, he was socially unfitted to join the minor gentry and small professional men at the bar of the Talbot or the Ship, even if he had had the money or the inclination to do so. Yet his living partly depended on networking, and maintaining at least the façade of gentility.

It was perhaps for this reason that he neglected contact with his own family, though they were still just a few miles down the road in Bagber. It seems that he never visited his father, who had continued to work his patch of land there. Curiously detached is the tone of a letter to Julia in July 1826, giving her the 'unpleasant information… of the death of my Sister, [Ann] who I believe caught her death from inhabiting a House the walls of which were damp from some repairs which had been made on it'. Presumably he did not go to the funeral. Nor did he refer to Ann's young child. He probably feared that a whisper round Mere concerning his low connections would damage his school.

So, unsupported by family or friends he pursued his lonely days. In winter he would rise with the light, make his way to school, teach all day and then return to his lodgings for supper, book and bed. He wrote to Julia: 'I am writing this Letter in my room where I have spent many a studious hour, and am accompanied only by a little Dog which is amusing himself by endeavouring to catch the Shadows thrown by the Candle by which I am writing'.[7] Spring and summertime were more spacious; after school he often took solitary walks out to Castle Hill or along the River Shreen.

*Above left:* Engraver's card, Mere. (Dorset County Museum)

*Above right:* Engraver's card. Barnes never worked in Bath. (Dorset County Museum)

Yet this solitary time was the making of him. Thrown back on himself, he began to discover his own inner resources and talents. His love of everything artistic now found new outlets. Letters to Julia were often accompanied by little poems and sketches depicting such scenes as a windy day, a card party or herself with a cat. In April 1825 he told her that he had been engraving a trade card for himself. Two have survived, one advertising 'W. Barnes, Copper Plate and Wood Cut Engraver, Mere', and the other 'W. Barnes Engraver, Bath'.[8] His aspiration to become an engraver was, he now admitted, an 'idle day-dream', though he had recently fulfilled some orders. Having invested in 'a very small and pretty copper-plate press' when he first arrived in Mere in 1826, he 'cut some little blocks for Mr Barter, a printer in Blackmore and was paid mostly in bookbinding and cheese'. A year later he engraved blocks for a Mr John Rutter of Salisbury.

The Christmas holiday of 1825 renewed his concerns about Julia's health. One day they started to climb Nailsea Hill together when she flagged and stopped. They had to turn back because she was 'so feeble and so ill'. His alarm was such that even after he had returned to Mere, she had to write to assure him that she was now much better and could climb the hill 'with very little difficulty'. He feared that she was tubercular.

In a letter written to her at about this time he once again professed his constant love, but this time there was a note of reproach, and even a touch of self-pity. The ardent lover was beginning to resent the length of their courtship:

> And thou, in absence, may'st discover
> How much remembered, and how dear
> Thou art to that unaltered Lover
> Who loves thee both from far and near
> Of late 'tis seldom he has viewed thee,
> And beauty too has smiled around him,
> And yet, through years, thou still hast found him
> Fond as when he first wooed thee.[9]

In the summer of 1826, the omens were not good. Julia was ill again, and this time so gravely that she was obliged to give up her teaching and go to 'Swanwich' (Swanage) for a long recuperation. For Christmas he sent her a copy of a lugubrious sonnet by Petrarch accompanied by his own translation.

In likening his state 'to a Ship in Distress', he declared himself to be 'laden with oblivion', while 'those two lovely eyes that lit my track/ Are gone, and reason in the waves is drowned/ And I cannot the destined haven find'.

This was a temporary poetic pose. Barnes was not really the despairing kind. He was too creative, and too energetic to allow adverse circumstances to depress him for very long. More interesting than his melancholic affectation here is the evidence that this obscure rural schoolmaster was translating all Petrarch's sonnets into English. Nor was Italian the only language he had studied alone by candlelight in his lonely lodgings. Years after he left Mere he recorded:

> I took up in turn Latin, Greek, French, Italian, and German. I began Persian with Lee's grammar, and for a little time Russian, which, as being wanting in old lore, I soon cast off. I luckily had a French master as friend in M. Charles Masson, an old French surgeon, who had heretofore been brought to England as a prisoner of war, and had married an Englishwoman of this neighbourhood, and was living in Mere. For some time I kept a diary of short daily notes in Italian or German for the sake of improvement in those languages.[10]

Evidently, he was developing quite prodigious language skills. But no one knew it. There was no one in his small circle of acquaintances even capable of guessing that he was already a formidable linguist, and certainly not the raw youths to whom he occasionally taught Latin as an extra for three guineas a year.

Despite his intense labour, after three years in Mere his financial situation and prospects had barely improved. It also came as a blow to his confidence when Julia reported her father's opinion that 'he thought it useless for you to waste your time in trying to establish a School in such a place as Mere'.[11] It seemed as if she agreed with him. Barnes too, if he were honest, had to admit that though the town had supplied him with a living, it was a poor one. He was also uneasily aware that another depression in farming or the cloth trade might close him down altogether. The way to prosper with a private school was to take boarders, but he was prevented from doing so because he was unmarried. Yet he could not get married because he was not prosperous enough.

One way out was to change his circumstances. In December 1826 he wrote to tell Julia that he had recently applied and failed to obtain the third mastership of a 'Classical and Mathematical School' at Plymouth. His references from Dr England (the Rector of Winterborne Came, near Dorchester) and four other clergymen had been well received, but at the last moment a more suitable candidate had come forward. The irony was that he had been rejected because the governors of the school now intended to take boarders, and it was desirable that the successful candidate should be a married man.[12]

Others, meanwhile, were getting on in the world. Back in Dorchester, his old flatmate Gilbert Carey had been given articles by Mr Coombs, which meant that some day he too would be a qualified lawyer. Barnes must have wondered with some bitterness if he himself should have stuck to the law. Nevertheless, Carey had not forgotten him and wrote to suggest that he should apply for the post of Inspector of Weights and Measures for Dorset. When this fell through, he recommended that Barnes should seek a clerkship at Pattison's Bank in Dorchester, at a salary of £1,000 a year. The only drawback to this application, he reported blithely, was that the candidate was required to supply two sureties of £2,000 each. There was no hope that Barnes could find them.

But by February 1827, things were looking up. Fortunately, one of his few supporters in Mere also happened to be a go-ahead local businessman. Charles Card so much admired Barnes's teaching abilities that he had said he wanted all of his seven sons to be educated at his school.[13] Card kept a shop opposite the old Market House. It was an early nineteenth-century version of a department store, on two floors, selling groceries, household goods, drapery and ironmongery. Card was related by marriage to the Jupeses who ran the local linen factory and, between them, the two families seemed to have had a finger in most business concerns in the town. Their prosperity, however, had been hampered by the lack of good local banking facilities. The nearest bank had been the Salisbury & Shaftesbury, but in 1810 its three partners were declared bankrupt. At this point, Card resolved to remedy the situation by setting up his own bank. It was not very impressive to look at, just another department in his shop, on the scale of a modern sub-Post Office, but it made Card the principal businessman in Mere, and a very useful friend to William Barnes.

What was more natural then that in deciding his future path, Barnes should have discussed matters with his friend Charles Card and that the latter should have tried to persuade him to remain in Mere? Card pointed out that since the proprietor of a local girls' school had just left the town, there was a new opportunity for Barnes to expand his academy. The only difficulty was that he would need a female teacher. Still doubtful about whether Julia's health was up to the work, and whether she was really willing to try, Barnes wrote to her at Radipole near Weymouth. He wanted to know just how far she was willing to commit herself: 'I would certainly take the Liberty of asking whether you would be inclined to do so or not. I mention this subject to you now that I may ascertain your sentiments upon it and make requisite arrangements. I would request you to state not only whether you would receive pupils but the very degree of Inclination or Disinclination you feel'.[14]

In March, he wrote again with exciting news: 'I am now in treaty for a House which is admirably adapted for a Boarding School'. Apparently the owner had some sort of objection to letting his property for a school, but Barnes thought this could be got over. In any case, he was also considering a second house for his – no, their – school. At last their plans were falling into place. It had been settled that they would be married and run a school together; he was to teach day boys and boarders, and she day girls, in the same premises.

Once the decision had been taken, things moved fast. On the last day of March he reported that he had been offered 'a large house' at twenty guineas a year but that the 'Gentleman who has been good enough to be my adviser' (Card) was at that time in London, but that when he had heard the gentleman's advice he would make up his mind. Apparently this house was more suited to their purpose than the other he had mentioned, though he considered its large garden a drawback. On Good Friday he told her that he was printing advertising cards for his school and that he looked forward to consulting Mrs Miles, presumably on the subject of bed linen. He added that 'a Gentleman of Mere [Card again] who understands Housekeeping much better than myself has kindly offered to put some Furniture in the House and I am to repay him when I have collected my Debts and find it convenient'.

Card's kindly encouragement had given him new confidence and this seems to have made him more popular in Mere. The sonnet of 1825 had slyly mentioned that 'beauty' had smiled around him, which suggests that he was now receiving invitations to local houses where there were young ladies. In April he was entertained by a Captain Jennings at Evershot, the company enjoying cards and 'Mr Martin's exploits as a Ventriloquist'. Though never a man for parties, Barnes was beginning to understand that such socialising was a necessary part of his business.

That month he leased a house and began gardening, though, as he explained to Julia, 'the Flower Garden will be neglected till I shall have a Wife'. He ordered bedsteads from the landlord's agent, and Card was to supply him with the bedding he needed for boarders, brown tick for the mattresses, sheets, counterpanes, bolsters and sacking, all at moderate prices. The news going round Mere now was that 'Mr Barnes has taken Miss Grove's House, and is going to keep a Boarding School, and marry a young lady of Bristol'.[15]

Years later he noted briefly: 'In 1827 I took Chantry House at Mere, and on a happy day – happy as the first of a most happy wedded life – I brought into it my most loveworthy and ever-beloved wife, Julia Miles, and then took boarders'.[16]

His solitary exile in Mere had lasted four years and seven months. They had been courting for nine years.

# 5

# THE UNIVERSAL GENIUS OF CHANTRY HOUSE

## —— 1827-1835 ——

One May Day morning in 1830, an observer might have witnessed a strange scene enacted in a Wiltshire garden. From an ancient house set on a slope, a figure in a blue flannel dressing gown padded down to a pond, fed by a little stream which overflowed into a waterfall. A few trees overshadowed the water and an early sun was already dappling the surface where midges were gathering in clouds. Pausing at the edge, the young man took off his robe and stood there in vest and drawers, with flat platforms strapped to his feet. When he stepped towards the shallows, a startled duck or two shot off across the adjoining fields.

A few onlookers stood around. There was a young woman with a baby in her arms, who more than once called out for him to be careful. There were also a few curious schoolboys, though this Easter holiday time had been especially chosen so that most of the pupils at Chantry House would be absent when their ingenious master tested out his latest invention. William Barnes was about to walk on water.

Or, rather, in it. Wading in breast high, he now struck out but at once appeared to be having trouble with his specially designed swimming shoes. One had come off. He had incorporated valves into the soles, which were designed to provide the maximum resistance when pushing the foot down, and the least when drawing it up so that, in this way, the swimmer would have more push. The idea was sound in principle but put too great a strain on the straps. Eventually, after various adjustments and two more trials, he gave up.[1]

A number of his other inventions proved more successful. These included a quadrant for taking angular measurements and an 'instrument for describing ellipses'.[2] As many other men have found, the early years of a happy marriage released a surge of creativity in him and made this time the most creative of his entire life. From dawn till dusk he was absorbed with his teaching, gardening, engraving, woodwork, music, reading and language study. Meanwhile he was writing pamphlets, articles and letters to the press. These activities were the harvest of those years of study when he had lived alone in Mere. Now came the revelation of what his daughter called 'his universal inventive genius'. That there were few to admire it seemed hardly to matter to him, so absorbed was he in his own creations.

The Barneses had been married in the Norman Church of the Holy Trinity, Nailsea, Somerset, on 19 July 1827, probably by the rector, the Revd Peter Guillebaud. Nailsea was now the home of the bride's family, and James Miles and his wife would have attended with any of the various brothers who happened to be around. It seems that John Barnes was not present. No doubt the forty mile journey from Sturminster would have been too difficult and expensive for him to undertake, even if he had been invited. Probably he was not. By this time, Barnes seems to have cast off any last links with his own family and been absorbed into the middle-class Mileses. His early attachments now embarrassed him.

Chantry House, his new school, was very old even at that time. The Grove family who had owned it were Royalists and loyal supporters of Charles II throughout the years of the Commonwealth. Their home had once served as a medieval chantry and had its origin in 1425, when Henry VI licensed the Dean and Chapter of Salisbury to award a certain piece of land on the south side of St Michael's Church for the common use of the chaplains. A chantry priest had lived there who had written a long poem entitled 'The Fantasy of the Fox', which was printed by Caxton's assistant, Wynken de Worde, in 1530. It tells of a priest who loses a pet fox and, in a vision, sees it captured and put to death by the people of Mere. When he wakes, he finds that the vision is true. Barnes probably never knew of this literary connection, but at desolate times in later life he might well have echoed the concluding words of the poem: 'Alas, my heart mourneth for pity and compassion. That reasonable people should be merciless'.[3]

After her marriage, the twenty-five-year-old Julia Barnes opened a girls' day school, and at the same time took over the management of the house. It was a rambling affair and therefore difficult to keep clean. There was a great parlour (the vestiges of Sir Johyn Thynne's medieval Great Hall), a little parlour, a buttery, at least two flights of stairs and two fireplaces, all on various levels. There was some wainscot, but the walls were mostly bare stone which made the place especially damp in winter. C.J. Wallis later described how forbidding he found the place when he was a pupil there:

> … A long, cold, dreary, one-storeyed edifice presenting to those looking from the front a somewhat gloomy and depressing view.
>
> The internal arrangements of Chantry House are singularly deficient in comfort. There is an air of isolation about the rooms as if familiar intercourse were forbidden; there are no cosy recesses, no quaint nooks and corners, no profusion of convenient cubboards. On one side of the building are situated the kitchen, with the usual offices attached to it, and a staircase leading to that part of the upper floor which then, for the most part, comprised the schoolroom and the boys, bedrooms. On the other side of a small room, then furnished as a parlour, and above it the apartments specially appropriated to Barnes and his family. The intermediate part of the building contains a large room – then the dining room – and a wide passage through the house.
>
> The schoolroom was situated on the upper storey of the house, and had a front aspect. This aspect… would, but for the presence of youth, have inevitably imparted a grave and solemn direction to the thoughts and feelings of the beholder. No counter-acting object was visible – the church and the churchyard were all that could be seen.[4]

These comments give no hint of the true charm of the building. Perhaps this is because many original features had been plastered and boarded over in Barnes's day, though the handsome timber roof was probably still visible from the interior of the Great Hall. The exterior of Chantry House, however, must always have been pleasing. Its structure may be understood at a glance, for it is in essence a symmetrical stone rectangle, very pleasing in its simplicity.[5]

Chantry House, Mere, with St Michael's Church behind. This watercolour was probably painted by Barnes. (Dorset County Museum)

Old prints and photographs of Chantry House, viewed from the south, often give a false impression because they appear to display a tower growing out of its roof. This is an illusion. The tower is actually that of St Michael's Church, just a few steps to the north. So close is the church that it was easy for Barnes to slip across for a moment or two to practise the organ. He did not need to go round to the north of the church, to the avenue of limes (or lindens) which lead up to the main entrance, because he had a little gate from his own garden which gave access to the nave.

The view from his classroom over the churchyard was a gloomy one, but the prospect on the other side was very different. Here was an open plot (or lea) of grassland that ran down to the pond. On first coming here, Barnes had thought this garden would be a distraction from his professional duties. But, in April 1827, even before he took formal possession of the place, he had planted a vegetable patch and began to clear thickets of brambles and weed. In following years, gardening became his chief form of exercise and one of his greatest pleasures. Entries in his Italian diary sometimes comprise a single word, 'zappando', meaning digging. Spring and summer evenings were spent planting and weeding, but he preferred to mow in the early mornings, before his pupils were up. These were the days before the mowing machine and grass was still cut by scythe. Barnes excelled at the work. Despite his aspirations to achieve a professional status, he had generations of farm workers as his forbears. His whole nature was expressed in the rhythm of the work: in the whetting of the steel; the swish of the blade; the steady, alternating swings; the clean, sweet cut; and the ordered falling of dew-fresh swathes as he progressed along the line.

Business improved as soon as the school opened at Chantry House. This was largely due to Julia, for she quickly became its public face as well as its manager and accountant. Barnes had always hated going cap in hand to prospective parents to beg for their custom. By contrast, Julia was proactive and good at networking. Parents were no longer confronted by a hesitant young schoolmaster who might easily be taken advantage of, but a forceful young woman who insisted on respect. Wallis reported that on 'momentous business occasions' she assumed 'an air of becoming pride and importance', imparted by 'an impressive dignity to her language'. In her husband, 'such qualities were conspicuous by their absence'.[6] And unlike him, she was socially ambitious.

It is doubtful whether the projected girls' boarding school ever got underway. On 11 June 1827, Barnes (or more probably, Julia) placed an advertisement in the *Salisbury and Winchester Journal* which does not mention girls:

BOARDING SCHOOL, MERE, WILTS

W. BARNES having taken a very commodious House, would be happy to Receive BOARDERS, after the Midsummer Recess. TERMS very moderate.
The course of Instruction embraces Reading, Writing, Arithmetic, Grammar, and Geography; (and extra) the Latin, French, Italian and Spanish Languages, with the Mathematics and Drawing.
This would be an eligible School for Young Gentlemen having a taste for the Fine Arts, or intended for professions connected with them.

It may be that this first advertisement was not as successful as they hoped, because another was placed in the same newspaper a month later, this time emphasising Barnes's 'Commercial Course of Tuition'. Most parents in Mere were concerned to prepare their sons for careers in trade, rather than the learned professions. This was a perennial problem for Barnes. His wish to emphasise an academic curriculum was at odds with the market for which he was catering.

Although there is little evidence, it is likely that Julia kept a girls' day school, at least until she was encumbered with her own children. There was no question of co-education. As an advertisement in the *Dorset County Chronicle* on 28 December 1827 explained, 'the size of the house enables W. Barnes's Academy for Young Gentlemen and Mrs Barnes's Establishment for Ladies to be kept quite separate'. A surviving account for a pupil named Miss Fry from Christmas 1830 itemises £1 3s 6d for tuition, with 6d extra for fire and stationary. Some notion of the curriculum may be gained from a list of class books for which her parents were charged: there was a Bible History (9d),

Silhouette of Mrs Julia Barnes. (Dorset County Museum)

a History of England (6s), a dictionary (3s 6d), a Grammar (1s) and a Glossary (1s). It has been deduced that Julia's fees were like those of her husband;'3gns p.a. plus books and stationary-and fire'. At this modest rate, the teacher would have needed at least seven pupils in order to earn even a farm worker's wage.[7]

At first sight, the Mere Academy might have appeared much like many other small private schools throughout England at this time. What was different was the curriculum and the master. In 1829 Barnes was advertising tuition in the 'Latin, French, Italian, Spanish, Portuguese, German, Swedish and Danish languages'. Just how many takers he had for Danish and Swedish must be a matter of doubt, but the claim was impressive and it was a good advertisement. What parents could not have guessed is that all these languages would be taught by just one man. For Barnes had become a linguistic marvel, able to teach himself to read and write one language after another. This was no ordinary schoolmaster.

As for Julia, she had taken on a tremendous workload. It was she who managed both the house and school. It was she who took on the catering and cleaning, the washing and mending of boys' clothes and bed linen, and the teaching of the girls' school. And it was also she who dealt with tradesmen, who were often difficult, and negotiated with the parents in arrears. What help she had in the house in these early days is not known, but it could not have been much because they could not afford it. Wallis testified to the fact that 'Barnes was grievously beset with poverty… onwards for many years'. Their daughter, Lucy, confirmed that they were very poor at this time, but, she adds, 'very happy'. Their happiness was increased by the birth of their first child, Laura Liebe in November 1828. Julia Eliza was born four years later in February 1832, and a son, Julius, in 1834. Each child was taken back to the Mileses home in Nailsea to be baptised at Holy Trinity.

This new life was one of responsibility and hard work for the Barneses. They did not have the luxury of taking to their beds when they were ill. Having almost no help, they just had to soldier on. And though Julia was occasionally unwell – Barnes's Italian diary in January 1834 recorded 'Giulia malata – giorno triste' – she seemed to thrive on this arduous life. So did he. On some days he wrote only one word: *Felice*.

Help was at hand, though occasioned by a tragic event. In 1832 Julia's father, James Miles, was living in Abergavenny, where he had now been posted. One day he was driving with one of his sons in a gig when both were thrown out. Miles died almost immediately, and his son shortly afterwards. As a result, Mrs Miles, who had once been so disapproving of Barnes, came to live with them at Chantry House. Another of Julia's brothers, the consumptive Cornelius, also joined them, perhaps to assist as an usher, though he died about three years later. But Mrs Miles lived on to be an invaluable help in the house to Julia. She was with them for over twenty years, until her death in 1853. So, in the end, the Mileses had good reason to be grateful to Barnes, whom they had once dismissed as not good enough for their daughter.

Removed from domestic concerns, he could now give greater attention to his teaching. In this he was remarkably imaginative and innovative, with ideas far ahead of his time. The school day at Mere began as it ended, with prayers. Boys were assembled in the classroom by a senior scholar who would act as usher, and Barnes entered at precisely nine o'clock, still in his dressing gown, often accompanied by a pupil carrying the apparatus he used for demonstration purposes. Lessons would start with a piece of dictation given to the whole school 'on any matter of science or history, botany, mechanics or any one of a hundred other things'. Boys were then required to parse and analyse every word of it, and 'to bring written notes on the following morning'. As the age range of his pupils was between five and sixteen, there were some who could not make much of all this, but over the years they were gradually inducted into the routine. Morning dictation was followed by work in groups, determined by the boys' ages and ability. Rather than the rote learning common at this time, Barnes preferred the Socratic method. By a process of question and answer, he tried to involve his pupils more closely, believing that by these means they would come to a truer understanding of the subject.

Afternoons were more informal. Weather permitting, he and his boys would go on educational walks, sometimes of six to eight miles. He usually set them specific tasks to complete, such as sketching botanical specimens, making notes on cloud shapes, observing formations of the rocks or exploring some place of historical interest. Mere definitions were not enough. His pupils had to have direct experience of what a word signified.[8] As far as possible, he believed that they should see, hear, touch, smell and taste the objects their notes described. This 'world-knowledge', he argued, of the 'forms of life and land, growth and ground, birds, beasts, insects, trees and flowers, weeds and minerals' was the 'groundwork' on which 'higher book-knowledge' was constructed.

Such novel approaches were based not merely on their success in the classroom but also on the master's sense of his own inadequacy. This was because Barnes was always conscious of the fact that he himself had enjoyed no education to speak of, and therefore feared that he might not have truly understood the matter in hand. Consequently, before he presumed to teach any topic he felt that he had to go to the very roots of it himself, in order to be sure of his authority. Nothing was taken on trust. It has been said that he kept a copy of Locke's *Thoughts Concerning Education* in his pocket, and though never a student of philosophy, he probably dipped into the *Essay Concerning Human Understanding* as well. Like Locke, he regarded himself as 'an under-labourer in clearing the ground a little, and removing some of the rubbish that lies in the way to knowledge'. His educational philosophy and classroom practice might have been modelled upon Locke's observation that knowledge 'had been more advanced in the world, if the endeavours of ingenious and industrious men had not been much encumbered with the learned by the frivolous use of uncouth, affected or unintelligible terms introduced into the sciences', whereas 'true knowledge of things was thought unfit or incapable to be brought into well bred company and polite conversation'.[9]

When coming into the classroom to give his morning lecture he usually carried a cane, but it was not an object of terror to the little boys because they knew that he used it merely to point out things on maps or diagrams. C.J. Wallis remembered only one occasion on which he himself had been punished. This was because, after repeated questioning, he refused to say whether or not he had completed the work assigned to him. Exasperated, Barnes finally seized him and shook him by the shoulders. Almost immediately, however, the schoolmaster seemed to regret his momentary lapse and sorrowfully directed the boy to leave the room. His gentleness gained him only respect. According to Wallis, the boys tended to revere him.

A practical problem he faced was the lack of suitable textbooks. In teaching across a wide age range, he had to leave boys to get on with their own work while he attended to others. And for this they needed primers offering examples and exercises to be worked through. So, overcoming his natural diffidence, he started to write them himself. Their publication was probably not an expensive undertaking, and he could always be sure of selling them by requiring them to be purchased by the parents. To turn their pages today is to hear faint echoes of voices from that schoolroom over 200 years ago. Not only do they provide an insight into Barnes's pedagogic practice, but also into the way his mind was moving.

The first came in 1829, with fifty pages, priced at 1s. The aim of the *Etymological Glossary* was to explain the origins of certain English words.[10] It took its origin in the inability of Barnes's rural pupils to understand much of the Latinate vocabulary then commonplace, which meant that he had had to waste considerable time in explaining hard words to them. But he considered that it was not good enough for them to simply memorise the meanings. He wanted them to understand the family resemblances between such terms so that they might be able to work out meanings for themselves, without need of a dictionary. At its most basic, this meant learning various Latin and Greek prefixes and suffixes.

An advertisement for the book described it as an 'Easy Exposition for the Use of Schools and Non-Latinists wherein the greater part of the English words of foreign derivation are so arranged that the learner is enable to acquire the Meanings of many at once.' The student was expected to learn by heart the Latin and Greek particles and 'numerical adjuncts' so that he might easily work out the meaning of many words in which they were utilised. An example was 'Dico, Dictus (Lat) to say, tell or speak'. From this 'root' the student might work out 'Contradict', v.=to say against, therefore, 'contradiction' and 'contradictory'. 'Dictate', v.=to tell what to do, will give him 'dictate', and 'diction'. Students would also be able to infer the meanings of such words as 'edict', 'predict', 'prediction', 'indict', etc. Confronted with puzzled lads, Barnes's first response to their incomprehension at the sight of such Greek and Latin forms in English was to explain them. In later years he took the view that these foreign words had no place in English at all.

In 1833 he published *A Catechism of Government in General and that of England in Particular*, which was probably one of the first textbooks of civics ever published for schools.[11] It was very relevant. Under the terms of the new reform bill, £10 copyholders and £50 leaseholders in the rural counties were now to receive the vote, and many of Barnes's pupils would eventually be among these. Consequently, he believed that they should try to understand political systems. Yet he had to be careful; parents would quickly object to any hint of political bias on his part. So he tackled the matter by catechising students on political facts:

> Q.- What is a limited monarchy?
> A.- A government in which the King cannot make any laws without the consent of the people.

> Q.- Where does this government exist?
> A.- In England, France, Sweden, Portugal, Hanover, Witemburg; etc.[12]

With ideas ranging beyond the immediate concerns of the classroom, he was now becoming not merely a teacher but a theoretical educationist. In 1834 he produced a twenty-three page pamphlet advocating 'a more common adoption' in the school curriculum of both mathematics and science.[13] But even this apparently safe subject was controversial. For, as Barnes was well aware, there were still many who regarded the study of mathematics as unsuited to the education of a gentleman and fit only for tradespeople and those few professional men who had need of them.

He begged to differ. Taking his cue from Plato, he argued that the elements of geometry provided a 'master-key' that 'opens all our investigation and comprehension. They are a great store of principles which can be applied to hundreds of different objects, and from which hundreds of propositions can be derived as infallibly true themselves'. Geometry and algebra together 'form a complete system of human reasoning'. In so arguing, he was suggesting a complete revaluation of the subject. Teaching mathematics, for him, was not just a matter of ramming multiplication tables into the heads of obdurate country boys. From what seemed petty calculations, he believed he could launch his students onto the entire sea of knowledge. This was because the study of mathematics was not for itself alone, nor simply an aid to the work of practical men. It was the guide not only to logical thinking, but also moral understanding. After all, Plato had decreed that no one should be admitted to his philosophical school 'without geometry'.

As if taking a hint from his own advocacy of mathematics, in the following year he issued a pamphlet illustrating their application, in which appeared actual calculations. No doubt he felt that he could safely assume the subject he addressed was both too humble, and too useful, to warrant the attention of the savants of Oxbridge. Here, his advice was offered to practical men like his father, who had found that farm gates, hung by rule of thumb, would often sag after a time or even come off their hinges. If, said Barnes, the place E on the vertical axis was one of the hinges, then there had to be 'some best place for the other hinge K'.[14] So, in nine pages illustrated with a diagram engraved by himself, he showed how to work it out.

By the mid-1830s, he was fast making himself a prodigious scholar. While keeping half an eye on the boys out playing in summer or clustered round the winter fire in the Great Hall, he could always find time for a book. His tastes were polymathic. In early 1830 he read: volumes of the *Histoire Naturelle* by George-Louis Buffon (1707-88); Josephus (AD 37-98?), author of *The Jewish War*, in Greek; Burns and Ossian; a history of Spain; German and Russian books; theology; and Rollin's *Ancient History*. The following year he looked into a history of France; the Latin text of the Roman historian Sallust (86-35 BC); logic; Hutton's *Mathematics*; Welsh grammar and literature; Shakespeare; Hebrew; and Blackstone's *Commentaries*. His diaries for 1832 and 1833 mention various Greek authors: Ovid; Herschel's *Astronomy*; Herodotus; and 'Hindustanee' writings.[15]

Obtaining access to these books cannot have been easy in an age when there were no public libraries. But Barnes, despite his habitual diffidence, systematically cultivated the acquaintance of anyone who could lend him a book or teach him something useful. Such a one was Major-General Henry Needham Scrope Shrapnel (1761-1842), inventor of an artillery shell which, on bursting, would scatter bullets over the enemy.

Like Barnes, Shrapnel was an outsider. Despite the fact that his invention was thought by some to have brought about the victory at Waterloo, he was not popular among many of his fellow officers, who considered his invention to be unsporting. Perhaps because of this, when Barnes first met him he had retired to the manor house in the west Dorset village of Puncknowle. This was in 1835, when Barnes went down to that village to make drawings of local antiquities. They soon became friendly. Their common passion was mathematics. Barnes subsequently dedicated his pamphlet on gate-hanging 'to Major-General Shrapnel, the greatest mathematician to whom the author has had the honour of being introduced, and to whose kindness much of his own proficiency in the exact sciences must be attributed'.

He learnt a lot from Shrapnel and was flattered by his notice. According to Barnes's daughter, there was a family tradition that he had been 'useful in aiding some mathematical calculations connected with the shell'. This must have arisen from one of Barnes's little jokes. It cannot have been true because Shrapnel's device was recommended to the Army's Board of Ordnance when Barnes was only two. Which is comforting, because it would be painful for the poet's admirers to learn that their gentle hero had helped to invent of one of the most barbaric weapons of his time. As for the socially ambitious Julia, she would have been only too pleased to shake the hand of a man who had shaken the hand of the King.

So creative were Barnes's powers in the early years at Chantry House that they found outlets in almost every aspect of his life. Music was another passion. He played the flute, piano and violin, sang with a good baritone voice and was, for a time, a voluntary organist at St Michael's. Then there were musical evenings with their new friends, Frederick Smith and his wife. Smith was the teacher of music and dancing to Barnes's pupils, and when Edward Fuller came up from Dorchester for a visit the old house resounded with the sound of a musical quartet. On 30 October 1832, Barnes noted in his diary: 'Suonando gli strumenti di musica col Sig, Cosens ed altri amici' and on 8 November he 'played musical instruments' at the home of a Mr Mitchell. He even turned composer, writing a waltz in the vein of Tom Moore, entitled 'There's a Charm in the Bloom of Youth'. Once he spent an entire morning composing a gloomy sonnet entitled 'The Mother's Grave', but cheered himself up in the afternoon by writing a comic song called 'Hopeful Youth'. And though he continued to write lugubrious verses in the style of Petrarch, the truth was that he could not disguise his bounding spirits. Domestic bliss and a sense of his own developing powers suffused him with happiness.

He was practical too. There was an old coach house attached to the school and he converted it into a workshop where, on long summer evenings, he would be hard at it with his new lathe, turning cradle legs or a wooden toy or a set of chessmen. Nor had he quite put aside his old loves of woodcutting and engraving. He cut blocks as illustrations to Phelps's *History of Somerset*, though this book never came out and he was not paid.[16] From any earnings that he did receive, he would buy a little present for Julia, a plate or butter knife or pair of sugar tongs or dozen teaspoons. She would find these pieces on the breakfast table, sometimes with her name etched on them.

Then, for a brief time, his imagination was set on fire by the drama. A troupe of comedians visited Mere and put on shows in his old schoolroom at the Market House. Caught up in it all, Barnes went to the play every night for a week and after the actors left, sat down and wrote a farce in three days. It was called *The Honest Thief*, and was acted at Mere on the 31 March 1833. He followed it up with a comedy, *The Blasting of Revenge; or, Justice for the Just*, which was performed at Wincanton on 27 April. Both plays have been lost, but some notion of the plot of the comedy may be deduced from the dramatis personae, which included: Lord Ethelstead; Truman, his tenant; Mrs Truman; Fanny Truman (with song); Marwell (Lord Ethelstead's steward); Henry Tuffman, a sailor; Holden (sheriff's officer) and Tom Guage, a merry exciseman. This was the theatre to which Dickens was soon to give expression, when Nicholas Nickleby met Vincent Crummles and the Infant Phenomenon. Its staple diet consisted of stirring scenes, melodramatic situations, noble sentiments, dastardly plots, music and fun. Such a change from Barnes's quiet life! No wonder he was momentarily entranced. With high hopes, he attended the opening night of his play but was disappointed. He noted in his diary: 'La premiera fu mal representata'. Nevertheless, he had made his first experiments in writing dramatic speech.

Though a conscientious churchgoer, he does not seem to have become intimate with his near neighbour, the Revd S.H. Cassan, Rector of Mere, though he wrote at least one sermon for him. The distance between them probably resulted from Barnes's anomalous social status. In Dorchester, the Revd Richman had befriended him somewhat in the role of a patron, one who was a superior not merely in age and education but also in class. But here in Mere, Barnes was an independent schoolmaster and no longer an appropriate subject for patronage, though his social position remained a doubtful one. Relations with Cassan, therefore, were probably awkward. Besides, the two men were of very different temperaments. Wallis described how they came into church:

> … there still lingers in my memory a contrast which, shortly before the service began, attracted even my boyish observation. With his head and body bent as if to avoid notice, and with steps so faintly audible that it seemed as though he sought to muffle them, Barnes slowly and meekly passed along the aisle to his allotted pew. In due time came the Rector whose progress from the entrance to the church to the pulpit attracted the marked attention of all present. The building reverberated to the sound of his quick, sharp step and sent a flutter of awe or fear to the hearts of the simple parishioners. His head, so far from being bent in saintly humility, was thrown back with apparently supercilious contempt; and the prevailing expression on his face seemed to be that of a man who feels that he is enacting a part altogether repugnant to his nature…[17]

The Barneses lived quietly. In their early years at Chantry House, they had neither the time nor the money for very much social life. Barnes was still on good terms with Charles Card, though the educational gulf between them probably put a limit on their friendship. Wallis could not remember anyone other than the Smiths visiting them in the evenings. With these friends, however, the whole Barnes family would go out nutting or for walks along the river. Julia sometimes attended 'Dorcas' meetings, evenings for ladies who made clothing for the poor, and where musical husbands would be admitted at eight o'clock; Barnes probably went along occasionally. But it was Julia who did the shopping in Mere. He rarely went out. Protected from the world by his wife, he preferred to stay at home, devoting his whole time to his school, his garden and cultivating his mind. He was almost a recluse.

# THEATRE, WINCANTON.
## BY PARTICULAR DESIRE.

On WEDNESDAY EVENING, April 27th. 1831,

Will be presented an entire new Drama in M. S. written by Mr. BARNES, Master of the Academy at Mere, entitled the

# Blasting of Revenge;
## Or, Justice for the Just.

Lord Ethelstead, Mr. PALMER,     Marweal, (his Steward,) Mr. S. DAVIS,

Trueman, (a Tenant of Lord Ethelstead,) by Mr. MURRAY,

Late of the Salisbury and Poole Theatres, who has kindly volunteered his service, for this Night only.
Henry Luffman, (a young Sailor,) Mr. MULFORD,     Holder, (a Sheriff's Officer,) Mr. M'LEAN,
Tom Gauge, (the merry Exciseman,) with a Song Mr. STANTON,
Mrs. Trueman, Miss MELVILLE,     Fanny Trueman, with a Song Mrs. MULFORD.

## An admired Air by Mrs. Mulford.

To which will be added an entire New Interlude, written by the Author of the Blasting of Revenge, called

# The Honest Thief.

Squire Richman, (a rich country gentleman,) Mr. M'LEAN,
Bob Truelove, (in love with Lucy,) Mr. S. DAVIS,     Lawyer Rhetoric, Mr. MULFORD,
Justice Drowsy, (Mayor of a small Borough,) Mr. PALMER,
Simon, (Servant to Squire Richman,) Mr. STANTON,     Constable, Mr. JONES,
Lucy Richman, Mrs. MULFORD,     Susan, (her Maid,) Miss MELVILLE.

A poster for two farces by Barnes. They were never performed again. (Dorset County Museum)

In later years, they were able to afford short holidays. They stayed with the Mileses at Nailsea, or at College Green, Bristol, with the parents of Wallis. Sometimes they took journeys into Dorset so that Barnes might make drawings of antiquities for various publications.[18] In 1831 he returned to Sturminster to sketch the church. Here he stayed with the 'impropriate Rector' or curate, the Revd Henry Lane Fox, with whom he had become friends. That he did so suggests that he must have made earlier visits to the town in preceding years, but he never mentions visiting his father. Perhaps this was because John Barnes had remarried and his son did not feel welcome there, or because the social gap between them was now so great.

After eight years at Chantry House, Barnes was thirty-four and balding. He cut a rather eccentric figure now as he went out to mow on summer mornings. Lost in thought, like some old Father Time, he would stand for a moment rapt, gazing down at the water, before beginning the slow rhythmic swinging of his scythe, carefully avoiding the skirts of his dressing gown. He was still happy, but perhaps not entirely content, for the years were slipping away and he had not made his mark. Far out beyond the meadows, the world was turning. While he had stood mowing here, news of great changes had occasionally reached Mere. They said that Greece had become independent – swish; that slavery had been abolished – swish; that a man named Michael Faraday had discovered something called 'electro-magnetic induction' – swish; that farm workers all over England were rioting in protest at their low pay, and there had been trouble at Tolpuddle – swish, swish. This last information now set off long-forgotten voices sounding in his head, though what they were saying he had not yet puzzled out. But his mind was teeming with such thoughts and he knew that he must write them down, if only to explain himself – swish, swish, swish.

# 6

# SOMETHING TO SAY

—— 1827-1835 ——

Shortly after William Barnes had left Dorchester in 1823, a new paper appeared there. It was the *Dorset County Chronicle and Somersetshire Gazette*, which offered four large, closely-printed pages every Thursday for 7*d*. The price was beyond the pockets of most local tradespeople and, conse-quently, its circulation was small. Its readership, however, was much larger, because such papers were often passed from one reader to another, descending from richer to poorer. The *Chronicle* quickly became influential, addressing itself chiefly to farmers, professional people and the business commu-nity, as well as the gentry and aristocracy, of which there was no shortage in Dorset.

Readers were offered national news, information on the Royal family, book reviews and chit-chat. The front page displayed advertisements for agricultural items and private schools, together with details of markets, crops and land sales. The *Chronicle* was a conservative paper in every sense of the word. An article on 31 January 1833 concerned the formation of 'Conservative associations in every part of the Kingdom, with the aim of preserving Church, state and Monarchy etc'. It opposed 'the infidelism of rule by ballot' which Simonds, the editor, considered 'unbecoming to the manly feelings of Englishmen'. He was also against the new mechanics' institutes, because 'education is a dangerous, possibly radical weapon to put in the hands of mechanics'. Opposition to Catholic eman-cipation was a continuing theme of the letters page. Correspondents, signing themselves 'Viator', 'A True Protestant' and 'A Briton', explained at length the full horror of giving papists the vote.

The paper also featured a good deal of literary material. There was a regular 'Varieties' item, with snippets of historical and antiquarian matters, and a 'Poetry Corner', which reprinted such harmless versifiers as Mrs Hemans and Barry Cornwall, and even the seditious Lord Byron (now safely dead). During 1825, for instance, readers were variously regaled with a translation of a Persian poem, an extract from Southey's *Tale of Paraguay* and a long passage from Tom Moore's recent biography of Richard Brinsley Sheridan. Such material not only provided the editor with free copy with which to fill up his columns, but also answered the real need of provincial readers to be informed about cultural matters. Simonds was shrewdly aware that many of his readers – especially his female ones – wanted to know more about such things. Famous writers were the celebrities of the day.

In November 1827, the editor received a letter from Mere, signed 'Dilettante', arguing that 'mel-ancholy is not incompatible with the poetic temperament'.[1] As evidence, the writer referred to Petrarch's '90 sonnets' and offered his own translation of a couplet from the poet's 'Rime in morte di Laura', while further alluding to the 'two Tassos in Italy and Camoens in Portugal'. Despite this display of erudition, his tone was diffident, even timorous, humbly begging leave even to agree with a previous correspondent. Aware that few of his subscribers were likely to take violent exception to such a harmless proposition, and even fewer able to contradict the writer, Simonds printed it.

This was William Barnes's first published piece, and it may be imagined with what pleasure its appear-ance was greeted in the little parlour at Chantry House. Because of his lack of formal education, he had long suffered a sense of inadequacy, with little confidence in his own powers. Now he had proof that one editor at least did not consider his opinions completely valueless. Emboldened, he risked another letter, this time concerning the languages of the ancient Romans and Saxons. It was headed 'Linguiana', and was soon followed by ten more on the same subject, all signed 'Dilettante' or 'W.B.'[2]

Barnes was cautious. Opinions were dangerous and, if his identity was revealed, they might threaten his living as a country schoolmaster dependent on the goodwill of parents. So, initially, he stuck to innocuous topics such as etymology and sheltered behind his pseudonym. His choice is revealing. According to the Shorter Oxford Dictionary, 'dilettante' means 'an amateur, (a) smatterer, one who toys with a subject', which accords with his habitual modesty. But in affecting this casual pose, he was doing himself an injustice because he was certainly no smatterer. This may have been a harmless duplicity on his part however, for he would have known that, in the original Italian, the word takes on a more serious meaning, something like 'connoisseur', or 'expert'.[3]

'Dilettante' soon proved himself a schoolmasterly sort of chap, with a passion for deducing historical facts from etymology. The Romans, he argued, must have taught the northern European nations how to make butter and cheese because their words for these items are derived from Latin. From 'butyrum' comes 'butter' (German), 'butter' (English), 'buttirro' (Italian) and 'beurre' (French). Moreover, the German, English, Spanish and Portuguese words for 'cheese' came from the Latin 'caseus'. Following this up, he traced the history of buttons and bellows by quoting from Caesar and Virgil.[4] In succeeding letters he drew on seven languages to discover the historical origins of corn-mills, chimneys, cord, compasses, biscuits, wine, watches, musical instruments and the days of the week. Each letter was a lesson, or rather several lessons, to show that history is best studied through comparative linguistics.

Of course he was showing off, but in a very harmless way. Even so, he was aware that his humble speculations might be slapped down by a university man. Sure enough, 'Qui-Quondam' soon replied from Basingstoke with the clear intention of putting this parvenu in his place. 'Sir', he addressed the editor, 'I have at various times been amused and interested by your correspondent who signs himself Linguiana, but though his various examples [of verbal derivations] are extremely pretty, yet they prove nothing and are little better than truisms'. It was hardly a surprise, he continued, that many English words were derived from Greek and Latin, as the author of 'Linguiana' was at so much pains to point out, because 'the analogy of language marks the intercourse of nations. I submit a few instances of the closest similarity between Sanscrit and Latin which appears at once extraordinary and inexplicable'. So saying, he provided a long list of Sanscrit and Latin words to demonstrate similarities between the two; for example, the Sanscrit 'pitara' and 'matara' resemble the Latin 'pater' and 'mater', etc. Human languages, he concluded, presented a 'vast hiatus', which would take more than the puny scholarship of one such as 'Dilettante' to sort out.[5]

In climbing to 'the fountain-head' of language, i.e. Sanscrit, 'Qui-Quondam' (who was almost certainly a clergyman) was pretty sure that 'Dilettante' could not follow. He was wrong. A reply, signed for the first time 'W.B.', appeared on 24 April 1828 and began:

> Sir, I willingly admit the truth of the observation made by your respected Correspondent 'Qui-Quondam' on my little articles entitled Linguiana that they prove nothing. I transmitted them to you with the most humble pretensions, thinking that as the facts of which they treated had amused my mind in my cultivation of some of the modern languages, the statement of them might interest some of your readers; and my expectation is more than fulfilled by their having attracted so favourable an attention from a gentleman of evident erudition.

This was neither mock-modesty nor irony, but genuine humility. Barnes, however, then amplified his account of linguistic resemblances by relating a list of German words to those of Sanscrit, thereby demonstrating that he too could read that language. Pressing his points still further, he attempted to explain such similarities by wide-ranging references to the climate of India, Arabian numerical terms, the Eastern doctrine of metempsychosis, the beliefs of Brahmins and the trading exploits of the Phoenicians. Was it not likely, he concluded, that the resemblances between many languages might not be traced to some original language from which they all derived? Game, set and match.

'Qui-Quondam's' pretensions to a superior level of scholarship had been sharply exposed. He took refuge in a pun: 'If I accused your intelligent Correspondent of Mere, of being a mere matter of fact man, it was not done to underrate his abilities, but to stimulate his evident powers of closer investigation'. Regretting any remarks which might have given pain to 'W.B.'s' 'modest worth', he speculated that the 'little palatable' offerings that 'W.B.' served up were only the skimmings of his literary studies. In this he was right.

Having gained confidence, Barnes now took a more provocative line and, in three 'Linguiana' articles, set out to challenge the fast-growing fashion in genteel society for people to employ French phrases and Latin tags in their everyday conversation. This affectation was thought by many to be a sign of superior culture, signalling that the speaker was of some education and therefore of an elevated social standing. Barnes detested it. Though few people in Mere or Dorchester were better able than he to talk Latin, Italian and French, he loathed their indiscriminate usage. Nor did he approve the tendency when new words were required (especially in the new technologies) for borrowing them from foreign languages, rather than fashioning them from English.

'Dilettante' explained why. Firstly, the very people who persisted in using foreign words often did not know how to pronounce them. They made mistakes when employing such terms as 'debut', 'eclat' and 'embonpoint'. 'Dilettante' remembered having heard the word 'corps' pronounced as if it referred not to a group of soldiers but a cadaver. Secondly, he observed that embarrassing mistakes were often made because foreign terms were not truly understood, as when a man he knew had been asked if a job involved manual labour, and replied 'no', only women were employed in it. Finally, he suggested that foreign tongues did not coalesce in sound and feeling with each other. Languages, he said, have characters of their own. 'German is remarkable for strength, the Italian for sweetness'. It was best not to mix them. English people should to stick to English. Not that he would have had the effrontery to put this to the public school men in the Ship Inn, with their imperfectly remembered Latin tags, nor simpering clerks attempting to impress young ladies with a phrase or two of Italian. But inwardly he was dismissive. Already, almost it seemed by instinct, he had conceived a highly individual notion of what good English was and these letters suggest where his linguistic ideas were later to lead him.

In 1828, 'Dilettante' and 'W.B. Mere' were joined by a third Barnes persona when he took to sending in anonymous poems. These were really little more than exercises in verse-making; mimicry. Mostly sonnets, often translations of Petrarch, they were fashionably lugubrious and grandiloquent. Their themes were usually disappointed love and/or the passage of time. In thought and diction they were entirely conventional:

## Human Life

Through waving boughs the wand'ring zephys sigh,
And passing onward, pass unseen away;
The sparkling stream is ever gliding by,
To meet the ocean in some beechy bay;
Aloft in air the clouds of summer stray;
The sun, in golden glory from on high,
In noiseless course sinks down the azure sky,
To end on western hills the waning day.

The air, the flying cloud, the rolling stream,
The sun that rises but to set again,
Are emblems of our life, a fleeting dream.

That, in the darksome nightwatch, cheats the brain,
O idle world! Why should I care for thee,
Thus passing through thee to eternity![6]

It was all a pose. In fact, he cared a good deal for the passing world, for his wife, his growing family and his new life. Far from melancholic, his temperament was normally cheerful and playful, as is shown by this bit of punning:

## Solution of the Charade from the Crypt

The proud survivor of the fight
Should moan the warriors slain,
The falling dew bespreads at night
The dead upon the plain.
Now tears are drops of dew you know
By many a bright eye shed,
And must be moan dew when they flow
In moaning for the dead.
So we may thus be pretty sure,
Sir Hilary cried at Agincourt,
(Having but little time to pray)
Moan dew, Mon-dieu (my God, Anglais.)[7]

In later years he used his *Chronicle* letters to try out all sorts of ideas in public. Sometimes he discussed topics that seem to have arisen in the classroom. Why did a watch-glass, with the convex side wetted, descend an inclined plane with a rotatory motion? Because, he said, of the diurnal motion of the earth.[8] What made the winds blow from certain directions at certain times? Well, he could offer a few thoughts on the subject to amplify those of Professor Airy at Cambridge, though, of course, merely for the 'consideration' of those who understood the subject better than himself.[9] He had so many observations to make and opinions to explore. Mildly eccentric but always learned, he regaled readers with his observations on folklore, ethics and culture. One example would be burial customs. Having a strong feeling for home himself, he noted the reverence that people 'feel for the spot which contains the bones of [their] forefathers'. In support, he quoted a Canadian Indian chief, who, when urged by Europeans to give up his land replied: 'Our forefathers are buried here, shall we say to their bones, arise and come with us into a strange land?'[10]

Sometimes he answered questions. When the editor asked for an explanation of the origin of the traditional mummers' plays, he was quick to oblige. These little dramas, he noted, were only performed at Christmas and always involved the defeat of a Turkish knight. Therefore, they must have derived from the Crusades. For support he quoted Tasso's *Jerusalem Delivered* in Italian and English.[11] Sometimes he dared to be a little more controversial, as in his consideration of the high pews then being introduced into churches to keep winter draughts off genteel persons, while the humbler sort were restricted to lower protection. Indignantly, he pointed out that whereas the sexton often caned little urchins for inattention, he would pass by the pews where affluent people sat and where, if the pews grew much higher in the future, he might find that 'a pack of cards instead of the Psalms of David will find its way into them'.[12]

And still the letters came. He wrote about cant, flattery, the building of Antwerp (having just come across 'a copy of a rather scarce book, Guicciardini's Italian work on the Low Countries, published in 1567'), finding an old medal in his garden, auctions, friendly societies and, rather grandly, on the 'origin, or revival and progress in Europe, of the arts, architecture, sculpture, painting and music', a progress he attributed largely to the church.[13]

For such a humane man, his opinions on social matters in his younger days were sometimes harsh. His innate sympathy for the work-folk in the fields was balanced with a hardening attitude towards criminals, outcasts and unfortunates. In one letter, 'Dilettante' argued that felons were far too leniently treated: 'The poor virtuous labourer's family, struggling against misery on the scanty earnings of 1s and in some cases 6d a day, can buy but little firing and less meat:– the rogue, by moderate exercise in nightly incursions, to steal wood, fowls, and sheep, obtains enough of both'. Even if the thief were caught and sent to a penal colony, Barnes still maintained that his life was comparatively soft. His lodging was a palace compared to the one he left behind; he had shelter and a fire, regular meals, adequate clothing and medical attention. He was not even obliged to work in the rain! 'Perhaps he works at the tread mill; that is not harder work than many kinds of field labour. We must confess he has lost his liberty – but then, to counterbalance that, he has no fear of starving, or of being houseless, and naked'.[14] That such criminals were often the same farm labourers he had defended, now driven to crime by starvation, seems not to have occurred to him.

To Barnes at this time, any thought of egalitarianism was anathema. Buried deep in his psyche was the assumption that social relations were still feudal, fixed and settled forever, as he argued in his letter on 'The Good Servant':

> The ancients tell us of a glorious age in which there was neither master nor servant; but mankind were all equals, and had everything in common. The continuance of this state of society is, perhaps, no more durable than possible…
>
> … to execute a great work many must work together under the one who designed it – which is subjection.
>
> The bad servant, who, instead of making himself profitable to his master, strives only to make his master profitable to himself, is a loathsome being.
>
> The good master treats his servant not as a being created expressly to work for another, but as a fellow man who happens to have been born in a low but necessary rank of society.[15]

Here, as in almost everything else, he was out of touch with the spirit of the age. Neither the new self-made capitalists, nor the growing band of working-class Chartists, would have agreed with him. Nor had he yet thought through the contradictions of his own position. For he himself had been born in a 'low but necessary rank of society', but by virtue of superior intelligence and hard work had changed his status. Was a 'good servant', such as his farm worker father, to remain content with serving others all his life? He himself had not.

The *Chronicle* had provided the first outlet for the liberation of Barnes's intellect, and the faded columns of this old provincial paper give hints of the sort of person he had become in early middle age. He was 'Dilettante', a modest language reformer and prodigious linguist; 'Anon', a solemn, sentimental sonneteer; and 'W.B.', a man of wide reading and deeply conservative temperament. He was all of these, and yet none of them. They had each said their say, but their voices were not entirely his. He had not found his own voice yet.

# 7

# TILLING THE GROUND

—— 1830-1835 ——

Lessons were over. Now, after play, the last reluctant boys had trooped into the house for supper, leaving their master alone in his garden. It was many hours since his morning mowing, and the interim had been fully occupied with routine tasks. Morning prayers. Multiplication tables. Spelling tests. Latin declensions. Meal supervisions. Private tuition. There were little boys everywhere. Slates. Inkwells. Dusty books. But now, before the light faded, William Barnes had come outside to take the evening air:

> I had been working in my garden. The sun was just below the horizon, and the dew was already on the smooth green walks, bordered by sweet-smelling roses and carnations. The stillness of the evening was broken only by the whistling of the blackbird, and the splashing of the water, when the trout sprung after the lively insects that floated in wild mazes over the ponds. I sat down on a rude seat I had formed beneath some old trees that darkened the twilight of the evening into an awful gloom, and as the smell of the bean-blossoms was wafted along the cool air, and I thought on the fruit and plants that were ripening around me, I exclaimed to myself, '*O fortunatos, sua si bena norint, Agricolas!*' How happy, if they but knew it, are they who till the ground...
>
> … And how much sweeter do things seem when they are the long-known productions of one's own soil, than when we buy them from strange hands! and how pleasing it is to know that, whether one prefers the red and juicy radish, or the cucumber that stretches its rough and bulky body on the warm earth, or whether one wishes for the crooked pear or the yellow apricot; all are within one's reach! and all one's own![1]

In many ways, he had everything he wanted here; his family, his books, his school, his church, his hobbies and his garden. But Julia was restless. Both she and her mother felt that it was time to move on to a bigger town, where he would have more opportunities for advancement. They still felt that he was wasting his talents in such an 'out of the way' place as Mere. Moreover, the future prosperity of his school was becoming doubtful because the economy of Mere was largely dependent on farming and, by the 1830s, the surrounding countryside was heaving with discontent. Currents of this had now begun to be felt in even so quiet a backwater as Chantry House.

This was because a great change was making its way swiftly through the rural counties of England. For centuries, commoners such as John Barnes and his forbears had enjoyed rights in certain arable fields, meadowland and also the wasteland scattered around villages. The fields were divided into strips, separated from each other by grass or furrows; some villagers owned a few and some many. Meadowland or lease was also divided into strips and used for pasture after the hay was brought in. The waste was open to all commoners and supplied grazing for cows, pigs and chicken; furze (or gorse) and sticks for fuel; and berries, mushrooms and all kinds of supplements to the rural diet.

But now, in many villages, these common lands were being enclosed by large landowners. Such measures were usually validated by Acts of Parliament, and their supporters had strong arguments for them. Strip farming, they said, was hopelessly uneconomic, requiring, as it often did, the cultivator to walk from one end of the village to another in order to work his various bits of land. Such a system could not hope to supply enough food to the fast-growing cities. Nor did it encourage great industry on the part of villagers, who could just about eke out a livelihood by working part-time for farmers and attending to their own property for the rest of the time. Moreover, they said that commoners had no inducement to bring new lands into cultivation because such endeavours were often beyond their capabilities. These apologists also employed aesthetic arguments; enclosures, they maintained, beautified the landscape, turning dreary wastes, bogs and marshes into fruitful landscape, pleasurable to the eye. The 'Report on Somerset' for the Board of Agriculture in 1795 even argued that enclosure was morally advantageous:

> Besides, moral effects of an injurious nature accrue to the cottager, from a reliance on the imaginary benefits of stocking a common. The possession of a cow or two, with a hog and a few geese, naturally exalts the peasant, in his own conception, above his brethren of the same rank of society. It inspires some degree of confidence in a property, inadequate to his support. In sauntering after his cattle, he acquires a habit of indolence. Quarter, half, and occasionally whole days are imperceptibly lost. Day labour becomes disgusting; the aversion increases by indulgence; and at length the sale of a half-fed calf, or a hog, furnishes the means of adding intemperance to idleness.[2]

In other words, a man was made better by having his rights taken away.

Bewildered cottagers took a different view. Often illiterate, they frequently knew nothing of the enclosure of their lands until the act had been passed. The only court to which they might appeal would be the local magistrates and these were very often the same people who were enclosing the land. Occasionally, however, a local community did make a protest, as in 1797 when the proprietors of a small common at Raunds, Northamptonshire, petitioned Parliament. It was a heartfelt cry from working people:

> That the Petitioners beg Leave to represent to the House that, under Pretence of improving Lands in the said Parish, the Cottagers and other Persons entitled to the Right of Common on the Lands intended to be enclosed, will be deprived of an inestimable Privilege, which they now enjoy, of turning a certain Number of their Cows, Calves, and Sheep, on and over the said Lands; a Privilege that enables them not only to maintain themselves and their Families in the Depth of Winter, when they cannot, even for their Money, obtain from the Occupiers of other Lands the smallest portion of Milk or Whey for such necessary Purpose, but, in addition to this, they can now supply the Grazier with young or lean Stock at a reasonable Price, to fatten and bring to Market at a more moderate Rate for general Consumption, which they conceive to be the most rational and effective Way of establishing Public Plenty and Cheapness of Provision; and they further conceive, that a more ruinous Effect of this Inclosure will be the almost total Depopulation of their Town, now filled with bold and hardy Husbandmen, from among whom, and the Inhabitants of other open Parishes, the Nation has derived its greatest Strength and Glory, in the Supply of its Fleets and Armies, and driving them, from Necessity and Want of Employ, in vast Crowds, into manufacturing Towns.[3]

A more law-abiding and patriotic plea could hardly be imagined. Parliament, however, took little notice of such appeals because it too was composed of the class doing the enclosing. So, between 1750 and 1850, well over 6 million acres were fenced off, about a quarter of all cultivated land in England.[4]

After enclosure, a hard-working commoner could no longer hope to improve his lot by acquiring more rights. He had ceased to be a 'peasant', because he owned no land. Henceforth, he would own nothing but his own labour. Reduced to a mere cash worker, he was now entirely dependent on his often fickle employer, but still bound to the soil which no longer guaranteed him a living.[5] While even Russian serfs owned their own bits of land, and American slaves – if only to preserve their strength and value – were adequately fed, many Dorset farm workers were close to starvation.

Before 1815, about half the land in Dorset had been let to tenant farmers; leases were often for life, or perhaps for a series of lives. But persuaded by the new move towards more 'efficient' farming, many large landowners wanted more control over their land, sometimes with the intention of farming it themselves. Once leases expired, they moved increasingly to call them in. Charles Rabbets was just such a tenant farmer who lost his land. In this way, many small farms became one large farm, and those who had worked them for generations now found themselves reduced to the ranks of day-labourers.

What made things worse was the lifting of the embargo on Continental grain following the end of the Napoleonic Wars. At once, foreign imports began to undercut British food. This was good news for industrial workers in great cities and in the mills, mines and factories, because it meant cheaper bread. On the farms it was a different story. Here, imported wheat meant less work, lower wages and, sometimes paradoxically, dearer bread. Moreover, there was simply not enough land in England to feed the rural population. The resentment of the farm workers was only inflamed by hearing of pheasants in the coverts, fed by 'boiled rabbits, chopped up small, sago, milk, rice, hard-boiled eggs (well minced of course), Indian corn and other delicacies'.

The introduction of new technology incensed them further. Steam threshing machines, for example, were hated not only because they reduced the number of people required for a job, but also because they were dangerous. While stoically resigned to injuries from traditional implements such as scythes and hooks, the work-folk objected strongly to those inflicted by the wayward belt and rotating drum of the threshing machine, and the exposed blades of reaping and mowing machines. Such injuries also resulted in further loss of work.

The upshot of all these developments was near starvation for many of the rural poor. Failure to feed his family forced the farm worker to apply for help from the parish. The Speenhamland Act of 1795 allowed for relief to be granted when wages fell below a certain level. This was to be calculated according to the price of bread and the size of the family. But the level of support was not a fixed one. It varied from one county to another and was subject to change. In 1795 the Berkshire magistrates had recommended an allowance of a 3½ gallon loaf a week for a man, and 1½ for every other member of the family. But from 1815 to 1835 rations were progressively reduced in many counties. In Dorset in 1826, an unemployed labourer was supposed to subsist on a 1½ gallon loaf a week, with a 1 ¹⁄₁₆ loaf for each other members of the family.[6] There was little the working man could do. Having lost his commoner's rights, or his little farm, he was now obliged to accept any wage the farmer chose to pay him, always supposing there was work to be had. He dare not move to another parish, which had no obligation to support him. Meanwhile, the farmer or landowner had no inducement to ever raise wages. If his workmen starved, then the parish would see to it.

Things were especially bad in Dorset. In the parish of Hazelbury Bryan in 1833, labourers were earning about 9s a week with beer while haymaking and harvesting, but no more than 7s at other times. The family income of a man working in the fields with three sons under fourteen, and his wife making buttons, amounted to no more than 13s 4d.[7] There was little left to save for the bad times when men had no work. One old labourer bitterly concluded, 'however much you worked and scrambled, the farmers just wiped their boots on you'.[8]

Despite this, for many years the rural population of the south-west of England remained stubbornly conservative in temper. If there were villains in the piece, they were inclined to complain about their traditional enemies – foreign imports, townsmen, new technologies and, as always, the weather. They felt that if only the authorities understood their plight, everything would be put right. What these workers wanted was not to change the system, but to get back to a golden age:

> Our venerable fathers remember the year
> When a man earned three shillings a day and his beer.[9]

Such memories were illusory. There had been poverty among landless labourers in Dorset as far back as the eighteenth century.

On the whole, Barnes shared the view that the present deplorable state of agriculture was a blip. To one of his conservative instincts, the world of his childhood seemed a fixture, a natural order of things that would endure for ever. Moreover, he disliked change, revered the gentry and instinctively supported authority. It only required humane measures, he felt, for the good times to come again and for the Blackmore society of his childhood to be restored. He had not yet understood how great a social tragedy was in the making.

That he was profoundly uneasy at the effect of these changes cannot be doubted, but there was little he could do about them other than to keep his head down, tend his school and watch events unfold.

But though he went into Mere as little as possible, he must have been aware of the distress around him in the little streets. Poverty on the land meant depression in the town and hordes of dispossessed country people now came crowding in. Mere had no public water, lighting or drainage systems, and the influx of ragged, penniless people was more than it could cope with. There was fighting at night in the alehouses and reports of stealing and violence.[10]

The news got worse. In August 1830 there were reports of public disorder throughout the southern counties. Riots in Kent quickly spread to Sussex and Hampshire. It was whispered that these agitations were led by a wild, romantic figure named 'Captain Swing', though in truth there was no such person. Rioters held protests, burned haystacks, smashed steam threshing machines and sent anonymous notes to farmers demanding a living wage. But though some were threatened, there was little actual violence to persons, except poor relief adminstrators who were sometimes put in carts and wheeled round the parish. Yet still there persisted the belief among many of the rioters that Parliament and the new King were really on their side, and would even pay for the damage they caused.[11]

That year, the troubles moved closer to Chantry House. There were more riots and machine-breaking throughout west Wiltshire, climaxing at Tisbury, just nine miles from Mere, where 400 rioters destroyed threshing machines until the arrival of a troop of yeomanry. A pitched battle was fought, the labourers armed with 'hatchets, hammers, pick-axes, sticks and stones', against the muskets of their opponents. One man was shot dead and twenty-five arrested. Elsewhere 'mobs' from Tisbury, Knoyle and Mere were reported to be assembling to break machines.[12]

As a child, Barnes had heard grown men talk of enclosures. John Barnes, Charles Rabbets and the neighbours were aware of the appropriation of grazing rights taking place in the Vale. They knew that 300 acres around Mappowder and Stoke Wake had been enclosed in 1807, and much of the grazing land lost to cottagers in Buckland Newton and Hazelbury Bryan about the same time. In 1810, 3,082 acres were enclosed around Mere. The *Salisbury Journal* reported:

> The inclosure of Milton and Mere Commons have excited much discontent. On Saturday se'enight
> nearly three hundred men from Gillingham and parts adjacent met on Maperton Hill and Pier's Wood
> and destroyed a long line of new fences. A troop of horse from Dorchester Barracks is now quartered
> in the neighbourhood, and the several ringleaders have been taken into custody. Four of them were on
> Friday lodged in Fisherton Gaol, whence they are to remain for trial till the next assizes'.[13]

But it was long after, in 1830, that ominous news reached Barnes from Sturminster. One Sunday evening, John Inkpen, the churchwarden, had stood up in St Mary's to read out a notice for the enclosure of Bagber Common. John Barnes, sitting in the gallery, would have understood at once that he was to lose the common rights on which his livelihood, status and independence depended. From then on, he too would have to live out his life as a mere day labourer, with only the workhouse to look forward to.

That November, there came news of unrest in Dorset. Labourers were said to be assembling at Winterborne Kingston and Bere Regis to demand a weekly wage of 10s. By the end of the month the demonstrations had spread to Wareham, Puddletown, Winfrith and Knighton. Mass meetings demanded higher wages, and there were outbreaks of arson and machine-breaking.[14] But by early December, the disturbances had been put down by the military.

Except in the Blackmore Vale. Here, disaffected labourers had crept along a network of deep lanes to meet and make their plans. They broke cover at last when echoing horns gave the signal for a mass protest on Castle Hill, at the foot of Bulbarrow, among the great beeches and ancient earthworks which commanded a view of the western approaches to the Vale.[15] On the 4th of the month, the fifty or so protestors unwisely moved down towards the old Stoke Common. In doing so they had to pass Castle Hill House, the home of the Williams family. Alarmed that they might break into his property (though they had given no sign of doing so), Mr Williams blocked their way with a force of special constables from Cerne Abbas, backed up by a troop of lancers. On seeing them, the labourers gave a great shout of defiance, intending to march on to break up machinery. But they were soon surrounded, and after a brief struggle, seventeen were arrested. In the subsequent trial at Dorchester, six men were condemned to death (later reprieved) and ten to transportation for seven years.

The failure of the Castle Hill rising marked the end of the Blackmore resistance. The labourers simply gave in. Bitterly, they now understood that the Vale was not large enough to feed its entire population, that enclosures were not to be resisted and that threshing machines had come to stay. So, despite attendant risks, men, like John and James Barnes before them, began to leave either to seek work in the cities or to emigrate.

For the next three years, however, sporadic reports continued from around the south of England of more fire-raising and machine-breaking. Barnes hated to hear of them. His was a quiet temperament. Besides, his political instincts were supported by his economic interests. The shopkeepers and the farmers who sent their boys to his school, the clergymen and businessmen on whose support he depended, were now exchanging horrified gossip about the riots. Julia herself had come back to school one day to report that Barnaby Rumsey, the father of one of her pupils, had been threatened by rioters.[16] And in 1831, Barnes had received a disturbing account of the situation in Wiltshire from his old friend, Gilbert Carey, recently appointed Clerk to the County Court at Calne:

> What alarms have we endured in this neighbourhood! ... Two or three fires seen at one time – Constables sworn and armed – the Military galloping about – mobs assembling and dispersing – machine breaking and taking to pieces in all directions...[17]

Knowing his dislike of radical politics, Barnes's acquaintances could all pretty safely assume that his loyalties would rest entirely with the authorities.

And yet, there was disquiet among many thinking people and he shared it. His publisher friend, John Rutter, now political agent for John Poulter MP for Shaftesbury, had organised a petition in that town against the transportation of the Castle Hill men, and Henry Hunt MP had proposed a general amnesty for them in the House of Commons.[18] Though both had failed, many observers remained uneasy.

Accounts of riots now appeared regularly in the long columns of the *Chronicle* or the *Western Flying Post*, beneath headings such as 'Disturbed State of the Country'. But whereas to genteel readers they suggested images of terrifying 'machine-breakers' and 'rioters', to Barnes they afforded glimpses of sullen, starving men, provoked to desperate action. And with a pang, he realised that these were his own sort, like the Rabbets, Bullens, Moores and Jeanes from Bagber. They were old friends and relations, and by and large he remembered them as good, hard-working people:

> I have known one who was toiling in the field, not only in the twilight of the morning, but when the moon shone from on high over the cottage, in which his wife and offspring had long been sunk into deep sleep.[19]

This was his father.

What was needed now, he felt, was that great landowners, such as Lord Rivers at Sturminster and James Frampton at Puddletown, should understand the sufferings of their work-folk and the causes of the unrest. Once they did so, he had little doubt that they would act to remedy things. After all, the great and good of the county – he was convinced that they were both – were of the same religion as their employees, and as such would surely recognise their Christian duty to show compassion. But to bring this about, the work-folk needed a voice.

In December 1833 he was not well. He had gone off in the first days of the school holiday to make sketches of local antiquities to serve as material for future engravings, but when he came home both he and Julia were taken ill. On 21 January, he noted, 'Giulia Malata, giorno triste'. It is likely that they both had flu, though he was convinced that he was suffering from 'an ailing of the liver'. Whatever its nature, some sort of infection was going around Mere which was so virulent that the Curate, the Revd R. Cozens, died of it on 30 January. Aware that Julia's constitution seemed too delicate to bear the work which she was called to do, Barnes was deeply concerned for her.

That winter Chantry House was a dismal place, with damp running down the walls and the wind blowing under the doors from the churchyard. Old Mrs Miles was hard pushed to keep things going in the kitchen, and there was a constant carrying of chamber pots down from the sick room. At last Barnes began 'up-halening' from his sickness and one day, when he was idly turning the pages of his battered copy of Virgil's *Eclogues*, he read:

> Tityre, tu patulae recubans sub tegmine fagi
> siluestram tenui Musam meditaris auena;
> nos patriae finis et dulcia linquimus arua:
> nos patriam fugimus; tu, Tityre, lentus in umbra
> formosam resonare doces Amaryllida siluas.

> (Beneath a shady tree you may rehearse
> At ease, my Tityrus, your simple verse;
> I'm forced to leave my country and to roam,
> My Tityrus from country and from home:
> You here can fill at leisure in the shade,
> With Amaryllis's name the woodland glade.)[20]

Meliboeus was speaking. He was heartbroken because he was going to lose his little farm. All Rome had been in a state of ferment since the assassination of Julius Caesar and now, following the battle of Philippi, the victorious armies were coming home. To pay them off, Octavius Caesar had promised them land and to get it, he announced that he would evict many of the families who had worked their lands for generations.

It was then that Barnes discerned that Virgil was describing much the same situation as that in which Dorset work-folk now found themselves. Meliboeus had been turned off his farm, just like Uncle Charles Rabbets. The notion set him musing. Could one write verses in the manner of Virgil, but describing contemporary evictions? A sort of Dorset eclogue? A moment's consideration, however, showed him that this would be impossible. A dialogue, in which labourers told of their hardships in polite English, would read as hopelessly false. They did not speak like that. Then a further thought came to him. Why not write the eclogue in the actual speech of the country people of his own day? It would not be difficult, because the dialect was always with him, coming unbidden at all times, whispering in his ear. He could still clearly hear those Bagber voices: Aunt Anne in a tantrum; Uncle Charles's hearty laugh; his father's sober accents; and the soft tones of his mother. And though unobtrusive, they were insistent.

He pondered and took his pen. The shepherd, Tityrus, and his friend, the small farmer Meliboeus, were still talking but their accents had changed. Theirs were now the voices of John Barnes and Charles Rabbets, no longer living in golden Arcadia but the grim world of rural Dorset. So he called them Thomas and John and just listened to them. John, it seemed, was off to sell his geese and cow. This was because, as he explains, 'they do mean to teake the moor in' (i.e. enclose it) and he would have nowhere to graze his animals:

THOMAS
… why 'tis a handy thing
To have a bit o' common, I do know,
To put a little cow upon in Spring,
The while woone's bit ov orcha'd grass do grow.

JOHN
Aye, that's the thing, you zee. Now I do mow
My bit o' grass, an meake a little rick;
An, in the zummer, while do grow,
My cow do run in common vor to pick

A bleade or two o'grass, if she can vind em,
Vor tother cattle don't leave much behind em.
Zo in the evenen, we do put a lock
O' nice fresh grass avore the wicket;
An' she do come at vive or zix o'clock,
As constant as the zun, to pick it.[21]

John then recounts how he used to let his geese run among the emmet (ant) hills on the common, how he fattened them for market, and how he plucked them to sell feathers and quills. When he needed fuel he went out onto the common with his hook and gloves and cut fuzz (furze) and briars, or he would send his children out to fetch a bag of dried cow dung. Thomas's response is bitter:

T'is handy to live near a common;
But I've a zeed an' I've a-zaid,
That if a poor man got a bit of bread,
They'll try to teake it vrom en.

His only hope was that that 'they' – never defined – might let out allotments to poor men. John hopes it is true, for otherwise he fears that he 'must goo to workhouse'. This contemporary eclogue was published anonymously in the *Chronicle* on 2 January 1834 under the title *Rusticus Dolens or Inclosures of Common*. Had Barnes been identified as the author, this criticism of enclosures would have been professional suicide.

A week later another eclogue appeared. 'Dilettante' had found a solution. He dared to recommend an extension of the 'excellent practice of letting out portions of ground to the poor'. In *Rusticus Gaudens – The allotment System*, John and Richard discuss the matter. The latter thinks himself lucky because he has been granted an allotment from the squire, 'a worthy man', who has rented out a few odd acres to the 'poor leabren [labouring] men'. That this same squire was probably the one enclosing the land which was the cottagers' by right, and is now charging them for its use, is a subtlety that has escaped Richard. His friend, however, has had no such luck where he lives:

JOHN
I wish the girt woones had a-got the greace
To let out land lik' this in ouer pleace,
But I do fear there'll never be nwone vor us,
An' I can't tell whatever we shall do;
We be a'most a starven, an' we'd goo
To 'merica, if we'd enough to car us.[22]

('ouer' – our; 'car' – carry)

The two then fall to itemising the ways in which an allotment provides food and exercise, and keeps folk busy and out of mischief. Wistfully, John concludes, 'I'd keep myself from parish, I'd be bound/ If I could get a little patch of ground'.

If Barnes's intention was to soften the feelings of employers and landowners, he failed. Shortly after *Rusticus Dolens* was published, events took place which revealed just how desperate were the work people and how obdurate their employers. On 1 March 1834, the government-supporting *Times* newspaper reported that six labourers from Tolpuddle had been condemned in Dorchester to seven years transportation after attempting to found a union to try to raise wages in order, as they said, 'to preserve ourselves, our wives and children from utter degradation and starvation'. They had been reduced to 8s a week, which was not enough for them to live on. Forming a union, or Friendly Society of Agricultural Workers, however, was not in itself illegal, and even *The Times* recognised that the basis of the trial was paradoxical:

> The formal charge against them was that of administering and being bound by secret and, therefore, unlawful oaths; whereas the real gravamen of their guilt was their forming a dangerous Union, to force up, by various means of intimidation, and restraint, the rates of labourers wages..The crime which called for punishment was not proved – the crime brought home to the prisoners did not justify the sentence.[23]

The trial of the Tolpuddle men probably brought embarrassment to Barnes in later life because he had personal connections at one time or another with three of the magistrates involved, James Frampton, the Revd J.M. Colson of St Peter's, Dorchester, and Dr William England, Rector of Winterborne Came.[24] But at the time, Anon kept quiet. After the *Chronicle* had published a comic piece entitled: *Rusticus Narrans – a Cousin Down from London* on 3 March, no more eclogues appeared for some months.

Now the treatment of the poor became even grimmer with the passing of the new Poor Law (the Poor Law Amendment Act). This changed the way in which labourers and their families were relieved. Previously, they stayed in their own homes, receiving bread from the parish. After the passing of the bill, they were forced into the new 'unions' or workhouses, each maintained by a group of parishes, where conditions were deliberately made harsh in order to dissuade applicants.[25] Unsurprisingly, new pockets of discontent emerged, some near Mere. At the end of the year, the *Chronicle* recounted how at Manningford Abbas in Wiltshire, Sir E. Poore had ridden out to confront a group of labourers promising them help to obtain 'a more adequate compensation for their labour' but that the 'mob' had gone on to Alton and smashed up a threshing machine.[26]

Many workers had little choice other than to up sticks and leave the farms their families had cultivated for generations. For those who could afford the voyage, emigration offered the best chance of working the land once more. But these partings brought great sorrow. In October, a new eclogue, *Rusticus Emigrans: Emigration* appeared, in which Robert meets Richard who is just off to Van Dieman's Land:

ROBERT
And how d'ye veel now Richat in your mind,
To leave your bethpleace and your friends behind?

RICHARD
Why very queer, I do I can't deny:
When I do think o' be'en piarted
Vrom al my friends var ever, I could cry
But var the shiame o' be'en so softhearted.
Here be the trees that I did use to clim in,
Here is the brook that I did use to zwim in,
Here be the ground where I've a–worked and played;
Here is the hut that I were barn and bred in;
Here is the little church where we've a prayed,
And churchyard that my kinsvolk's buones be laid in;
And I myzelf, you know, should like to lie
Among 'em too when I do come to die;
But 'tis noo use to have zich foolish wishes;
I shall be tossed, I' may be to the vishes.[27]

After this was published, anonymous eclogues continued to appear from time to time. Some were comic; *A Bit o' Sly Coortin* was a wonderful depiction of the tiffs and makings–up of village lovers, in little dramas enacted by thousands of country couples since the days of Shakespeare. Some like *Rusticus res Politicas Animadvertens: The New Poor Law* and *Two Farms in Woone*, offered social commentary. Yet his chief aim was to elicit compassion for work-folk, with sympathetic pictures of their lives, as in *Father Come Home*:

WIFE
Your supper's nearly ready. I've a-got
Some teaties here a-doen in the pot;
I wish wi' all my heart I had some meat.
I got a little ceake too, here, a-beaken o'n
Upon the vier. 'Tis done by this time though.
He's nice an' moist; vor when I were a-meaken o'n
I stuck some bits of apple in the dough.

CHILD
Well, father, what d'ye think. The pig got out
This mornin; an' avore we zeed or heard en,
He run about, an' got out into gearden,
An routed up the groun' zoo wi' his snout![28]

Such loving depictions re-endowed these lives with value. Almost without intending to, Barnes was becoming the true witness of those who had tilled the ground for many generations, the vanishing peasantry of England. Their voices were heard once more in his verse. Hitherto, their language had no literature. Here was the beginnings of one.

# 8

# FOOTHOLD: DURNGATE STREET

## — 1835-1837 —

On the evening of 26 June 1835, people in Durngate Street looked up to see two or three tranters' carts, piled high with household effects, rolling to a halt. A clean-shaven man of medium height climbed down from the leading one, followed by a slight younger woman cradling a baby, and two little girls in the charge of a matron in her sixties. They were exhausted. Up at first light, they had been trundled nearly forty miles that day, from Mere on the banks of the Stour, through the Blackmore Vale, over the great chalk uplands and down into the valley of the Frome, by way of Gillingham, Shaftesbury, Blandford and Puddletown. And though the man was familiar with the route, to the others it must have seemed a journey to the end of the world.

The wagon pulled up in front of the door of a rather modest house. On entering, the man at once started to direct the carriers where to put things. It was not only furniture and the usual domestic items they lifted down, but also a considerable number of bedsteads, desks, stools and classroom fittings. Meanwhile, the women busied themselves with feeding the children and finding milk for the baby. The Barnes family had arrived in Dorchester.

Barnes summarised the reasons for moving:

> Mere was out of the way for pupils, and I had always yearned for Dorset and Dorchester, and as I had strengthened my teaching power, and was told by friends at Dorchester that there was an opening for a boarding school, I put my hopes of after life in work at that place.[1]

These friends included his previous employer, the solicitor Thomas Coombs, George Jacobs the bookseller, George Clark the printer, and Frederick Smith and his wife, who had also moved their fashionable academy for 'dancing, deportment and music' from Mere to the county town. The deciding factor, however, had been the continued pressure for the move by Julia and her mother.

Yet Barnes had left Chantry House with a heavy heart, and in his troubled later years, remembered their days there as an idyllic time. Shortly before leaving, he had walked round the garden once more:

## To A Garden – On Leaving It

Sweet Garden! peaceful spot! no more in thee
Shall I e'er while away the sunny hour.
Farewell each blooming shrub, and lofty tree:
Farewell the mossy path and nodding flower:
I shall not hear again from yonder bow'r
The song of birds, or humming of the bee,
Nor listen to the waterfall, nor see
The clouds float on behind the lofty tow'r.

No more, at cool-aired eve, or dewy morn,
My gliding scythe shall shear thy mossy green:
My busy hands shall never more adorn,

My eyes may no more see, this peaceful scene.
But still, sweet spot, wherever I may be,
My love-led soul, will wander back to thee.[2]

They had taken the Durngate house without seeing it. It stood in a narrow turning running east-wards from South Street, down towards Fordington and the open fields beyond.[3] Though it probably derived its popular name, 'Wood and Stone Lane', from a public house, Durngate Street must at that time have been a respectable quarter, otherwise Barnes could not have expected parents to send their sons to his school there. Nevertheless, just across the river ran Mill Street, notorious for disease, poverty and prostitution.

The removal to Dorchester was a calculated gamble by the Barneses to try to gain a foothold in a more thriving educational centre than Mere. The county town was the focus of the region's eco-nomic life and many local trades and professional people, and even the gentry, sent their sons to the schools there. And apart from its enhanced business opportunities, the place had always retained a romantic feel for Barnes and Julia. Having met and courted there, returning with their young family had a feeling of appropriateness about it.

Pondering this removal in verse, Barnes imaginatively re-cast himself as a farm worker. After all, if he had been obliged to move for security of employment, then so had his labourer on 'Lady Day'.[4] And though he had hired a tranter, whereas the working man would have piled his goods onto a wagon, when it came to it, they both had to endure their precious belongings being stared at by strangers:

## Leady-Day, An' Ridden House

Well, zoo, avore the east begun
To redden wi' the comen zun,
We left the beds our mossy thatch
Were never more to overstratch,
An borrow'd uncles wold hoss Dragon,
To bring the slowly lumbren waggon,
An' when he come, we vell a-packen
The bedsteads, wi their rwopes an' zacken;
An' then put up the wold earm-chair,
An cwoffer vull ov e'then ware,
An vier-dogs, an copper-kittle,
Wi' crocks an' saucepans big an' little;
An' fryen-pan, vor aggs to slide
In butter round his hissen zide,
An' gridire's even bars, to bear
The drippen steake above the gleare
O' brightly-glowen' coals. An' then
All up o' top o' them agean
The woaken bwoard, where we did eat
Our croust o' bread or bit o' meat,-
An' when the bwoard wer up, we tied
Upon the reaves, along the zide,
The woaken stools, his glossy meates,
Both when he's beare, or when the pleates

Do clatter loud wi' knives below
Our merry faces in a row;
An' put between his lags, turn'd up'ard,
The zalt-box an' the corner cupb'ard.
An then we laid the wold clock-cease,
All dumb, athirt upon his feace,
Vor we'd a-left, I needen tell ye
Noo works 'ithin his head or belly.
An' then we put upon the pack
The settle, flat upon his back;
An' after that, a-tied in pairs
In woone another, all the chairs,
An' bits o' lumber wo'th a ride,
An' at the very top a-tied,
The children's little stools did lie,
Wi' lags a-turn'd toward the sky;'[5]

('reaves' – the ladder-like wooden framework on the sides of a wagon)

It was the schoolmaster, however, rather than the labourer who, previous to his arrival, had placed an advertisement in the *Chronicle* to declare his hope that 'from his experience, character and acquirements… [the inhabitants would] give him such measure of support as will enable him to gain the object of his fondest wishes – a permanent and happy residence in the delightful town of Dorchester'.[6]

Details of the proposed school had also been set out as an advertisement in his pamphlet on hanging gates and bridges. There he styled himself a 'teacher of Mathematics, classics and modern languages' who, after ten years of 'constant experience and study', begged to inform parents that he was now about to open an 'eligible school' in Durngate Street, Dorchester, for a limited number of 'select pupils', to prepare them for the 'Commercial Mathematical, or Learned Professions, or the Naval or Military Colleges, or Universities'. Testimonials were available from 'a great Mathematician', Major-General Shrapnel, as well as from the Revd S.H. Cassan, Vicar of Bruton, and the Revd W. Dyer of Mere.[7]

It worked. 'Boys', he noted, 'came in very hopefully, and we soon had a fair and fast-filling school'. His terms were twenty-two guineas per annum for a boarder under twelve years of age and twenty-four for older ones. Day pupils paid five guineas. Special tuition in preparation for college entrance, or in mathematics or languages, cost an extra four guineas. Mrs Barnes, 'herself a Mother', was to have care of 'young gentlemen' under six years of age, at a cost of four guineas. Pupil numbers were to be limited to forty. Optimistically, Barnes could calculate that with perhaps sixteen boarders and twenty-plus day boys, he could hope for an annual income of about £500. His advertised fees, however, were not absolute but often a basis for bargaining. Nor were payments assured. As he had discovered in his early years in Mere, fees were often paid late or not in full, and sometimes not at all.

Fortunately, he had come at the right time. Even before he had arrived, one well-wisher had written:

Dorchester 18th April 1835

Dear Sir,

I have just seen your advertisement in the *Dorset Chronicle*. I was glad to see it because I think there is an opening here for a good school. I am unhappily incapable of judging, but from all I have seen and heard of your proficiency from a scholastic point of view, I must auger well of your settlement in this Town. You may, perhaps, wonder at receiving a Letter so unceremoniously from an individual with whom you have never communicated by Letter. But I am sure you will not take offence. If among Friends, Farmers and others, I can see an opportunity of helping you to a Pupil, I will gladly do so…

A sketch by Barnes of boys playing. (Dorset County Museum)

> I do feel great interest in the success of a self-accomplished Scholar. When I say there is a good opening,
> I ought to explain – Mr Cutler's is an expensive School – I dare say, (I suppose there is no doubt that he
> is an able Master). Watson's is certainly a school for the middle classes; but as to his competency to teach
> I am wholly uninformed. I rely upon your good name. Ours is a Town in which the inhabitants are well
> off; it is so with the neighbourhood; and if the local public are well acquainted with your capabilities as
> an Instructor of Youth, as those who know you best must be, your success wd be certain.
>
>                                                                                    Josiah Pople

Watson's was a 'School for Young Gentlemen' that offered a course in 'Classical, Mathematical, French and Commercial Education'. Cutler's was Dorchester Grammar School in South Street, with fees of '40 gns per Annum, washing 3 gns'. Barnes's prices, therefore, were very competitive.[8]

Pople was right in thinking that Dorchester was going through a phase of prosperity. Nevertheless, the town was surrounded by miles of open country and local businesses depended largely upon agriculture for their prosperity. These included not only the hay-merchants, saddlers and farriers, but also the solicitors, schoolmasters and provision merchants. Any depression in farming would eventually hit them too. Throughout his long career as a schoolmaster, the financial stability of Barnes's various establishments was always subject to the ebb and flow of agricultural fortunes. Moreover, the nature of the Dorset economy largely determined local politics. There was strong support in the county for the Corn Laws, which levied taxes on foreign imports.

The Durngate Street house was poky or, as Barnes put it, 'strait-pent'. Because of the school's very success it quickly became overcrowded both with his own children and scholars, swarming and clattering through every room. He soon found himself yearning for the tranquillity of Chantry House. One of his scholars, C.J. Wallis, later noted that 'he evidently regretted his former freedom and quietness – the pleasures he had found in mowing his little lawn and in cultivating his large garden'.[9] At Chantry House he had lived independently, without the constant scrutiny of his neighbours. Recollections of it provided the impulse for his most famous poem:

## My Orcha'd In Linden Lea

'Ithin the woodlands, flow'ry gleaded,
By the woak tree's mossy moot,
The sheenen grass-bleades, timber sheaded,
Now do quiver under voot;
An' birds do whissle overhead,
An' water's bubblen in its bed,
An' there vor me the apple tree
Do lean down low in Linden Lea.

When leaves that leately wer a-springen
Now do feade 'ithin the copse,
An' painted birds do hush their zingen
Up upon the timber's tops;
An' brown-leaved fruit's a-turnen red,
In cloudless zunsheen overhead,
Wi' fruit vor me, the apple tree
Do lean down low in Linden Lea.

Let other vo'k meake money vaster
In the air o' dark-roomed towns,
I don't dread a peevish measter;
Though noo man do heed my frowns,
I be free to goo abrode,
Or teake agean my hwomeward road
To where vor me, the apple tree
Do lean down low in Linden Lea.[10]

('moot' – the bottom of a felled tree, with its roots)

His daughter later wrote that this poem was prompted by a visit he paid to his birthplace in Blackmore. Evidence suggests, however, that he had Chantry House in mind. It was at the Chantry that he first tasted the bliss of freedom. The 'lea' was probably the greensward he used to mow; the 'lindens' the avenue of limes leading up to St Michael's Church. For all that, 'Linden Lea' is not really a precise location at all but a country of the mind.[11]

School days in Durngate Street were much like those in Chantry House, often beginning with a morning 'lecture' to all the boys, usually on a scientific subject. There were no forms as such, for Barnes taught the whole school at the same time and the age range was from five to about seventeen. As at the Chantry, smaller boys had to try to make something of the lecture as best they could, though Barnes had become adept at explaining things to them all.

For two years he undertook all the teaching himself. Then, in 1837, he felt sufficiently confident about his finances to appoint two assistant teachers: Julia's brother, Julius, and a boy from the school, C.J. Wallis, who joined him in the (largely unsuccessful) hope of improving his own knowledge of the classics. Wallis was not merely a pupil and assistant, but also an admirer and a friend, so much so that in later years the Barneses sometimes stayed with his parents at College Green in Bristol. That Barnes was now able to afford such additional help is an indication of the improved fortunes of his school. This added assistance enabled him to engage more in the lucrative extra tuition mentioned in an advertisement, in which he offered: 'Mathematical Studies, including Drawing with Linear or Isometrical Perspective', 'a course of Latin and Greek reading', as well as 'French, Italian, German or other modern European Language'. All the advanced work was undertaken solely by Barnes himself, so that it must have seemed to parents that he knew and could teach practically anything.

If a father were ambitious for his boy to enter a naval college or the military seminary at Addiscombe, then he could be sure that Mr Barnes would be able to coach the lad in the mathematical and engineering expertise he might require.

At this time, the growth of British power in India was beginning to present a new challenge to schools such as Barnes's. Young Englishmen who wished to enter government service in that country were now required to compete for places by public examination. And though English had become officially pre-eminent there, the vast majority of the inhabitants spoke only their own languages, so candidates with some knowledge of these were especially useful. Barnes was ready to meet the challenge. For some time he had been studying the languages of the Subcontinent, and was therefore able to inform parents that he could 'render valuable service to Gentlemen going out to India, by teaching them to read the Asiatic Character, and the Rudiments of that essential and all-sufficient Language in Asia, the Persian as well as the Hindoostani'. Not that he was yet entirely proficient in these tongues, but as happened so often, he found someone living locally who could tutor him. Colonel Besant, of the Native Bengal Infantry and author of *The Persian and Urdu Letter-writer*, became a friend with whom 'for some years [he] read a little Hindustani and Persian almost every week'.[12] Later they went on to explore together 'the laws of Manu and other Sanskrit' works. One of Barnes's first pupils in Dorchester was C.V. Cox, who studied Hindustani with him before entering Addiscombe, and profited so much from it that he eventually became a general in the Indian Army.

## Literature.

### POET'S CORNER.

#### My Orchet in Linden Lea.

'Ithin the woodlands, flow'ry-gleaded,
 By the woak tree's mossy moot,
The sheenen grass-bleades, timber-sheaded,
 Now da quiver under root ;
An' birds da whissle nuver head,
An' water's bubblèn in its bed,
,An' there vor me the apple tree
Da lean down low in Linden Lea.

When leaves that leately wer a-springèn
 Now da feäde 'ithin the copse,
An' painted birds da bash ther zingèn
 Up upon the timber's tops ;
An' brown-leav'd fruit's a-turnèn red,
In cloudless zunsheen, auver head,
Wi' fruit vor me, the apple tree
Da lean down low in Linden Lea.

Let other voke meäke money vaster
 In the air o' dark-room'd towns,
I don't dread a peevish meäster
 Though noo man da heed my frowns,
I be free to goo abrode:
Or teäke ageän my hwomeward road
To where, vor me, the apple tree
Da lean down low in Linden Lea.

The original version of 'Linden Lea' as it appeared in the *Dorset County Chronicle*, 20 November 1856. (Dorset History Centre)

This was a period of 'unremitting exertion' for Barnes. Apart from his hours with Besant, the work of setting up and teaching a new school left him little leisure for writing. During 1835, W.B. supplied only five Petrarchan sonnets to the *Chronicle*, and even these were probably written before he left Mere. Yet somehow he found time to acquire a new interest, in archaeology. And he soon became involved in a dispute concerning some 'hard brittle stuff' resembling peat, which a local dentist named Maclean claimed to have found among bones in a barrow on Ridgeway Hill. When planted by a local gardener named Hartweg (who was told nothing of the origins of the material) this ancient 'stuff' germinated and grew leaves. It turned out to be a mass of raspberry seeds, presumably left undigested in the colon of an ancient Briton. Maclean's integrity was subsequently challenged, but Barnes, who knew him personally, publicly vouched for his honesty. And from the discovery he concluded that 'the Britons fed freely on the wild fruits of the land'.[13]

He also undertook yet another responsibility. At Mere, the Revd Cassan first put it into his head that he might seek ordination in the Church of England. Clearly, Barnes was suitable in many ways. He was pious, hard-working and scholarly. But he was so tender-hearted that all suffering upset him dreadfully and he could hardly bring himself to face it. Even so, when the Revd J.M. Colson at St Peter's urged him to undertake the task of voluntary district visitor to the Dorchester poor, he agreed. Never before had he attempted such work. It required him to call at hovels where he found people starving, hopeless and sick with disease. In confronting these sights, however, his eyes were first opened to the plight of the urban poor, and his social conscience – latent till now – was thoroughly awakened. This first experience of pastoral work strengthened in him the desire to become a priest one day.

Meanwhile, his thoughts turned to acquiring a university degree. For both academic and social reasons, this was considered highly desirable in a schoolmaster. Most of Barnes's Dorchester competitors were graduates, and he was at a disadvantage when advertising because he could not print BA after his name. Because of this, it was only his close friends or those who knew him by repute who would have understood that the new Dorchester schoolmaster was almost certainly a far better scholar and teacher than most MAs, Cantab. or Oxon., in the whole county. Nevertheless, he now took the advice of Cassan and applied to Oxford University for admittance to an extended degree course, probably in divinity. Like Jude Fawley, he was rejected.

His solace was his family. In January 1837, Lucy Emily, his third daughter and fourth child, was born. Then tragedy struck. Their little boy, Julius, still an infant, died suddenly. The cause of death is not known and Barnes left no note of the event. The register of All Saints' Church simply records: '17 May (1837): Julius Barnes, aged 3 years'. And among Barnes's papers there survives an account:

> F. Oliver, King's Arms Inn, Dorchester, 17 May 1837
> pr. Horses for the Funeral of the
> late child of Mr Barnes. 10s.6d.

When Barnes's daughter, Lucy Baxter, came to publish a life of her father in 1887, she did not refer to the death of her small brother. It therefore seems that it was rarely, if ever, mentioned in the family. She may not have been aware of it. Probably, he found it too painful to talk about.

Except in his poetry. Here he was able to confront things which he found unbearable in life, such as the terrors of a mother left alone at night with a sick child.[14] Or the grief of parents at the death of a little son:

## The Turnstile

> Ah! sad wer we as we did peace
> The wold church road, wi' downcast feace,
> The while the bells, that mwoaned so deep
> Above our child a-left asleep,
> Wer now a-zingen all alive

Wi' tother bells the meake the vive.
But up at woone pleace we come by,
'Twer hard to keep woone's two eyes dry:
On Stean-cliff road, 'ithin the drong,
Up where, as vo'k do pass along,
The turnen stile, a-painted white,
Do sheen by day an' show by night.
Vor always there, as we did goo
To church, thik stile did let us drough,
Wi' spreaden arms that wheel'd to guide
Us each in turn to tother zide.
An' vu'st ov all the train he took
My wife, wi' winsome gait an' look;
An' then zent on my little maid,
A-skippen onward, over jay'd
To reach agean the pleace o' pride,
Her comely mother's left han' zide.
An' then, a wheelen roun', he took
On me, 'ithin his third white nook.
An' in the fourth, a sheaken wild,
He zent us on our giddy child.
But eesterday he guided slow
My down cast Jenny, vull o' woe,
An' then my little maid in black,
A-walken softly on her track;
An' after he'd a-turn'd agean,
To let me goo along the leane,
He had no little bwoy to vill
His last white earms, an' they stood still.[15]

('drong' – a narrow way between two hedges or walls)

Despite their grief, life for the Barneses had to go on. By now their foothold in Dorchester was secure. New scholars continued to come into the school in pleasing numbers. So in the last months of 1837, William and Julia agreed that they would need to move again to bigger and better premises. The question was: where?

# 9

# ALMOST A GENTLEMAN

## ⸺ 1830-1840 ⸺

Mr Sylvanus Urban lived at 25 Parliament Street, Westminster, which was convenient for his business. 'Urban' was not his real name. It was merely a literary convention. But, judging by the number of letters that dropped into his mailbox almost every day from all over the country, this fictional person was very popular indeed. In the 1830s and '40s, more than a few of them were written by William Barnes.

The true identity of the Mr Urban was John Bowyer Nichols, a printer, publisher and distinguished antiquary.[1] Among his numerous publications were the third and fourth volumes of Hutchin's *History & Antiquities of Dorset*, which appeared in 1811 and 1815, and which were followed by a number of other county histories. He probably first heard of Barnes through their mutual acquaintance, John Rutter, for whose *Delineations of the North-Western Division of the County of Somerset* Barnes had supplied thirty-two engravings. So it was perhaps with the encouragement of Rutter that Barnes was persuaded to submit letters to one of the most august journals of the day, *The Gentleman's Magazine*, nominally edited by Mr Urban.

The *Magazine* was a monthly subscription publication, devoted to scholarship and the fine arts rather than politics and current affairs. Each issue presented about 100 close-printed, double-columned quarto pages given over to reviews of, and long extracts from, recently published books. An interest in the classical world was assumed in its readers and the *Magazine* included frequent articles on ancient civilisations, with passages in Latin and Greek. A typical issue quoted lengthily from Bishop Monk's life of the eighteenth-century critic, Bentley, and proffered an essay on 'Macaronic' poetry with extracts in Greek. The tone was heavy and the language ponderous. An article begins: 'To account for the various advantages attendant on biography were an act of superrogation'. It was not a specialist journal but one devoted to polite letters generally, offering as much information as any cultivated gentlemen of leisure might reasonably require. Mr Bennet, of *Pride and Prejudice*, might well have been a typical subscriber, perusing its columns in the tranquillity of his study. The editor knew his readership very well. It was largely composed of just such people as Bennet, living quietly on their investments and taking an interest in the world of scholarship. The only gesture towards contemporary life was provided by the stock market prices printed at the back.

Exactly 100 years old when Barnes's first letter appeared in June 1830, the *Magazine* was still a prestigious publication with a national readership, though admittedly it was a bit old-fashioned.[2] But then so was Barnes, despite the fact that he was not yet thirty. For him, the *Magazine* supplied an ideal intellectual home; solidly respectable, erudite and culturally conservative. Moreover, he shared its pronounced interest in classical history, literature, languages and antiquarian matters.

Bowyer Nichols was a plain-dealing man, like Barnes, but rather more shrewd. Required to fill up so many pages every month, he relied upon free copy from his contributors to do so. This was the advantage of maintaining the convention that most of the articles were letters addressed to Mr Urban. Yet though Barnes was not paid for his contributions, he would, no doubt, have considered himself sufficiently rewarded by simply appearing in columns once graced by Dr Johnson himself. As for any commercial advantage he might have gained from his new-found prestige, he was far too unworldly to think in such terms. But now he wanted to be known and so he discarded the signature 'Dilettante' in favour of 'W. Barnes' below the thirty-eight items he contributed to the *Magazine* during the next fourteen years.[3] For, unlike his letters to the *Chronicle*, these enhanced his status as a

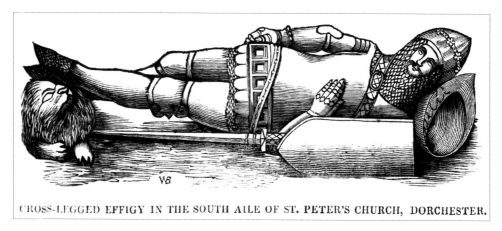

CROSS-LEGGED EFFIGY IN THE SOUTH AILE OF ST. PETER'S CHURCH, DORCHESTER.

Effigy of a knight, engraving by Barnes. (Dorset County Museum)

scholar and afforded him a national readership of highly educated men. By becoming a regular correspondent, he had both found a suitable audience and joined the national intellectual conversation.

There was one further advantage. As one who professed to educate young gentlemen, Barnes had always had to be extremely reticent about his social origins as the son of a labourer. Now, in becoming a contributor to a journal specifically addressed to gentlemen, his own claims to that rank seemed to have been confirmed. Surely it followed that one who wrote for *The Gentleman's Magazine* must be a gentleman himself. Or almost. At any rate, it was proof that despite his lack of formal education, he was now acknowledged to be a clever man. And though there were few in Mere to recognise his achievement, it is most unlikely that Julia would have let it go by entirely unnoticed. She would have wanted their genteel neighbours to know that venerable doctors and professors in the universities were regularly reading the opinions of their local schoolmaster in the columns of a learned periodical.

Many of his early articles consisted of descriptions of sites of antiquarian interest in the surrounding countryside, which were accompanied by his own engravings. Preparing these pieces must have entailed a considerable amount of work and taken a good deal of his spare time. At first he chose locations inexpensively close to home but in later years, when he was more affluent and could afford to hire a vehicle, he travelled farther afield. In April 1832, his engraving of the parish church at Mere appeared in the *Magazine*. Over the next few years there followed prints of Thornhill Obelisk at Stalbridge; Napper's Mite in Dorchester; the church at Sturminster Newton; Nailsea Church; the sculptured cross at Stalbridge; General Shrapnel's mansion at Puncknowle; the Roman amphitheatre at Dorchester known as Maumbury Rings; the judge's house at Dorchester; and Henry Fielding's house at 'East Stower' (or 'Stour'), though he engraved this from a drawing.

By the mid-1830s, letters from 'W. Barnes' of Mere had become familiar to this small but discriminating national audience.[4] In remote rectories, in the libraries of learned societies and even on the tables of sedate gentlemen's clubs, his name was now (slightly) known. Few of his readers can have doubted that W. Barnes was something of a polymath, one who had a supply of information and interesting ideas about almost everything. This was because, in late Georgian England, the separation of academic disciplines and the professionalising of scholarship were in their relative infancy, and laymen like Barnes might still hope to make useful contributions to various branches of the arts and sciences.[5] He had many such observations to make.

History was one of his favourite subjects. In due course, readers were treated to his speculations – they were mostly such – on the Celts in Spain; on the Belgae, Aquitani and Celti; on the peopling and languages of Britain and Ireland; and on Phoenician intercourse with the British Isles. His approach was almost always etymological, considering it valid to make historical inferences by tracing the origins of words.

This remained true even when concerning Egyptian hieroglyphics. Following Napoleon's expedition to that country in 1798, there arose a great interest among scholars in all things Egyptian. Like other readers of *The Gentleman's Magazine*, Barnes would have followed news of attempts by researchers to decipher the inscriptions made by this ancient people. There was even a Dorset dimension to the story, for in 1821 that paper reported that Mr William Bankes was bringing an ancient obelisk back to Kingston Lacy, his home near Poole. Then, in the following year, came the news that Jean Francois Champollion had found the key to decipher the hieroglyphs on the Rosetta Stone. Such reports set Barnes thinking. In December 1831 he blithely informed the *Magazine* that although he had not yet seen Champollion's *Precis du Systeme Hieroglyphique des anciens Egyptiens*, he 'should like to know whether the learned [had] ever tried to decypher the Egyptian symbols by supposing them to represent only the modifications of the organs of speech, instead of words; or, in short, that they are letters, as much as those of the Hebrew alphabet'. Well, yes, Champollion had considered this proposition, as well as innumerable other possibilities. Clearly Barnes had not the slightest idea of the immense labours involved in trying to read the hieroglyphs.[6] But his comically naïve enquiry reveals just how much he wanted to play a part in the national – even international – debate on such scholarly topics.

But though the number of Barnes's antiquarian and historical contributions to the *Magazine* throughout the 1830s and '40s is impressive, it must be admitted that there is nothing especially original about them. True, his range is extraordinary, reaching from Latin pronunciation to the songs of the ancient Romans, from the biography of Aesop to Hindu science, and from the 'reed' used in the Crucifixion to the harmonic proportions of church architecture. But these articles might have been composed by any number of gentlemen with speculative minds and not enough to do.

There was one topic, however, on which Barnes was fitted to make an unique contribution; philology. By the late 1830s he had taught himself to read at least fourteen foreign languages. There was no linguistic matter in which he was uninterested, and no language that he was not prepared to try to learn. And over the course of the next decade he developed an extraordinary cumulative argument concerning the history and the possible future development of the English language. It had been the theme of that first letter to the *Magazine*, to which Mr Urban gave the title, 'The Unnecessary Corruptions of the English Language'.

Its argument reprised that of the 'Linguiana' pieces in the *Dorset County Chronicle*, i.e. that the 'contemptible' system of Gallicising, Latinizing and Hellenizing the English language was then so common among the middle classes that within a few years the native language was 'likely to be understood by only a few professors of the dead and living language'. It objected to the common contention that foreign languages were more expressive than English or could supply terms for which the vernacular had none. Such a view, Barnes believed, was 'scandalous to the English nation', and a servile acknowledgement of national inferiority. The fact that the Italians had supplied their musical terms to the English was no proof that they had taught them the art itself. Foreign terminology, he insisted, rendered the English language 'less simple, less perspicuous, less pure, less regular, and fit only for learned people to converse with each other'. Such usage caused 'great toil and obstruction to the teacher of youth, and [kept] the pupil learning words when he should be learning facts'. Moreover, many people simply did not know how to pronounce the foreign words they employed.

All this he had argued before, but he now went on to suggest how to combat such 'corruptions'. There were two ways. The first was simply to avoid using foreign words at all by using English ones. For 'protége', we should say 'ward'; for 'aid de camp', 'under general'; for 'canaille', 'rabble'; for 'escritoire', 'writing-chest'; for 'billet-doux', 'love-note', and so on. Secondly, words for which there were no English equivalents might be replaced by compounding true English words. The suffix 'stead', for example, which means 'place', could be used to provide many useful expressions, so that for aviary we might say 'birdstead'; and for menagerie, 'animalstead'. Similarly, the English 'lore', meaning 'learning' or 'doctrine', could replace the Greek 'logy'. 'Ornithology' would become 'birdlore'; 'osteology', 'bonelore'; 'geology', 'earthlore'; and – interestingly – 'philology' would become 'wordlore'. From these compounds he derived such nouns and adjectives as 'birdloreman' and 'birdlearned'. Concluding, he humbly hoped that his 'observations [would] meet the eyes of some scholars who [might] be better able, and no less willing than [he was], to stop the decline'.

What lay beneath these proposals was his yet unformulated assumption that there was such a thing as a 'pure' English language which, though threatened by linguistic importations, might still be reclaimed. Stimulus to such notions was provided by a holiday in June 1831 that he took with the family to visit the Mileses in Abergavenny. He later noted, 'I was quickened with a yearning to know more of the Welsh people and their speech'.[7] True to form, he tried to go everywhere and learn everything. He climbed the mountain Blorenge, went fishing, spent time 'studying Welsh on the shores of the Usk' and walked twenty miles to Llangelly and Nant-y-glo. So fired up was he by all this that when back at Chantry House, he began studying the Welsh language, its literature and history, and even subscribed to a Welsh newspaper. Eventually, his new enthusiasm resulted in letters to Mr Urban on 'The Identity of National Language and Manners' and 'The Origins of Language'.[8]

The concept of a 'pure' language was partly stimulated by the Welsh experience. Welsh, in his view, was derived from the ancient Britons and had come down, virtually unchanged, to modern times. Yet, despite the venerable antiquity of their language, Welsh speakers employed no foreign terms, such as derivations from Greek, Latin or Norman French. Their language was unsullied, pure unto itself, and served as the medium of a noble literature. A 'pure' language was, therefore, a possibility. And if this were true for Welsh, why might it not also be so for English? By 'English', he was progressively coming to mean the speech of King Alfred's Wessex.

Meanwhile, his attack on 'corrupt' English became progressively more combative in tone. Such corruptions, he insisted, had been allowed to infiltrate the language for several reasons: conquest; a want of English words to meet the developing needs of modern science, arts and technology; the carelessness of translators; and the 'pomp of smatterers' (i.e. snobbery), who wished to appear familiar with other languages. Nevertheless, it was surely better to say 'truth' instead of 'veracity', and 'cover' rather than 'envelope', and to employ vernacular stems, such as 'back', 'fore', and 'out' to construct a purer English. In this way 'backshine' might replace 'reflection'; 'foretake', 'anticipate'; and 'outroam', 'excursion'. Difficult foreign words, such as 'telescope', 'polygamist', and 'biography' could be dropped for the more homely 'far-seer', 'many-wedder', and 'life-writ'.[9] Sometimes, however, almost alarmed at his own daring, he would draw back a bit and deny that he ever hoped that his compound words were likely to come into general use. He was, he maintained, merely a 'linguistic conservative', not wishing 'to work any great change in the English language', but merely demonstrating how it might be self-enriched.[10]

And there, in the early '30s, his argument rested for a while. So far it had progressed in a number of steps which may be summarised as follows:

1. That contemporary English had become 'impure' by the common usage among the middle classes of words of foreign origin, especially Latin and French.

2. That this alien usage was an impediment to understanding. Many of those who used such expressions did not fully comprehend them, and the practice effectively debarred working people from understanding what was said, especially from the pulpit or in the classroom.

3. That, nevertheless, there was a 'pure' form of English which all native speakers understood and which might be retrieved.

The next step in his thinking came almost a decade later, in a letter to the *Magazine* in June 1840. It marked a great leap forward. Mr Urban gave it the title 'The Dialects of Dorsetshire Compared with the Anglo-Saxon'. To understand just how bold it was, it is necessary to consider for a moment the consensus view of middle-class people concerning local dialects such as those of Dorset. In the early nineteenth century, there was an opinion widespread among many – though never clearly formulated – that the dialect was merely a failed attempt by inadequate people to express themselves in standard English. It was the linguistic consequence of stupidity; the broader the dialect, the more stupid the speaker.

Of course, this view was not confined to Dorset. Barnes later quoted the opinion of an eminent philogist that 'the poor landfolk of our shires [have] only about two hundred words in their vocabulary'.[11] An even more dismissive view regarded the dialect as something akin to sounds made by farmyard animals. The notion was that the rural work-folk spent so much time with their animals that their speech approximated to the lowings, bleatings and gruntings of their constant companions. To genteel people, the merest hint of dialect was evidence of, in Thomas Hardy's words, 'those terrible marks of the beast'.[12] Quite literally.

This contempt for their speech had even communicated itself to the work-folk themselves. In his *Glossary of the Dorset Dialect*, published many years later, Barnes included the word 'ninnywatch' or 'nunnywatch', as used by an old countryman. When asked about its meaning, an enquirer was told: 'tant got noo meanen, sir, 'tis only oone o' they words we poor folk do use'.[13] This suggests that many dialect speakers had lost all confidence in the efficacy of their language. Snobbery and derision had induced them to believe that their words had no meaning at all, which raised the extraordinary notion that there could be a language without a semantic content. The Dorset dialect, it seemed, was an example of this, a language without meaning, incapable of furnishing expressions of sufficient consequence and precision to function effectively.[14]

It was against this background of ignorance and prejudice that Barnes's letter on the Dorset dialect appeared. It contained a strong and passionate defence of the qualities inherent in the dialect, for which he now made several astonishing claims. He even had the nerve to compare it with classical Greek:

> It is a broad, bold, rustic shape of English as the Doric was of the Greek, rich in humour, strong in raillery, powerful in hyperbole, and altogether as fit a vehicle of rustic feeling and thought as the Doric is found in the Idyllia of Theocritus.

Most breathtaking of all was a contention made in passing, almost as if it were a statement of the obvious:

> This [Dorset] dialect, which is purer and more regular than that which has been adopted as the national speech, is, I think…

'Purer' than standard English because it was closer to Anglo-Saxon; 'more regular' because it derived its grammar from that language, which observed its own rules of procedure rather more faithfully than did standard English. Far from being a failed attempt at English, the Dorset dialect was the purest form of it and a language in its own right.

What emerged from all this was startling and apparently paradoxical. If one were to believe Barnes, the language spoken by the work-folk in the fields was etymologically and grammatically superior to that of the professional and middle classes in Dorchester. This was not a safe opinion for a man who depended for his living on teaching country boys to speak correct English. Nor did it serve to promote his modest aspirations to gentility. Fortunately for him, not many people in Dorchester at that time would have read and understood the implications of his article, nor did Barnes himself at first fully comprehend just how dangerous they were. He had not yet perceived the tension between his theories and practice, though this was to prove of great consequence in later days.

# 10

# ESTABLISHMENTS: NORMAN'S HOUSE

## —— 1838-1847 ——

Back a bit from the braying coach horns and the town pump, South Street took on a more countri-fied air. Here, pedestrians might safely saunter past the Napper's Mite almshouses and Dorchester Grammar School ('Hardye's') to peer into the windows of dark little shops. Barnes's sometime pupil, Frederick Treves, remembered a 'gracious medley of red brick and grey stone, of fine doorways and tiled roofs… there was one house behind high gates that had a carriage drive… at another place the garden broke in upon the street'. He recalled a cobbler in horn spectacles making boots and little boys staring through railings at the peacocks. Here too, strolling down to Fordington, were gentlemen in tall hats and side-whiskers accompanied by ladies in crinolines, poke bonnets and flowing veils with their ringlets and chignons. Occasionally, farmers' wagons and haycarts lumbered magisterially down the street.[1] Towards the end of 1837, Norman's House, a fairly spacious, two-storey building on the east side became available for rent. It had an annexe at the rear suitable for a classroom and playrooms. In the following January, Barnes moved his school there.[2]

This was a time of change. A young Queen had ascended the throne; the Chartists were demand-ing universal male suffrage, annual elections and a secret ballot; the railways were opening up the country; communications were about to be transformed by Professor Wheatstone's electric telegraph; and a man named Isaac Pitman had introduced a new system of speedwriting called 'shorthand'. In due course, Barnes's life was to be touched by all these changes. One day he would glimpse the Queen close up; the Reform Bills would give him the vote; and the railways were to bring him new educational opportunities. Wheatstone and Pitman, too, would play a part in his story. In the New Year of 1838, however, he was busy settling in and welcoming new scholars. Within two years he had forty: twenty-one boarders and nineteen day boys. Somehow, he had become not only a teacher and scholar, but also a successful businessman.

Emboldened by this progress, he applied once again for university entrance. This time he was suc-cessful, and was enrolled as a 'Ten Year Man' at St John's College, Cambridge, for a bachelor's degree in divinity. All he had to do, it seemed, was to keep his name on the college books, reside there for a few terms and pass certain tests. Though he well understood that this would be a protracted and expensive business, it gave him a long term goal and the hope of achieving greater recognition for his talents.

Meanwhile, the schoolroom routine continued. Treves remembered one of Barnes's nine o'clock lectures to the whole school:

> It was on logic. I sat on a form with other boys and was required to write for dictation the following sentence. 'Logic is the right use of exact reasoning'. This is the first important contribution to the sum of knowledge that I ever received. For a boy of seven it was undoubtedly strong meat. It was, I am hardly ashamed to say, hardly intelligible. The lecture that followed only served to add mystery to the text. I formed the idea that logic was some form of medicine, physic as administered in those days to the young, being my conception of something unpleasant and incomprehensible that was supposed to do the taker good. It is curious that the sentence never faded from my memory. It was for years a kind of cryptic utterance full of mystery, a sort of Abracadabra, a thing that was purely cabbalistic, that had some powerful

inner meaning unknown to the multitude. I found myself muttering it with reverence and awe. I tried it upon other boys of about my own age and found that it affected them solemnly.

If any boastful boy endeavoured to impress me with his learning I replied: 'Logic is the right use of exact reasoning'. Some boys, the more profane and heedless, kicked me for my precious saying, while others were apparently moved by an utterance that resembled the formula of an incantation such as may have been used in the 'Arabian Nights'.[3]

Another former pupil, the Revd J.B. Lock, sometime tutor in mathematics and physics at Gonville and Caius College, Cambridge, explained how the schoolmaster strove to make scientific studies both comprehensible and memorable:

I was sent to his school in South Street when I was about eight years old, and I can still picture to myself the old school-room in which once a week Mr Barnes used, punctually at nine o'clock, to give the whole school a lecture on practical science. His lecture on electricity – he gave us some sharp shocks with a frictional machine – on the physical geography of the Alps, on the steam-engine – he showed us a model which his son, Egbert Barnes, had made – on bridge building – he had a model arch in wooden bricks – I can still remember in detail. We had each, big and little, to write an abstract of the lecture in the most approved modern fashion. It seems worth recalling that such lectures were given in Dorchester thirty years ago, just such lectures as are now given in most of the great public schools in which such subjects were still untaught much less than thirty years ago. These lectures of my old master were as wonderfully adapted to his audience, as they were clear and accurate in substance.[4]

South Street, Dorchester, in the nineteenth century. (Dorset County Museum)

Placing a considerable emphasis on science in his curriculum, Barnes backed it up with practical experience. In good weather there were walks in the surrounding countryside, sometimes joined by members of his family. Boys were encouraged to collect such items of interest as rocks, fossils, plants, flowers, insects or birds' eggs. On one expedition to Yellowham Wood, where there was much tree-climbing in search of nests, he called out, 'Come down Blair, we are going on now'. 'I'm coming directly, sir', replied the boy with his mouth full of eggs; but at that moment the branch on which he was sitting cracked and he came down abruptly with a good deal of clutching at branches to break his fall. After he was sure the boy was not hurt, Barnes added, 'You kept your word, Blair; I like a boy who speaks the truth'.[5]

The improvement in his fortunes, and consequent relief from years of financial anxiety, enabled Barnes to relax the anxious earnestness which had long characterised his manner. As a result, his innate geniality and wry humour became much more apparent, especially with his pupils and, later on, with his own children. Soon there were more of these. In 1838 his daughter, Isabel, was born, then came William Miles in 1840, and finally Egbert in 1844. Always childlike himself, Barnes would play the 'bear' for them and chase the little 'dogs' round the parlour. In her charming vignette of early Victorian family life, Lucy Baxter remembered him inducting her brothers into games such as marbles, 'ring-taw' and also top whipping, in which they competed to see who could keep them spinning longest.

He was the gentlest of fathers. The children were rarely scolded and never smacked. Lucy could recall only one occasion when they were seriously punished. This was when the four older ones were accused of breaking the branch of a fruit tree and, on their persistent denial, locked in a room. Unperturbed, the children continued their games in this 'prison' until their father, heavy with guilt, came to release them, having discovered the real culprit was one of his students.

They were a musical family. On Sunday evenings the children would sit on their little stools round the fire joining in hymns with their parents. On weekday evenings they would listen to William and Julia sing duets from opera: 'Drink to me' and 'O Pescator dell'onda', etc. Barnes formed a little quartet to play pieces by Beethoven and Haydn. Frederick Smith was first violin, the cellist and viola player were recruited from the St Peter's Church choir, and Barnes himself supplied the second violin or the flute. Sometimes, when quite young, his daughter Julia performed on the piano, for she had revealed very early promise of an exceptional musical talent. Lucy remembered the younger children waking at night to hear 'beautiful harmonies' coming up from the rooms below.[6]

The Barnes daughters were educated at home and his sons in his own school, though the two communities were often intermixed. His task in teaching so many children of all ages was a complex one and, eventually, he felt prosperous enough to take on another usher, Isaac Hann. Much of the teaching was still done by himself and he had to find a way of ensuring that boys were getting on with their work while he attended to others. The obvious way to do this was to have them working from textbooks. So, finding many of these unsatisfactory or too expensive, Barnes resumed the practice of writing his own and published a series of paper-covered primers. They never seem to have had a sale much beyond his own school, but there it was guaranteed because he could require parents to buy them as essential 'set-books' to accompany his lessons.

Something of his workaday life may be glimpsed in the pages of these little books. No copy of his *Corrective Concordance or Imposition Book* appears to have survived, but its pious tenor is suggested by an advertisement which announced that, 'All Scripture is given by inspiration of God, and is profitable for doctrine, for reproof, for correction, for instruction in Righteousness'. (2 Timothy III 16) Parents would have been reassured.[7]

Much more ambitious in scope was *An Investigation of the Laws of Case in Language* which, astonishingly, claimed to take 'the first step towards a system of universal grammar', from the most basic processes of human thought.[8] This involved extending the usual six noun declensions in Latin to nine! One commentator has observed that 'here was an obscure schoolmaster demanding a complete revolution in the approach to language teaching, ignoring the traditional framework, accepted for centuries as fundamental truth, inviolable as Holy Writ'.[9] For all that, the attempt to fashion the key to all languages in a pamphlet of a mere fifty-two pages might be considered a little ambitious.

## RELATIVE STANDING OF PUPILS
### AT
### Mr Barnes's School, Dorchester
#### PERIODICAL REPORT

| PUPILS. | Divinity. | English Language and General Knowledge. | Arithmetic. | Writing. | History. | Geography. | Classics. | Modern Languages. | Drawing | Geometry. | Place on the Tropograph. |
|---|---|---|---|---|---|---|---|---|---|---|---|
| Plowman, Major, . | 1 | 1 | 1 | 6 | 1 | 13 | 1 | 1 | | 1 | 1 in the Whites. |
| Stickland, . . . | 5 | 9 | 6 | 8 | 8 | 20 | 2 | 6 | | 2 | 1 |
| Eldridge, . . . | 3 | 4 | 7 | 15 | 11 | 12 | 9 | | | 3 | 1 |
| Harding, Major, . | 10 | 6 | 4 | | 9 | 14 | 10 | | 3 | 4 | 1 |
| Cross, . . . . | 4 | 3 | 14 | 7 | 2 | 1 | 29 | | | 6 | 1 |
| Browning, Major . | 9 | 2 | 19 | 17 | 3 | 2 | 24 | | | 7 | 2 |
| Card, Minor, B . | 7 | 8 | 2 | 10 | 7 | 7 | 11 | 3 | | 8 | 1 |
| Bishop, . . . . | 8 | 7 | 10 | 26 | 5 | 21 | 5 | 8 | | 5 | 1 |
| Symes, B . . . | 2 | 5 | 3 | 5 | 4 | 6 | 4 | | | 9 | 1 |
| Bascombe, B. . . | 18 | 14 | 11 | 30 | 10 | 17 | 8 | 4 | | | 1 |
| Simonds, . . . | 16 | 12 | 22 | 25 | 21 | 11 | 7 | | | | 1 |
| Durden, Minor . | 11 | 11 | 23 | 1 | 16 | 9 | 16 | | | | 1 |
| Warne, . . . . | 6 | 10 | 17 | 22 | 12 | 4 | 3 | 2 | | | 1 |
| Legg, B . . . | 21 | 23 | 8 | 11 | 14 | 10 | | | | | 1 |
| Saunders, B . . | 31 | 24 | 12 | 20 | 24 | 30 | 28 | | 6 | 12 | 1 |
| James, B . . . | 12 | 26 | 20 | 24 | 26 | 27 | 17 | | | | 1 |
| Harris, B . . . | 17 | 15 | 5 | 2 | 6 | 3 | 14 | | | 10 | 1 |
| Tassell, . . . . | 14 | 21 | 9 | 16 | 25 | 28 | | | | | 1 |
| Plowman, Minor . | 13 | 19 | 30 | 18 | 20 | 19 | 15 | | | | 1 |
| Gaulton, . . . | 27 | 20 | 28 | 27 | 28 | 25 | | | | | 3 |
| Scutt, B . . . . | 19 | 17 | 18 | 13 | 18 | 5 | | | | 11 | 1 |
| Nobbs, B . . . | 15 | 13 | 13 | 3 | 13 | 16 | 13 | | 1 | | 1 |
| Harvey, Minor . | 26 | 27 | 16 | 32 | 29 | 8 | 22 | | | | 1 |
| Fox, Minor, B . | 28 | 25 | 32 | 29 | 22 | 22 | 21 | | | | 1 |
| Harding, Minor, . | 37 | 39 | 29 | 37 | 32 | 29 | | | | | 1 |
| Thatcher, B. . . | 22 | 22 | 24 | 19 | 23 | 24 | 19 | | | | 1 |
| Smith, . . . . | 38 | 34 | 33 | 33 | 33 | 33 | 26 | | | | 1 |
| Lambert, . . . | 39 | 36 | 38 | 39 | 37 | 39 | | | | | 1 |
| Clark, Minor, B . | 23 | 18 | 15 | 9 | 17 | 15 | 12 | 7 | 2 | | 1 |
| Pope, B . . . . | 20 | 16 | 26 | 23 | 15 | 18 | 6 | | | | 1 |
| Lucas, . . . . | 32 | 30 | 21 | 12 | 27 | 26 | | | 5 | | 1 |
| Clark, Minimus B | 24 | 29 | 34 | 21 | 35 | 31 | 23 | | 4 | | 1 |
| Clark, Major, B . | 25 | 28 | 31 | 14 | 19 | 23 | 18 | 5 | | | 1 |
| Tullidge, Minor . | 34 | 37 | 35 | 36 | 34 | 36 | | | | | 1 |
| Browning, Minor . | 36 | 35 | 39 | 34 | 36 | 37 | | | | | 1 |
| Symes, Minor, B . | 30 | 32 | 25 | 28 | 31 | 34 | 27 | | | | 1 |
| Symes, Minimus, B | 29 | 31 | 27 | 31 | 30 | 35 | | | | | 1 |
| Wright, Minor . | 33 | 33 | 36 | 38 | 39 | 32 | 20 | | | | 2 |
| Urquhart, Minor . | 35 | 38 | 37 | 35 | 38 | 38 | 25 | | | | 1 |
| Burgoyne, . . . | 40 | 40 | 40 | 40 | 40 | 40 | | | | | 1 |
| Devenish, . . . | 41 | 41 | 41 | 4i | 41 | 41 | | | | | 1 |

THREE GENTLEMEN *in Oriental Languages and other particular Studies.*

\* The Tropograph, which Mr. BARNES has adopted with the best effect for registering and correcting the conduct of his Pupils, is a tablet on which each boy has a pin moveable in a line of 24 holes, through 4 colors, white, red, blue, and black. His pin sinks a hole for a reprehensible act, but may be worked up again by a voluntary task. The numbers in the last column (the Tropograph column,) show the place of the Pupil's pin—counting the holes from the top.

*The lowest numbers are the most creditable in all the columns.*

Dorchester, *March*, 1846.

W. BARNES.

Record sheet from Barnes's school. (Dorset County Museum)

Yet Barnes was so learned by now – in his book he says he had drawn upon 'twelve or fourteen languages' – his mind was so quick, so apt to note linguistic analogies, so eager to formulate new systems of thought, and so enthusiastic to communicate them, that it is impossible not to admire the attempt. Nor were his ideas solely hypothetical, for he employed them in his own classroom. He was an exceptional teacher. His pupils were only ordinary boys and no doubt many were often perplexed by his explanations, yet his record as a language teacher was highly successful, as proved by the fact that many of his pupils, and some among his own children, became proficient linguists. Whether other teachers could be equally effective when employing his methods must remain a matter of doubt.

He was always logical. In another little book, this time on arithmetic, he observed that whereas rival texts provided ample working examples, they did not explain things adequately.[10] This one did. A student was not asked to square a number before telling him what a square was. Nevertheless, the chief function of the book was to provide questions which Barnes spent many tedious hours working through with his students: 'A gentleman left his estate to his three children, one of whom sold 2/5 of his share for £2,620. What was the estate worth? Ans. £19,650.'

Intriguingly, the scrupulously honest Barnes practised a mild deception on the title page of his *Laws of Case* and in following books by describing himself as 'W. Barnes, (of St John's College, Cambridge)'. This seemed to imply that he was a graduate of that institution. However, he was not yet a graduate and he may not even have visited the college at the time. He was only 'of' the college because his name was on its books. That he should have done this reveals the sense of inferiority he felt in not having a degree and how much this new college connection, however tenuous, meant to him.

By the 1830s and '40s, his habit of publishing school books had become routine. And so innovative was his mind that his daily work of explaining complex things to little boys pushed his own thoughts further and further along the seams of every subject he taught. Especially language, which he examined in his most ambitious text, *Elements of English Grammar, with a set of Questions and Exercises*.[11]

Though he divided this book conventionally into sections on orthography, etymology, grammar and prosody, he took nothing on trust and started from the most basic concepts: 'Letters are characters used to spell words'. 'The letters used to spell the words of a language, are called the Alphabet of the language'. Whereas a less thoughtful teacher might have been content to simply repeat familiar grammar lessons, he did not. Everything that he wished to present to the pupil he thought through again himself. Consequently, he gave an almost philosophical consideration to the subject. This sometimes caused difficulties. Though much of the book would have been within the understanding of the average pupil, there were passages in which Barnes struggled to explain what would have already been clear to a less complex mind. For example:

> When a second sure action is named as the subject of the first, the second may be joined to the first in the indicative mood, with its noun in the nominative case, by the conjunction that; or may be put after the first in the infinitive mood, with its noun in the accusative case; as 'I know that John is a good boy'.

Well, yes.

Published in London by Longman and partners rather than the usual Dorchester printers, and running to 112 pages, Barnes probably had greater aspirations for this book, hoping perhaps that it would become a nationally-recognised primer and employed in many schools. He was disappointed. *The Elements of English* did not sell widely and failed to bring in a nice little income. Nevertheless, in making this survey of the structure of English, he had involved himself in a searching scrutiny of the language of a kind rarely undertaken by many teachers or poets. And it provided the basis for later work which was to mark him out as an original linguistic thinker.

For his mind was open to all new ideas. At one time or another, he enthused over such innovations as the decimal system, the ten-month-year, the phonetic alphabet, the coming of the railways and Pitman's new system of shorthand. When his friend, William Colbourne, wrote to tell him about Pitman's book, *Phonography* (1840), he was astonished to receive a reply in this very same shorthand.[12]

Now, great changes were felt in Dorchester and afternoon expeditions from school were given increased momentum by a tremendous upheaval in the local countryside. The railways were coming. Soon armies of 'navvies' began to prepare a standard-gauge (4ft 8½in) single track from Southampton to Dorchester. It was opened on 1 June 1845 by the London & South Western Railway, and soon there were plans to extend it to Weymouth. Meanwhile, there was talk of the construction of a broad gauge (7ft) line by Brunel's Great Western Railway Company from Bristol to Weymouth, via Yeovil and Dorchester.[13]

There was a renewed public interest in antiquities. Over in Lyme Regis, a cabinet-maker's daughter, Mary Anning, had already become a local celebrity for the 'curiosities' she had collected from eroding coastal cliffs.[14] Now it was Dorchester's turn. Would-be archaeologists, including schoolboys from Norman's House, followed the railway diggings to harvest a rich supply of fossils. At last, a public meeting was called to consider how best to take advantage of the situation. On 15 October 1845 it was resolved:

1st. That, in consideration of the importance of this district to natural history and both British and Roman antiquities, and more especially at this time, when the disturbance of the surface of the country in the formation of railroads is likely to bring to light specimens of interest in these several departments of science, it is advisable to take immediate steps for the establishment of an institution in this town containing a museum and library for the county of Dorset…

5th. That the Right Honourable Lord Ashley, M.P., be requested to become president of the institution.

6th. That the Rev. C.W. Bingham and Mr. William Barnes be appointed honorary secretaries, and Herbert Williams, Esq. treasurer.[15]

A property was taken in Back South Street to house the collection and items poured in from round the county: British and Saxon antiquities, stuffed animals, cases of butterflies, an ichthyosaurus and the fin of a plesiosaur from Purbeck, rocks, fossils, flora and fauna. The Dorset County Museum was established.

So was Barnes. By his election as secretary, his scholarship and reputation were at last given some official recognition in the town. He had already enjoyed a small coup as an archaeologist when he had identified what he described in *The Gentleman's Magazine* as 'the so-called Kimmeridge Coal Money'. Recent excavations into the clay strata of the Isle of Purbeck had thrown up hundreds of 'whorls of black shale with square holes in the centre'. Eagerly the archaeological community responded with all sorts of explanations of the origins of these strange objects: they were pieces of prehistoric money, carried about hung on strings; they were weapons of war; they were curious splittings of the shale deposits. Barnes disproved all this. He showed conclusively that the 'coal money' in fact consisted of turnings from a modern lathe.

Now he threw himself into the business of the museum. As if to prove himself an authority, he was soon engaged in correspondence with some very learned people. Professor Anstead wrote from the Geological Society to offer his services in identifying Dorset specimens; Mr J.R. Jones of the same institution declared that the fossils Barnes had sent him were 'a very interesting group of the brachiopod species'; Mr Dale wrote excitedly to enclose some rare butterfly specimens. Barnes replied as an equal, a fellow cognoscente.

Then alarm bells began to ring. Slowly it dawned on people that with the proposed extension to Weymouth, the railway workings threatened to destroy one of the county's most important antiquarian sites. Maumbury Rings, just south of Dorchester, consisted of two circular banks of earth, the inner of Neolithic origin and the outer dating from the seventeenth century. The Romans had used them as an amphitheatre; they had served as a Civil War fort; and, in the eighteenth century, as a place of public execution. Barnes had published an article about the site in *The Gentleman's Magazine* in May 1839. Anticipating the danger, he and two museum colleagues alerted the Archaeological Association. As a result of such protests, the London & South Western line to Weymouth was diverted to the east of the Rings.

In the spring of 1846 he received a letter from a fellow antiquarian, William Colfox of Bridport, concerning another threat. Brunel's proposed broad-gauge line from Bristol now threatened to cut through Poundbury, the Roman camp to the north-west of Dochester, which was notable for its aqueduct which had curled twelve miles around adjacent hillsides to bring water to the town. Barnes reassured Colfox. Steps had already been taken. He and his colleagues were petitioning Parliament against it. And when it was found that they were too late in this, they tried another approach. His friend, Charles Warne FSA, wrote to Brunel personally to state their case. The great man was sympathetic. In the event, the Bristol to Weymouth line, which finally opened in 1857, was tunnelled beneath Poundbury and swung just west of Maumbury Rings. In all this activity, Barnes had been to the fore, attending meetings, writing letters and petitioning. That these sites still survive is partly due to him.

Such successes simply fuelled his energy. There was a new zest to him now, and a new confidence born of achievement. In active middle age, it seemed there was nothing he could not do, no height which he could not climb. And at last he had the means and some leisure to pursue his manifold interests. He even thought of taking a trip abroad.

His old friend Edward Fuller had several times suggested that they should go together for a holiday to Paris, the Rhineland or southern Germany. These plans had been dropped, however, when Fuller's young wife became ill. She died of consumption in 1838. Then Fuller himself contracted the disease. So, like John Keats before him, he decided to go south to seek the sun and stave off death. What he needed was a companion, someone who could see him safely on his journey and who could, incidentally, speak French. Barnes was the obvious choice. But in March 1840, his son Miles was born and he could not leave Julia. In the meanwhile, Fuller's health deteriorated. A few months later, Barnes's notebook recorded, 'This day I have lost my early and much loved friend, Edward Fuller, who died at Staple Grove, near Taunton'. Fuller left him £100 as 'a token of long-standing friendship'.

It was more than twenty years since they had first met in Dorchester, had strolled the banks of the 'crow-studded' Frome, talking excitedly of their ambitions and had enjoyed their musical evenings together. Only dialect was adequate to express Barnes's sense of loss:

## The Music o' The Dead

When music, in a heart that's true,
Do kindle up wold loves anew,
An' dim wet eyes, in feairest lights,
Do zee but inward fancy's zights;
When creepen years wi' with'ren blights,
'V a-took off them that were so dear,
How touchen 'tis if we do hear
The tuens o' the dead, John.

When I, a-stannen in the lew
O' trees a storm's a-beaten drough,
Do zee the slanten mist a-drove
By spitevul winds along the grove,
An' hear their hollow sounds above
My sheltered head, do seem, as I
Do think o' zunny days gone by,
Lik' music vor the dead, John.

Last night, as I were gwain along
The brook, I heard the milk-maid's zong
A ringen out so clear an' shrill
Along the meads an' roun' the hill.

I catched the tuen, an' stood still
To hear't; 'twer woone that Jeane did zing
A-vield a-milken in the spring,-
Sweet music o' the dead, John.

Don't tell o' zongs that be a-zung
By young chaps now, wi sheameless tongue:
Zing me wold ditties, that would start
The meadens' tears, or stir my heart
To teake in life a manly part, –
The wold vo'k's zongs that twold the teale,
An' vollow'd round their mugs o' eale,
The music o' the dead, John.[16]

('lew' – shelter)

It was another five years before Barnes finally crossed the Channel. An advertisement in the *Chronicle* had announced an excursion to France by 'The Poole, Isle of Purbeck, Isle of Wight, and Portsmouth Steam Packet Company's splendid Packet, "Water Witch", leaving from Poole on 20 June 1845.' At 6 p.m. on the Friday he sailed from Poole to Le Havre, arriving back the following Tuesday morning. Three clear days in France! It was the first – and only – time that this great linguist visited a foreign country. It might have been supposed that the trip would have been a memorable experience for him. Apparently not. Perhaps he suffered from sea-sickness, or disliked French food, or objected to the French Sunday. Whatever the reason, he rarely spoke of it again.[17]

Eighteen-forty-six was an anxious year. Rumour had it that the Tory Prime Minister, Sir Robert Peel, was contemplating the removal of the levy on agricultural imports. Iron masters and mill owners in manufacturing towns were clamouring for cheap bread for their employees and did not much care where it came from. In June the rumour proved true. Import duties on foreign cereals would be reduced from 1849, with an interim levy until then. The towns had triumphed. Farming, for centuries the basis of the British economy, was now demoted to a merely supportive status. In Dorset, many feared that this would bring disaster to every local business, including the schools. Barnes had reason to be concerned. With fewer parents able to afford his fees, his school might fail.

In May 1846 came news which promised to resolve the problem. The Revd Richard Cutler, master of Dorchester Grammar School, was to retire. Barnes decided to apply for the post. If he were appointed, he would be able to conduct the two schools in tandem, while slowly running down his own school, thereby solving any problem of reduced recruitment. He had a great deal of support. At least three local clergymen wrote on his behalf to the 'feoffees' (governors) of Hardye's, as did the editor of *The Gentleman's Magazine* and Colonel Dawson-Damer, who had recruited several other Dorset MPs to the cause. In addition, 104 prominent citizens of Dorchester wrote to the chairman, the Earl of Shaftesbury, 'to recommend Mr. William Barnes of this town to fill the vacancy', urging the success of his system of education, his eminence as a classical scholar, linguist and mathematician, and his ability to teach Oriental languages.

His supporters were quietly confident. Such an outstanding man could hardly be overlooked. True, the regulations stated that candidates should be members of either university, but was not Barnes 'of St John's College, Cambridge'? It said so in his books. As for the chairman's wish to maintain the tradition of appointing a man in holy orders, this was no problem. It was widely known that Barnes was seeking ordination. On 30 May the feoffees met. They chose the Revd Thomas Ratsey Maskew BA, Curate of Swyre, Classical Prizeman of Trinity College, Cambridge, and author of *Annotations of the Acts of the Apostles*.

Why was Barnes passed over? The arguments that he was not a graduate or yet a clergyman were probably mere pretexts for those who opposed him. It is more likely that suspicions had been raised when it became known that he was the author of certain dialect verses which had been regularly appearing in the *Chronicle*, a fact which seemed to confirm the whisper of his lowly origins. Moreover, these verses were actually written from the point of view of labouring men – people capable of rioting and rick-burning. Could the author of such pieces be considered politically trustworthy? Was Barnes 'sound'? Was he really 'one of us'? On the whole the feoffees thought not. So they played safe and chose a mediocrity.

Up until the Hardye's debacle, Barnes had been a coming man. This was his first major setback, a bruising one which was to have a knock-on effect for the rest of his life. His reputation never recovered. At first an object of pity, he then became one of slight suspicion. Even some of his erstwhile supporters for the headship began to doubt him. There was covert speculation; perhaps the feoffees had discovered something to his detriment that had led them to reject him.

In reaction, his thoughts turned to another profession, one he had been considering for years. A decade before, the Revd Cassan had encouraged him to apply for ordination in the Church of England and, since then, his religious impulse had, if anything, become stronger. Now, supported by the Revd Colson of St Peter's, he resolved to do so. On his intention becoming known, in January 1847, Colonel Dawson-Damer of Came House, the father of one of his pupils, offered him the 'living' of Whitcombe, about three miles from Dorchester. Traditionally included in the parish of Winterborne Came, Whitcombe was not a curacy, but a 'donative' worth £13 a year. The Rector of Came, the Revd George Arden, made no objection when the Bishop of Salisbury wanted to cede it to Barnes.

The business of taking orders involved a number of examinations. So, in February 1847, he took the train to Salisbury, where he found temporary lodgings in two 'prettily furnished and cheerful rooms' and prepared himself for the ordeal. He was required to write a sermon from a given text, and then to turn a long passage into Latin. This was followed by an interview with the bishop which he found 'encouraging'. On a later day, he had to summarise the arguments from Hooker's *Ecclesiastical Polity*. Such tasks should have been no problem for a scholar of his distinction, and it was probably simply because he was nervous that he found them 'rather severe' and 'stunning'. But he passed. Ordained at Salisbury on 28 February, he was now the Reverend William Barnes. Julia was unable to be there. She had had to stay behind to keep the school running. But she took the short train ride from Dorchester to Wool to meet him. His journey had been rather longer – from a poor cottage in Bagber nearly fifty years before.

Whitcombe was tiny. Just a little church, a barn and seven or eight thatched houses set in the fields a few yards back from the Wareham road. The antiquarian in Barnes would have rejoiced to discover that King Athelstan (*c.* 966) had awarded it as part of the endowment of Milton Abbey and it had been administered by one of the monks. After the Reformation, it passed to the impropriators of the abbey, the Tregonwells, and thence to the Damer family. In one of the bell openings of the handsome little tower is a stone marked 1596, while other parts of the building are twelfth century. There are two fourteenth- or fifteenth-century wall paintings, though he probably never saw them because they were painted over in his day. One served as a hidden emblem of his own life; it showed St Christopher carrying the burden of the infant Christ. No more suitable parish than Whitcombe could have been found for Barnes's first ministry. And so, for some years following, he trudged out there every Sunday and in all weathers to minister to the Damers and their work-folk.

John Thorne, the Blackmore artist, painted a portrait of Barnes at this time (see page 11). He is depicted as if about to give one of his famous nine o'clock lectures. A clean-shaven, balding man in his mid-forties, his face is intelligent, gentle and earnest; his manner reflective, as if he were thinking profoundly. One hand holds a book, the other is pointing something out; behind him are what appear to be scientific instruments. He is formally dressed, for the painting was partly intended as an advertisement, designed to impress prospective parents. It says: 'This is a man to whom you may safely entrust your boy'.

What the picture does not display is his sense of humour. His infectious laughter at a shared joke in the classroom still sounds now, after nearly 200 years. In early middle age he was a delightful and light-hearted companion, with a gift for friendship with a chosen few such as Fuller and Frederick Smith. The latter's two sons were placed at his school and the younger, Boyton, became a noted composer.

Music was the focus of the Barnes's social life, and the quartet of earlier years was revived at Norman's House. Frederick Smith was first violin; Barnes, second violin or flute; Thomas Patch, cello; and Mrs Bonifas, piano. They were even persuaded to give a public concert in the upstairs room of the Antelope Hotel. Such a thing had not been known in Dorchester before, and the musicians were anxious that they might not get through the advertised programme. On the evening, the large room was packed. Each item was greeted with rapturous applause and there were frequent encores. The *Chronicle* reported that, 'the members acquitted themselves in a manner far exceeding the most sanguine expectations'. [18]

But, after his rejection at Hardye's, Barnes became more emotionally vulnerable, more quick to take offence or see a slight, even when one may not have been intended. An incident that took place beneath the chestnuts of one of the Dorchester 'walks' was especially upsetting to him. Here he and Hann used to promenade on Sundays in their best clothes. It was a Dorchester custom, and they were expected to nod to parents and local notabilities. Among the strollers on one occasion was no less a person than the soon-to-be Emperor of the French, Napoleon III. He had been obliged to escape to England, and was staying with Damer. That morning, when passing them, whether by accident or mischievousness, the Emperor's cane slipped between Hann's legs and tripped him. Always 'peppery', the usher made as if to strike the Frenchman, and it was only with the greatest difficulty that Damer and Barnes parted them and smoothed things down. But, though the offence had been offered to Hann, it left an unpleasant taste in Barnes's mouth. It seemed to show a lack of respect for them both, somehow mocking their pretensions to gentility.

Barnes was well used to snubs. Parents and tradesmen were discourteous at times, and gentlefolk patronising. Though rarely bitter, this normally gentle and generous man confided his response to a commentary he kept on cant phrases then fashionable in Dorchester:

Whitcombe Church. (Dorset County Museum)

'Behaving with spirit':

Trampling on the poor and helpless, blustering with one's equals, and fawning with one's superiors, to get all possible good from them.

'Well married':

Said of a lady married to a man who has plenty of money in his pocket, but little wit in his head, and neither love nor grace in his heart.; and which lady spends part of her time in assumed cheerfulness, and the residue in dread, bickerings, vexation and tears…

'A clever man':

One who turns snuff boxes with a fancy lathe, recites scraps of plays and can buff the pianoforte.

'Common Report':

The lies of the day: originating from envy or hatred or love of excitement.[19]

But such sharp judgements he had to keep to himself. He had his livelihood to think of.

In the meantime there was a business decision to be made. He could still not be sure how the repeal of the Corn Laws would affect his school. Business uncertainty in the town had already reduced his boarders to seventeen. The question was, should he hang on at Norman's House, with the threat of Hardye's across the road renewing itself under Maskew? Or should he expand his own school so that it might become the unrivalled academy in the town? Up till now the Barneses had flourished wonderfully. By 1845 they probably had £1,000 in savings, a prodigious achievement for their joint industry. But what should they do with it? Hoard it against hard times, or invest it in a further enterprise? As always, Julia was his guide. Incensed at his rejection by the Hardye's feoffees, and always jealous for her husband's reputation, she urged him to be bold. So they looked for larger premises.

The following year, Frederick Smith discovered a suitable house for him. Barnes noted: '1847. This year I bought a Life-hold House, late Hawkins in South Street, Dorchester, for £700'.[20] It was on the west side of the street, almost opposite Napper's Mite. With ample room for his family and boarders, and a garden for recreation, it was ideal. They moved in that summer. He was now a property owner and the next edition of Kelly's *Post Office Directory to Dorchester* listed him among 'the gentry'.

It was not his only purchase. Some years before, he had made a loan to a farmer in Blackmore who, suspicious of the postal service, had paid him periodically in alternate letters, each containing one half of a £5 note. When the money had been repaid in full, Barnes decided that he wanted to retain a last contact with the area following the death of his father. So, he asked his old employers, Dashwoods, the solicitors in Sturminster, to act as his agents. On their advice, he took a trip to the Vale and subsequently bought two fields there: three acres comprising 'All that Freehold Meadow or pasture land called Creedman or Honey Burts' and 'All that piece of meadow land called Mogg's Mead' of just over an acre. Lying on either side of the Frome, these were the haunts of his childhood.

He bought them on a whim. Julia probably disapproved, because he had no particular plans other than to let them for grazing. But he had never forgotten that the Barneses had once owned – and lost – their property in the Vale. True, these were not the same fields but, at last, by hard work he had managed to regain land there. Just to own it. He was exultant:

## I Got Two Vields

I got two vields, an' I don't ceare
What squire mid have a bigger sheare.
My little zummer-leaze do stratch
All down the hangen, to a patch
O' mead between a hedge an' rank

Ov elems, an' a river bank.
Where yellow clotes, in spreaden beds
O' floaten leaves, do lift their heads
By benden bulrushes an' zedge
A-swayen at the water's edge,
Below the withy that do spread
Athirt the brook his grey-leav'd head.
An' eltrot flowers, milky white,
Do catch the slanten evenen light;
An' in the meaple boughs, along
The hedge, do ring the blackbird's zong;
Or in the day, a vlee-en drough
The leafy trees, the whoa'se gookoo
Do zing to mowers that do zet
Their zives on end, an stan' to whet.
From my wold house among the trees
A leane do goo along the leaze
O' yellow gravel, down between
Two mossy banks vor ever green.
An' trees, a hangen overhead,
Do hide a trinklen gully-bed,
A-cover'd by a bridge vor hoss
Or man a-voot to come across.
Zoo wi' my hwomestead, I don't ceare
What squire mid have a bigger sheare![21]

('clotes' – yellow water lillies; 'eltrot' – cow parsley; 'zives' – scythes)

It was not an ambitious capitalist or landowner that wrote this, nor a clergyman, scholar or professional man. It was a peasant.

# 11

# VOICES FROM HOME

—— 1838-1846 ——

William Barnes had a secret. Most of his time at Norman's House was inevitably taken up with his school and family, as well as his voluntary work as secretary to the museum. But he kept something back. After lessons, he would frequently retire to his study and spend some hours writing. Then he would slip round to the *Chronicle* office and push a paper through the letterbox. Preferably, this was after dark because he did not want to be seen.

He was writing dialect poems and they were promptly published in the *Chronicle*.[1] George Simonds, the editor, would have recognised the handwriting, but he told nobody. And although the authorship of the poems became a general talking point in Dorchester, no one else knew who had written them, not even Julia. And not until some years later did Barnes's children find out that he was the author.

For about five years, from December 1839, he wrote over 100 of these anonymous poems, at times supplying Simonds with a new poem every other week. Almost all were sub-headed, '(IN THE DORSET DIALECT)'. Soon, the verses became a regular fixture in the paper and were given extra prominence. Whereas the eclogues had never been headed 'original verse', nor printed in the 'Poetry Corner', the new generation of dialect poems were given the imprimatur of both. It was official. The writer was both original and a poet.

The first of these poems was called 'The Unioners' (later re-titled 'The Times'.) Structurally, it showed little advance upon his previous eclogues, being a series of rhymed couplets that filled almost an entire column of the paper. It was political. Two farm workers, Tom and John, were depicted debating the wisdom of throwing in their lot with the 'leaguers', i.e. radicals, such as the Chartists and trades unionists. Tom, the malcontent, complains that:

> Bread is so high an' wages be so low,
> That, after worken lik' a hoss, you know,
> A man can't earn enough to vill his belly.[2]

His solution to poverty is to support the Chartist demand for universal suffrage and annual elections. He believes that when the poor have power, they will remedy their own situation:

> Vor if a fellow midden be a squier,
> He mid be just so fit to vote, an' goo
> To meake the laws at Lon'on, too,
> As many that do hold their noses higher.
> Why shoulden fellows meake good laws an' speeches
> A-dressed in fust-in cwoats an cord'roy breeches?
> Or why should hooks an' shovels, zives an' axes,
> Keep any man vrom voten o' the taxes?
> An' when the poor've a-got a sheare
> In meaken laws, they'll teake good ceare
> To meake zome good ones vor the poor.

('fust-in' – fustian; 'zives' – scythes)

Responding, John recites a fable in which, by promising corn, the crow gets the pig to grub up the land for him. But when he does so, the pig is unable to pick up the seeds and the crow gets the lot. According to John, the 'leaguers' and trades union men were just like the crow. They would exploit farm workers for their own ends. Better, says John, to trust 'frien's near hwome', the squire and the parson. Better to keep quiet than to make things worse, 'i-ma-be, by a riot'.

'The Unioners' is an extraordinarily astute analysis of the question posed to farm workers all over England at that time. Should they submit to their lot, relying on the good intentions of their employers, or should they resist and organise a stronger bargaining position for themselves? The former course had already failed in many cases, as the Tolpuddle labourers had discovered. Nevertheless, the quietist, John, had the last word, so that the editor of the *Chronicle* could breezily conclude that 'we trust that the plain good sense of John may be usefully instructive to his fellow labourers'.

In later years, Barnes admitted that this was the only one of his poems that he regretted writing, for his opinions had changed. Yet he hardly needs to have recanted. On examination, Tom, the union man, has by far the better of the argument. He contemptuously dismisses such fables from 'childern's books' of 'silly pigs an' cunnen rooks', and questions whether the squire and parson really are their friends. Had the conservative, Simonds, considered the piece more closely, he might have been less eager to print it.

Dialect verses came to Barnes unbidden. When once he took up his pen, the tumult of his Dorchester day faded and voices from his old home in Bagber once again began to whisper in his ear. So, week by week, he wrote down the common talk of carters, shepherds, farmers' sons, milkmaids, smallholders, country fiddlers and Blackmore girls out chatting on summer evenings. He remembered 'Uncle and Aunt', 'Grammar' who loved to tell tales to the children, faithless Jeane of Grenley Mill, and the 'witch', Moll Brown. He recalled driving the common, consulting gypsies, playing ghosts and visiting Shrodon Fair. He told stories of ghosts, harvest homes, weddings, country fairs, tricks and jokes. He glimpsed again the yellowing of the corn, the appearance of an old wagon and the fall of the light on early morning fields. Almost every feature of the lives of the rural poor he artfully rendered into verse, to provide a unique record of that bygone time. That was why Thomas Hardy later described these poems as 'a complete repertory of forgotten manners, words and sentiments'.[3]

One poem recounts the felling of a tree. A 'romantic' poet at this time might have exploited the occasion to express his sense of identification with nature, ending with a poignant meditation on the brevity of human life. Not so Barnes. His poem stressed the communal nature of the event, using the life of the tree to document those of the people who have lived beneath its branches. His tone is matter-of-fact. One villager simply tells another all about it. And, in keeping with the folk tradition, the tree is not presented as a mere object, but a sentient being:

## Vellen o' the Tree

Aye, the girt elem tree out in little hwome-groun'
Wer a-stannen this mornen, an' now's a-cut down.
Aye, the girt elem tree, so big roun' an' so high,
Where the mowers did goo to their drink, an' did lie
In the sheade ov his head, when the zun at his heighth
Had a-drove em vrom mowen, wi' het an' wi' drith,
Where the hay-meakers put all their picks an' their reakes,
An' did sqot down to snabble their cheese an' their ceakes,
An' did vill from their flaggons their cups wi' their eale,
An' did meake theirzelves merry wi' joke an' wi' teale.

Ees, we took up a rwope an' we tied en all round,
At the top o'n, wi woone end a-hangen to ground,
An' we cut near the ground, his girt stem a'most drough,
An' we bent the wold head o'n wi' woone tug or two;

An' he sway'd all his limbs, an' he nodded his head,
Till he vell away down like a pillar o' lead;
An' as we did run vrom en, there, clwose at our backs,
Oh! his boughs come to groun' wi' sich whizzes an' cracks;
An' his top were so lofty that, now he is down,
The stem o'n do reach a'most over the groun.
Zoo the girt elem tree out in little hwome-groun',
Wer a-stannen this mornen, an' now's a cut down.[4]

('het' – heat; 'drith' – drout; 'snabble' – to snap up hastily or greedily; 'ees' – yes, 'o'n' – of him, i.e. of it)

By contrast, the village on a summer's evening is a picture of tranquillity:

## Evenen in the Village

Now the light o' the west is a-turned to gloom,
An the men be at hwome vrom ground;
An' the bells be a-zenden all down the Combe
From tower, their mwoansome sound.
An' the wind is still,
An' the house-dogs do bark,
An the rooks be a-vled to the elems high an' dark,
An' the water do roar at the mill.

An' the flickeren light drough the window-peane
Vrom the candle's dull fleame do shoot,
An' young Jemmy the smith is a-gone down leane,
A-playen his shrill-vaiced flute.
An' the miller's man
Do zit down at his ease
On the seat that is under the cluster o' trees,
Wi' his pipe an' his cider can.[5]

Until now, Barnes had restricted himself to rhymed couplets which were both repetitive and limiting in their effects. But, as the poem above reveals, he was beginning to experiment with new stanza forms. His extensive reading of ancient Greek, Roman, Persian and Welsh poets, as well as Petrarch and the moderns, was now called in to give greater variation and subtlety to his verses, and to determine just how far the despised rustic language could be stretched for artistic purposes. From his exemplars he learned how to push his poems into new forms, with variations of rhyme endings, internal rhymes and stanza shape. The result was a bold and unique combination of material and form. 'Primarily spontaneous, he was academic closely after', according to Thomas Hardy.[6]
   Just how technically innovative he had become, is revealed by:

## The Welsh Nut Tree

When in the evemen the zun's a-zinken,
   A drawen shiades vrom the yoller west;
An' mother weary's a-zot a-thinken,
Wi' vuolded yarms by the vire rest,
Then we da zwarm, O,
Wi' sich a charm, O,
So vull o' glee by the welshnut tree.

A-leaven father indoors, a-leanen
   In his girt chair, in his easy shoes,
Ar in the settle so high behine en,
While down bezide en the dog da snooze,
Our tongues da run, O,
Enough to stun, O,
Your head, wi glee by the welshnut tree…[7]

('welshnut' – walnut; 'yoller' – yellow, 'ar' – or; 'settle' – a high-backed wooden seat)

Original of 'The Welshnut Tree', *Dorset County Chronicle*, 8 December 1842. (Dorset History Centre)

What did Barnes's first readers – the Dorchester shopman, the farmer's daughter, the landed proprietor, and the parson in his rural rectory, pouring over the columns with a reading glass – what
did they make of these poetic oddities turning up in their local paper? Initially, they thought they
were jokes. For, though the editor of the *Chronicle* had considered 'The Unioners' to be 'usefully
instructive' to labourers, he could not help adding that that he was sure that 'the dialogue [would] be
amusing to our readers'.

Amusing. Of course. Imitations of the local dialect were good for a laugh among the gentlemen
taking their port in the King's Arms. Some of them were quite good at it. The Revd Frederick
Urquhart, the Rector of Broadmayne, was for a time one of those suspected of being the author of
these verses. The rumour was not diminished by his anonymous letter to the paper with a mock-
serious correction:

> Sir- The Dialogue headed 'Rusticus Dolens' in your paper of the 2nd instant is inimitable and doubt-
> less caused great merriment to those who really understand the Dorset dialect. Now, Sir, from 27 years
> constant residence in a country village of your county, I consider myself a tolerable good judge of the
> lingo. I would therefore in kindness point out two errors, which might be avoided in any future effusion
> the writer may favor us with. In the first line 'morn' should be written 'murn', and the word 'vor', which
> occurs very often, should be written 'var'. These alterations may appear trifling; but Sir, I am a stickler for
> the purity of our native dialect, which must plead the apology of
>
> Your obedient Servant, CRITIC[8]

The joke, readers perfectly well understood, lay in the preposterous notion that the uncouth gabble
that comprised this 'lingo' could have any kind of 'purity' or correctness at all.

Had he been the despairing sort, Barnes might well have been cast down by such incomprehension. Admittedly, some of his poems were intended to be good-humoured and even comic, but
that comedy was always to be derived from the context and not because the dialect itself was to be
regarded as intrinsically absurd. Then again, in assuming that dialect verse was always ridiculous and
therefore comic, Urquhart and his like had failed to notice the range of emotion and experience
displayed by the poems. Such as pathos:

> Poor Jenny wer her Robert's bride
> Two happy years, an' then he died;
> An' zoo the wold vo'k meade her come,
> Vorseaken, to her maiden hwome.
> But Jenny's merry tongue were dum';
> An' round her comely neck she wore
> A murnen kerchief, where avore
> The rwose did deck her breast.
>
> (From 'The Rwose That Deck'd her Breast')[9]

> When wintry weather's all a-done,
> An' brooks do sparkle in the zun,
> An' naisy-builden rooks do vlee
> Wi' sticks toward their elem tree;
> When birds do zing, an' we can zee
> Upon the boughs the buds o' spring, –
> Then I'm as happy as a king,
> A-vield wi' health an' zunsheen.
>
> (From 'The Spring')[10]

And mature reflection:

> Why thik wold post so long kept out,
> Upon the knap, his earms astrout,
> A-zenden on the weary veet
> By where the dree cross roads do meet;
> An' I've a-come so much thik woy,
> Wi' happy heart, a man or bwoy,
> That I'd a meade, at last, a'most
> A friend o' thik wold guiden post.
>
> (From 'The Guide Post')[11]
>
> ('wold vo'k' – old folk, i.e. her parents; 'murnen' – mourning; 'athirt' – across; 'a-froze' – frozen; 'knap' – a small hillock; 'astrout' – stretched out stiffly; 'dree' – three; 'woy' – way)

As time went on, the attitude of *Chronicle* readers changed. At first objects of patronising derision, by their sheer ingenuity the verses eventually compelled a wry admiration, and then a sneaking local pride. Odd though they were, they were Dorset's own oddities. What other county had produced such things? But the dialect was still an obstacle to their acceptance as true poetry. Few readers would have read Barnes's article in *The Gentleman's Magazine* in which he had attempted to prove the dialect's authenticity. Nor would they have approved of his conclusions had they done so. Had they suspected that he had written 'What Dick and I Done', for example, they might well have decided that he was not the man to teach their sons grammar.[12]

As for the authorship of the poems, the rumour mill went grinding on and the names of various possible authors were canvassed round the town. Beside Urquhart, candidates included: the Revd Lord Sidney Godolphin Osborne, who had written a number of letters to *The Times* in which he deplored the plight of farm labourers and their families, and an unnamed 'Archdeacon of the Established Church'. That these candidates were all clergymen was perhaps because they were among the few educated men who came into regular contact with the labourers and their families. So the gossips were partly right.

Then, early in 1844, the secret was out. The identity of the author was at last revealed with the appearance of a book that collected 128 poems from the columns of the *Chronicle*. The title page announced: '*Poems of Rural Life, in the Dorset Dialect: with a Dissertation and Glossary.* By William Barnes'. Nothing quite like it had ever appeared before. It was, and remains, the most original and probably the most accomplished book of dialect poetry ever written by an English author.[13]

Arranged in a seasonal scheme – spring, summer, autumn and winter – the structure of the book was perhaps influenced by John Clare's *Shepherd's Calendar*. The scheme ensured that a full record was presented of the rural year. Here are poems featuring 'lady day', 'club-walking' at Whitsun, hay-making, thatching, mowing, harvest time, Guy Fawkes Night and Christmas revels. Not all the poems fitted easily into the seasonal frame and Barnes was obliged to include a fifth section entitled (in the first edition) 'Miscellaneous Pieces'.

Because of his extensive first-hand knowledge of rural life, his depictions are meticulous in their accuracy, as in that about the technically complex business of haymaking:

## Hay-Carren

> 'Tis merry ov a zummer's day,
> When vo'k be out a haulen hay,
> Where boughs, a-spread upon the ground,
> Do meake the staddle big and round;
> An' grass do stand in pook, or lie

In long-backed weales or parsels dry.
There I do vind it stir my heart
To hear the frothen hosses snort,
A-haulen on, wi sleek-heair'd hides,
The red-wheeled waggon's deep-blue zides.
Ay; let me have woone cup o' drink,
An' hear the linky harness clink,
An' then my blood do run so warm,
An' put sich strangth 'ihin my earm,
That I do long to toss a pick,
A-pitchen or a-meaken rick.

The bwoy is at the hosses head,
An' up upon the wagon bed
The lwoaders, strong o' earm do stan',
At head, an back at tail, a man,
Wi' skill to build the lwoad upright
An' bind the vwolded corners tight;
An' at each zide o'm, sprack an strong,
A pitcher wi' his long-stemmed prong,
Avore the best two women now
A called to reaky after plough...[14]

('staddle' – a wooden frame-work, or a bed of boughs, upon which a rick is made so as not to touch the ground; 'pooks' – cones or ridges of drying grass; 'weales' – ridges of grass smaller than 'pooks'; 'sprack' – lively, springy, active; 'to reaky' – to rake up)

Haymaking in Dorset in the nineteenth century. (Dorset County Museum)

This account is not offered to an outsider. The speaker is one of the work-folk talking to a friend, who will not only understand the technicalities of the job but will share in the sheer pleasure it affords. In the 'Dissertation' to his book, Barnes explained his motives:

> [The author] has not written for readers who have had their lots cast in town-occupations of a highly civilized community, and cannot sympathize with the rustic mind, [for] he can hardly hope that they will understand either his poems or his intention…
>
> [But]… If his verses should engage the happy mind of the dairymaid with her cow, promote the innocent evening cheerfulness of the family circle on the stone floor, or teach his rustic brethren to draw pure delight from the rich but frequently overlooked sources of nature within their own sphere of being, his fondest hopes will be realised.[15]

In other words, his poems were not simply about farm workers, they were addressed to them.

How far this was a realistic aim is a matter for speculation. Many Dorset farm workers were literate, but access to the poems was difficult. At this time, they earned only about 7s a week, and the *Chronicle* cost 7d. If they saw the poems at all, it would only have been in handed-down copies. But the book itself cost 10s, which would have put it beyond the pocket of almost all the people Barnes said he was writing for.[16] Some may have borrowed it.[17]

With parental pride, the *Chronicle* gave the book two long reviews, one on 16 May 1844, and – no doubt to push further sales – another on 16 October. It declared:

> This is real poetry… a description so full of truth and feeling that each resident in the county will at once fancy it the picture of his own home, every line conveying to his own mind what he sees, hears and feels in his evening walk through the village at this time of year.

In keeping with the paper's politics, the anonymous reviewer regarded the poems chiefly as exhortations to respectability and contentment. They are free of any coarse vulgarity and urge the village labourer, in the words of Bishop Hacket, to 'Fear God and be cheerful'. Barnes, it declared, had successfully employed language to produce, 'a series of portraits of which (though we never saw the individuals) we seem to know the originals'. Their effect would be to persuade the peasant reader to obedience and to count his blessings, 'perhaps… hardly conscious how many advantages he possessed: he was not alive to the real dignity of his simple position'.

For once the *Chronicle's* radical rival, the *Sherborne and Yeovil Mercury*, agreed with it, and in so doing made the first of many comparisons of Barnes with the great poet over the border:

> Since the days of Burns we believe that no provincial dialect has been honoured by becoming the vehicle of true poetry, in any degree approaching this, and we have every reason to hope that Mr Barnes's simple lays will embalm the good old-fashioned language of Dorsetshire, and secure it a memorial as long as the Doric and Scotch shall be unforgotten.

Unlike the *Chronicle*, however, the *Mercury* believed the poems were especially valuable in keeping alive 'the interest in the affairs of the poor', and giving farmers and landlords 'a more intimate acquaintance with their feelings and habits and a more sincere sympathy with their wants'.[18]

Few of the national literary journals noticed the book. The sole comment in the *Literary Gazette* was that it must have been written by someone of extensive scholarship, an observation suggesting that, having failed to make much of the poems, their reviewer had merely flipped through the 'Dissertation' and 'Glossary'. But Barnes's friends, the Nicholses, editors of *The Gentleman's Magazine*, did not let him down. They treated the publication as a major literary event and made every effort to promote it. The issue for December 1844 contained a fourteen-page notice, and reprinted fifteen of the poems in full. Moreover, the unsigned article (probably by Gough Nichols) was given especial prominence at the front of the journal. The reviewer admitted in all honesty that the poet had been a contributor to the magazine for many years, but that he did not know him personally.

This extremely perceptive review was the first to perceive Barnes's most significant claim to be considered a major poet, that his work was original in both thought and language:

> Poets like all other persons, must have their thoughts strongly affected and acted on by the sympathies of their own times, and by the minds of their contemporaries… But we are bound in fairness to say that in Mr Barnes's poems we can trace no footsteps of the submissive or sequacious follower of any poetic school or model, but that of true nature and passions. The poet's heart is at home – his scenery is all domestic – his circle of description of home growth, confined to his own fields and boundaries, and the little village scenes, the household cares, and employments, the innocent pleasures, the gentle sorrows and joys, the rural pastimes, the business and amusements – he places before us, and throws into dramatic form, and invests with personal interest, are all drawn from the characters familiar to him.[19]

The *Magazine's* reviewer was right in his conclusion concerning the absence of poetic influences. No doubt, as a young man exploring the Revd Henry Richman's library, Barnes had read the pastoral verse of Shakespeare, Pope and Oliver Goldsmith. More importantly, he would also have come across George Crabbe's 'The Village' and later Robert Bloomfield's 'The Farmer's Boy'. But though Crabbe, like Barnes, had witnessed the grinding poverty of the rural poor and seen landlords drive out their tenants, his verse retained the 'smooth alternate' rhymed couplets and poetic diction that constituted the stock in trade of poets in his time.[20] Bloomfield's poem had been enormously successful and justly celebrated for its vivid descriptions of rural life, but he too preferred rhymed couplets and a diction far removed from rural dialects.[21] As for William Wordsworth, who had declared in his *Lyrical Ballads* the intention to write in 'the real language of men', he did no such thing.[22] In later life, Barnes may have come across *The Shepherd's Calendar* by his near-contemporary John Clare, who certainly employed many dialect terms, but not the cadence and syntax of the rural idiom.[23] All these poets were primarily descriptive but, because Barnes was concerned to present people talking to each other in their own language, his work is dramatic. In so doing, he had no poetic progenitors at all. He was, said Gerard Manley Hopkins, 'straight from nature and quite fresh'.[24]

Despite the *Magazine's* support, sales were slow. In May, John Russell Smith, Barnes's London publisher, wrote to say that he had sold very few copies. He advised that a little money might be spent on advertising. But at this time, what money Barnes had was mostly tied up in his school. He needed a patron and, as luck should have it, he found one. In April 1844, he was invited to join a house party at Frampton Court, near Dorchester, the home of Richard Brinsley Sheridan MP, a grandson of the dramatist. This was at the request of Sheridan's sister, the Hon. Mrs Caroline Norton.[25] She was curious about him. For some years the family had noticed the queer little rhymes that had appeared in the *Chronicle* – Mrs Norton fancied herself as a mimic and no doubt would have entertained the family with her readings of them – and now that the identity of the author was known, they wished to inspect him. Barnes politely declined. He was, he wrote, 'unaccustomed to society'.

Which was true. He was not used to the sort of company gathered at Frampton Court. Among the guests were: the 'Bishop of the Diocese, Bishop Dennison; Philip Pusey, editor of the *Royal Agricultural Journal*, Dr. Buckland, afterwards Dean of Westminster, Fonblanque the editor of the *Examiner*, Archdeacon Huxtable, two Sheridan sisters, Mrs Norton and Lady Dufferin, and other members of the family'. Disappointed, Sheridan wrote again, to say that his sisters and others in the house admired Barnes's poetry and were anxious to make his acquaintance, and that he and his wife would feel greatly honoured by his acceptance of their invitation. Greatly honoured! Barnes was overwhelmed and a little intimidated. Apart from General Shrapnel, he had never had anything to do with grand people. He probably worried that he did not have the right clothes to wear, especially at dinner. It also seems that Julia was not included in the invitation, which was awkward, especially as he relied upon her advice in social situations. Nevertheless, he went.

The Sheridans probably expected to be confronted with a rubicund farmer or a foxhunting cleric. In the event, Caroline Norton was confronted with a balding, rather shabby, unprepossessing, middle-aged schoolmaster, but one who, on acquaintance, turned out to be a gentle, modest, sweet-natured man. Always a radical family, the Sheridans were artistic and a little bohemian, in the spirit of their famous grandfather, and, up to a point, prepared to overlook social differences. But though he was initially rather shy, it transpired that Barnes could talk about almost any subject, because he had a fund of information on all sorts of things. Dr Buckland, especially, was very impressed with his knowledge of geology. As for languages, they discovered that he wrote and/or spoke almost every foreign language they could name, and many they had never heard of. He was more than quietly impressive, he was intriguing. Charmed, the Sheridans urged him not to leave before the whole party broke up.

Following that visit, the Sheridans became his lifelong admirers and supporters. His special friend, however, was Caroline Norton, herself a poet, and author of such popular pieces as 'The Arab's Farewell to his Steed', and 'Not Lost but Gone Before'. Years before, her unorthodox behaviour had nearly destroyed a government. In 1836, her husband, George Norton, a Tory MP, had brought a legal action against the Whig Prime Minister, Lord Melbourne, for 'criminal conversation' (i.e. adultery) with Caroline. Norton lost, Melbourne got off, and his government survived. But Caroline's reputation was almost fatally damaged. For many years she had been regarded by society as a scandalous woman. Since that time, she had been estranged from Norton and had supported herself by writing melodramatic poems. She had also engaged in what seemed an interminable struggle to retain her earnings and win custody of her three sons. This house party at Frampton was one of the many efforts of her intensely loyal family to help her regain her reputation. And at last they were having some success. Only recently, and probably due to Melbourne's string-pulling, she had been admitted once more to the Royal drawing room.

Of all this, Barnes was probably unaware. Or if he knew anything about Caroline's shady reputation he chose to ignore it. To him, she was a great lady, a kind friend, a supporter of his poetry and a source of advice. For her part, she was amused, flattered and rather touched by his naïve regard. She was a notorious flirt who could not resist charming any man she met, though not all succumbed. Tennyson, for example, who was once sat next to her at a dinner table, considered her 'dangerous, terrible, beautiful'. Barnes, however, never spotted the danger and he too was smitten. When safely back in South Street, he wrote her a sonnet:

Frampton Court, Dorset, the home of the Sheridans where Barnes first met Caroline Norton. (Dorset County Museum)

## To the Hon. Mrs Norton

When first I drew with melting heart alone,
(O gifted vot'ry of the tuneful Nine)
Entrancing melody from songs of thine
Sweet echo'd words of one as yet unknown;
How much I wondered what might be the tone
Of her true voice, as yet unanswering mine,
And what the hue with which her eyes might shine,
And what the form in which her soul was shown
To sons of men. How busy fancy brought
Before me lineaments of love and grace.
But who can tell what joy was mine at last,
When I beheld the object of my thought
In bright reality before my face,
And found the fairest of my dreams surpassed![26]

Once again Caroline had conquered. She replied sedately, saying that she would place the poem in a book of autographs she was collecting for her little boys. History does not record the comments of Mrs Barnes.

The friendship continued. In June of that year Barnes went up to London for a few days, partly to call upon his publisher but also to accept an invitation from Mrs Norton to spend the weekend at her house, 24 Bolton Street, Mayfair, or the 'Palazzo Boltoni' as she persisted in calling it. He arrived on Saturday, the 22nd, and knowing that he was interested in science, she took him at once to meet the physicist Professor Charles Wheatstone, of King's College, who demonstrated to them the workings of his galvanic telegraph between London and Slough. Barnes found it all very interesting, declaring that this would give him new material for his weekly science lectures in school.

They later took dinner with a group of Caroline's friends especially chosen for their social tact. It was all very exciting. Barnes wrote to tell Julia that he had taken in 'Lady –, and dined with Lord – son of the Earl of –' (he considered that to put the full names of these people in a letter to his wife breached the code of hospitality). Lord – had told him that his book 'was making quite a sensation in the west end of the town'. Then to the opera, though Barnes was restive during the last act. He later admitted to Caroline that he had been shocked that they had stayed out into the early hours of the Sabbath.

The Sheridan influence helped sales. Copies of Barnes's book were stored in Dorchester by Simonds and twice that year, Russell Smith sent for another fifty copies. And long after this, the Sheridans continued to promote his work. Barnes never forgot their help. Thirty-five years after his visit, he inscribed a copy of a new edition of his poems:

TO MR AND MRS BRINSLEY SHERIDAN, WITH A HAPPY MEMORY OF THEIR INVITATION TO FRAMPTON COURT, IN APRIL 1844, TO MEET MRS NORTON:-

Sweeter to me
Your early praise
Than now could be
A crown of bays

W. BARNES

But Caroline Norton's support came with disadvantages. Buoyed up by the sales of her own work and supremely confident that she knew the ways of the world, she nagged Barnes to 'cocknify' his poems to make them more accessible to the general reader. By this she probably meant that he should put them into standard English rather than the speech of Sam Weller. He submitted by continually re-editing his poems. As a result, in 1846, John Russell Smith brought out Barnes's next book, *Poems Partly of*

*Rural Life (In National English)*.[27] It was not successful. Whereas his dialect poems went through eleven English editions before 1905, his book in 'national English' was reprinted only once. Mrs Norton was wrong. She had mistakenly identified his true strength as his weakness.

In 1846, however, the Dorset dialect was considered by many to be no more than an embarrassing relic. The coming of the railways had brought London ways and expressions to the county and many socially aspiring people were learning to despise the local speech. One such was Mrs Jemima Hardy. Four years before the publication of *Poems of Rural Life in the Dorset Dialect*, she had given birth to a boy in the cottage she shared with her husband, a builder, in the hamlet of Higher Bockhampton, near Dorchester. But though both Jemima and her husband spoke with broad accents, her son Thomas, later remembered that the dialect 'was not spoken in his mother's house, but only when necessary to the cottagers, and by his father to the workmen'.[28] People going up in the world wanted nothing to do with Barnes's old homely talk.

# 12

# WILDERNESS

—— 1847-1850 ——

Two golden beasts stand pawing each other over the ancient gateway of St John's College, Cambridge. They are yales; heraldic creatures with the tails of elephants, the bodies of deer and the heads of goats with reversible horns. Walking beneath that archway for the first time on the evening of 26 May 1847, William Barnes understood at once the provenance of these creatures. For, as an antiquarian, he would have known that they derived from the coat of arms of the founder of the college, Lady Margaret Beaufort. Above the yales stands a figure which was even more familiar to this newly ordained Anglican priest.[1] It is the apostle after whom the college was named. With an equivocal smile, St John stands in blue and pink, with a golden eagle at his feet. His left hand, enwreathed by a snake, holds a poisoned chalice. Legend has it that he had extracted the venom from the serpent and then drank it safely.

Barnes had come a long way. The Southampton & Dorchester Railway Company had not yet opened the line to the county town, and his journey that May would have necessitated a drive to Moreton or Wool in order to catch the London train.[2] Fortunately, the North & Eastern Railway had recently completed the link between London and Cambridge so that the second leg of his journey was easier. Even when he arrived in Cambridge, however, with his heavy portmanteau, he discovered that the newly opened station was situated in the fields beyond the town. None of the waiting cabs were for him. He was a poor student and had to economise. So he was obliged that evening to take the long walk through the 'ugly and dirty' little thoroughfares, before passing up Trumpington Street and beneath the astounding archway of St John's.

Yet nothing could detract from this moment. He had worked for years in provincial obscurity to get here. And now, at last, he was entering one of the intellectual centres of the nation, a place heaped with the learning of the ages where scholarship and intellect were revered. That evening, he walked through the older college courts, then down towards the Cam to inspect the Bridge of Sighs, and finally to the Backs, from whence he might turn to take in the vista of New Court, glowing honey coloured in the evening light. It was all delightful.

Among its other functions, the university served as a seminary for Anglican priests, even though it offered no first degree in divinity. The degree of BD, for which Barnes was registered, was a post-graduate qualification, intended in the Elizabethan statutes for those who were already MAs. Originally, the statutes assumed that candidates would be in residence and would fulfil a rigorous programme, attending lectures and completing various tests. There was, however, an alternative route. A medieval ruling had allowed monks and friars over the age of twenty-four to proceed to the degree, provided that they devoted themselves to study and undertook certain oral examinations. True, this regulation had also assumed residence, but by the seventeenth century this requirement had fallen into disuse. Permanent residency was excused, provided the candidate kept certain terms in college.[3] Barnes was just such a candidate and not unusual at St John's. This college in particular accepted many ten-year men, mainly older Anglican priests who desired a degree. One old collegian recollected that the typical ten-year man was usually 'a worthy but uninteresting person'. By 1850 there were forty-eight such worthy persons on the books at the college, by far the highest in the university. It appears that their fees were often waived.

There is no record that Barnes was required to undertake any course of 'distance learning' before going up to Cambridge. He submitted no essays and worked through no reading list. Nor were there any written examinations for him to pass when he got there. What he had to do was to spend three

Gateway to St John's College, Cambridge, which Barnes attended from 1847-1850. (Private collection)

terms in college; to preach two sermons, one each in Latin and English; to undertake two 'opponencies', i.e. public theological debates, in Latin and another one in English; and to satisfy his tutors in certain interviews. What constituted 'terms' was probably a matter of agreement. These were not necessarily concurrent with those of the undergraduates. This meant that Barnes was able to contrive that, as far as possible, he went up to Cambridge when his own pupils in Dorchester were on holiday. There was a drawback to this system, however, for in college vacation times it was difficult to get examiners to make themselves available to witness his sermons and debates. One sorry tale told how a candidate had delivered his Latin sermon, only to subsequently discover that his professor had not been in church to hear it. Even when these tests could be arranged, they were formidable.

After twenty years of marriage, Barnes still doted on his wife and, to such an uxorious man, this first extended separation came hard. It was hard for Julia as well, but perhaps for a different reason. Whereas for him the parting was a matter of sentiment, for her it meant a much increased workload. While at St John's, he often did not have enough to do; she, by contrast, was almost overwhelmed with responsibilities. To make up for their parting, they corresponded almost daily. Fortunately they could now afford it. When they were courting all those years before, a letter sent by post from Mere to Dorchester was prohibitively expensive. But now, thanks to Sir Rowland Hill, a letter of less than half an ounce went for the cost of a mere penny stamp. Added to this, Julia had informed him that the railway to Dorchester would open a few days after his leaving home. Evidently the new technologies were conspiring in their favour. He wrote to her on 1 June:

My Dearest Julia,

You have been so naughty as not to write to me yesterday and I am fearful that you will be so gay today as to forget me. Well, I am glad the railway is opened as it makes me two or three hours nearer to you. I have been, tell the children, to the Botanic Gardens, which contains some rare shrubs and other plants though it is as plain as a kitchen garden. I have seen also the geological Museum containing a rare collection of paintings and the University Library containing, I should think, 30 or 40 thousand volumes.

Give my love to all the children and your mother. We have a choral service at our Chapel again tomor-
row evening. You would enjoy it so much. I shall think of you there at 6 o'clock. I am very glad your
mother likes our new house so much.

I am, My Dear Julia,
Your affectionate husband,
Wm Barnes.[4]

Next day he wrote again with good news. He had already composed his English sermon which was
to be given at the University Church of St Mary's, 'before the Vice-Chancellor, Regius Professor of
Divinity and the great men of the University who sit weighing every word of it'. He also hoped to
get his Latin sermon written. It was even possible that it might be heard that term. An invitation to
take his dessert with his tutor seemed to auger well for his prospects.

Meanwhile, the college was 'thin' because 'nearly all the men had gone home'. Had he realised it,
this was no misfortune. It is difficult to imagine the pious and desperately earnest William Barnes
living easily alongside the drinking, hunting and fishing crowd that comprised the less reputable
section of St John's. Nevertheless it was a rather lonely life, with few people around to talk to. He
walked about the town, watched haymaking in the college grounds, worked at his Latin sermon,
attended services in the chapel and invited a fellow student and his wife to tea. He picked up a
friendship with another priest, Mr Pickard, who had sponsored his ordination and was the uncle of
his pupil, Octavius Pickard Cambridge. They visited each other's rooms and Barnes agreed to read
services for him at the hospital, and also to conduct one or two services at St Edward's. Nevertheless,
he was lonely and homesick. He confessed to Julia that he would be glad when his term was all over:
'But still, I confess, I am very happy'.

These desultory days were soon to end. The first sign of this was an immense tent being put up
in the college grounds. The cost of its hire and erection was, Barnes reported excitedly, more than
£100. Quite by coincidence, he had arrived at a time when the university was about to witness one
of the greatest events to take place there in the century. Prince Albert, the Prince Consort, was to be
inducted as Chancellor of the university, and the Queen herself would be coming. By 28 June the
Cambridge inns were asking a guinea a night during the installation, while tickets for the celebra-
tory fête were the same price.

Barnes was present that afternoon when Victoria arrived in the Great Court of Trinity. He told Julia:

It is a mercy that you have a husband with sound limbs as we have had such a squeeze in Trinity College
as you can hardly conceive. Members of the University, up to many hundreds, possibly nearly two thousand, assembled in the outer square to receive the Queen, who arrived soon after one o'clock, and on its
being announced that we were to go into the Hall to present our addresses to her, a great rush was made
to get in. I went in with an impetuous wave that carried all before it; and in which Doctors with their red
robes were pushed into scarecrows, and Masters had their hoods torn off and your worthy admirer got his
silver chain broken. We wore bands and pretty things they were made in the scuffle.

I got up to the head of the hall near the Queen before she withdrew. Our noble old college has appeared
in its glory today. We have had two Halls [dinners], one for the pensioners and sizars at four o'clock, and a
Fellow's Hall at six, when I sat down to a superb dinner with about 200 sons of our Alma Mater; most of
these men come up from the provinces for the Installation…

Uneasily aware that he must avoid unnecessary expenditure, he did not go to the fête, nor did he
attend the special concert featuring Jenny Lind, the 'Swedish Nightingale', then at the height of her
fame. However, he did manage to fight his way through the 20,000 crowd into the Senate House,
and saw the Queen while she listened to the Installation Ode, read by proxy, but partly written
by another St John's man, William Wordsworth. Later, he walked through the grounds of Downing
College 'within three or four' steps of the Queen herself. This exciting event reinforced his optimism.

Things seemed to be going so well now. He had even preached his 'clerum', i.e. Latin sermon. The only shadow over things was his constant worry about how things were going in Dorchester.

For Julia had been left to manage the school on her own during the last weeks of the summer term. She was not without practical help; in all domestic matters – the running of the house, the catering for family and boarders, the laundry, the provision of clothes and linen, and the shopping – she was supported by her daughter, Laura, now aged nineteen, and old Mrs Miles, now seventy-five. Meanwhile, the teaching was done by the experienced usher Isaac Hann, together with a young assistant named Morgan. But the ultimate responsibility was Julia's. This was not only the care of her six children and the twenty or so boarders, but the overall running of the school, together with the seemingly endless queries from parents. And, if this were not enough, in the summer of 1847 it was she who had to prepare for the removal from Norman's House to their new school.

To all this she brought the determination and strength of character which had proved so successful in their joint endeavours for many years. However, her bodily strength was not as great. There were constant worries over her health. So when Barnes first went up to St John's, his emotions were vacillating between the sheer joy of getting there at last and the concern, even guilt, that had deserted his post as schoolmaster and left his darling wife to bear a load too great for her. He wrote to tell her that he would be relieved when the school term had ended, because its continuance had caused him 'uneasiness', and added uncertainly, 'I trust it will all be for the best'.

He was just not used to being without her. When he heard that Dorchester Station had at last been opened, he told her that his chief comfort was that it 'brings me 2 or 3 hours nearer to you'. She was the more prosaic of the two, and had far too much to do to indulge in such sentimentality. But Barnes, while mooching about St John's courts, constantly yearned for her. So torn were his emotions that he could not decide whether he preferred her to remain happy while he was away, or to be miserable without him. College chapel was a comfort. He could go there and think about her. In the week ending 4 June 1847, he attended chapel ten times more than was required, and in the following week, eight times more.[5] There was one particular time each week when he wanted them to think of each other. It was six o'clock on Sunday evenings, when he was going into the college chapel and she was leading the children into St Peter's for evensong.

There were also more practical considerations for them to consider. In successive letters, Barnes issued a stream of instructions concerning the school and the move to its new premises. He himself had designed a classroom to be built at the rear of Hawkins's, and he ordered the builder, Mr Lucas, to go over the property with the drawings in his hand. And, yes, Mr Hann was to take young Besant's health into consideration, and yes, Master Clark was to have new clothes, even though his father has not yet paid his bill. In reply, Julia tried to ease his anxieties. Mr Lucas foresaw no difficulties in building the new schoolroom just as he had designed it, and old Mrs Miles had declared the new house a 'perfect palace'. Meanwhile, she reported, the school went on nicely, the pupils were good boys who had spent their half-holidays playing cricket, and Mr Hann said that he was not to worry about things. Reassured, Barnes replied, 'In all things but the thoughts of my charge and you at home I am as happy as the day is long'. As the boys were good, he authorised Hann to excuse them lessons twice a week, and 'give them full half-holidays'. But though he meant well by the gesture, such lordly generosity from afar was eventually to store up troubles for him.

Yet despite Julia's cheerful assurances as business manager, she was beginning to become concerned about their financial situation. Setting up a new school necessitated greater economy, even in small things. Accordingly, though unsure of the propriety of a lady making bids in public, she went on her own to the auction of Hawkins's effects in order to bid for the window curtains, which would save buying new ones. She also hoped her presence might prevent damage to the walls. Barnes's approach was rather less practical. He pondered the advantage of ordering inexpensive paint from a London wholesaler. And after the Installation ceremony at St John's, he even considered bidding for the very carpet trodden by the Queen herself, 'that is, if they are selling it off cheaply'.[6] In the event, he did not.

That they should have had money worries at the time of their greatest prosperity was caused by their sudden change of circumstances. Hawkins's, or 40 South Street, had come upon the market suddenly, and they had felt they must snap it up quickly. This accounted for £700 of their savings, while

Barnes had already laid out £360 more in the quixotic purchase of the two fields in Blackmore. In the process, he seems to have forgotten his easily made promise of a loan to an old friend which had now become due. This was 'assistance to the extent of £600' to William Carey, once his fellow clerk at Coombs, to help him with the purchase of a house. Carey now wrote to say that he had long been expecting the money and was disappointed that he had not already received it. Barnes admitted to Julia that he hardly knew what to reply. The upshot was that at the end of June he sent Carey £200, which he could ill-afford. Carey died two years later and it is not known whether Barnes ever recouped the money. Some time after that, he was also obliged to call in part of a loan he had already made to his brother-in-law, Samuel Thatcher, which vexed Julia because it brought tension with her family.

It was all getting too much for her. At the end of the school term, Laura wrote to say that her mother was 'so tired and poorly with a bad cold that she [was] not able to write'. Barnes could only advise Julia to 'walk out constantly, so as to get rid of your face-ache, which I think arises from the delicate state of your nerves from too much confinement'.[7]

On 9 July, he at last went home after seven weeks of absence. Julia met him at Poole Station and they took the train home to Dorchester for the first time. They comforted themselves that the omens were still good. She seemed to have completely recovered her strength and the children were all well. His report was also optimistic. He had just completed one of the three prescribed terms, and he had already preached both his English and Latin sermons. His tutor was pleased with him. So in the following year he might hope to complete his degree and style himself 'BD'. In the meantime, he threw himself at once into the preparations for the new school term, which was to start on the 29th. The removal of his school across the road was now planned for October.

January 1848 found him back at Cambridge. His intention was to complete at least one of his acts or opponencies that term. His enforced absence from home, however, was now beginning to raise difficulties for the school. He had naively assumed that his pursuit of a degree would be an additional recommendation to parents, who would be impressed that their schoolmaster was away studying at St John's College. Not all were. Some of the more down-to-earth Dorchester citizens took the view that the schoolmaster was taking money to educate their sons while absenting himself, and that therefore they were not getting their money's worth. A Mrs Pugh declared that she would not send her sons back to school until Barnes returned. He replied that, 'if she would rather keep the boys back a fortnight she might do so, but that they could work without me. However I hope I shall soon come home. My term is half over today'. Lack of new applications for school places was also a matter for concern. He advised Julia to say that he was happy 'to hear of enquiries after terms'. It was no longer a seller's market, and he was being forced to bargain.

He was even more worried that winter about Julia's health. He wrote to her to say that he hoped she was still getting strong and taking exercise.[8] Meanwhile his stay at St John's produced little more than the completion of another term. By the end of February he was relieved to hurry home, now catching the night mail from Nine Elms Station, Battersea, at 8.50 p.m. and arriving in Dorchester at 3.30 a.m. the following morning. 'Leave the door unlatched,' he instructed Julia, 'or better leave the window unfastened'.

Cambridge was still a novelty to Barnes at this time. He loved to walk the college courts and visit the ancient library. But whatever pleasure he derived from these things had become marred by a nagging sense of guilt. For one thing, there was the expense of it all to consider. Then again, when he thought about it, he had to admit that the parents might have reason to complain. By his absences he was, perhaps, letting them down and putting his school at risk. Above all, he was fearful that he was asking too much of Julia, and thereby endangering her health. Despite these fears, he was back again at St John's in May, even before the end of the school term. On the 30th he wrote:

My dear Julia,
I had the happiness of receiving your letter today at the Hall where we have a College Post Office. I am truly happy to find that you are going on pretty well. In all things but the thoughts of my charge and you at home I am as happy as the day is long. I have bought a surplice (cheap) which it was necessary for me to have on white days when we all go in surplices to Chapel.

Our men will soon shrink here now as many will go off after their examination which is now going on. I shall have to undergo an examination with the Regius Professor of Divinity when I take my degree. He has given me his subjects now so that I shall have time enough to read them before my last term.

Dearest Julia,
Your most affectionate husband,
Wm Barnes.[9]

By his 'charge' he probably meant his costs in Cambridge. As a relatively poor ten-year man he had been excused university fees, but there were still his college expenses to find. For the month ending 16 June 1848, the College Buttery book reveals that he paid 8s 8d for 'sizings', i.e. for meals in Hall, 6d and a ha'penny for letters, 1d and a ha'penny in chapel fines (for some reason he appears to have missed some services) and 1s for the weekly charge, which was a contribution to the college running costs.[10] And though he might try to economise, it was difficult for him to do so by dining in his rooms, because any leftovers of food fetched from the college kitchens became the traditional 'perks' of the 'gyps'. Besides that, a ten-year man usually dined at the Fellows' table.[11] Added to his expenses were the cost of his railway tickets and cab fares across London. Thus, the cost of his academic expeditions mounted and the frequency of his visits to St John's contributed to his financial worries.[12]

The one positive benefit he gained from the business was access, for the first time in his life, to an academic library. He, who had had to beg and borrow books all his life, might now draw on the resources of one of the finest collections in the country. It might be expected that his reading at this time would have been confined to the theological texts his professor had recommended. Not so. He was still primarily a philologist. On 29 June 1848, he noted that his borrowings had included: *Grammatica Lapponica*; *Apercue de la langue des Iles Marquises*; *Elements Grammatica Tyzoena*; Lattain's *Egyptian Grammar*; and *Elemens de la Grammatica Mandehoud*.[13]

So his days were spent reading, practising debates with other candidates and wondering how things were going on at home. Sadly, he finally had to admit to Julia that in this, his third term, there was very little chance of his completing his two opponencies. Presumably the tutors were out of Cambridge that summer. Because of this, he had to keep a further term that autumn, and had to rush up and down to Cambridge more than once for the purpose. At last, on 19 October 'before Dr. Olliphant', he debated with a Mr Cole of Trinity College the 'questions': 'Testamentum vetus novo contrarium non est' ('The Old Testament is not contrary to the New') and 'Male sentiunt qui veteres tantum impromissiones temporarias sperasse confingunt'. ('They think evil who merely invent ancient myths to inspire temporary hope'.) Having performed successfully, his domestic and professional responsibilities required him to go home immediately. But once again, he had to return to Cambridge in November to complete another term. His letter on arrival gives some insight into his days at St John's, where he lodged in an old building often allocated to impoverished scholars:

St. John's College,
November 1st, 1848.

MY DEAREST JULIA,

I came up exactly the way I marked out, but from the slipperiness of the rail I was late in London, and arrived at the Eastern Counties station at the last minute.

Mr. B. (my tutor) had found me a room and sent in a sack of coals and a bedmaker ready to receive me, and a porter met me at the lodge to show me the way to my abode. I am in that part of the college which men call 'the wilderness', one side of the first or oldest court.[14]

I ascend to my room by a dismal dusty decayed staircase of dark oak, trodden by gownsmen of many generations. My room is large and lofty, and is partially lighted by a great window with stone mullions, but unluckily the fireplace is in the same wall as the window and therefore in a dark corner, so that I can hardly read in the luxurious attitude in which I indulge myself at home, with my feet on the hobs, or with my nose roasting over the grate. I guess the room might have been so built to give the students a hint of the difference between light and heat.

I am making something of my time by reading. You might have found me if you had come this morning with a huge folio (the works of an ancient church father) before me. I wish I could do as well as possible at my examination, and can have from the library books that I should not and could not buy.[15]

Rushed off her feet with the demands of parents, pupils, ushers, boys and her own family, this world where her husband had to 'make something' of his time must have seemed very remote to Julia. But soon after he wrote this letter, he was back in action, debating with a Mr Minen of Sidney Sussex College, when once again it seems he performed well. At home, however, problems were beginning to overwhelm his wife. Barnes it seemed was continually away, and the business could not stand it, even if she could. So, though he still had not completed all the requirements needed to graduate, when he returned he promised her that he would not go back to St John's the following year.

By this time, his visits to the college had lost all their glamour and become an irksome chore. He had already completed more than the required three terms in residence, had preached his sermons and successfully performed his acts, yet still he had to go back again, presumably for his examination by the Professor of Divinity and to fulfil various administrative requirements. He might have resented these enforced attendances less had he thought that he was spending his time usefully and actually learning something new, but there is little evidence of a programme of studies prepared for him.

When he returned to college for his fifth term in January 1850, he cut a very lonely figure, a rather withdrawn, middle-aged man in clerical garb, housed in that dusty old pile the Wilderness, walking the lawns across the courts to visit the library or to hear a service in chapel, where the choir would sing the 31st Psalm, 'Incline thine Ear' as set by Himmel. Having no formal academic requirements to meet, he attended lectures in mineralogy as well as divinity, and borrowed philological books from the library. They included: David's *Modern Greek Grammar*; J. W. Pol, *Bohmusche Sprache*; Ziegenbalg, *Grammatica Danubica*; Vassalle, *Grammatica Maltez*; *Evangelia Gothice and Anglo-Saxonice*; Endlicker's *Chinesischen Grammatik*; Blazewicz's *Wallachian Sprache*; *Armenian Grammar*; *Albanesan Sprache* (Xylander); *El Arte del Bascuenze*; and *Chaldee Grammar*.

After a year's absence, he now knew few in college, and perhaps only one or two tutors remembered him. Yet there were some people who did. It is characteristic of Barnes that, wherever he went, his instinctive humanity and implicit egalitarianism endeared him to working people. It was the college servants who went out of their way to welcome him back. He wrote to tell Julia: 'Miss Cardless, my first bedmaker, called to see me today and Mrs Todd, my last bedmaker, yesterday. They were very glad to see me. Mrs Todd said: "La, sir, we've been looking for ye this term or two"'. They also helped him to make himself at home. He added that he was just going to bake and make his toast and brew his tea. 'You would', he told Julia, 'smile to see me in the woman's office [he means preparing food] at my tea and breakfast'.

There was a change now in his feelings about what he had once described as 'our noble old college'. Those with whom he had once identified himself proudly as 'our men' and 'superior minds', he now perceived to be, in the main, rather ordinary, rowdy youths:

Jan 27th 1850

My Dearest Julia,
I sit down after Chapel to talk a few words to you though I have little new to tell you. We have had a good anthem tonight from Haydn's 'Creation'. I went yesterday to the Senate House to the great yearly Congregation at which the outgoing men take their B.A. Degree. There was, as usual in this Congregation, a great uproar with the undergraduates who get into the galleries and greet some of the public men with cheers or groans. At sight of one of the examiners who had set the men a hard paper

they gave him three groans and at the first glimpse of the Master of Trinity College they shouted 'Billy Whistle' and began to bark like dogs. One of them, most like a Trinity man, proposed three cheers for 'The Pigs' – St. John's. I suppose there were fifteen hundred in the house…[16]

This was the term in which he hoped to take his degree but there were new difficulties. Barnes's status as a clergyman had previously absolved him from paying university fees, probably because the assumption of the authorities had been that indigent 'ten-year' clergymen occupied church property and had insufficient capital for them to be charged. But now that Barnes himself was the owner of a lifehold property, 40 South Street, worth £700, the university administrators raised the question of whether he was, after all, liable to pay. It is not clear if their query related only to the period after his purchase of the property in 1847, or even further back to his registration in 1838, though it was probably only the former. Nevertheless, even the possibility of having to pay fees was a severe shock to him, and raised the prospect of his having to require repayment of the whole of his loan to Samuel Thatcher to raise the money. Anticipating the worst, he tried to call in the loan but reported to Julia that three days after the stipulated date he had still not received the remittance. What he needed now was a clear ruling on the fee question. Without such a ruling he could not proceed to his degree. But though he trudged from one office to another at Cambridge, he could get no one to give it to him. He was walking in a wilderness.

It seemed that the college and university authorities were entirely indifferent to his situation. He now perceived that what was such a desperate matter to him was of little concern to these people. Despite the heroic struggles he had made to get there, the fellows and tutors had turned their backs on him as a person of little consequence. St John's people simply could not imagine, and did not care, what he and his faithful wife had endured in order for him to gain a degree. It was vexing and humiliating. In February he wrote to tell Julia that this was, 'the second week of my shame'. Once the degree business was over, he promised that his 'diligence afterwards [would] leave no reason for complaint'. Yet once again he had to return to Dorchester empty handed.

His anxiety was well-placed because there were now more difficulties with the school. The younger usher, Morgan, had fallen out with Hann and had to be dismissed just at the time when he was most needed to cover for Barnes. There were also signs of a decided reaction by parents, even more incensed by the schoolmaster's frequent absences, and his announcements of yet more half-holidays. The number of boarders had dropped to eighteen and the total roll below forty, the lowest since he had first set up school in Dorchester. The balance had now swung strongly in favour of the parents, and some took advantage. A Mrs Chick, to save money, wanted her two day-boy sons to bring bags of bread and cheese to school rather than to eat the meal provided. Barnes was against it but was obliged to ask Julia whether they could offer her a deduction. Another mother, Mrs Paul, sent her son back early but Barnes advised Julia to let him stay to fill up the numbers. A Mrs Com was always complaining, and a Mrs Williams, a 'crabbed old maid' according to Barnes, wrote an offensive letter and began to stir up other parents in protest, claiming that the boarders were not properly fed at the school. When Mrs Pugh repeated Mrs William's complaints, Barnes wrote her 'a strong answer… telling her of the utter falsehood of the charges contained in the letter of the busy Mrs Williams, and begging her to ask herself whether the boys looked to be starved when they went home'. Worst of all, Mrs Guppy refused to pay her account. There was nothing he could do about this as he was 'quite at her mercy, as she has no tangible property and I am fearful she is too cunning to be much affected by epistolary communications for money'.[17]

His situation in Cambridge was equally desperate. Back once again in May, he tried to sort out the various administrative impediments to taking his degree. Then at last came good news. There had been a ruling from the university authorities that his position as a householder would not prevent his fees being waived. So, thinking that all was settled, he returned once more to Dorchester. But he had not allowed for the inefficiency of the university officers. He could not, of course, graduate while still owing sums to the university, and now they claimed he had not paid a bill for £15. After an exhausting and dispiriting protest on his part, they discovered they had accidentally torn up his cheque. Even after that, there was another hold up because an essential certificate 'by some oversight' had lacked the signature of the Regius Professor of Divinity. In the event, he was obliged to return to Cambridge for the seventh time in October, in order to graduate. He noted: 'At last, in 1850, at a more trying cost of time in residence in Cambridge than even of money, I took my degree'.

What benefit did Barnes derive from his excursion into university education? The degree itself was his principle objective and its possession now promised to enhance immeasurably his social and academic status. Never a one for 'networking' though, he does not appear to have made any significant friendships nor useful contacts in his time at St John's. Nor did the study of divinity seem greatly to have stimulated his intellectual curiosity. It was simply an academic course to be gone through. His more profound interest was in philology and the only way in which this benefited was in his access to the college library. Indeed, his private reading when in residence seemed to consist almost entirely of philology, and this bore fruit in his later writings, though there is no indication of research at St John's into Anglo-Saxon, which language had a marked relevance to studies.

It was in the first flush of enthusiasm for college life that Barnes had written to tell Julia that there were 'many superior minds here'. So there were and his was one of them. Yet no one seemed aware that they had a great scholar and an original artist come among them. He reported that the fellows were very kind but no tutor or professor took a personal interest in him. An unassuming man, without money or influence, and living in the Wilderness with so many other shabby old clergymen, it was always unlikely that he would be noticed much at St John's, and he was not.

Barnes never returned there. He went home to Dorchester and took up his old life just as if he had never been to Cambridge at all. It was not immediately apparent then what his time there had cost him, personally, professionally and financially. In later years, he rarely seems to have mentioned his time at St John's. Perhaps this was because, when he walked out of that gateway for the last time and looked up once more at the smiling saint, it was with a feeling that he had already tasted something of the bitterness at the bottom of his cup.

# 13

# ANGLO-SAXON ATTITUDES

## —— 1846-1852 ——

Fortunately, Barnes's time at Cambridge did not entirely succeed in stifling his creative thinking. On arriving home, he would find packets of books from Gough Nichols, with the request that he should review them for *The Gentleman's Magazine*, and while juggling the competing claims of family, school and the university, somehow he still found some time to do so. Because he usually wrote them during the summer or Christmas holidays, his reviews often appeared immediately afterwards, in the September/October or January/February issues. And although he was still not paid for the work, free review copies rapidly began to fill the shelves of his little study on the top floor of 40 South Street.

As a priest, he was well-qualified to review a new study of St John's Gospel, and to understand the mundane problems of 'Female parochial schools'. As a linguist, he was thoroughly competent to write reviews on *Hebrew Grammar*, the *Analytical Hebrew and Chaldee Lexicon*, and a *Ready Guide to French Composition*. As a man of letters, he could be entrusted to have informed opinions on a recent anthology of prose and verse and an account of English history.

But what is astonishing is that Nichols entrusted Barnes to review books on subjects in which he had no qualifications at all; economics, for example. How was a mere student of theology, with no formal qualifications in economics, to assess such works as: *A Financial, Monetary and Statistical History of England*, a *History of the Bank of England*, and *The Nature and the Use of Money*? Yet review them he did. As for science, it might have been assumed that the editor of this leading intellectual journal could have chosen from many eminent experimenters to provide reviews in this field. But no; it is Barnes's name that appears below notices of works on *The Philosophy of Geology*, *The Correlation of Physical Forces* and the structure of the universe.

He was an editor's dream. He seemed to have well-informed and original opinions on almost every academic subject, and Gough Nichols was very ready to exploit the talents of this provincial polymath. Yet in the long run, it was Barnes who profited most from these diverse studies. For in writing them, he began to formulate his many insights into language and society, and to fashion these into a consistent whole. He was working out how to live.

This is not to say that he had abandoned his poetry. His verse still had its admirers and by 1847 the first print run of his book was almost sold out and there was sufficient demand to justify a second edition. So he set to work, rearranging the order of the poems, as well as including three new ones: 'Gwain to the Fiair', and the two 'piarts' of 'Shrodon Fiair'. Some items were partly rewritten, presumably to make them more accessible to the non-dialect reader, as Mrs Norton had advised. An example is 'The Milk-Maid o' the Farm':

First Edition, 1844

   I be the milk-maid o' the farm:
   I be so happy out in groun',
   Wi' my white milk-pail, in my yarm,
   As ef I wore a goolden crown.

   An' I don't zit up hafe the night,
   Nar lie var hafe the day a-bed:

An' that's how tis my eyes be bright,
An why my cheaks be alwiz red.

Second Edition, 1847

O Poll's the milk-maid o' the farm!
An Poll's so happy out in groun',
Wi her white pail below her yarm
As if she wore a goolden crown.

An' Poll don't zit up hafe the night,
Nar lie var hafe the day a-bed;
An' zoo her eyes be sparklen bright,
An' zoo her cheaks be bloomen red.[1]

There is a charming sprightliness about the milkmaid when she speaks for herself, which is lost by distancing her in the third person. There is also a loss of authentic 'feel' in such feeble phrases as, 'An' zoo her eyes' which replaces the vernacular, 'An' that's how 'tis'. This loss of immediacy was to become a feature of many of the 'translations' into 'national English' which he made later on.

The second edition of *Poems of Rural Life in the Dorset Dialect* is a bigger book than the first, because of the enlargement of the 'Dissertation' from thirty-seven to forty-nine pages and the 'Glossary' from ninety to ninety-eight pages. The latter is curiously described as 'A Glossary of the English Language', though it is, more accurately, a list of local dialect terms. It was a cooperative venture. On the last page of the first edition there appeared a notice to readers:

> The Author, being convinced that his Glossary is still imperfect, would be thankful to his Dorset read-
> ers for any Provincial Words he may have omitted. He must not omit to mention that the Rev. C. W.
> Bingham, M.A., of Sydling St. Nicholas, Mr John Sydenham, Author of the History of Poole, &c. and Mr
> Isaac Hann, of Dorchester, have each kindly contributed to its present copiousness.

Bingham is thanked again in the later edition, along with E.J. Vernon of Newchurch, Isle of Wight, author of *A Guide to the Anglo-Saxon Tongue*; Henry Ker Seymour MP of Hansford House; and F.A. Carrington 'of the Oxford Circuit'. Notably absent, however, are thanks to those who actually spoke the dialect. It seems that Barnes still had not confidence enough at this time to name his informants among the working people themselves. After all, they were not 'authorities'.

Nevertheless, this 'Glossary' was an important piece of verbal conservation, one of the first serious attempts in English to record the fast-disappearing dialects of the south-west. Barnes was even prepared to throw his net beyond Dorset itself, though most of the words and phrases included were from his home county. And by supplying etymologies for his entries, he anticipated the *Oxford English Dictionary* by many years. Sometimes when doing so he was guessing, but mostly he drew upon his own vast linguistic knowledge, referring in passing to: Anglo-Saxon, Gothic, Icelandic, German, Dutch, Danish, Swedish, Old English, the Northern Counties, Scottish, Latin, Greek, French, and – intriguingly – Herefordshire.

But one among these languages was of more significance to him than all the others put together. Increasingly, he found the roots of many of his Dorset dialect terms in Anglo-Saxon. Indeed, though the 'Glossary' was meant to reduce the linguistic difficulty of the poems for the general reader, he actually introduced into it characters from the Anglo-Saxon alphabet to give a closer idea of the correct pronunciation of dialect words. Both editions quote Saxon sources copiously. In the first he recorded:

Pure – AS Pur. Sound. Quite well.
'How b'ye?' – 'Pure, thenk ye'.
Quag – AS cwacian, to shake. A quagmire which shakes when walked on.

Riames – AS Ream, a ligament, a skeleton, the frame or ligaments of anything.

Riddle – AS Hriddel, A kind of coarse sieve.

Ruf – AS Hrof. A roof.

Scram – AS Scrimman, to dry up, wither, distorted, awkward, 'How scram ya da handle it'.

In the second edition he added:

Hummick – a heat or sweat. Is it a diminutive of AS homa, which is appplied to erysipelas?

He continued to collect dialect terms and expand his glossaries for the rest of his life. And though he published many other books and papers on philology, it is likely that this record of one of the ancient dialects of England will in the end prove to be his most valuable contribution to language studies.

Fired up with enthusiasm for Anglo-Saxon, he now began to teach it in school. As usual he wrote the textbook for his pupils. This was *Se Gefylsta* (*The Helper*) which came out in 1849.[2] Not that there were hordes of Dorchester parents thronging the school doorstep, imploring him to teach the language to their boys. He did so just because he wanted to. And he must have kept the subject going for some time because, in 1866, the publishers brought out a second edition. This was ushered in with a delicious solecism. His first edition was advertised as a 'first class-book' of the language. The new one announced itself as a 'first-class book', a claim not at all in accordance with the author's natural modesty.

One reason for his advocacy of Anglo-Saxon was familiar; he wished to show how closely it was related to the Dorset dialect. In so doing, he was validating both the dialect speech itself and his own poems. But a more personal motive arose from the mortification he still felt at being passed over for the headship of Hardye's. As a result of this, he now took against both grammar schools as such, and the curriculum they taught. For it seemed to him that the chief effect of these schools was to promote the Latinate corruption of the English language. His task, therefore, was to help restore it to its origins.

In this he was, probably unknowingly, aligning himself to that small group of scholars who had long pressed for a return to an older, 'purer' form of English, drawn mostly from its Saxon origins. Sir John Cheke, for example, in a letter to Thomas Hobbes in 1557, declared that, 'I am of the opinion that our tung shold be written cleane and pure, vnmixt and vnmangled with borowings of other tunges'.[3] Barnes too advocated this purist doctrine:

He (the author) believes, though possibly few but Teutonic scholars will be of his mind, that Anglo-Saxon (English) has not been cultivated into a better form, but has been corrupted for the worse, since King Alfred's days. English has lost many of the case-endings and other inflections of its old form, and cannot therefrom, if it may from aught else, have become a more excellent language than the Anglo-Saxon… and the praise of greater richness which some bestow on English must be lessened by the truth that Anglo-Saxon, like German, had within itself the elements of the utmost richness; and that we have thrown away many of its good words to take in their stead less intelligible ones from the Latin and Greek.[4]

Not that he always adopted pure English himself; he was not yet confident enough to do so. His own procedure was often self-contradictory, as revealed by the the full title of this little book, *Se Gefylsta* (*The Helper*): *An Anglo-Saxon Delectus*, where 'delectus' is Latin for school book. Elsewhere, he ties himself up in Greek knots to explain to pupils the simple notion that, in speech, words and syllables are often shortened:

There is a tendency in all languages to an immutation of words by syncope, aphaeresis, and apocope of vowels and consonants, and crasis of vowels; and thence we have new forms of innumerable English words differing more or less from their older ones in Anglo-Saxon.

Which must have made the matter as clear as day to his long-suffering pupils.

Meanwhile, the effects of the Hardye's debacle rumbled on. It resulted in a loss of confidence and a deepened sense of vulnerability. It also lost him friends and supporters, including George Simonds who, as editor of the *Chronicle*, had given him his first platform as a poet and was also part-publisher of his books of verse. This became clear in late 1847, or early in the next year, when they quarrelled because Simonds had decided to take his son away from Barnes's school to send him to Maskew's grammar school. This rubbed salt in. Incensed, Barnes now presented Simonds with a bill demanding a quarter's fees in lieu of notice. Simonds retaliated with charges for printing the poems in 'national English'. After checking his own accounts, Barnes replied, 'William Barnes cannot owe Mr. Simmonds anything on account of the publication of the *Poems in the Dorset Dialect* or the English Poems as Mr. S. published them at his own risk, on the condition of having half the profit of the edition if there should be any'. For good measure, he added that he had discovered that Simond's printing charges were exorbitant and that his bill contained errors in dates. Loftily, he concluded: 'Willam Barnes gives Mr. Simmonds notice that he does not any longer take the *Dorset County Chronicle*'. This was foolish. He had made an enemy, and an influential one at that.

The dispute forced him to find outlets other than the *Chronicle* for his occasional journalism. One was the *Poole & Dorset Herald*, whose editor, Sydenham, was the father of a pupil and probably paid him for his contributions. In April and May 1849, there appeared in the paper seven articles collectively entitled *Humilis Domus: Some thoughts on the Abodes, Life and Social Conditions of the Poor, especially in Dorsetshire.*[5] As author of the dialect poems, Barnes was already reckoned by some to be an authority on the lives of the rural work-folk. Here, once again, they were his subject, but from exploring their experiences in verse, he now turned to examining the economic basis of their lives. And in discussing the subject, his thinking took a new trajectory. The results were startlingly radical, and entitle *Humilis Domus* to still be regarded as both an original approach to social reform and a founding text of the environmentalist movement.

He begins by explaining that the home is uniquely important for providing rest, shelter and the opportunity for wholesome family life. But, he observed, this was no longer true in Dorset. The present time was one of dreadful hardship for the rural poor. Land clearances, enclosures, the deliberate demolition of cottages and the amalgamation of many small farms had all conspired to reduce the number of homes available to farm workers. So, from want of work or housing, they were obliged to leave their native parishes to seek these things elsewhere. But this bred resentment in the new parishes because, when the next source of work dried up, incomers became a liability on local poor rates. So families were 'encouraged' to move on again. As a result, a destitute population was being shuffled around the county and herded into the few hovels that were left. Such overcrowding bred 'many evils, moral and spiritual'. Ignorance, squalor, drunkenness and (he implied) incest were the inevitable result of such housing conditions.

Who was to blame? He was not afraid to raise the question. Was it the children of the poor themselves, he asked, 'young women or men [who] have been bred up from childhood in the poisonous conditions of an unseemly house life, and have necessarily yielded to their sad effects'? Or was it the fault of their parents, or their employers? Or was it perhaps 'the head of the nation, who holds God's people in his charge'? That he should even have posed such questions was risky.

Such observations were not unusual. Other writers had complained about the state of the rural poor.[6] What marked Barnes out was his solution. Briefly, he considered that a partial alleviation of the problem might result from adopting national or county rating, rather than a parish one, but having raised the prospect of what looks like a national insurance system, he dismissed it as merely cosmetic. The real answer, in his view, was to ensure that each labourer's family was provided with adequate housing and enough cultivable land to be self-sufficient.

In working out how this could be done, he resorted to arithmetic. On 19 April, readers of the *Herald* were confronted with columns of calculations based on the census returns for 1841 concerning the number of farm labourers and their families in Dorset, and the amount of agricultural land that might theoretically be available to them in the county. Barnes's conclusion was uncompromising. If these families were to be properly housed and made self-supporting, 'there should be a labourer's cottage to every 130 acres of land'.

What was he suggesting? That the enclosures should be reversed? The commons re-established? That the land should be returned to the people? No. He did not go that far. He merely did the arithmetic. But he had raised the possibility of an England in which half-starved farm workers and hopeless factory operatives no longer trudged the lanes looking for work. Instead, his readers glimpsed a landscape stippled with small family farms, worked by sturdy yeomen. This was his vision of the good life.

An instinctive conservative, he habitually looked to the past for remedies to present ills.[7] Never once in *Humilis Domus* did he question the existence of 'the upper classes, who are freed from labours for the body of man, that they may take care of his mental nature'. As for 'the worthy landowner, the protector of the poor, and the pattern of civilised man… [and] of the mind-labourer, the upholder of intelligence and ideality: their life is a source of blessing to the world'. Yet a kernel of radicalism was becoming visible in his contention that every class had its appropriate work to do. Everyone, he believed, should be a 'labourer' of some sort. He noticed that, in using the phrase 'the unproductive classes', some contemporary commentators seemed to have in mind only out-of-work labourers and machine operatives. Far more 'unproductive' in his opinion, was: 'The consumption of a gay and insolvent spendthrift… his horse and carriage, and wine and grogs, and meats and cigars, and clothing, and firing, and travelling, are all more costly, as the production of many hands'.

Especially objectionable to him was the Malthusian argument, often repeated at that time, that the poverty of many labourers and their families was an inevitable consequence of over-population, and that the only answer to it was emigration. Even as Barnes wrote, the population of Ireland was draining away as many inhabitants emigrated to America to avoid starvation brought on by the potato famine. One early advocate of emigration was Richard Eburne, in his book *The Pathway to the Plantations*, published in 1624, which complained of the over-population of England, though Barnes calculated that it had been no more than about 5½ million in the early seventeenth century. 'Bee not to much in love with that countrie wherein you were borne', Eburne counselled, 'that countrie which bearing you, but seemeth, and is indeed, weary of you. She accounts you a burthen to her, and an incumbrance of her, &c.'

Such sentiments provoked Barnes to outrage. Why should the poor man be bullied out of his home? What right had anyone to invite others to leave their own country? His reply was one of the most deeply-felt expositions of true patriotism ever penned. Love of one's country, he derived from love of home:

> For what is England, that she should be dear to me, but that she is the land of my own county! Why should I love my county, but that it contains the village of my birth? Why should that village be hallowed in my mind, but that it holds the house of my childhood.

For all the stirring quality of his prose, however, it cannot be denied that his economic solution, of a return to a prosperous peasantry with its clusters of small-holdings extending across the whole country, was simply not possible. By the mid-nineteenth century, neither in Dorset nor England as a whole, was there sufficient land to sustain the agricultural population. Emigration was the only remedy, either to great industrial cities or to the colonies. But rather than face up to this, he elected to put his faith in a God who would always provide, just as he had done when the national supply of firewood was replaced by coal.

Forced emigration supported the new imperialism. Barnes loathed both. Bitterly, he quotes Eburne again who recommended that in accordance with the biblical edict, 'we should multiply and replenish the earth' by settling in other lands. Replying, Barnes declared that he could not understand the logic of this view, because, surely, the commandment applied equally to the 'red men of America, and the darker ones of Australia or New Zealand' who were also the children of Adam, and who were, no doubt, already multiplying and replenishing their own country until 'we went and stopped them'. He considered the reply that 'yes, but we could do it better', no excuse for appropriating the lands of others.

Above all, he rejected the argument that Europeans had the right to colonise other lands simply because they were Christians:

> Mr. Eburne thought that there was no bar why the king of England might not 'by any lawful and good meanes, seize into his hands, and hold as in his own right, whatsoever countries and lands were not before actually inhabited or possessed by any Christian state'; as if Christians could draw from the positive precept, the new commandment of their Divine Saviour 'to love one another', the negative one that they might plunder all men not yet within the fold of the Church. It is to be feared that as a nation, we have to answer for much unrighteousness towards weaker tribes.

Regrettably, he lived too early to debate these matters with Rhodes or Kipling.

*Humilis Domus* provoked such an interest among readers of the *Herald* that Sydenham soon asked him to supply another series of articles, presumably on a topic of his choice. His request came at his busiest time, when he was still involved with his university studies as well as trying to keep the school on course. Though never able to resist an opportunity to put his ideas to the public, Barnes was now obliged to cast around to find a topic that would take very little of his time. Luckily, he had recently come into possession of a diary, kept during the years 1697 and 1701 by a John Richards of Warmwell, a hamlet a few miles from Dorchester. So, from October 1849 until the end of the year, *Herald* readers were presented with extracts, which Barnes had merely to copy out and send to the editor with a few added comments. The series was entitled 'Dorsetshire 150 Years Ago'.[8]

A bucolic Pepys, Richards records a wealth of detail about small farm life in the seventeenth century as well as his personal doings:

> Wednesday the 10th of January 1699. This morning I agreed with Jno Battercomb my under carter, to live with me another year for £4.10s pr. ann. wages.

> 26 June, 1699. – Last night the gout came into my left foot, and all this day it was very troublesome, but much worse Tuesday 27th ditto abt noon this day I applied 5 leaches to it. next day ye 28, was very severe and all yt night much worse not permitting a moments sleep.
> Munday the 2 ditto (1698) meeting old Loder this day at the Antelope yard at Dorchr. I took him thence to Mrs. Bakers Coffee-house, and told him my inclination to purchase Watercomb, and that if he could bring it abt. I would give him cinq ps d'oro. [Barnes comments, 'i.e. 5 pieces of gold, Guineas we may suppose, cunning, if not naughty Mr Richards'.]

Richards was a model of just the sort of independent farmer that Barnes admired. Canny, good at business and skilled in all the arts of husbandry, he was also public spirited, a humane employer, benevolent and pious. Not merely practical, he was both literate and cultivated, for having travelled as a merchant he spoke Italian, and there could be few higher recommendations to Barnes than that. Day in and day out, Richards's life was taken up with going to market; superintending the movements of stock; horse shoeing; aiding animal births; and feeding and shearing of animals. His thoughts were taken up with such matters as his 'feminine mousers, and emasculations of his tom-cats... the sittings of broody hens, [and] the lending of ferrets and wedges... [the] tipping of ploughshares and grinding of scissors'. He was a loyal parishioner and would dine unsnobbishly with his less genteel neighbours. All this signified the good life to Barnes, pleasurable in itself and useful to humanity. For him, Richards and his kind were the salt of the earth.

Consequently, what he found especially objectionable were contemporary notions of 'progress', as exemplified in the writings of people like Thomas Babington (afterwards Lord) Macaulay. His essays, Barnes maintained, held that:

> Richards's generation, or that of earlier times, [was] most excessively below our own in education, knowledge and manners, so that it is believed that our fourth or fifth fathers, as the Anglo-Saxons would

have called them, were in mind but little above their hinds, if they were rural squires, and little above the lowest savages, if they were hinds.[9]

Begging to differ, he doubted whether the onward march of history had brought any improvement at all. It was true that the 'gaffers' and 'gammers' of Richards's time had to be content with lumps of bull's beef as charity, but:

> He [did] not seem to have found his land overwhelmed with poor's rates, nor needed the bayonette and the bludgeon to shield his house from a plundering, if not bloodthirsty, mob of famished operatives. His wife jogged with great patience over the rough and lonesome roads of the land on a pillion, instead of flying on the pillowed sedile of a railway carriage, but yet he knew not of dense populations of wan and weakly operatives, who could hardly win a scanty livelihood by twelve or fourteen hours of daily labour.

Far from the concurring with the idea of progress, Barnes believed that things had got worse. England was not improved by enclosures and industrialisation, by absentee landowners, capitalists, trades unions and Chartists. Better by far was an older England, where the land was worked by small tenant farmers and their men, whom they recognised as their workmates. In that un-enclosed Eden, there was enough land for all, and it was so thickly forested that in Dorset, 'a squirrel might then jump on trees from one village to another'. More personal and humane, it was a society of a vigorous, self-supporting peasantry, beholden to no one, and speaking a homely dialect, rooted in the practical activities of their daily lives. Like his uncle and aunt in Bagber years before.

And the Anglo-Saxons.

# 14

# TWO SUMMERS

## —— 1851-1852 ——

With clattering, clanking and great snorts of tortured steam, the locomotive pulled up at the platform. Awestruck and still rather alarmed at the sight, people hung back a moment before rushing forward to find their seats in the carriages. Here were small tradesmen and their wives, craftsmen, and professional people, farmers and dealers in agricultural machinery. Chattering excitedly, they pushed and shoved their way in, anxious matrons and knowing youths, affable countrymen and families with children, a sea of voluminous skirts, bobbing bonnets and nodding top hats. Some were searchers after knowledge, and others mere pleasure-seekers. Many had never been on a train before. But now they were all bound for London on the special excursion. It was six o'clock in the morning on 1 July 1851 at Dorchester's new station.

In the midst of the crush there appeared a family group of obviously impeccable respectability. The balding, middle-aged clergyman began at once to search for their seats, while a rather anxious-looking, slightly built matron and two excited young women followed on behind. For William Barnes was off to London, accompanied by his wife, Julia, and their two elder daughters, Laura Liebe, now aged twenty-three, and Julia Eliza, eighteen. These women had kept the school running during his recent absences in Cambridge. This trip was their reward.

At last they had arrived in middle-class society. Barnes was now a clergyman, a scholar, a successful schoolmaster and something of a local celebrity. His wife and daughters would have been proud to be seen in the company of such a genial gentleman. The Barneses were travelling purely for pleasure, a notion that had not hitherto played a great part in their family history, but one it seemed that they could now afford. The women wore their Sunday best and Barnes had discarded his old dressing gown for a smart, though appropriately sober, clerical outfit.

Arriving in Battersea at three o'clock in the afternoon, they immediately set about their sight-seeing. Even before they retired to their Pimlico lodging-house that night – their landlady was an old Dorchester acquaintance – they had already visited Westminster Abbey, the National Gallery and the House of Lords. Such a day, devoted entirely to enjoyment, was a novelty to them all, though Julia, if not the others, had already discovered that such pleasures can be exhausting. And there had been a moment of real terror. Not used to watching out for London traffic, one of the girls had nearly been run over. Tragedy was narrowly averted when Julia jerked the girl away from under the plunging feet of the horses while the driver desperately fought to pull them back.

The following day was one of the most memorable of their lives. They rose early and left their lodgings at 9.30 a.m. by cab. Trotting northwards from Pimlico for a mile or so through the little streets, they soon joined a growing stream of hackneys, hansoms and carriages of all descriptions making their way towards Hyde Park. Following huge crowds, they eventually passed through a set of ornate gates, and it was then that they had their first glimpse of what they had come to see. An immense structure emerged, gleaming high above them. It was taller than the ancient elms around it; indeed it enclosed some fully-grown trees. They knew this because they could see inside it, for it was made of glass. They had arrived at Joseph Paxton's 'Crystal Palace', the enormous pavilion which housed the Great Exhibition.

They spent the entire day there. Fortunately, the original charge of 5s per person per day had now been reduced to 1s, so that the cost was not excessive for a family of four. And once inside, there was so much to see. Thousands of exhibits had been gathered from all over the world; handicrafts, pictures, pottery, jewellery, furniture and all kinds of inventions. There was the 'Day dreamer' easy chair in papier mâché, the patent freezing machine, the 'Lady's mechanical escritoire in white wood' from Switzerland, which enabled the owner to write while either standing or sitting, and the 'Lion in Love' sculpture from Belgium which represented the savage beast having his claws pulled out by a young girl whose beauty had captivated him.

Perhaps they joined the crowd looking at the machines. The *Daily News* had originally suggested that this part of the exhibition would be of little interest to many visitors but, as it turned out, on some days it drew the largest crowds. Among the most popular of the items in the American pavilion was the McCormack reaper. Crowds of farmers, some still wearing smocks, had come up to London especially to inspect the new machines which promised to change the face of farming and do away with the worst drudgery of rural labourers. Among the crowd gathered round, Barnes spotted an old acquaintance from Dorset. It was Job Rose, a miller who lived near Fontmell Magna in the Blackmore Vale, and a pillar of the local Wesleyan chapel. Rose was a convivial man who weighed over twenty stone, and had a cheerful disregard for the under-fed cockneys he had encountered. His perennial joke was that he had lost weight because he could not get enough to eat since coming to London. On his return to Dorchester, Barnes wrote up Rose's visit in dialect verse, though changing the miller's name. The resultant piece is a good joke and yet another variation on the time-honoured debate between rustic and townee. It is also a little piece of social history.

## John Bloom In Lon'on

(all true)

John Bloom he wer a jolly soul,
A grinder o' the best o' meal,
Bezide a river that did roll,
Vrom week to week, to push his wheel.
His flour wer all a-meade o' wheat;
An' fit for bread that vo'k mid eat;
Vor he would starve avore he'd cheat.
'Tis pure', woone woman cried;
'Aye sure' woone mwore replied;
'You'll vind it nice. Buy woonce, buy twice,'
Cried worthy Bloom the miller.

Athirt the chest he wer so wide
As two or dree ov me or you,
An' wider still vrom zide to zide,
An' I do think still thicker drough.
Vall down, he coulden, he did lie
When he were up on zide so high
As up on end or perty nigh.
'Meake room,' woone naighbour cried;
''Tis Bloom,' woone mwore replied;
'Good morn t'ye all, bwoth girt an' small,'
Cried worthy Bloom the miller.

Noo stings o' conscience ever broke
His rest a-twiten o'n wi' wrong,
Zoo he did sleep till mornen broke,
An birds did cal 'en wi' their zong.
But he did love a harmless joke,
An' love his evenen whiff o' smoke,
A-zitten in his cheair o' woak.

'Your cup,' his daughter cried;
'Vill'd up,' hi wife replied;
'Aye, aye; a drap avore my nap,'
Cried worthy Bloom the miller.

When Lon'on vo'k did meake a show
O' their girt glassen house woone year,
An' people went bwoth high an' low,
To zee the zight vrom vur an' near,
'O well,' cried Bloom, 'why I've a right
So well's the rest to zee the zight;
I'll goo, an' teake the rail outright.
'Your feare,' the booker cried;
'There, there,' good Bloom replied;
'Why this June het do meake me zweat,'
Cried worthy Bloom the miller.

Then up the guard did whissle sh'ill,
An' then the engine pank'd a blast,
An' rottled on so loud's a mill,
Avore the train, vrom slow to vast.
An' oh! at last how they did spank
By cutten deep, an high-cast bank
The while their iron ho'se did pank.
'Do whizzy,' one o'm cried;
'I'm dizzy,' oone replied;
'Aye here's the road to hawl a lwoad,'
Cried worthy Bloom the miller.

In Lon'on John zent out to call
A tidy trap, that he mid ride
To zee the glassen house, an' all
The lots o' things a-stowed inside.
'Here, Boots, come here,' cried he, 'I'll dab
A zixpence in your han' to nab
Down street a tidy little cab.'
'A feare,' the boots then cried;
'I'm thcre,' the man replied;
'The glassen pleace, your quickest peace,'
Cried worthy Bloom the miller.

The steps went down wi' rottlen slap,
The swingen door went open wide:
Wide? no; vor when the worthy chap
Stepp'd up to teake his pleace inside,
Breast-voremost, he wer twice too wide
Vor thik there door. An' then he tried
To edge in woone an' tother zide.
'Twon't do,' the drever cried;
'Can't goo,' good Bloom replied;
'That you should bring thease vooty thing!'
Cried worthy Bloom the miller.

'Come,' cried the drever, 'pay your feare;
You'll teake up all my time good man.'
'Well,' answer'd Bloom, 'to meake that square,
You teake up me, then, if you can.'
'I come at call,' the man did nod.
'What then?' cried Bloom, 'I han't a-rod,
An can't in thik there hodmadod.'
'Girt lump,' the drever cried;
'Small stump,' good Bloom replied;
'A little mite, to meake so light,
O' Jolly Bloom the miller'.

'You'd best be off now perty quick,
Cried Bloom, 'an' vind a lighter lwoad,
Or else I'll vetch my voot, an kick
The vooty thing athirt the road.'
'Who is this man? they cried, meake room,'
'A halfstarv'd Do'set man', cried Bloom;
'You be?' another cried;
'Hee! Hee! woone mwore replied,
'Aye, shrunk so thin, to bwone an' skin,'
Cried worthy Bloom the miller.[1]

('vo'k' – folk, people; 'athirt' – across; 'perty' – pretty; 'a-twiten o'n' – worrying him; 'het' – heat; 'pank'd'
– panted; 'rottled' – rattled; 'drever' – driver; 'I han't a-rod' – I have not ridden; 'vooty' – little, trumpery;
'hodmadod' – clumsy thing)

There was one particular exhibit that Barnes was especially anxious to see, so they made for it first thing. It was a life-size statue they found in the American pavilion, Hiram Powers's sculpture, 'The Greek Slave'. It was probably the most popular piece of American art in the mid-nineteenth century. This was not hard to account for, because the slave-girl herself, shackled to a post with her hair tied back, was completely naked. Powers himself had supplied a gloss: 'The Slave has been taken from one of the Greek islands by the Turks, in the time of the Greek Revolution... her father and mother and perhaps all her kindred have been destroyed by her foes'. Her history was suggested by the fact that she wore a cross and a locket, the former evidence that she was a Christian and the latter that she had had a sweetheart. But here she was, in the hands of barbarians and, by implication, to be sold for sex.

   Not that Barnes and many of his fellow Victorians were publicly anxious to explore this last thought. They were gravely enjoined by the commentary to note the slave's apparent resignation in the face of such misfortune which, they were informed, indicated that that her nature was superior to suffering because of her inward purity. There was a coded political message here, because any depiction of the inhumanity of slavery, especially from the United States, acted to promote the abolitionist cause. Barnes would have solemnly explained the significance of it all to his wife and daughters, one of whom remembered that the statue had made a 'great impression' on him. So much so indeed that he bought a plaster replica of it and took it home, where he kept it on the mantlepiece in his study.

   There was no pause in their exertions. The next morning they were up early again for a boat trip down the river, taking in London Bridge and landing at Greenwich, where they inspected the Great Hall of the Naval Hospital. This was of particular interest to Barnes because the walls and ceiling had been painted by a Blackmore man, Sir James Thornhill, who had lived not two miles away from Bagber. Barnes's mother, Grace, had been a great admirer of the artist and he could still remember her taking him as a child to see Thornhill's obelisk to honour the succession of George II. It was through his mother's reverence for Thornhill and the arts that he had derived his own early love of such things.[2]

There was so much to see and so little time. Their fourth day in London was their last, probably because the special fare for excursions to the exhibition was valid only for weekdays. Even so, before leaving they took in the British Museum where Sir Austen Henry Layard's discoveries, sculptures and bas-reliefs from Ninevah and other Assyrian cities were objects to wonder at and talk about. Then it was a cab to Nine Elms to catch the 3.30 p.m. train. They arrived back in Dorchester at 10 p.m. that night.

For Barnes, as for thousands of his respectable contemporaries, the Great Exhibition marked a high point in Victorian optimism. There is no doubt that he identified with this expanding vision of progress. It was one in which science and technology would transform the future for all, bringing endless improvements, especially for the poor in the form of relief from much backbreaking toil. In his regular 'lectures', he had tried to explain to his pupils not only the basis of the new scientific ideas, but also their significence for daily life. If only he could have taken the boys with him to the exhibition, to lead them inside that translucent palace while the sunlight lit up its countless marvels of technology! It was a vision of a radiant future, and one he was determined to take home with him.

Inevitably, life back in Dorchester seemed a little flat but, as usual, he was very busy. The fortunes of the school were improving and with them his financial situation, so that there was more money for small luxuries. Julia had discovered an interesting old tapestry in a cottage in Fordington and had a section of it cleaned and mounted to hang on the wall of his study. In return, he presented her with a carved and gilded table, while Laura received a japanned box. He also invited the Blackmore Vale artist John Thorne to come to Dorchester to paint family portraits, one each of himself and Julia, and perhaps of some of the children. The painter probably stayed at a local inn. An alcoholic and not entirely reliable, Thorne might have been a difficult customer to manage within the confines of a boarding school. A few years later, he drank himself to death.

Lessons at Hawkins took place in the new red-brick, slate-clad schoolroom at the back that Barnes had designed himself. It proved so satisfactory that this 'temporary' structure was not demol-ished until 1952. Above the fireplace was painted a passage from his own poem, 'The Church an' Happy Zunday':

Ah! ev-ry day mid bring a while
O' ease vrom all woone's care an' tweil,
The welcome evenen, when t'is sweet
Vor tired friends wi'weary veet
But litsome hearts o' love, to meet…[3]

The main part of the house was restricted to domestic purposes. At this time it accomodated twenty-eight boarders, five staff and nine members of the family. Fortunately, Barnes could now afford greater help from ushers, which allowed him more time for his writing. This took place in the little study he had fitted out at the top of the house, in which he had installed a coke stove. On one occasion it was nearly the end of him. By chance, Julia went up there to consult him only to discover her husband unconscious from the fumes. She got him out just in time.

What with his school, church duties and his role as secretary to the museum, he was kept busy in the autumn of 1851. He also had some extra calls on his time that year, for while he was away at Cambridge a number of his fellow clergy, such as Fred Urquhart, had helped by covering for him at Whitcombe. Now it was payback time and he found himself taking services at other local churches. Yet he still found the leisure to become Chairman of the Dorchester Total Abstinence Campaign.

The new term proved difficult. In August, what was called the 'fever' was sweeping the town, and a number of the boys went down with it. It was cholera.[4] Soon more boys became ill, some with measles and others with an unidentified fever. Then one boy died. Throughout this time, Julia and her daughters stoically attended the sick boys and kept things going. Things got still worse. Laura went down with a fever, so the Barneses were obliged to call in Mrs Stickland from Sturminster Newton to act as resident nurse for a number of weeks. In September, Barnes himself became ill but the redoubtable Julia nursed him back to health.

*Above left:* Rear of Barnes's school at 40 South Street, Dorchester. (Dorset County Museum)

*Above right:* Julia Barnes, portrait by John Thorne, *c.* 1845. (Dorset County Museum)

Though she never complained, however, it became evident that she was very weary. Slowly, their situations were reversed and he began to look after her. Soon, her state of health concerned him so much that on 15 January 1852 he resigned the donative of Whitcombe after five years. The long walk out to the hamlet every Sunday was proving onerous and distracting at a time when he was increasingly concerned for Julia. He had to relieve her of her household duties so that she might rest quietly on Sundays.

In late April, she was obviously exhausted but would still not go to bed. Only on 3 May did she at last agree to see Dr Cowdell, who discovered what he referred to as 'an ulcer on the breast'. He was quite confident that he could cure it but, after nineteen days of painful blistering, he had to admit defeat and Sir Benjamin Brodie was called in. He immediately diagnosed breast cancer. The tumour, he said, was inoperable. Her case was hopeless. All he could add by way of comfort was that had he been called in earlier, it would have made no difference.

Nurse Dent was now in regular attendance for Julia. Barnes also spent much of his time upstairs by her bed, holding her hand while she smiled at him wistfully. On 5 June he resumed his Italian diary: 'Infelice, mia moglia malata'. But he still had to attend to his school duties. And though he rarely appeared in the classroom there were other obligations to be fulfilled. When almost overcome with grief, he was obliged to umpire cricket matches and accompany boys on their afternoon walks.

On 12 June, Julia's forty-seventh birthday, he presented her with a little inlaid table as a present. She could barely smile her thanks. On the 20th, a Sunday, he had to be away from home almost all day to honour an agreement made long before to take two services at Frampton. When he returned and rushed up to the sick-room he found her only just alive. The following morning she moved her lips slightly and whispered to Laura, 'A great change is coming'.

Monday 21 June 1852 was Midsummer's Day and a year since their happy trip to the Great Exhibition. But now the summer sunshine had turned black for him. That evening he made a diary entry, the anguish of which still resounds across the years:

Oh, day of overwhelming woe! That which I greatly dreaded has come upon me. God has withdrawn from me his choicest worldly gift. Who can measure the vastness of my loss? I am undone. My dearest Julia left me at 11.30 in the morning.

# 15

# BEREFT

—— 1852-1853 ——

William Barnes did not have a breakdown as a result of his wife's death. He could not afford to. But he came very close. Evidence of the toll it took on him may be deduced by contrasting John Thorne's portrait of 1846 with a photograph taken, probably by John Pouncy of Dorchester, in 1852, the year of Julia's death.[1] Thorne had depicted him as a smartly-dressed, clean-shaven schoolmaster, whose upright stance and benign expression suggests an active enthusiasm for his profession. Six years later the camera told a shockingly different story. Dressed in an old cassock and wearing a curious beret affair, Barnes slumps defensively, his eyes avoiding the camera. He has put on weight and his face is fringed with a straggly bit of beard, not yet entirely white. His look is reflective, severe, weary. It suggests a man in profound depression. Within a few short months, the once lively Mr Barnes, so full of life and cheerfulness, had metamorphosised into the figure whom, for years after, Dorchester people pityingly referred to as 'old Barnes of South Street'. Yet he was still only fifty-two.

There is no surviving account of Julia's funeral, but her interment took place in the tiny churchyard of St Peter's, alongside High West Street. There they stood, the mourners, men in stove-pipe hats with crape ribbons and women in their stiff, black bombasine, among them Barnes with his six children clustering around him. The health of Julia's mother, old Mrs Miles, was perhaps too fragile for her to be able to attend.

Shortly after the ceremony, family members and friends received a mourning card from the bereaved husband:

## Julia

My Julia, my dearest bride,
Since thou hast left my lonely side,
My life has lost its hope and zest.
The sun rolls on from east to west,
But brings no more the evening rest,
Thy loving kindness made so sweet,
And time is slow that once was fleet,
As day by day was waning.

The last sad day that show'd thee lain
Before me, smiling in thy pain,
The sun soar'd high along his way
To mark the longest summer day,
And showed to me the latest play
Of thy sweet smile, and thence, as all
The day's lengths shrunk from small to small,
My joy began its waning.

And now 'tis keenest pain to see
Whate'er I saw in bliss with thee.

The softest airs that ever blow,
The fairest days that ever glow,
Unfelt by thee, but bring me woe;
And sorrowful I kneel in pray'r,
Which thou no longer, now, canst share,
As day by day is waning...[2]

That the poem was written in standard English was probably because Barnes felt that the circumstances of the funeral demanded a more formal response than dialect would have permitted.

One small mercy afforded by the circumstances of Julia's death was that it took place during the
school vacation. The loss would have been even more unendurable to Barnes had it occurred during
term time, with small boys running about the place, laughing, shouting, and calling from the yard
below. The respite given by the holiday enabled him to retire to his study where he could give himself
over to the first paroxysms of grief, though very soon he was to find some solace in composing the
mourning card. For while these verses measured the depth of his desolation, in the very act of writing
them he gave a sign that his instinctive response was to be creative and imaginative. Even so soon after
her death, he was able to derive a certain gloomy consolation from the conceit that Julia's last smile
came when the sun was at its zenith, and that the subsequent shortening of the days matched the
diminishing nature of his own happiness. To him, these parallels seemed more than concidental.

On Laura Liebe, now twenty-three, and Julia Eliza, twenty, would fall the heavy load their mother
had borne for years. Of the other children, Lucy was fifteen, Isabel was fourteen, William Miles was
twelve and the rather sickly Egbert was nine. They were all to be kept hushed so as not to disturb
their father. These, together with old Mrs Miles, made up the family. Others sleeping in included
Isaac Hann, the senior usher, and perhaps an assistant teacher to replace George Brown, who had
left at Easter. The household was completed by Jane Brown, the cook, and two live-in maids. The
handyman probably came in daily.

Though always an affectionate father, it appears that Barnes did not initially look to his children
for comfort. In the selfishness of grief, his impulse was to get away from everybody, to be left on
his own, so that he might indulge himself in memories of his wife without the intrusion of other
people. He needed to absorb the full calamity of his loss, and to meditate the history of their life
together. He shaped out his feelings in the dialect:

Barnes in the 1850s after
the death of his wife.
The photo is probably
by Pouncy. There is a
marked deterioration
in his appearance in
comparison with the
Thorne portrait of
1845. (Dorset County
Museum)

## The Wife A-Lost

Since I noo mwore do zee your feace,
Up steairs or down below,
I'll zit me in the lwonesome pleace,
Where flat-boughed beech do grow;
Below the beeches' bough, my love,
Where you do never come,
An' I don't look to meet ye now,
As I do look at hwome.

Since you noo mwore be at my zide,
In walks in zummer het,
I'll goo alwone where mist do ride,
Drough trees a-drippen wet;
Below the rain-wet bough, my love,
Where you did never come,
An' I don't grieve to miss ye now,
As I do grieve at hwome.

Since now bezide my dinner-bwoard
Your vaice do never sound,
I'll eat the bit I can avvword,
A-vield upon the ground;
Below the darksome bough, my love,
Where you did never dine,
An' I don't grieve to miss ye now,
As I at hwome do pine.

Since I do miss your vaice an' feace
In prayer at eventide,
I'll pray wi woone sad vaice vor greace
To goo where you do bide;
Above the tree an' bough, my love,
Where you be gone avore,
An' be a-waiten vor me now,
To come vor evermwore.[3]

In identifying here with the grief of a countryman, Barnes may well have been recollecting his own father, thirty-six years before. John Barnes had also been made a widower in his early fifties, and perhaps he too had preferred to be out in the fields rather than sitting gloomily at home.

In the first weeks after Julia's death, Barnes's friends did their best to distract him. Frederick Smith would call to play chess with him, a Mr L. took him for drives and the chaplain of the prison arranged little dinner parties for him. His sister-in-law, Elizabeth Thatcher, came over from Nailsea in September to stay for a while, and then took two of the younger ones back with her for a holiday.

Music was an especial comfort. On 27 October some of Barnes's friends arranged the first of a number of madrigal evenings to amuse him. His hosts were talented musicians. One of them, Thomas Patch, subsequently became organist at Wells Cathedral and later at St Peter's in Dorchester. Lucy Baxter remembers his bass voice rolling out 'Oh ruddier than a cherry', and Purcell's 'Mad Tom'. By contrast, the girls secretly agreed that George Arden, a 'young surgeon', possessed a beautiful baritone.[4] The soprano voices of the two older Miss Barneses completed the little choir, and the musical talents of Julia Eliza were apparent to all. As for Barnes, Lucy recalls him in his armchair by the fire with his eyes shut, listening intently to 'Blow gentle gales' and 'When winds breathe soft'. And cast down though he was, his musical nature was so pronounced that even at that time of grief he could hardly resist joining in such pieces as 'Ye spotted snakes', though it might be anticipated that certain tender passages in the love songs would have proved upsetting to him.[5]

When not alone in his study, he contrived to be out of the house as much as possible as a relief from this 'forlorn' life. There were drives and walks, and he was eager to undertake services for his clerical friends. On a rare Sunday when he was not kept busy, he recorded in his diary, 'supp'd at Mr. S's; very sad. My sabbaths, which were so happy with J. at my side, are now my saddest days'.

One distraction was in collecting old paintings. Barnes's friend, John Pouncy, encouraged and advised him in this, and the new hobby kept him busy and helped to stem the flow of melancholy thoughts. So he began to venture in to the recesses of dark little shops to poke about for bargains. Afterwards, he would spend hours cleaning up his purchases and reframing them. He is said to have had a good eye and that he identified and acquired work by a number of past masters, including those of Gainsborough and Richard Wilson.[6]

Now, for the first time since he was a boy when his inn-sign was the talk of Bagber, he tried his hand again at painting. With his palette-box slung from his shoulder, he would walk in the woods to discover a picturesque scene. Having found one, he would settle down to make a watercolour record of it – in a rather slapdash way if we are to believe his daughter Lucy. The results were not a success. She thought that the sketches he made at this time were 'low and melancholy in tone and colour', depicting nature at her saddest, which is not to be wondered at.[7]

The real test of his resolution came in mid-July when the school reopened and twenty or so lively young boarders came whooping back. He had dreaded it. How was he to endure it all, their animal high spirits and shouts of reunion, the allocation of rooms, the heaving of trunks upstairs, the laying out of their clothes, the ordering of dining places and the tedious checking that each scholar had brought with him the requisite knife, fork and spoon, together with six towels? These were the routine matters which Julia had managed for many years. And afterwards he was required to greet the assembled school and announce the arrangements for the morrow when the day boys would come in. How could he face it? Yet he had to. The school was his only source of income. As a father of six, he could not afford to fail.

Older pupils would have noticed changes from the first day of school just a year before. Then they were welcomed by the bustling and maternal Mrs Barnes; now they were greeted by Miss Laura and Miss Julia, who did not seem entirely sure of what to do. When in doubt the girls had to refer to old Mrs Miles, who seemed the only one to have the answer to the many practical problems that arose. As for the schoolmaster himself, he seemed quiet and withdrawn. Classroom directions were mostly given by Mr Hann.

What became slowly apparent to the more perceptive boys was that with the death of Mrs Barnes, the heart had gone out of the enterprise. The success of this small private school had always been built on the partnership between the two of them. She had supplied the practical domestic skills and the talents needed in dealing with parents; he had provided scholarship, an extraordinarily wide curriculum and a unique talent for teaching. Now that the partnership had ended, there was no way in which her role could be replicated. Certainly, her daughters could not do it. Moreover, Barnes's vocation for his profession had come to an end. He could still teach well, and he was just as conscientious as before, but he could not disguise the fact that he had lost his enthusiasm for it.

A great weight of responsibility now fell on the two older girls. Laura, in particular, had no choice but to become the substitute mother to her younger siblings. Furthermore, she and Julia Eliza were expected to run the house and manage the school as well. All the work of shopping, planning menus, nursing sick pupils, dealing with tradesmen and washerwomen, mending clothes and superintending staff was now down to them. They hated it.

This was partly because they both had ambitions to lead wider lives. Laura was pious, and there had been some talk of her entering a religious order or, by contrast, of studying painting abroad. Julia Eliza had high hopes of a musical career. What were to become of these plans? They hardly dared to think. Their youth seemed to have ended abruptly with the death of their mother and their prospects had entirely changed. There seemed now nothing for them to look forward to but a life of unending drudgery, helping their bereaved father to run a provincial school. To make matters worse, the atmosphere in the house was so gloomy that they hardly ever dared to appear light-hearted or to enjoy a little innocent fun. For all that, they were dutiful and affectionate girls and genuinely wanted to comfort him, even to the extent of sharing in his scholarly enthusiasms. Laura's diary entry for 11 February 1853 reads: 'Julia's birthday. Julia, on this day, with much perseverence, completed her task – that of being able to read and translate three chapters in the Greek Testament, and for a reward father intends to teach her Hebrew today'.[8]

At every opportunity, Barnes left the class to the care of Hann and retired to his study, as far away as possible from the high spirits of his pupils. He would go up there whenever he could, to lose himself in a reverie, revisiting in memory his life with Julia. Especially vivid were recollections of their early days when, despite her father's prohibition, he had courted her along the river banks. He was an eighteen-year-old impecunious lawyer's clerk, and she just a very young girl. When he reached for his pen to record that time, however, once again his poetic imagination transferred the scene from Dorchester to Blackmore, from the Frome to the Stour, and his memories of Julia became absorbed into those of his earlier life. In a poem written about this time, he reinvented the first occasion on which he had caught sight of her. Rather than stepping down from a stagecoach, she was depicted sitting in a boat. But the emotional effect upon him was just as powerful:

## The Bwoat

Where cows did slowly seek the brink
O' Stour, drough zunburnt grass, to drink;
Wi' vishen float, that there did zink
An rise, I zot as in a dream.
The dazzlen zun did cast his light
On hedgerow blossom, snowy white,
Though nothen yet did come in zight
A-stirren on the strayen stream.

Till, out by sheady rocks there show'd
A bwoat along his foamy road,
Wi' thik feair maid at mill, a-row'd
Wi' Jeane behind her brother's oars.
An' steately as a queen o'volk
She zot wi' floaten scarlet cloak,
An' comen on, at every stroke,
Between my withy-sheaded shores.

The broken stream did idly try
To show her sheape a-riden by,
The rushes brown-bloom'd stems did ply,
As if they bow'd to her by will.
The rings o' water, wi' a sock,
Did break upon the mossy rock,
An gi'e my beaten heart a shock,
Above my float's up-leapen quill.

Then, lik' a cloud below the skies,
A-drifted off, wi' less'nen size,
An' lost, she floated vrom my eyes,
Where down below the stream did wind;

An' left the quiet weaves woonce mwore
To zink to rest, a sky-blue'd vloor,
Wi' all so still's the clote they bore,
Aye, all but my own ruffled mind.[9]

('sock' – shock; 'a-drifted' – she drifted; 'clote' – the yellow water lily, nuphar lutea)

Though she had indeed floated from his eyes, his imagination was already busy transmuting that loss into art.

Throughout the ensuing months and years, she was never far from his thoughts. On 19 May 1853, he noted in his diary: 'Sad for my dearest wife'. On the 28th: 'Heavy-hearted for my astounding loss'. On the first anniversary of her death: 'This day twelvemonths I began this diary. Oh, day of sorrow! which has lasted until now'. For years after he would frequently end each day's entry in his diary simply with her name, 'Giulia', written, as his daughter said, 'like a sigh'.[10]

Christmas 1852 at South Street was a subdued affair. And it was soon followed by a new anxiety. Old Mrs Miles fell ill. Born Isabella Leader, she was eighty-one years old and had been an invaluable member of the Barnes household since she had first joined it at Mere twenty years before. For much of her time with them, she had taken charge of the catering in their various schools, and had continued to do so even until quite recently. Then, after Julia's death, she had become for Laura and Julia Eliza a unique source of practical advice and help in their running the establishment. But now her health rapidly deteriorated. She died on 23 February 1853. As a result, an even greater weight of responsibility fell on the two older girls. Thoughtlessly perhaps, their father confided to them, 'I sink a step lower in sadness'.

# 16

# THE LANGUAGE OF MANKIND

—— 1852-1854 ——

It was work that saved him. However, it was not work which was commercially advantageous. Barnes was never much of a businessman and did not know how to go about recruiting pupils. As far as he was concerned, the education he offered was to be judged on its merits, and promoted chiefly by word of mouth. Julia would have understood that this was not enough, but he was oblivious to all such considerations. No, it was into poetry and academic work that he now put most of his creative energy. He still wrote poetry but because of the quarrel with George Simonds it was not published. From time to time he would put another manuscript in a drawer, and there the poems lay.

In July 1852, he received a disturbing letter from his London publisher. John Russell Smith reported that he had had difficulty in getting hold of copies. For an unknown reason, the printer, George Clark, had given up trading and the remaining unsold copies of the second edition of *Poems of Rural Life* had been sent to the auction room, presumably to be knocked down for a derisory sum. Of the (probably) 500 copies, 402 were left. Russell Smith advised that all remaining stock should be put into his keeping. Barnes replied at once giving the necessary authorisation. In September he received a letter from the hapless Clark himself, apologising for what had happened, explaining why his own efforts to contact Barnes had been frustrated and confirming that Russell Smith was now in possession of the whole stock, for which the printer hoped 'a speedier sale' than of late.[1]

Meanwhile, Russell Smith had again written to say that he was starting a new quarterly to be entitled the *Retrospective Review*, the first issue of which was to come out that October. Barnes was invited to contribute. The *Review* had been founded principally to research Early English manuscripts. Modern authors were banned, as were controversial religious topics. The last pages of each issue were to be devoted to the printing of previously unpublished manuscripts in Anglo-Saxon, Norman or Early English.

Barnes jumped at the chance. This was all very much his sort of thing, and it was not difficult for him to find suitable material. Even better was the fact that he was to be paid. The rate was £2 10s for an article of sixteen octavo pages, of which at least one third was to be of original composition rather than quotation. This was not an insignificant consideration because, worryingly, his school roll was falling and any extra income came in useful. Of course, he might have been better advised to spend his time hobnobbing with prospective parents in Dorchester, but he was too shy and academic a man for this to come easily and, moreover, he had a lifelong distaste for commercial dealings. On the other hand, parents learning of his articles might well have thought that the schoolmaster would have done better attending to the needs of their boys rather than shutting himself up to write articles about musty manuscripts.

Fortunately, he already possessed a small collection of these, from which he furnished copy for the *Review*. He recycled articles that had appeared elsewhere, such as those on Eburne's 'Plaine Pathway to Plantations' and the diary of John Richards. A copy of Joseph Glanvill's *Vanity of Dogmatizing* (1665) in his possession supplied another article, while the madrigal songsheets passed round by his friends at their impromptu concerts were also subjected to his critical comments.[2]

Yet this was mere journeywork. His great project, started just a few months after Julia's death, was the *Philological Grammar*. He always believed that even more than his poems, it was his crowning achievement. Certainly, it is one of the most extraordinary books of the nineteenth century. It is also pretty well unreadable. But Barnes believed in the book because he had put so much of himself into it. Enormous in scholarship and profound in argument, the *Grammar* was his vindication, the absolute proof of his abilities. It also revealed a breathtaking and apparently limitless intellectual ambition. Though in all personal matters Barnes was essentially a modest man, he was never overawed by scholarly orthodoxy. Apart from theology, he recognised no field of rational enquiry to which he might not make a contribution.

His subject here was language, considered from the most fundamental standpoint. Lucy Baxter later explained the origins of the book:

> William Barnes had been led to the design through the readings of many years. It dawned upon him when he began, in the days at Chantry, to compare Anglo-Saxon with English, and in Abergavenny, when he was so struck with the purity of Welsh. It grew upon his mental view when he discovered that the same laws of case ruled the fourteen different languages he had studied at Mere, when he wrote his pamphlet. Then he began to investigate further rules of grammar and wider laws, when his leisure time at Cambridge threw open to him the treasures of the University library, and he studied that polyglot list of books. The more he studied philology the more he felt sure that the science of grammar would be simplified by a clearly expressed epitome of these rules which are found in all tongues…[3]

Probably no major English poet ever pondered the nature of language as deeply as Barnes did here. His book was an examination not merely of English, but of the basic grammatical principles common to all languages, and he believed that he had discovered them. One is reminded of Edward Casaubon in *Middlemarch*, with his search for the key to all mythologies. There, however, the comparison ends, because Casaubon never completed his work, whereas Barnes finished his book in about a year. It came out in the spring of 1854, price 9s, published, as usual, by the long-suffering John Russell Smith. According to the title page, the argument was: 'Grounded upon English, and formed from a comparison of more than sixty languages, being An Introduction to the Science of Grammar, and A Help to Grammars of All Languages'.[4]

In the 'Preface', Barnes argues that, 'if we would make Grammar truly worthy… we must seek to conform it to the universal or to some common laws of speech, so as to make it the science of the language of mankind, rather than the Grammar of one tongue'. To which the reader might reasonably enquire how this could be. After all, humankind has invented innumerable languages and they are all different, with their own vocabularies and grammatical conventions. How could one grammar describe them all? A partial response is provided by the author's proud list of the sixty-seven languages on which the book drew in order to illustrate his arguments. These included not only classical and modern European tongues, but also such exotics as: 'Illyric, Sanscrit, Mongolian, Arabic, Finnic, Magyar, Cree, Chippeway, Greenlandish, Japanese, Malay, Maori, Hawish of Hawaii, Bisaya of the Philippine Islands, Tonga [and] Kafir'. He knew what he was writing about.

Lucy wrote that on first opening the book, 'one feels in a strange land'.[5] This is partly because Barnes illustrated his grammatical observations with hundreds of examples taken from many languages. A brief glance at any page reveals that this is no conventional grammar, but one whose writer has meditated the nature of language at a fundamental level. He begins from first principles, with concise, enumerated statements that follow one from the other. His tone is that of a patient, elementary schoolmaster who is struggling to make deep matters as clear as day:

1. Grammar is the science of speech.

2. Speech is the formation and utterance of breathsounds, by which men communicate thoughts to one another.

3. Breathsounds of language may be either pure breathsounds, or clipped or articulate breathsounds.

Yet even here, at the beginning, he has complicated matters (though, to be fair, he would argue he was simplifying them) by Saxonising his vocabulary. Most readers would have been puzzled by such unfamiliar terms as 'breathsounds' and 'clippings', by which he meant vowels and consonants. True, much of the book is still expressed in the customary grammatical terminology, as in the headings of the sections on 'Orthography', 'Etymology', 'Syntax' and 'Prosody', but here, for the first time in one of his philological books, he combines them with his own peculiar version of Saxon terms. This endows the text with a distinct oddity. And pressing the case for 'purity' in English, he repeats his now familiar attack on the 'slavery' to foreign expressions exhibited by the genteel speech of his own day. Rather than 'hieroglyphics', 'braille' and 'euphemism', he argues that we should say 'sight-speech', 'finger-speech' and 'name-changing'. 'Exaggerate', 'programme' and 'flexible', could be replaced by 'greaten', 'foredraught' and 'bendsome'.[6]

The section on 'Orthography' is just as radical. From a consideration of the anatomical operations involved in speech, he goes on to categorise its sounds: 'The clipped breathsounds of the English language are made by motions of the organs of speech, embodied with 16 pure breathsounds, as there are in English 16 voicesounds, 8 long and short, 8 close and 8 open'.[7] Current spelling practice, he rejects; because of its 'looseness and untruthfulness', it is often not an accurate representation of the spoken word. This is the schoolmaster talking. Having for years tried to teach spelling to little boys, he was well aware of confusions caused by 'the k clipping of knave, knife, knocker, know; or the gh clipping in bright, fight, high, light, plough, right; or the l clipping in should, would'. Cautiously, he advocates a degree of spelling reform and also helpfully reproduces Pittman's phonetic alphabet.

What prompted the writing of this book were the many resemblances in word formation that Barnes discovered in his study of languages. These suggested to him that beneath apparent linguistic differences, there was a basic sub-structure to all language. Furthermore, at a time when many peoples throughout the world were dismissed by his fellow Victorians as 'primitive', the notion accorded with his humane ideas that all languages, and therefore all people, were valuable. In a small way, this obscure clergyman was working to reverse the catastrophe of Babel by rediscovering the common language of mankind. It was a noble endeavour.

It is the section on 'Etymology', or word formation, which is at the heart of his project. What he needed to show was that there were general rules for linguistic construction in all languages. To do this, he resorted to symbolism to represent verbal units. For example, a noun is 1, an adjective 2, and a verb 3, and and ★ an unspecified syllable. Armed with this notation, he now attempted to reduce the principles of language to what looked rather like a form of algebra. For example:

In Latin the form of this noun is (2+★do), (2+igo), (2+a), (2+monium), (2+itudo), (2+★tas), (2+itia), (2+ies), (2+or).

| | | | | |
|---|---|---|---|---|
| dulcedo | rubigo | scientia | duritia | sanctimonium |
| parcimonium | lassitudo | longitudo | aegritudo | altitudo |
| coecitas | capacitas | durities | aequor | calor.[8] |

If Barnes's readers were not frightened to death by this, they were unlikely to be reassured by his attempts at explanations:

In the construction of expression for the formations of compound words, we may betoken by a dot a breathsound which is not now a word in itself; so that (1+.) would be the form of a word compounded of a noun-root and such breath-sound afterset to it, as 'manly', 'golden'; and (2+.) and (3+.) would betoken such forms as, as those of 'whiteness' and 'runner'; (.+1) would betoken the form of 'ex-king'; and a figure with a dot over it might be taken as a mark of a word formed from a root with a breathsound or clipping set within it, as (3), which would betoken the form 'l-inm-acat', from the root 'lacat', to go, in Bisaya.[9]

Despite such obscurantism, Barnes persisted in maintaining that, in the final analysis, his system was more comprehensible than its rivals because it was closer to perceived reality. For example, he increased from six to twelve the cases of nouns familiar to Latin students. But in defending this apparently unnecessary complication, he argues that his categorisation accords more truthfully with 'the logical relations of things… in nature'. The complexity of the human experience of the world necessitates a certain grammatical structure. That was why he had increased the number of cases, as in:

266.    Case 8.-Locative Case

A thing named as the place of another or its predicate, is in a case which may be called the locative or 'where' case.

This case is classed in Latin under the ablative case-form, and in Greek under the dative; but in Russian and Bohemian it is mostly marked by a form called the propositional case-form. In Basque it is mostly marked by the case-ending – an; it is the commemorative case in Armenian, in which its ending is e; and it is the inessive of the Finnic and Syrjaen tongues, in which its case-ending is -yn, and ssa, ssa, issa, issa; while in Lapponic it is -esn or -en, and in Hungarian -ban,-ben. In Chinese its mark is a preposition 'iuu', as in 'Iu t'ang shang'; 'he sat in the hall'.[10]

The above is only part of one paragraph and there are 591 paragraphs in the 'Etymology' section alone. And so he proceeds for 312 pages, with detailed explanations and examples of word formation adduced and compared from a host of languages.

Perhaps only the final passages of the book, those devoted to verse form, have had a lasting significance, and this is chiefly because of the light they throw on the author's poetic technique. For here Barnes offers a uniquely informed study of the subject drawn from many languages. Few poets have devoted a greater consideration to this topic than he did. In the passages on prosody he discusses such matters as the effect of syllable length in Latin and Greek verse, vowel emphasis in Anglo-Saxon and Teutonic poetry, and accentuation in Spanish, Irish and Welsh, together with the effect of various rhyme schemes in 'Persian, Kafir, Italian, Spanish, and Portuguese poetry', as well as many others. Here we observe the workings of the Welsh clipping-rhyme or 'cynghanedd', the Persian 'tujnis-i-mokurer' and Hebrew parallel line techniques. In commenting on Barnes's verse, Thomas Hardy once wrote that though he was 'primarily spontaneous, he was academic closely after; and we find him warbling his native wood-notes wild with a watchful eye on the predetermined score, a far remove from the popular impression of him as a naif and rude bard who sings only because he must'.[11] Hardy is right. It is the resultant combination of artful verse-patterning and dialect, the mix of the scholarly and the demotic, that is the unmistakable mark of Barnes's verse, and it is in the *Philological Grammar* that the linguistic sources of his art are revealed.

If he never truly expected others to follow him in pursuit of the universal language chimera, he was not disappointed. Lucy loyally claimed that 'the author had… so reduced the study of grammar to general rules, that [the student] could win, with the help of a dictionary for the root words, to learn to read or write a foreign language in a few weeks'. But there is no record of anyone ever doing so. Indeed, it seems probable that no one at all except Lucy ever tried to work through the copious and labyrinthine explanations in the *Philological Grammar*. As for Barnes's declared intention to aid the study of languages, this was obviously unrealistic. A reader would already need to know a good many languages in order to profit from the innumerable comparisons between them. A young linguist would have been far better off getting to grips with the actual languages than attempting to master Barnes's commentary on them, which only served to introduce a 'long linguistic confusion' into the learning process.

In his heart, Barnes knew that this book would not revolutionise the teaching of languages. It might be reckoned, therefore, that in writing the *Philological Grammar* he exhibited an obstinate indifference to the patience of the reading public and wilfully wasted his own time and talent. It was not so. For the truth is that he wrote the book to please himself. And because he had to. It was an answer to his inner needs. Sitting alone at night in his little study, his desk littered with dictionaries, lexicons and the notes he had made long before in the library of St John's College, for a short while he could forget the petty vexations of every day, as well as his grief.

There was, moreover, an intellectual pleasure in it all. Barnes was a system builder, and wanted to try whether the mass of notions concerning language which had come crowding into his mind over many years might be organised into a coherent whole. Having believed, after the death of Julia, that he would never experience joy again, the completion of this curious book seems to have given him an uncharacteristic flash of intellectual pride and, importantly, self-vindication. Such a book would surely silence those petty snobs in Dorchester who still muttered that the publication of his dialect poems was clear evidence that the schoolmaster was reverting to his ignorant social origins.

How was the book received? With respectful neglect. There were one or two reviews. The *Phonetic Journal* described him as 'an able advocate of the phonetic representation of language' and added that 'his handsome volume is such a contribution to English literature as is not made above once in a generation'.[12] And the *Edinburgh Review* commented that 'Mr Barnes's work is an excellent specimen of the manner in which the advancing study of Philology may be brought to illustrate and enrich a scientific exposition of English Grammar'. All of which suggests that reviewers were baffled by it and had given it no more than a perfunctory inspection. No doubt the algebraic appearance of some of the pages frightened many of them off. If so, they deserve sympathy. The great number of grammatical points and illustrative examples often makes the argument intellectually indigestible. At best it is a book to be dipped into.

Yet what an extraordinary performance it is! Almost every page reveals a wealth of insights and a vast knowledge of different tongues. It is also a supreme intellectual achievement by an obscure provincial scholar working alone. Far from the universities, the learned societies and the intellectual centres of the nation, Barnes had laboured at this forgotten masterpiece. In other circles, a man might have been awarded a university chair for such a performance, but after a brief look at his book, academia nodded and turned away.

The manuscript of the *Philological Grammar* was sent to the publisher in the middle of 1853. Throughout the following year, Barnes was occupied with correcting the very complicated proofs. Eventually, on 24 February 1854, he received the first copy from the printer. Russell Smith had guessed, probably correctly, that it was a loss-making deal, but generously offered £5 for the copyright. Barnes took it.

# 17

# RADICAL SHIFT

—— 1853-1859 ——

A widower with young children has no option in life but to soldier on. In the decade following Julia's death, William Barnes did just that, but these were the most difficult years of his life. They were especially marked by a decline in the fortunes of his school and the increasing radicalisation of his opinions. And the two were linked.

Painfully aware that without meaning to, he seemed to have inflicted a life of drudgery upon his eldest girls, by way of a reward for their help he took them for a few days holiday to the Isle of Wight in July 1853. Sixteen-year-old Lucy, meanwhile, was away from home, probably staying with the Mileses in Nailsea. So when Barnes got back, he wrote to tell her about their holiday. And ponderous and forced though his humour might be at times, the letter reveals just how hard he tried to keep his children cheerful:

MY VERY DEAR L.

I am very happy to find that you are enjoying yourself so highly, though I am most bewildered with the thoughts of your pleasures, past, present, and anticipated. Your dances on the green, and frolics in other places, blowings of cornopeans, squeaking of flutes! tweedling of fiddles! Laughings of girls! glee singings! hoppings, skippings, and jumpings! Oh, it makes me quite giddy to think it all!

Your sisters will tell you of our trip, and how we saw the Princess Royal swimming in the sea, and went on board the Victory, and how I stood up where Nelson fell – am I not a great man![1]

It was probably money worries that restricted them to a holiday at home the following year, so the family stayed in Dorset and went on outings. On 29 June, they were all up by five o'clock for an early breakfast before climbing into the carriage which was to take them to Barnes's old home in Blackmore. In her diary, Lucy recorded this 'memorable day', when under clear skies and a 'brilliant' sun, the carriage drove the thirty-odd miles through birdsong before entering 'the vale of sunny slopes, shady lanes, woody dells, picturesque trees and rivulets – not forgetting the cottages which are scattered about'.[2] The young Barneses had always regarded Blackmore as their ancestral home, but although they had glimpsed that landscape in their father's poems, none of them had ever been there. Each sight was familiar yet new.

At Sturminster they let the carriage go and began their walk across Bagber Common. Lucy was dismayed to discover the 'new, stiff straight road' now built across it and the ugly brick houses adjoining. On the site of her father's birthplace, she was even more disappointed to find not an ancient farmhouse, but a modern brick villa. It was only when the road gave way to a lane overshadowed with elm trees that she felt that she had entered Eden. Walking ahead, Barnes pointed out to his children the settings of some of his poems: the house of 'Poll's Jack Da' (Jackdaw), the 'Haunted House', and the 'Girt Wold House of Mossy Stwone'. Then at last they came to the banks of the Liddon, with its bridge and the water lillies in bloom. Beyond this was Pentridge Farm, where as a boy Barnes had played with his Rabbets cousins. Here, the farmer came out to greet them and insisted that they walk in and taste his cider.

Eventually, they came to one of Barnes's own fields, with a 'dear little brook' running through it. Here they sat eating their sandwiches until the rain came on. So they sheltered under a hedge for a while, but when the downpour got heavier they ran under an elm tree and 'sang glees and danced' until it was over. From there, they walked along a winding path to Newton and on into Sturminster, where they dined on a large pike caught in the River Stour. Afterwards they looked into the church and inspected 'the very font' at which Barnes was christened. The appearance of their celebrated poet among them seems to have gone unnoticed by the inhabitants of 'Stur', save for one man, aged about sixty, who ran after them to tell them that his grandmother was dead. Afterwards, they had tea with their friends the Colbourns, and at seven o'clock set off homewards in the carriage.

Such days were exceptional. There were few excitements that term, though the school routine was relieved on one occasion by the visit of an ex-pupil, Major C.V. Cox, who enthralled the boys with stories of his sixteen years service in India. Seeking further interests, Barnes now became the Appeal Secretary to the St Peter's Church Restoration Fund, where he was assisted by an able young barrister named Frederick Cosens. Another diversion was provided by his growing interest in the antiquities of the county. Soon, his local knowledge was freely offered to the archaeologist Charles Warne, who was in process of compiling his illustrated map of Dorsetshire.[3] Warne became a close friend and invited Barnes to stay for a few days at his home in Milborne St Andrew, but an unfortunate occurrence prevented this.

That autumn there was a fresh outbreak of cholera in Dorchester occasioned by convicts having been housed in the town barracks. Despite Barnes's attempts to quarantine his pupils, one became ill. The infection proved to be rheumatic fever, but the lad had to be sent home. Soon it became advisable to send all the boys away for the Christmas holidays. This was a blow to the school and to Barnes's income. Even worse was the fact that he himself became seriously unwell. He had contracted erisypelis, or St Anthony's fire, which resulted in high fevers and deep red blotches on his skin. While assisting the boys in their packing, Laura also had to nurse her father. He got worse. Nights of pain were accompanied by high temperatures, gout and blood-poisoning. It was articular rheumatism. And strong though his constitution was, the illness left an alarming legacy.

On 18 December he dictated a reply to Warne, explaining his predicament:

> My Dear Sir, I write to you by an amanuensis, for your kind letter found me on a sick bed from an attack of Erisypelas and rheumatism in the hands and feet and I am now on my back with my right hand swollen into a lumpy fist which is a very unhandy writing machine. Gladly will I take the pleasure of spending two or three days with you if I can effect it but I cannot at present say when I shall be free.

The damage done to his hand by the rheumatism proved permanent. It meant giving up any attempt at painting and drawing; even writing was difficult. Lost forever was that beautiful copperplate which had once secured him a job as a solicitor's clerk. It deteriorated into a scrawl; characteristic, but often barely legible, so that correspondents were obliged to puzzle out his manuscripts. A friend, Charles Tennant, wrote to him some years later:

> It has taken me two days to make out Cincinatus in your last letter and but for those five acres of yours in the Vale of Blackmore I never should have made it out… But I like your handwriting because it is like your own and unlike anybody's else. It puts me in mind of a fly escaped from drowning in a bottle of ink and crawling over your paper…[4]

By the New Year of 1855 he was well enough to spend a week or two with Warne in London, where they visited the British Museum and the National Gallery, called on an official of the Society of Antiquaries and attended a meeting of the Syro-Egyptian Society. Enjoying such company provided Barnes with an intellectual stimulus, but once again anxious parents concluded that his interests were anywhere other than in his school. Besides, he had let himself go, so that such absences, together with his shabby appearance, suggested that he had no respect for Dorchester notions of what was seemly in a clergyman and schoolmaster. This impression was now enforced by a new activity.

Over the years, a number of letter-writers to the conservative *County Chronicle* had expressed their opposition to the working mens' institutes that were opening round the county. Their arguments were familiar. The education of the working classes, it was claimed, was misplaced and possibly dangerous. The working man (it was always a man) who was taught to read and think would become dissatisfied with his lot. He was likely to lose interest in his work, argue with his employer and perhaps agitate for a change in the social structure. Such men were dangerous.

Despite these objections, there were some gentlemen and employers who encouraged the movement. These included William and Thomas Colfox, who had supported the formation of the Bridport Mechanics' Institute in 1831; William Charles Macready, the retired actor; and later the Reverend Nares Hennings at Sherborne. From the first, Barnes was an enthusiastic supporter. In 1851 and '52 he accepted invitations to lecture to working men in Weymouth and Sturminster Newton, his chosen subject being the Anglo-Saxons. And though there was still no institute in Dorchester, in 1853 he enthusiastically contributed to a lecture programme at the County Museum with a talk on 'Light and Heat', based upon his school science lectures, following it up with another on political economy entitled 'Labour and Gold'.

In 1855, he learned that some young men in Dorchester were trying to form a 'Working Men's Mutual Improvement Society'. Always acutely conscious that he had himself only narrowly avoided a life of manual labour with a 'dearth of mental stimulation', he stepped forward at once to help them. Soon he was averaging about eight to ten lectures a year to working-class audiences in the town, charging no fee. This did not go down well with some of the parents. It seemed to them that Barnes had transferred his allegiance from their sons to the working men. While they were paying good money for him to educate their children, he was expending his time and energy in giving education away free to labourers. One commentator has described it as 'professional suicide'.

Then came further occasions when the school had to be closed due to illness. Frequently scholars would leave for the holidays and never return. The knock-on effect meant that Barnes could not afford as much help in the classroom as previously. Ushers did not come cheap. And though he could still rely on the faithful Isaac Hann, he admitted in a letter to Warne that he was now occupied 'six days in the week of school work, and clerical work on the seventh'. Exhausted and overworked, he was caught in a downward spiral. Unsurprisingly, the number of pupils was steadily diminishing and his income falling. This came at the very time when he most needed money to educate his own children.

By 1855, Laura Barnes was twenty-seven, with much of her young womanhood already drained away in menial work for the school. Her hopes of becoming an artist of some kind had been abandoned because she was needed at home. Selfishly, her siblings took it for granted that she would not marry but would always look after their father. By contrast, Julia Eliza was still determined to undertake a singing career but she needed further training, possibly abroad. Lucy, now eighteen, was a dreamy, imaginative girl, interested in art and just starting a novel. Seventeen-year-old Isabel was the least talented but the most attractive of all the sisters. There seemed a good chance that she at least would marry, perhaps to a local tradesman who could keep her in comfort. As for the boys, Barnes had already decided, come what may, that William Miles, then fifteen, would follow him to St John's College. Egbert, still only twelve, was already revealing a marked interest in mechanical matters. Barnes was determined that his children should have their chances, but where was the money to be found?

Meanwhile, he resumed his Persian lessons with Major Besant, continued his reading in Hindustani and kept a diary in Spanish. And once more he applied to Cambridge University, to be allowed to take his doctorate, though it is difficult to see how he could have coped with the extra workload. Fortunately for him, he was turned down. Unable now to paint, he made up for it by theorising about colours. Nature, he maintained, never makes a mistake. To test his theories, he would collect leaves, mosses, fruits and flowers, and group them together to try the visual effect, concluding that in nature strong colours rarely touched each other. He published his conclusions in the *Art Journal*.[5] In later years, the colours of his book-bindings were chosen to conform to his views. So were the colours of his daughters' frocks, though what they thought about it may only be imagined.

The summer holidays this year he spent inexpensively by accepting invitations to stay with local antiquarians. He visited Osmington and Glanville's Wooton, and also Stourton Caundle, where he was entertained by an elderly lady (name unknown) at her large country house. Her drawing room was hung with portraits by Lely and Reynolds, and in what she called her 'book-room', he discovered texts with intriguingly antique titles such as: *Ye Arte of Ingenyouslie Tormentynge* and *Tears from Ye Bottle of Jonas Mickelthwayte*.

On Michaelmas (29 September) 1855 came a dreadful blow. His trusted assistant, Isaac Hann, gave notice. It quickly became apparent that he intended to set up a rival school in Dorchester. Hann cannot be blamed. He had watched the slow decline of Barnes's business and had reason to fear for his own employment. He guessed correctly that when William Miles eventually graduated from Cambridge, his father intended that he would take over the school. In which case, Hann had to look to his own future. Having resigned, on 1 November he advertised in the *Chronicle* his 'Classical, Mathematical and Commercial School', to be opened after the Christmas vacation, offering English, French, Latin, Greek and mathematics, with the aim of preparing 'young gentlemen' for the universities, the military and naval colleges, and the various professions and trades. The house he had chosen was in Salisbury Terrace, not far from Barnes's. Significantly, he described his terms as 'moderate'. He was going to undercut his old employer. The confidence signalled by this notice proved well-founded. Within five years he had removed to a more prominent locale in North Square and taken on four assistant masters.[6] By contrast, Barnes's latest advertisement in the paper was a humble affair: 'Education, Dorchester, Professional and Other Courses. By W. Barnes B.D.'

Hann was not his only competitor. In 1850, the highly respected Isaac Glandfield Last kept a British School (Nonconformist) in Greyhound Yard. Three years later he removed to South Walks where he set up a 'commercial academy' for more advanced pupils. One of these was the fifteen-year-old Thomas Hardy, who received an excellent education there, including supplementary tuition in Latin. Last was strong on technical as well as classical learning and it was this, as well as lower fees, that probably induced Hardy's parents to prefer his academy to Dorchester Grammar School or William Barnes's.[7] Nor were the two Isaacs the end of Barnes's competitors, for there was also 'Mr. Watson's School for Young Gentlemen'. Furthermore, new schools were being opened even in smaller towns. Dorset boys could now be sent by rail to Sherborne, Poole, Weymouth, Bridport and even Taunton for their education.

Hann's defection was a cruel blow. The man had been a family friend as well as a colleague. But though Barnes refrained from publicly commenting on it, privately he was incapable of understanding how anyone could prefer financial advantage to the much greater rewards of friendship and trust. To him, personal disloyalty seemed like a self-contradiction, in that it was ultimately self-defeating. It discarded a greater good for a lesser. With a growing loathing of the commercial ethos of Victorian life, he wrote a poetic commentary on it, and in so doing invented a new proverb:

## Zellen Woone's Honey To Buy Zome'hat Sweet

Why, his heart's like a popple, so hard as a stwone,
Vor 'tis money, an money's his ho,
An' to handle an' reckon it up vor his own,
Is the best o' the jays he do know.
Why, vor money he'd gi'e up his lags an be leame,
Or would peart wi' his zight an' be blind,
Or would lose vo'ks good will, vor to have a bad neame,
Or his peace, an' have trouble o' mind.
But wi' every good thing that his meanness mid bring,
He'd pay vor his money,
An' only zell honey to buy zome'hat sweet.

He did whisper to me, 'You do know that you stood
By the Squier, wi' the vote that you had,
You could ax en' to help ye to zome'hat as good,
Or to vind a good pleace vor your lad'.
'Aye, aye, but if I wer beholden vor bread
To another', I zaid, 'I shoud bind
All my body an' soul to the nod ov his head,
An' gi'e up all my freedom o' mind'.

An' then, if my pain were a-zet wi' my gain,
I should pay vor my money,
An' only zell honey to buy zome'hat sweet.

No, be my lot good work, wi' the lungs well in play,
An' good rest when the body do tire,
Vor the mind a good conscience, wi hope or wi' jay,
Vor the body good lewth, an good vire,
There's noo good o' goold, but to buy what 'ull meake
Vor our happiness here among men;
An' who would gi'e happiness up vor the seake
o' zome money to buy it agean?
Vor 'twould zeem to the eyes ov a man that is wise,
Like' money vor money,
Or zellen woone's honey to buy zome'hat sweet.[8]

('popple' – pebble; 'ho' – care; 'lewth' – shelter; 'lags' – legs)

Fortunately, despite all his critics, rivals and misfortunes, Barnes could still count on the support of a number of parents who admired him for what he was: a teacher of exceptional ability and total integrity. Among these were his old friends the Frederick Smiths, who brought prestige to his school with their dancing lessons. They had now become the highly successful proprietors of a chain of dancing academies, with branches in Weymouth, Wimborne, Poole and Sherborne. Another Dorchester family which never flagged in its loyalty was that of the Locks, who over the years supplied him with three pupils, one of whom became a judge and another a professor of divinity at Oxford. Then there were influential county supporters such as the Dawson-Damers of Moreton House, who were grateful for Barnes's private tuition of their son, Seymour, who eventually became the Earl of Portarlington.

It was during the school vacations that Barnes sometimes found relief from his worries. At Christmas 1855, he was able to take a few days off and to pay a visit to Mere, probably visiting Chantry House, where he and Julia had started their school together. The following summer he visited the Mileses in Wales, and made a walking tour of the vales of the Taff and Neath. This was partly a working holiday because he wanted to renew his study of the language in preparation for a book he was to write on the Ancient Britons, whom he regarded as the ancestors of the Welsh people.

On Monday 23 February 1857, there came what Lucy called a 'white cross day'. That evening Barnes made a routine visit to the working men's institute in Dorchester to chair a debating class. After a 'very interesting discussion on dreams, clairvoyance, etc.' he was taken aback when one of the young men approached:

[and] presented to him a framed testimonial and a handsome pencil case. They spoke of his kindness in giving them lectures and instruction, and in encouraging their society when it was first begun, and looked down on by many people. One of the working men, named Cole, spoke wonderfully well, every word showing a refined mind and good feeling.

Barnes's reply came on the spur of the moment, but the words he then used were to have a lasting effect on his fortunes. On rising, he 'began by sympathising with them, and said that he himself was not nursed in the lap of luxury, but was *like themselves, a working man* [my italics] so he cheered them on the path they had chosen, of cultivating their minds and refining their tastes'.[9]

This single utterance revived the question of Barnes's social status. His new habit of consorting with working men had not gone unnoticed. It seemed to some that the focus of his interests had now moved from *The Gentleman's Magazine* to the working men's institutes. Moreover, the very same issue of *Kelly's Directory* which had listed him as a clergyman, and therefore one of the gentry, had confused the matter by also including him as a proprietor of a school among the tradesmen.

There was a *Chronicle* reporter present at the institute that night who had come to cover the presentation. But though he did not publish the exact words of Barnes's reply, word soon got round the town of what had been said. Nothing could have done more harm to his school. 'So much,' aggrieved parents might have complained, 'for the pretensions of the Revd William Barnes BD'. All that education, and all that time spent at Cambridge, could not really disguise the influence of his lowly origins. He had admitted it himself. He was still just a working man. How then, the question followed, was he fit to teach their boys to be young gentlemen? Not surprisingly, he failed to recruit a single middle-class pupil for the next two years.

Public misgivings were reinforced by some of his sermons. Previously, he had largely confined himself to conventional homilies expounding biblical texts and promoting brotherly love. But there were times when he could not refrain from condemning the iniquities of contemporary society. Such occasion came in September 1849, in a sermon at Whitcombe, during the cholera epidemic in Dorchester.[10] 'Why was this happening?' he asked. One cause was surely the overcrowding of people in hovels in order to make greater gain for the landlords. Were not such racketeers as much to be blamed for the contagion as the dirty people, the drunken husbands and lazy housewives? Well knowing that many of the worst hovels in the town were owned by the Duchy of Cornwall, his congregation would have understood who he was getting at.

As the years went by, Barnes became increasingly outspoken. In December 1856, Mayor Ensor of Dorchester invited him to join a panel to address a public meeting to protest about income tax. He had simply assumed that his assembled speakers would join the chorus to complain of the unfairness in the way that new taxes bore down on property owners and the middle classes generally. Ensor got more than he bargained for. Barnes took the side of wage earners because they did not have the advantage of avoiding tax by using expense accounts. In particular, he singled out the unfairness of businessmen who used these accounts for their own private expenditure. His remarks were greeted by silence.

In the following year came the Indian Mutiny. Discontented sepoys had captured Meerut prison and marched on Delhi. The garrison at Cawnpore was massacred in July, and the women and children captured. Such reverses shocked opinion in England so much that a Day of National Mourning was proclaimed for 15 October. It was intended to be observed in every parish church. When the day came, Barnes mounted the pulpit at St Peter's to tell the truth as he saw it. He had always considered imperialism to be inimical to Christianity. Now he let rip:

> This is the day for deep searching into our sins… Missionary work will never be done by the sword, nor by the sceptre, nor the civil power. They may make thousands of hypocrites, but no conversions. Do missionary work with a missionary spirit and not for our gain in an easier trade. Look at the power we hold in India – yet look at the evil that has arisen.

Imprisoned in their pews, the assembled dignitaries had to sit and listen to this tirade while phrases such as 'arrogantly boastful Englishmen', 'the nation going towards Mammon', 'missionary work with the sword' and 'our Satanic arguments' resounded round their ears. All this in a county town which acted as the prime recruiting area for the 39th of Foot (whose motto was *Primus in Indis*)! All this from the mild-mannered parson whom they had trusted to prepare local boys for the Indian service![11]

Undeterred, Barnes continued to devote much of his spare time to the education of working men. True to his familiar practice, he would give a series of lectures and then write them up as a textbook, as he did with his *Notes on Ancient Britain and the Britons*, published by John Russell Smith in 1858.[12] Simply because he had always believed in the importance of Barnes's work, this long-suffering man had brought out what he described as 'one abstruse book after another', expecting little immediate profit. Now, the best terms he could offer him were a few free copies. *Ancient Britain and the Britons* consisted largely of notes on the food of these people, their tattooing, clothes, houses, customs, bards, literature, etc. Characteristically, Barnes was concerned to refute the then conventional view that Britons were merely barbarians wrapped in furs. They were, he maintained, people of high culture. It was almost as if he were defending his Dorset labourers.

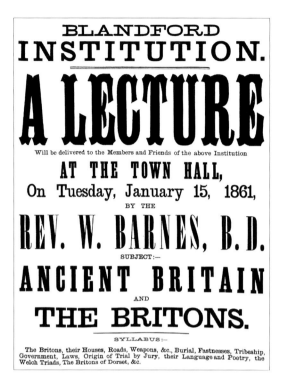

Poster for a lecture. (Dorset County Museum)

His next book was much more controversial. *Views of Labour and Gold* was a polemical foray into the dangerous and (for him) new territory of political economy.[13] The book was not much more than a disjointed collection of his lecture notes, yet there was a consistent theme running through it which was uniquely that of the author. It was unique because his views owed nothing to anyone else. Rather than drawing on the great authorities such as Adam Smith, Bentham, Malthus and Ricardo, he relied on cuttings from the newspapers and recycled passages from his own *Humilis Domus*, especially those concerning the desirability of small farms.

No politics or religion; that was the rule of the the working men's institutes. But Barnes was concerned not with party politics so much as the fundamental principles that govern society. Nevertheless, he was undoubtedly encouraging his students to make a critical analysis of the economic conventions under which they lived, and his conclusions were often radical and, some might have said, seditious. This was especially so because he espoused the labour theory of value just as wholeheartedly as John Locke or Karl Marx. 'Labour,' he insisted, 'is capital'. Though some might argue that supply and demand was the determinant of value, this was not so. For example, there was as great a demand in England for water as brandy, yet brandy was of more value. Nor was scarcity the measure: 'There is in England less weasel flesh than beef, and less badger quarters than quarters of mutton, and yet the commercial value of weasel flesh and badger joints is less than that of beef or mutton'. No. It was the amount of work required to produce goods that determined their value, and this was true even of money itself. Labour, he told his working men, was the product they brought to market.

Remembering how the little Blackmore 'farmlings' had been swallowed up by landowners, he argued that the victims of takeovers owed no thanks to those people who later offered them work: 'The kindness which is done by capital when it affords employment to people from whom, by monopoly, it has taken their little businesses, is such as one might do to a cock by adorning his head with a plume made of feathers pulled out of his tail'. He remembered how his own father had been reduced to the labouring class and placed entirely at the mercy of his employers. Such treatment often brought ominous results. For example, a pious labourer refusing to work on Sundays might well be subject to the 'circumstantial thralldom of anger of capital' and dismissed.

Some might have wondered whether Barnes was seeking to undermine the foundations of society with such teachings. He was not. Nowhere did he attack the Victorian social system itself. Throughout his life he retained a reverence for the gentry and aristocracy, provided that they fulfilled their 'higher' role in promoting the welfare of mankind. What he was doing was propounding 'a radical and pro-phetic vision of economic justice'.[14] It was not social structures, he argued, that determined the moral worth of a society, it was the motives and behaviour of individual men. 'It is often said', he wrote, 'that the interest of capital and labour are identical, and so in truth they are as long as they are kept so by Christian kindness'. Both employers and servants owed each other the duty of Christian love. It was this which justified their relationship. Mere profit making, which excused all kinds of inhumanity, could not be condoned. Nor should there be any need of union action to persuade employers to treat their workers well. Trade unionism and capitalism were two sides of the same coin. He rejected both and wished to replace them with an exalted notion of Christian love.[15] Of his near contemporaries it was, perhaps, only Tolstoy who preached a similar message.

*Labour and Gold* is not merely contentious in its opinions but decidedly odd in its expression. Barnes had his own vocabulary: 'By the social law of the All-wise, a man cannot win any unlimited quantity of another's labour for a given quantity of his own. Every man's labour is rated in the market by the labour that brings, or could bring, all kinds of life-gear against it'. His examples are equally eccentric, though they still give the book a certain curiosity value. Here we may learn that there were 100,000 workers in the Woolwich Arsenal during the Crimean War, that the inhabitants of the Philippines built their houses of Nipa grass and that the ancient Spartans liked to eat black pudding.

Predictably, the book provoked little comment save for a notice in the *Athenaeum* which observed that, 'The opinion of such a Scholar and Clergyman of the Established Church, on subjects of political economy, cannot fail to be both interesting and instructive'. Whether the reviewer had actually read the book was not clear. Its publication, however, did gain Barnes one new friend. A Mr Charles Tennant, a Liberal economist and sometime MP for St Albans, wrote in April 1859 to praise the book's 'Christian Philosophy'. His favourable review of the book eventually appeared in the *Financial Reformer*.

Not that it did Barnes much good, for his prose books were never such as to bring him much profit, and his finances continued to deteriorate. In April 1858 there was more sickness in the school and boys had to be sent home. One again, some never returned. Lucy remembered her father coming into the room one day with yet another letter from a parent withdrawing a pupil for no stated reason. 'What a mockery is life', he said. 'They might be putting up a statue to me some day when I am dead, while all I want now is to live. I ask for bread, and they give me a stone'.[16] Tradesmen he had dealt with for years now received his reduced orders or cancellations with disdain. Some snubbed him in the street.

Relief came in the summer vacation of 1858 when the Rector of Winterborne Came, the Rt. Hon. Revd George Lionel Dawson-Damer, asked Barnes to act as his locum for a few weeks. Only a few miles from Dorchester, the parish included the hamlet of Whitcombe where he had previously been pastor. Meeting his old parishioners once more was like a homecoming for him, and life in the pretty thatched rectory was a dream of rural peace in contrast with his vexatious Dorchester days. What was more, the Rectory offered free lodging at a time when 40 South Street was being repainted and it would literally have made them sick to stay there. The whole family went to Came, and Laura wrote in her diary:

21st June: Willie, Isabel and myself finished the evening by walking arm in arm round the garden giving vent to our joy in song.

28th June: How charming this country life is! The perfect peace and happiness of it is doubly pleasant to us who have anything but a tranquil life at home.

Hoping to make themselves useful, Lucy and her sisters attempted to take choir practice with six local children, but it turned out that none could sing and three could not read. Pastoral duties had clearly not been among Damer's priorities. Despite this little setback, their time at Came was an idyll. The living was in the gift of another member of the rector's family, Captain Lionel Seymour Dawson-Damer, once a private pupil of Barnes's. He had been heard to say that should the living ever become vacant, he would offer it to his old schoolmaster. But Barnes did not like to let his mind dwell on this. Promises are easily made; it was just a pipe-dream.

Their homecoming to South Street was grim indeed, especially because of the smell of lead paint everywhere. The new term was due to start on 25 July and that morning Barnes went down to the schoolroom to greet his scholars. Later, Laura entered and was 'surprised to find Father sitting on his stool alone in the large room, not a boy at any of the desks!' He looked up and observed quietly, 'You see, I am at my post'. He stayed there for two hours. Laura noted, 'Father wanders about looking miserable, and sits all day in the empty schoolroom with no pupils, and the house, though very light and roomy, seemed to hang over us like a cloud of trouble'.

Some comfort came in the summer of 1859 when one of Barnes's pupils, Thomas Hooper Tolbort, came out first in languages and second in English in the Oxford public examinations. This brilliant pupil had been intended to work in his uncle's chemist shop in South Street, but now a much greater prospect opened out to him. So he continued to study privately with Barnes for the Indian Civil Service examination. Tolbort was especially friendly with two other clever young men, though neither of them had been among Barnes's pupils. One was Horace Moule, son of the Rector of Fordington. The other was the sixteen-year-old Thomas Hardy, now a pupil architect in the South Street office of John Hicks, next door to Barnes's school. Hardy was a studious youth and, along with a colleague, still pursued classical studies in his leisure moments in the office. In later years he remembered that he would 'often run in to ask Barnes to decide some knotty point in dispute between him and his fellow-pupil', and that Barnes would usually decide the matter in his favour.[17] Another attraction for Hardy at the school in South Street was young Lucy Barnes, whom he remembered as having a 'sweet disposition, but [was] provokingly shy, with plenty of brown hair, a tripping walk [and] a face pretty rather than handsome'.[18]

Though briefly distracted by the apparent admiration of such talented young men, Barnes was now haunted by the grim reality approaching – financial disaster. His only significant income was failing. True, a few day boys drifted in later that term, and a routine of sorts was cranked up, but the absence of scholars on that first day had been a profound shock to him. Signs of decline were everywhere. In the previous September his school cricket team had beaten the grammar school XI by four wickets. In 1859 he was unable to field a team.

Deciding now that he should concentrate his energies on boosting his finances, he resigned his post as secretary to the museum after thirteen years and concentrated on supplementing his school income. He wrote a guide to Dorchester for a local printer, though this cannot have brought him much profit. More remunerative was preaching. Acting as locum for other clergymen entitled him to fees. But because he could not easily afford a cart, on Sundays he often exhausted himself by walking long distances, such as the eleven miles to Puddletown and back. When taking services as far away as Nether Cerne or Piddlehinton, however, he was obliged to hire a cart and this reduced the value of his fees. Nevertheless, in 1858 preaching brought in £65.

It was not enough. His savings were shrinking alarmingly. What he needed was a secure income. To obtain it, he decided to sell the school and seek employment elsewhere. And so, much of the New Year vacation in 1859 was spent writing for posts. In February he applied for the principalship of the Diocesan Training College at Winchester, which was worth £250 p.a. Perhaps because of his age, or reputation for eccentricity, he was turned down. The post of assistant principal was offered to him, but at a mere £100 a year, he could not afford to accept it. He applied for the post of head of Bath Grammar School. He was rejected. He applied for the chaplaincy at Dorchester Gaol, and later that at the Dorchester Workhouse. He was rejected. In despair, he applied for the chaplaincy of Forston Lunatic Asylum.[19] Once again, he was rejected.

He was desperate. There seemed no way forward. For the first time the unthinkable had to be faced, and not only by him but by his children. Yet it seemed inconceivable to them that their own father, who had worked so hard to rise in the world to become a scholar and a gentleman, now might be made bankrupt. Would the Church of England allow one of its priests to become destitute? There seemed a very real prospect of it. If it happened, what would become of them all? Such fears began to haunt the minds of the entire family.

# 18

# PERFORMANCE

—— 1853-1859 ——

Since his quarrel with the editor, not a single dialect poem by Barnes had appeared in the *Dorset County Chronicle* for twelve years.[1] Nor apparently did he choose to publish his verse elsewhere. So, by the mid-1850s, it must have seemed to his admirers that the flow of his writing had ceased and that the *Poems of Rural Life in the Dorset Dialect* which had appeared as long before as 1844 was a one-off. The truth, however, was that he never stopped writing them. For him, they were a habitual form of self-communion, almost a weakness. And because he could not prevent himself, he simply wrote the poems and put them away unread.

Yet throughout the time his business affairs were going from bad to desperate, his literary stock had risen in inverse proportion. This was because a few faithful admirers continued to promote his interests. Among them were Mrs Norton and her Sheridan relatives and the veteran actor William Charles Macready, whose friends included Charles Dickens.[2] Macready had retired to Sherborne, where he was helping to revive the local literary institute, and in 1855 he invited Barnes to give a science lecture there, though his real interest was probably in Barnes's poetry.

While in Sherborne, Barnes met a local clergyman who professed great enthusiasm for his poems. Shortly afterwards he received a letter from this man, who had taken it upon himself to give a public reading of them:

SHERBORNE, Jan., 1856

My DEAR SIR,

I am much obliged to you for your kind acknowledgement of my poor endeavour to make known at Sherborne the beauties of your Dorset rhymes, and delighted that I did not do them an injustice. I never saw anything like the reception of this selection, and I hope it will increase sale of the book. I believe the audience would have sat patiently to hear the whole volume; as it was I kept them an hour and half beyond their usual time. Miss Macready sent for the poems next day... last night I was at a party where I was pestered for a few more specimens... I very much regret I had not asked you the other day to read one or two to me...
I am, etc. etc
EDWARD NARES HENNING

It was cheering to discover that even twelve years after the publication of *Poems of Rural Life* his poems were still appreciated. However, the letter also gave him matter for reflection. Previously, he had conceived of his audience as composed of a few genteel booklovers silently turning the pages, or perhaps a family of cottagers laughing together over Father's reading of 'What Dick and I Did' in the light of a guttering candle. But now he had learned from Henning that the poems made excellent performance pieces on the lips of a suitable reader. And if Henning could perform them, why should he not do so himself?

There were good reasons. Especially cogent among them, perhaps, was the fear that that his hard-won status as schoolmaster and parson might be compromised if he were heard speaking dialect in public. There was probably some such failure of nerve. So for two years more he confined himself to scientific and economic matters in his lectures. Sometimes at one of the institutes he might be asked to read a poem or two, and this he would willingly do, but only when the serious business of the evening was over.

Then, in about 1856, George Simonds was succeeded as editor of the *Chronicle* by William Wallace Fyfe, an admirer of Barnes. As a result, on 11 September, his great silence ended. Readers opened the pages to find 'The Bit of Ground at Huome', an eclogue in the familiar Barnes style. Twelve more poems were to follow in as many weeks. They included 'My Orchet in Linden Lea' and 'The Leane'. This last poem vividly articulated Barnes's growing loathing of the contemporary push for profit at all costs and the primacy of commercial values. It has claims to be regarded as one of the first great environmentalist poems in the language:

## The Leane

They do zay that a travellen chap
Have a-put in the newspaper now,
That the bit o' green ground on the knap
Should be all a-took in vor the plough.
He do fancy 'tis easy to show
That we can be but stunpolls at best,
Vor to leave a green spot where a flower might grow
Or a voot-weary walker mid rest.
'Tis hedge-grubben, Thomas, an' ledge-grubben,
Never a'done
While a sov'ren mwore's to be won.

The road, he do zay, is so wide
As 'tis wanted vor traveller's wheels,
As if all that did travel did ride
An' did never get galls on their heels.
He would leave sich a thin strip o' groun',
That, if a man's veet in his shoes
We a-burnen an' zore, why he coulden zit down
But the wheels would run over his tooes.
Vor 'tis meake money, Thomas, an teake money,
What's zwold an' bought
Is all that is worthy o' thought.

Years agoo the leane-zides did bear grass,
Vor to pull wi' the geeses' red bills,
That did hiss at the vo'k that did pass,
Or the bwoys that pick'd up their white quills.
But shortly, if vower or vive
Ov our goslens do creep vrom the agg,
They must mwope in the garden, mwore dead than alive
In a coop, or a-tied by the lag.
Vor to catch at land, Thomas, 'an snatch at land,
Now is the plan;
Meake money wherever you can.

The childern wull soon have noo pleace
Vor to play in, an if they do grow,
They wull have a thin musheroom feace,
Wi' their bodies so sumple as dough.
But a man is a-meade ov a child,
An' his limbs do grow worksome by play,

An' if the young child's little body's a-spwëil'd,
Why, the man's wull the sooner decay.
But wealth is wo'th now more than health is wo'th;
Let it all goo,
If t'ull bring but a sov'ren or two.[3]

('knap' – a small hillock; 'stunpolls' – idiots (lit. stone heads); 'never get galls on their heels' – never walk; 'sumple' – supple)

So great now was the flow of poems that it can only be accounted for by his taking some out of store, as well as writing new ones. Nevertheless, fresh verses came pouring out of him. Between September 1856 and September 1859, the *Chronicle* published no fewer than 144 poems.[4] They were now given pride of place in the paper, sometimes furnishing the whole of 'Poetry Corner'.

When he had a sufficient number of poems, he put them together in a new book. John Russell Smith's edition of *Hwomely Rhymes: A Second Collection of Poems in the Dorset Dialect* (1859) included 105 new poems.[5] There was no falling off in quality. Once again, almost all of the poems derived from memories of his boyhood in Blackmore, and these were rendered just as fresh and undimmed as in the previous collection published fifteen years before.

Brought to life again were the old coaching days:

## The Stage Coach

Ah! when the wold vo'k went abroad
They thought it vast enough
If vow'r good ho'ses beat the road
Avore the coach's ruf;
An' there they zot,
A-cwold or hot,
An' roll'd along the groun',
While the whip did smack
On the ho'ses back,
An' the wheels went swiftly roun', good so's;
The wheels went swiftly roun'…[6]

Here were portraits of familiar rural types, such as the bashful country boy, unused to company and overcome with embarassment:

## The Shy Man

Ah! good Meäster Gwillet, that you mid ha' know'd,
Wer a-bred up at Coomb, an' went little abroad;
An' if he got in among strangers, he velt
His poor heart in a twitter, an' ready to melt;
Or if, by ill luck, in his rambles, he met
Wi' zome maidens a-tittren, he burn'd wi a het,
That shot all drough the lim's o'n, an' left a cwold zweat,
The poor little chap were so shy,
He wer ready to drap an' to die.[7]

Here also were old country tales recounting the reversals and sheer unexpectedness of life, such as that of the farmer's daughter who, when ordered to stay at home while the others went out to the fields, answered the door to her future husband and so left her home forever:

## Minden' House

'Twer when the vo'k wer out to hawl
A vield o' hay a day in June,
An' when the zun begun to vall
Towards the west in afternoon,
Woone only wer a-left behind
To bide indoors, at hwome, an' mind
The house, an' answer vo'k avore
The geate or door, – young Fanny Deane.

The air 'ithin the gearden wall
Wer deadly still, unless the bee
Did hummy by, or in the hall
The clock did ring a-hetten dree,
'An there, wi' busy hands, inzide
The iron ceasement, open'd wide,
Did zit an pull wi' nimble twitch
Her tiny stitch, young Fanny Deane…[8]

('ruf' – roof; 'so's' – souls, i.e. people; 'het' – heat; 'o'n' – of him; 'bide' – stay; 'hetten' – hitting, striking; 'dree' – three)

By this time, Barnes's range as a poet was pretty well defined. Neither party politics nor sexual passion were his concerns. Nor was religion. Although he was deeply religious and a poet, he was not a religious poet; perhaps because he never seems to have experienced doubt. His subjects were love and death, family life, rural people, farm work, village customs, the seasons and changing times. No one, not even John Clare, has presented so full a picture of the lives of agricultural workers in the fast-fading, pre-industrial world. Barnes was enabled to do this simply because although by 1859 he was a Victorian businessman, exhausted by grief and disappointment, his imaginative responses still remained rooted in recollections of his early years in the Vale and the talk he had heard there. His vision rarely extended beyond that time. With the exception of a few poems, chiefly touching on the death of his wife, all the rest are inspired by his Blackmore days.

Apprehensive about slow sales for his new book, Barnes now suggested to Russell Smith that perhaps it should be published by subscription. More sanguine than he, the publisher offered to take all the risk and even to buy the manuscript 'right out' for £40. It had dawned on him that the dialect poems were a better commercial bet than the prose works. After some hesitation, Barnes turned him down but agreed to accept £15 in return for allowing him to bring out 400 copies. In the event, Barnes never did sell the copyright to his poems, which was fortunate because these were the only writings of his that proved commercially valuable.

Meanwhile, some of his Dorchester friends were making strenuous efforts to help his financial circumstances. The young barrister Frederick Cosens, who had been his assistant in the St Peter's Church Restoration Fund, now collected the signatures on a large parchment of 'all the magistrates and others of the County' for a petition to the then Prime Minister, Lord Palmerston, requesting a Civil List pension for Barnes. These financial awards were granted from the Royal Bounty to persons of merit who were experiencing financial distress. The covering letter was written on 14 November 1859 by William Wallace Fyfe. Interestingly, despite the radical tendency of some of his writings and the support of Liberals such as the Sheridans, Barnes was presumed by many to be a Conservative. Therefore, when Fyfe wrote to the Liberal Prime Minister, he found it necessary to observe that whatever his lordship's party politics, he was sure that 'as an admirer and patron of polite literature', he would not be prejudiced against a 'good and deserving man'. In a lengthy letter, he sketched out Barnes's achievements and situation. Barnes was, he said, 'of advanced age' (he was fifty-eight!), in Holy Orders, with a large family, and was a schoolmaster whose income was 'not eminently remunerative'. Despite this, whenever required, he had willingly come forward to deliver public lectures throughout the county to the working classes. Fyfe concluded that nothing would be more popular locally than the bestowal of the 'full Literary Pension' on the poet.

Barnes himself never sought the pension. Indeed, throughout the whole of his life he never canvassed a personal advantage for himself. An innate delicacy prevented him from ever advertising himself personally, or seeking a favour. Yet it seems from an entry in Laura's diary that when the family eventually got to hear of the petition, he did not oppose it. He probably regarded the news with mixed feelings. On the one hand, it was almost a public acknowledgement that he was a financial failure, driven to depend on charity. On the other, the award of the pension would be both a sign of national recognition and a practical help. So, for a time he lived in hope, but on hearing nothing of the matter month after month, he put it out of his mind.

There was nothing doubtful, however, about the honour done to him by two eminent Frenchmen at this time. Prince Lucien Bonaparte, who was a distinguished dialect scholar, visited him twice in 1859, putting up at the Antelope Hotel. The Prince came especially to consult him on the local speech, and also to request that he should obtain translations of the 'Song of Solomon' in the dialects of Wiltshire and Somerset. Barnes himself was to undertake the translation into Dorset. The task resulted in a poignant outpouring of erotic nostalgia from this still uxorious man in his seventh year as a widower:

> How comely your vootsteps wi' shoes, prince's da'ter! the jeints o' your thighs be lik' jewels, the work o'
> the han's o' the skillfullest workman.

> Your neavel is lik' a roun bowl not empty o' liquor; your belly a-roun' heap o' wheat a-bounded wi' lilies.

A limited edition of *The Song of Solomon in the Dorset Dialect* was published in 1859, and as payment Barnes received a box of about thirty scholarly books.[9]

Another French admirer was the Chevalier de Chatelaine, who had actually translated a number of Barnes's dialect poems into French and now wrote to ask permission to publish his versions in an anthology entitled *Beautes de la Poesie Anglaise*. The Chevalier confided that whereas he believed that he had had success with some of Barnes's poems, he had failed with 'The Wold Wall'. This was because he was convinced that 'votre charmant dialect etait souvent intraduisable'. Some of these French translations were published in the *Gazette de Guernsey* and afterwards copied in other French papers. The Chevalier became a personal friend and later, accompanied by his wife, visited Barnes at South Street.

Flattering though such attention was, it did very little to help Barnes's financial fortunes. And though it might have been thought that the mere sight of Prince Bonaparte's coach pulling up outside the school would have increased his social status locally, this was not necessarily so. Most Dorchester people would simply have been bemused by the appearance of such a splendid equipage, and at a time when the French were suspected of preparing another invasion, some were probably hostile.

Then came promising news. Charles Tennant wrote on 2 October 1858 inviting Barnes to give a private reading at his house in London. He said he wanted to introduce the poet to his friends, some of whom might prove useful in promoting the poems. Tennant continued:

> I have long thought that the Dorsetshire folk have not shown a due appreciation of their own poet by
> allowing him to have been so long in comparative obscurity. But he has only to make his appearance in
> the great metropolis to insure for Barnes, the Dorset poet, a celebrity equal to that of Burns, the Scotch
> poet, whose hundredth anniversary is now about to be celebrated.

Echoing a remark of Lord Byron's he added, 'if we do this well, you will wake one morning and find yourself famous'.[10] A further letter from Tennant revealed that a friend of his had met Mrs Norton in Scotland, where they had discussed the event.

There then seems to have been a change of plan because, in March 1859, Caroline Norton wrote to Barnes to say that her friend the Duchess of Sutherland had agreed to make Stafford House available for the reading, presumably in place of Tennant's. Caroline had now ordered copies of the poems from Russell Smith to be sent to the Duchess and to her other 'friend', the Rt. Hon. Sidney Herbert, Secretary for War in Lord Palmerston's cabinet.[11] It was rumoured that Disraeli might attend and even the Queen herself. The occasion was fixed for the first week in May 1860. At last Barnes might dare to hope that success in such company might earn him a national reputation and perhaps restore his financial fortunes. This was his great opportunity.

But he needed to prepare for it. Chief among his concerns was that he was not an experienced poetry performer. Preacher, yes, lecturer, yes, but not performer. He had never given an extended reading of his own work, and felt he needed a rehearsal prior to his London appearance. What better place then than his own town? Accordingly, in October 1859, he arranged to read a selection of his poems in the Town Hall in Dorchester. His hosts were his old friends, the members of the working men's institution, and they were to bring their families along. Indeed, everyone was welcome. Lucy Barnes left an account of the occasion:

> It was an evening to be remembered. The hall was thronged almost to suffocation with rich and poor, and seldom has an audience been more excited by various emotions. At one moment the whole mass of people would be breathless with interest at such descriptive poems as 'Jeanes's Wedden-day in Mornen', 'Grammer's Shoes;' the next women would be sobbing audibly over 'Meary Ann's Chile', or 'My Love's Guardian Angel;' then hey presto! sorrow would flee away, and the multitude of faces relax into smiles, with now and then a burst of hearty laughter, at 'What Dick and I done,' or 'A Bit o' Sly Courten'. It seemed to one of the poet's children that the crowd of human beings was a magic harp on which he played, bringing forth at his will the emotions he chose… If this seems exaggerated, let it be remembered that it was the first time a Dorset audience had heard its feeling, language, and daily life portrayed in its own common speech, and the effect was all the greater from the newness of the emotion.[12]

Thomas Hardy also witnessed Barnes reading his poems, perhaps on the same evening. As a nineteen-year-old youth, he may well have accompanied the charming Lucy, who was some three years older. Be that as it may, he too left a memorial of a Barnes reading:

> The effect, indeed, of his recitations upon an audience well acquainted with the nuances of the dialect – impossible to impart to outsiders by any kind of translation – can hardly be imagined by readers of his lines acquainted only with English in its customary form. The poet's own mild smile at the boisterous merriment provoked by his droll delivery of such pieces as 'The Shy Man', 'A Bit o' Sly Coorten,' and 'Dick and I' returns upon the memory as one of the most characteristic aspects of a man who was nothing if not genial; albeit that, while the tyranny of his audience demanded these broadly humorous productions, his own preferences were for the finer and more pathetic poems, such as 'Wife a-lost,' 'Woak Hill,' an 'Jay a -past'.[13]

But the reading at Stafford House never took place. At the last moment it was postponed because of the illness of a member of the Duchess of Sutherland's family.

It did not matter. Perhaps to his surprise, Barnes had discovered himself to be a performer. Even more importantly, he had found his true audience. From this time on, his lectures on scientific subjects were pretty much abandoned. It was the dialect poems his audiences wanted to hear, and over the years his readings became familiar and popular events round the county and beyond. One of his admirers was the Revd J.J. Lias. When a literary critic in *The Times Literary Supplement* later dared to opine that that Barnes had 'no public and never had', Lias responded indignantly: 'In his lifetime he had a public. It was the Dorsetshire peasantry'.[14]

Lias was right. It was not Mrs Norton's aristocratic friends who furnished Barnes's most faithful audience; it was the working people of Dorset. And they first discovered him on that memorable evening in the Town Hall. For his listeners, some barely literate, he had supplied a living literature, their own experiences in their own language. And in so doing, he had at last found his own voice.

# 19

# DELIVERANCE

## — 1859-1862 —

Eighteen-fifty-nine was for Barnes a year of acute anxiety or, as he expressed it in his diary, 'un anno molto ansioso'. Seven years previously he had been a prosperous, happily married man with a fine young family, a thriving school, prospects of professional promotion and a growing reputation as a poet and scholar. Now he found himself a passed-over, penurious widower, struggling to maintain a fast-failing academy, with six young people dependent on him. How had this happened? He tried to puzzle it out in a poem:

### Jay A-Pass'd

When leaves in evenen winds, do vlee
Where mornen air did strip the tree,
The mind can wait vor boughs in spring
To cool the elem sheaded ring.
Where orcha'd blooth's white sceales do vall
Mid come the apple's blushen ball.
Our hopes be new, as time do goo,
A-measur'd by the zun on high,
Avore our jays do pass us by.

When ice did melt below the zun,
An' weaves along the stream did run,
I hoped in May's bright froth to roll,
Lik' jess'my in a lily's bowl.
Or, if I lost my loose-bow'd swing,
My wrigglen kite mid pull the string,
An' when noo ball did rise an' fall,
Zome other geame wud still be nigh,
Avore my jays all pass'd me by.

I look'd, as childhood pass'd along,
To walk, in leater years, man-strong,
An' look'd agean, in manhood's pride,
To manhood's sweetest chaice, a bride:
An' then to childern, that mid come
To meake my house a dearer hwome.
But now my mind do look behind
Vor jays; an' wander, wi' a sigh,
When 'twer my jays all pass'd me by.

Wer it when woonce, I miss'd a call
To rise, an' seemed to have a vall?

> Or when my Jeane to my hands left
> Her vew bright keys, a dolevul heft?
> Or when avore the door I stood
> To watch a child a-gone vor good?
> Or when zome crowd did laugh aloud;
> Or when the leaves did spring, or die?
> When did my jays all pass me by?

('blooth' – blossom; 'avore' – before; 'jess'my' – jasmine; 'heft' – weight)[1]

His sons and daughters were now desperate to get on with their own lives, but careers cost money and his savings were running out. Two options were open to him. He could retrench and hope that things would improve, or else realise what assets he had and launch his children on the world. To his credit, at the very time when his various applications for employment were rejected, he chose the latter course. As a result, this close-knit family had begun to break up.

By this time, only Laura and Lucy remained with him. Laura had by now accepted the fact that that she would never have a career, never marry and never leave home. True, she had once sent to learn the terms of entry to a 'House of Mercy' but, having received the information, she paused to consider and came to the conclusion that providence had appointed her to be her father's helpmate, to keep his home together, so she did not apply.

Meanwhile, when Egbert was barely sixteen, Barnes had written to Daniel Gooch's railway works to obtain a five-year apprenticeship for him. The premium of £150 was formally accepted on 22 October and shortly afterwards the boy went to Swindon. Many years before that, Gooch had agreed with Brunel, the chief engineer of the Great Western Railway, that this hitherto small Wiltshire town should be 'our principal engine establishment', and in due course it had indeed become the mechanical heart of Brunel's Great Western Railway. It was very exciting, therefore, for young Egbert to be joining such a prestigious company, even though he soon found that the fumes and heat of the clanging engine shops gave him a cough and made his head ache.

Julia was even more ambitious. At twenty-seven, this bold, talented woman was more than ready to begin her professional career as a singer. Well-schooled by her father in modern European languages and with Frederick Smith as her voice coach, she now wished to extend her musical experience, preferably on the Continent. Fortunately, Smith had recently studied in Paris and made useful contacts in the musical world, and it was probably through him that she got her chance. On 23 May 1859, Laura noted, 'Julia to go to Brussels for six months', presumably to teach and to sing. She must have made an impression there for, having come home briefly for Christmas, on 6 February she was off again. Now she had a sponsor. Incredulously, Laura records, 'Julia awarded a singing master in Berlin for six months by Princess Frederick William – all done for Julia by her kind friends Mr Belsom, the English chaplain in Berlin and Frau Zimmerman, through our Father's name and works; truth is stranger than fiction'. This was all rather mysterious – and expensive. For even though the professional training seems to have been offered free, there were still fares, accommodation and pocket money to be supplied, presumably by Barnes.

Since the departure of Isaac Hann, William Miles had become his 'father's right hand' at the school and Barnes relied on him more and more. He increasingly looked to the young man as the hope of the family, and intended him for an academic career. After all, William had received a much better start than he had and therefore might hope to rise further. Whatever it cost, Barnes was determined that the boy should follow him to Cambridge University and become a scholar and a gentleman. Then he might also become a clergyman, and perhaps take over the school. As it turned out, the urgent need of an usher delayed William's career for a time, but eventually in January 1859 he entered St John's College. It cost Barnes £50 for that month's fees alone, which must have depleted his savings severely. Perhaps it was at this time that he sold his fields in Blackmore to raise the money.

Meanwhile, his other hope, though he hardly liked to acknowledge it even to himself, lay in the application for a Civil List pension. At first his supporters had seemed optimistic, but as the months went by and he heard nothing of it, his expectations faded.

Then came an entirely unexpected piece of good fortune. Of all Barnes's children, the least gifted was Isabel. Though she was remarkably pretty, she had neither Laura's strong moral qualities, nor Julia's talent and determination, nor Lucy's intellect. Without any personal fortune to tempt a suitor, her sisters rather assumed that she would remain a spinster, helping Laura with the house and school.

They had underrated her. She had put her attractions to work formidably. On 14 December 1859 Laura recorded, 'Mr Shaw engaged to Isabel'. Mr Shaw, it turned out, was a very good catch. Like Barnes, he was a St John's man and a clergyman. Unlike Barnes, he was well off. Joseph Richard Shaw came from the north of the country but was currently the curate at Nether Cerne, near Dorchester. He was likeable, genial and very fond of Isabel. What was not so immediately apparent was just how how well off he was, nor where his money came from. But Barnes soon learned. In order to ensure that his daughter would be supported rather better than she had been accustomed to, he became privy to Shaw's business affairs. And he discovered that although Shaw had only recently come to Dorset, he was already engaged in a number of commercial ventures locally. He had agreed a mortgage with the Revd Frederick Moule on the 'Prebendal Parsonage House and Heriditaments at Fordington', and arranged a loan of £1,000 to Peter Weston Ayles, the Weymouth shipbuilder.[2] Closer acquaintance revealed Shaw to be even wealthier than first appeared. It seemed that Isabel was about to make a very advantageous marriage. At last Barnes could count on having at least one of his children satisfactorily off his hands.

The happiest day of 1860 for the Barnes family came at Midsummer, with Isabel's wedding. Because money was so tight, professional caterers were out of the question. For some days previously, the four sisters had been busy making cakes, jellies and blancmanges to be set out in the schoolroom as refreshments for the the wedding guests. Then, on 21 June, Barnes walked arm in arm with his daughter up South Street and over the road to St Peters's Church. Waiting on the steps was his old friend the Revd Morton Colson, who had conducted Julia's funeral service there exactly eight years before. But now, on this bright morning, Barnes could dare to hope that the long years of misfortune were coming to an end. Shortly afterwards, Isabel left for Westmorland with her new husband, where he was to take up the living of Brough under Stainmore. Barnes proudly wrote to tell his friend Warne that Isabel was 'a good wise girl and very happy. Her husband is a steady young clergyman with some private property'.

Among the new pupils in 1860 was the seven-year-old Frederick Treves. In later days he penned a picture of Barnes, who by now had adopted the eighteenth-century costume he was to favour for the rest of his life:

> My recollection of the poet and philologist is that of the kindest and gentlest of men. His appearance was peculiar. He had white hair and a long white beard, and always knee-breeches and shoes with large buckles. Out of doors he donned a curious cap and a still more curious cape, while I never saw him without a bag over his shoulder and a stout staff. During school hours he was in the habit of pacing the room in a reverie, happily oblivious of his dull surroundings. I remember once that some forbidden fruit of which I was possessed rolled across the schoolroom floor, and that I crawled after it in the wake of the dreaming master. He turned suddenly in his walk and stumbled over me, to my intense alarm. When he had regained his balance he apologised very earnestly and resumed his walk, unconscious that the object he had fallen over was a scholar. I have often wondered to which of his charming poems I owed my escape from punishment.[3]

No doubt when recollecting this, Treves understood very well that his old schoolmaster must have had many things other than poems to occupy his thoughts at that time. Yet astonishingly, amid all the turmoil and vexations of his life, Barnes was indeed still writing poetry.

To his great relief the school revived a little, so that on 20 September he felt able to write once again to his archaeologist friend Charles Warne, explaining that he had had a very unprosperous time in the previous two years and that he had not wished to be in touch until he had better news. Turning to other matters, he reported the latest archaeological finds in Dorset: four skeletons near the Culliford Tree, one with a necklace of unknown substance, and a fine urn which had turned up at Winterborne

(Came?). A week later he wrote again with more such news: a sewer had just been dug in his South Street garden, and the men had found a Roman rubbish pit there. They had unearthed Samian and black pottery, frescoed plaster, a bone hair-pin and a stud.[4] Concerning the Civil List application, he could not say whether the news was good or bad: 'I am told that Lord Palmerston has promised another of the Ministers – my friend in the case – that he will place my name on the Civil List. He has sent me, through the Lords of the Treasury, £30, as of Her Majesty's Royal Bounty. It is, however, still an anxious time'.[5]

One small piece of financial help now came very opportunely. A friend, Charles Tennant, had introduced his name to David Masson, editor of *MacMillan's Magazine*, who wrote to offer him £1 a page for any articles he chose to supply. There was no difficulty here. Barnes's mind was so crammed with curious bits of knowledge that he could have churned out any number of such articles with no difficulty at all. His first essay, on 'Beauty and Art', appeared the following May and elicited a cheque and reply from the famous proprietor himself:

> I have only been able to look [the article] over partially as yet, but have read enough to convince me that
> I shall have a great admiration of it, as our editor told me I should – the style and thought seem so fresh
> and genuine... I am Dear Sir, Yours very respectfully, Alexander MacMillan.

Whether or not this entrée to *MacMillan's* was part of a covert charity on behalf of his well-meaning friends is not clear. If so, Barnes never suspected it.

The year ending brought not only comings and goings, but some alarming portents. Egbert turned up unexpectedly from Swindon. All his enthusiasm for his job could not disguise the fact that the smoky atmosphere of the Swindon workshops was undermining his health. But after Christmas, Barnes doggedly packed his bag to go on a few days' lecturing tour of the working men's institutes, before school started. Laura noted rather bitterly that, as usual, it was 'for no return but expenses'. Soon Julia left for London again, probably to take up a position as a lady's companion while she was look-ing for work as a professional singer. William departed for St John's. Then, on 16 January 1861, came a letter from Isabel revealing that Joseph Shaw was very ill. He had contracted tuberculosis when nursing his elder brother in Cambridge. Though just married, the shadows were already gathering round this young woman. She now found herself nursing a sick husband in a silent rectory in a bleak country, where she knew no one.

Her sisters rallied round. Immediately after hearing the news, they agreed that Laura should go up to the Lake District to support Isabel. She remained there for the next four months. Even Lucy 'left for Tytherington' for a time. Now Barnes had no help in the schoolroom, and precious little in the house as well. He was almost alone on his sixtieth birthday on 22 February. Calling a month later, the Census enumerator recorded the inhabitants of 40 South Street as: William Barnes, 'Clergyman without cure of souls, schoolmaster, etc'; Lucy, two servants, the cook, Jane Hall, the housemaid, Sarah Townsend, and seven boarders. This sparse little household was all that was left of the once flourishing school. Yet despite the lack of pupils, Barnes became so overworked that Julia was brought home for a while to help out.

Then, at last, came good news. A Dorchester admirer of Barnes named John Cox was one day scanning a newspaper when his eye happened to fall on an item that caused him to jump up imme-diately. Snatching up his hat, and pausing only to recruit another friend, he marched round to the school and knocked at the door. Lucy takes up the story:

> There came an April day, when the only daughter who was at home was arranging some primroses she
> had just brought from a long country ramble, when two gentlemen entered, saying they had come to
> offer their hearty congratulations to Mr. Barnes.
>   'On what?' asked the girl, wondering.
>   'On having received a Civil List pension of £70 a year,' and they showed her a Daily Telegraph with
> the list of newly-granted pensions, and there truly was her father's name as one of the chosen recipients.
>     'Let us go and tell father directly,' said the girl, hastily taking up her hat; 'he is gone to the station to see
> a friend off '.

So she and her two friends set off in eager haste to bring the good news, which to him was a veritable godsend. The official notice from Lord Palmerston followed the next day, April 17th, 1861, and then began to pour in letters of hearty congratulation from all the county'.[6]

The congratulations included one from his old supporter Richard Brinsley Sheridan MP, as well as friends that he did not know he had, such as the influential John Floyer, sometime Mayor of Dorchester.

In replying to Palmerston's letter, Barnes, with characteristic modesty, accepted the honour, hoping that his future writings might not disgrace the 'literature of Her Majesty's kingdom', and trusting that 'those works in the dialect of [his] own county [might] promote peace and goodwill among her rural subjects in the west'. The news brought only small relief, however, because though an extra £70 a year was sufficient to ease his financial situation, it was not enough to transform it. Nor was it payable until eighteen months later, i.e. August 1862, and he needed help right away. Yet for a brief time, this unassuming man was able to bask quietly in the glow of eventual recognition, and could take comfort in the financial relief to come.

His pleasure did not last long. The following post brought news that Joseph Shaw had died at Sedburgh, Cumbria, on 14 April 1861. He was just twenty-seven. The letters coming to South Street over the next few days were a touching mixture of congratulations and condolence. Shaw was buried in Brough on the 18th. It was too far for Barnes to attend, even if he had been free to do so, but he was reassured to know that the ever-reliable Laura was with her sister. Nine days after the funeral, both women arrived home in Dorchester. Isabel had been married for barely ten months.

Once again three of the four sisters were living together in their father's house. Yet their relative situation was now different. Three months before he died, and understanding full well how ill he was, Joseph Shaw had made his will and nominated Barnes as his sole executor. He had left his whole estate 'Unto my dear wife, Isabel Shaw'. Consequently, her status had changed significantly. Whereas, the year before, she had been merely one of four impoverished spinster sisters, now she was a young and attractive widow. And she was rich.

Lucy, who was a natural optimist, noted that the New Year of 1862 had dawned brightly, though whether she was referring to the weather or her hopes is not clear. Careworn Laura saw things differently, but resolved to appear cheerful for her father's sake: 'There seems a mist over this world to me – I must put on happiness and hopefulness; we have had so many bitter disappointments'. Yet there was now a feeling of anticipation stirring among the Barneses, a sense that things could not go on as they had been. There would have to be a change. Meanwhile, after both William and Julia had arrived home for the holidays, the days were spent visiting friends. Julia came home with a letter to Barnes from a Mrs Elizabeth Jennings of 11 Langham Street, West London, who thanked him 'for allowing me to have your daughter whom I so much admire and esteem'. Within a few weeks, however, Julia departed to London again. Meanwhile, Barnes went off on his annual tour of the working men's institutes, this time to Sherborne, Weymouth and Blandford. His lecture title was 'Trial By Jury', though it appears that his listeners were more interested to hear his poems.

It was on 15 January, when Barnes was dining with a fellow clergyman, that he heard that the Revd Lionel Damer, Rector of Winterborne Came, had resigned to take up another parish in the Midlands. At once the question arose of whether Captain Damer would remember his promise to offer the living of Came to Barnes. But as the days passed with no word of it, friends suggested to him that he should remind the squire of his promise. He flatly refused. He said he would not stoop to do so: 'If it is Captain Damer's wish that I shall have the living he will give it to me, if not, the forcing him to maintain a word perhaps forgotten, perhaps repented of, could bring no happiness to him or me'.

There followed a fortnight of anxious waiting until, at last, there came a letter:

MORETON HOUSE, Jan. 30th, 1862
MY DEAR MR. BARNES,

I am not unmindful of my promises I can assure you, and I have delayed till this day, when I was officially assured of my cousin's resignation of Came living within the next six months, to offer for your acceptance the same, which I do with the most heartfelt pleasure in the world, hoping you will long live to enjoy it. I may hope to see you next week in Dorchester. Remember me kindly to all your family, and with Mrs. Damer's best wishes,

Believe me,

Very truly yours,

SEYMOUR DAWSON DAMER

Next day Damer was on the doorstep to enquire personally whether Barnes were willing to accept the living. Was he? He was. It was deliverance.

In just a few hours everything had changed. The sense of relief throughout the entire household was almost palpable. Having for so long slaved to keep things going, Barnes's daughters were now elated, aware that the 'mantle of responsibility, which had rested so heavily on their shoulders… was slipping off, under the sunny rays of a more congenial future'.[7] For the first time since the death of their mother ten years before, cheerful laughter was heard coming from the house.

Barnes's long bondage to the school was over. At last he was free of financial anxiety. In years to come he would be able to count on a small but adequate income to support a middle-class standard of living. He would have the Civil List pension of £70 p.a, together with a stipend of £200. The Rectory came rent free. He had come to love this house when he had lived there briefly as Lionel Damer's locum. And it brought with it a new life. Instead of schoolroom drudgery and troublesome parents, he would now have the care of a country parish, where the congregation would include his old friends from Whitcombe.

Though away in London, by some mysterious means Julia had already learned of his good fortune. She scribbled a hasty note: 'My dearest darling Papa. You will see that I have heard of what has happened as soon as you, but how Eh?' She continued, assigning new roles to them all:

> Laura will have enough to do now. My quiet sainted Lucy will look after the sick – Dear Laura in the schools etc., will find enough in her great mind. I often wish Laura had means to educate one of her great talents – Music or painting – perhaps it may not be so impossible. Dear Isabel will be the Lady Benevolent of the Parish. Dear Willie the blushing young curate etc. Egbert the Rector's youngest son and organist.

She excepted herself: 'I am a wandering star but slipped out of my orbit'.

It was true that she was already moving beyond the sphere of her staid family. Seeking to impress her father, she confided that she was about to call on Madam Sartoris, though whether as a guest or for singing lessons is not revealed.[8] The daughter of the actor Charles Kemble, and niece of Sarah Siddons, Adelaide Sartoris had been painted by Lord Leighton and was at the centre of London artistic life at the time. How Julia had got in with her is not known, but clearly she was mixing in elevated, though perhaps rather raffish, artistic circles. All of which resulted in a knowingness her provincial sisters at times found exasperating. But one thing was clear; Julia would never settle down again in Dorset. In April she was home again briefly, and planning a trip to Florence. For this she required more money and so the family debated it. William, Lucy and Isabel were against the idea but Laura and Barnes himself supported her, believing that she was right to continue to cultivate her fine voice. Presumably he dipped into the last of his savings to find the fare.

It was a spring of mixed fortunes. Following the news from Captain Damer, Barnes was 'very poorly', perhaps as a reaction. There was yet another infection going round and Julia said that the school house was like a hospital. And though Egbert went back to Swindon, on the 9 May William Miles came home early from St John's, unwell from what was politely called 'over-reading and anxiety'. The phrase suggests that either he had failed his examinations or had had some sort of breakdown, or both. While at home he received more bad news. Anticipating his graduation he had applied for a clerical post in Jamaica but now a letter came with the news that he had been rejected.

Poetry was still Barnes's solace. From time to time, a dialect poem of his had appeared in the *Chronicle*, and in the spring of 1862 he was busy correcting proofs for another book. That year, John Russell Smith brought out a third collection of his *Poems of Rural Life in the Dorset Dialect*, with ninety-five new items. Once again, there was no falling off in standard. The volume contains some of his most memorable verses.

By this time he had settled his thoughts concerning the wisdom of writing in dialect. He saw now that Mrs Norton and all those well-intentioned friends who had for so long urged him to adopt standard English were mistaken. Though he was master of over seventy languages, including 'Englandish', he now recognised that his true artistic idiom was the dialect. He knew the drawbacks – that it was not widely understood and often alienated the sort of people who bought poetry books – but even so, he could choose no other:

> To write in what some may deem a fast-wearing out speech-form, may seem as idle as the writing of one's name in snow of a spring day. I cannot help it. It is my mother tongue, and is to my mind the only true speech of the life that I draw.[9]

Meanwhile, he played out his days as a teacher with the few remaining boys in the dusty classroom. His passion for education having long gone, he remained a conscientious tutor to the last, still given to the occasional, charming little spurts of enthusiasm for which many of his pupils remembered him. More interesting to him than the routine classwork, however, were the one-to-one tutorials with his brighter private pupils, including Thomas Hooper Tolbort, whom he had been coaching in the languages of the Subcontinent, in preparation for the Indian Civil Service examination. But all this had now come to an end. On 20 June 1862, his final classes were dismissed and the last boys sent home. It was forty-four years since he had first set out for Mere, and now his career as a schoolmaster was over. He did not regret it. The trials and vexations of recent years had taken too great a toll.

Yet there was one consideration that upset him. He was increasingly aware that in a few weeks time he would be quitting forever the South Street home that he had first made with Julia fifteen years before. In leaving the house, he felt that he was somehow leaving her. He put his thoughts into a poem, one of such intense pathos that Thomas Hardy later wrote that it would still be read 'when much English literature will be forgotten'.[10]

## Woak Hill

When sycamore leaves wer a-spreaden,
Green ruddy, in hedges,
Bezide the red doust o' the ridges,
A-dried at Woak Hill;

I packed up my goods all a-sheenen
Wi' long years o' handlen,
On dousty red wheels ov a waggon,
To ride at Woak Hill.

The brown thatchen ruf o' the dwellen
I then were a-leaven,
Had shelter'd the sleek head o' Meary,
My bride at Woak Hill.

But now for zome years, her light voot-vall
'S a-lost vrom the vlooren,
Too soon vor my jay an' my childern,
She died at Woak Hill.

But still I do think that, in soul,
She do hover about us;

To ho vor her motherless children,
Her pride at Woak Hill.

Zoo – lest she should tell me hereafter
I stole off 'ithout her,
An' left her, uncall'd at house-ridden,
To bide at Woak Hill-

I call'd her so fondly, wi' lippens
All soundless to others,
An' took her wi' air-reachen hand,
To my zide at Woak Hill.

On the road I did look round, a-talken
To light at my shoulder,
An' then led her in at the doorway,
Miles wide vrom Woak Hill.

An' that's why vo'k thought, vor a season,
My mind wer a-wandren
Wi' sorrow, when I were so sorely
A-tried at Woak Hill.

But no; that my Meary mid never
Behold herzelf slighted,
I wanted to think that I guided
My guide vrom Woak Hill.[11]

('dousty' – dusty; 'to ho vor' – to care for; 'lippens' – whispers)

The last months at South Street were spent packing away the evidence of many years of family life. As well as furniture, they were to take to Came hundreds of books, framed paintings, folios of pictures and 140ft of book-shelving. What items remained of the school, the dog-eared lesson-books, cracked inkwells and old desks were to go to Ensors, the auctioneers. On 30 July, the outgoing rector, Lionel Damer, called round with best wishes and the keys to their new house. On 7 August, wagons arrived to cart off their goods to the Rectory. In his diary, Barnes wrote: 'Rid house for Came'.

Then, even while they were packing, there was great news, both gratifying and rather vexing to one who had been convinced that his career as a schoolmaster had been a failure. *The Times* newspaper had come out with the names of the eighty successful students in the Indian Civil Service examinations. The list was headed not by a pupil from one of the famous public schools, but by Thomas William Hooper Tolbort. His master's name was also printed: William Barnes of Dorchester. Barnes's response was typically modest: 'I told them it took two to do it'. Nevertheless, he was soon 'deluged with letters, offering pupils', which prompted his reflection that, 'When I was drowning no one offered me help; now I have come to land, hands are held out to me'.

He was not to be tempted. Though his career as a teacher had ended triumphantly, it really was at an end. He took no more pupils. As for the South Street house, it hung on the market for over a year and was finally sold 'at a great loss [in] the worst time for house property ever known in Dorchester'. It was bought by a Mr Fitch, who announced that he intended to start up another school there.[12]

# 20

# IN PARADISO

### ⸺ 1862-1870 ⸺

Situated a mile and a half from Dorchester on the Wareham Road, the Old Rectory of Winterborne Came is still an idyllic place. Writing in Italy, just a year after her father's death, Lucy Baxter remembered the 'thatched cottage with wide eaves and wider verandah, on whose rustic pillars, roses, clematis and honeysuckle' entwined. It had 'a flowery lawn in front, and a sheltering veil of trees at the side. The poet's study was in a room on the upper floor, which overlooked the sunny fruit garden'.[1]

The house is surprisingly large for the priest of such a small parish. This is because between 1804 and 1836 it was the home of a much more splendid cleric than Barnes. William England was not only the Rector of Came but sometime Archdeacon of Dorset, Rector of Owermigne and West Stafford, and also had the dubious distinction of being a magistrate involved in the trial of the Tolpuddle Martyrs. Consequently, the thatched roof and verandah are deceptive in suggesting rural humility. For this is no early Victorian sprawl, incrementally distended by extra rooms, outbuildings and Gothic embellishments. On the contrary, the building is simple, bold and ambitious, a two-storey box with central hallways, a porticoed inner fanlight, an elegant balustrade, four main rooms on the ground floor and four above. There is also a coach-house behind, though Barnes kept no carriage.[2] Yet when descending the graceful staircase or entering the elegant sitting room, his daughters were reminded daily that in coming here they had achieved a new social status. They were translated from the urban middle class to the rural gentry.

Instinctively modest, Barnes never troubled himself with such notions. After all, his new parish was not a rich one, with only a few houses. Yet unusually, it had three churches. Set among the fields, and hard by Came House, stood the secluded thirteenth-century church of Winterborne Came, with cottages and gardens grouped round. Here 'the "shrouded" elm trees and low-boughed oak trees appeared like ancient bards blessing the opulent pastures'.[3] In spring the ditches were ablaze with flowers and the lanes pungent with the smell of wild garlic. A mile or so away stood the little church of Whitcombe, Barnes's old 'curacy', with its farm house and cottages. Finally, there was a ruined stone wall and pointed window in a field, which was all that remained of the medieval church of Winterborne Farringdon. Barnes sometimes said that whereas he went to his other churches to preach, he went to Farringdon to pray.

There were also two grand residences. Came House was a splendid mansion in its own park, adjacent to the parish church. It was the home of Captain Dawson-Damer MP, Barnes's patron and the owner of the estate. Curiously, though Dawson-Damer was an old pupil and undoubtedly wished Barnes well, there is no indication that they were ever especially close. It was very different, however, with the Williams family, the owners of Herringston House. Here Barnes found new friends. For many years Mrs Williams regularly welcomed him in from his parish walk to take tea with her in the Queen Anne parlour, or perhaps beneath the enormous plaster barrel-vaulted ceiling in the Great Hall.

Barnes's arrival at Came served, if possible, to strengthen his simple faith. It was, he said, 'a living before which I know not any which I should have chosen'. That he had finally arrived in this blissful place only strengthened his conviction that all the setbacks and rejections he had suffered in past years were part of God's plan for him. In his scrapbook he pasted a skit on a popular song of the day, probably written by a pupil:

Winterborne Came Church. (Private collection)

## In Paradiso

A schoolboy sat by Napper's Mite,
Tho' long the sun had set.
He seemed with grief o'er-burdened quite
His cheek with tears was wet.
'An' where,' I asked, 'is that old Boy
To whom all languages were joy,
Who every tongue did know?'
He pointed Eastward out by Came,
And sobbed – (he scarce the words could frame)
In Paradiso – In Paradiso.

'He left me here alone', he said,
'An uninstructed Boy;

The teacher from his Pupil fled
To dwell in peaceful Joy
No more my Tutor will he be,
No more, alas! he'll punish me;
I own that I was slow.
Damer has borne him from the school
o'er Came's glad parish folks to rule,
All at his ease, oh! all at his ease, oh!

I mourn not that he's gone away
Nor kick up any shine;
For his return I do not pray,
Nor usefully repine,
For as I sit beside the street,
Whilst Busses nearly crush my feet
As they pass to and fro
I see there's no-one I can blame,
I hear he's settled down at Came,
Oh that't sho'd be so; oh that't sho'd be so. [4]

He took possession of the Rectory in August but it was not until 4 November, when he went to sleep at the bishop's palace at Salisbury, that he was instituted priest of Winterborne Came by Walter Kerr, the Lord Bishop. On 1 December he enacted the traditional ceremonials in his own parish, which required him to ring the bell and be presented with a sod of earth. Then his parochial work began in earnest. It was his intention that his parishioners should be visited every week and, accordingly, he divided the parish into four, of which he took two and his daughters – he called them his 'curates' – the other two. The following week the order was reversed.

Lucy remembered that:

Whitcombe whose people received their former curate with joy, [lay] a mile from Came along the high road. There is a long hill leading to it, between the cliffs of a deep cutting, where the fiercest winds and the hottest sun share the times of year between them. Up this long hill the parson and his daughters would toil through rain or snow or sunshine every week, greeted when they appeared on the summit with the triple harmony of the village church bells. In summer a roof of blue overhung the deep cleft of ruddy soil, whose banks were covered with wild flowers – pinks, crow's-bill, golden pennyroyal, and tender silver-weed – and the poet read sermons on them all…

Barnes would start out to visit his parishioners with a leather bag slung round his shoulder and over his cassock:

In the bag were prayer books, or at need a pocket font, or a communion service. Sometimes the well-filled pockets of the cassock coat bobbed against the comely stockinged legs – for they were apt to be full of sweets for the children – or now and then a doll might be seen with its head peering out of the clerical pocket. Thus accoutred he trod sturdily beneath the hawthorn trees, and across the shadows of the great elms in the park, and knocked with his stick at the cottage doors when he reached them. [5]

So, for the first time since he left Bagber as a boy, Barnes found himself living again among the working people of the farms. Much of his time now was spent trudging the lanes, calling in at the cottages and listening to the talk. His empathy with them was apparent from the start. The labourers of Came and their wives sensed at once that their new parson was not of the usual sort. Here was no well-meaning, but utterly alien, sprig of the gentry. This was a priest who seemed to understand their way of life. Lucy continues:

The housewives were always glad to see him, and poured out all their confidences, sure of comfort and sympathy. If he did not come on the usual day they met him with a half reproach next time, 'Ah, sir, we thought you had forgotten us'. The children would creep nearer and nearer, peeping into those big pockets from which 'goodies' were wont to come. I do not believe a child, however shy, was ever afraid of our parson... One of the women remarked to the writer, 'There, miss, we do all o' us love the passon, that we do: he be so plain. Why, bless you, I don't no more mind telling o' un all my little pains and troubles than if he was my grandmother.' Here she blushed. 'I don't mean any disrespec', miss, but o'ny to show how he do understand us, and we do seem to understand him.'

There was a great deal of coming and going at the Rectory during the following years. In the 1860s the Barnes children were all at home at one time or another. Laura was in charge of the house; Lucy and the widowed Isabel continued to live there for many years; and from time to time, both the sons were at home. William was still recovering from his 'over-reading' at Cambridge, while Egbert rested from the rigours of Gooch's engine-shops. Only Julia took every opportunity to get away.

She had contrived to be absent in Italy when the family moved into the Rectory, probably having taken a position as a lady's companion while pursuing her musical career. In June 1863, however, she turned up again in an agitated state, complaining of being 'out of health in the warm climate of Florence'. This was a pretext. The reason that she was so upset was that she was struggling to decide between a musical career and love. Love won. Within six weeks she had recovered her health, and informed the family that she was to be married. The banns were read at the British Episcopal Church in Florence in September, and even before the final reading, her bridegroom arrived at the Rectory. He was William Charles ('Charlie') Dunn, a well-respected English dentist in that city. On the 29th of that month, the Revd Ponton married Julia to her Charlie at Winterborne Came. They left immediately, to return to Florence.

Julia was right in fearing that marriage would put an end to her singing career. In September 1866, Charlie wrote to tell Barnes that he had become a grandfather for the first time and the child had been named William in his honour. Within a year another son, Edward, was born and then, in 1869, a daughter named May. There is no record that Julia ever returned to the Rectory, and Barnes probably never saw his daughter again. The link with Florence, however, was not broken, for in later years there were frequent summer visits from Barnes's 'Italian' grandchildren.

These were not only Dunns. When Julia was expecting her second child she felt the need for female support and wrote to ask that one of her sisters should come out to Italy. Lucy was chosen. But she could hardly travel unaccompanied, and it was fortunate that, by chance, one of Charlie Dunn's friends from Florence, Tom Baxter, was on hand to escort her from the French coast to that city. In some mysterious way, however, the two seem to have prolonged their trip, for they took over two weeks to get to their destination. And when they finally arrived in Florence, they announced they were engaged.

The pair seem to have anticipated some opposition to their union from Barnes, though at the age of thirty, Lucy was free to do as she wished. Their doubts arose from the fact that Tom Baxter was an apothecary, which in Victorian times was thought of as a trade rather than a profession. Was Lucy not marrying beneath her? At any rate, Charlie Dunn felt it necessary to write to Barnes to reassure him, declaring that he had known Baxter for twenty years, adding:

> He has not the polish of a man of society for a very good reason, he is not and never has been and never, I imagine, will be a man to seek or wish to enter society, but for what constitutes really a gentleman... kindliness of heart, courtesy, forbearance and cultivation of mind – I know very few indeed who could stand a favourable comparison with him.

Barnes left the decision to Lucy, but was no doubt gratified when Baxter himself wrote later to say that he had an annual income of some £500 and savings of more than £1,000. In fact he was much better off than Barnes himself, whose fears for the future of his children were probably as much derived from his own experiences of poverty as from considerations of social status. So, Lucy was married to Baxter on 14 April 1868 in Florence, and on 26 April the following year, her daughter, Grace, was born.

She was brought over in August 1869 for a visit to her grandfather. Grace was the first of four Baxter children and as the years went on, they too joined the other young 'Italian' visitors to Came.

Baxter's apprehension that he might not be considered socially acceptable as a son-in-law of the Rector of Came was not without grounds. For, despite Barnes's humanity and sweetness of disposition when ministering to the working people, there is some indication that in later years he became protective of his hard-won social status. After all, he had been welcomed by 'society' in London, and could consider himself a friend of members of the gentry such as Tennant and Mrs Williams. It is also probable that the highly proper 'Miss' Barnes, i.e. Laura, and Isabel Shaw, the wealthy widow, would have encouraged him to remember who he was and to avoid 'low' connections.

An indication of this stiffening social attitude is revealed by Barnes's treatment of his younger son. Egbert was the only one of his children to enter what might have been considered a socially-dubious occupation, that of a railway engineer. When he finished his apprenticeship, he married Jane Creasy of Swindon, the daughter of a mere pattern-maker. The couple then went to live in Battersea, and Egbert obtained work on the construction of the new underground railway. But his father did not attend Egbert's wedding at St Marks in Swindon, and there is no record of any later correspondence between them. True, he baptised their first child, William Egbert Creasy Barnes, in 1867, but in later years, when the unfortunate and unhealthy Egbert drifted into poverty, though both his 'Italian' brothers-in-law lent him money, the family at Came largely ignored him.

Barnes, meanwhile, was required to act as sole executor of the will of his late son-in-law, Joseph Shaw, who in 1861 had left his entire estate to Isabel. Immediately following her husband's death, she had come home, and because she was still only twenty-two, she was probably glad to let her father manage her business affairs. This he did for many years, with the help of Henry Lock, the Dorchester solicitor. Much of Shaw's investment had been in loans to people in the Weymouth and Dorchester area, and there were many decisions to be made. As for Isabel, though she may not initially have been aware that she was a considerable heiress, as the details of Shaw's business were revealed, this slowly became apparent to her. This caused tensions, for she was well-off while living in a household where her father was still hard-pressed financially, and where her brothers and sisters were practically without an income. The rector, of course, was the soul of rectitude. He would never have diverted Isabel's income into his own household expenses. But the presence of a rich little widow living in a cash-strapped home was an anomaly, and the total control of her finances would have been a temptation, if Barnes were the type ever to be tempted.[6] He was not. Ruefully, he wrote to J.F. Furnival of the Philological Society in January 1863: 'P.S. I might have joined your society had I not too many children to have spare guineas.'[7]

William ('Willie') Miles, the older son, had finally been ordained in 1865, but had lived on at his father's house with no obvious prospects. Then, on 6 September 1866, when Barnes was walking home along Herringston Lane after a visit to the Williams family, he met the Revd Derrithorne Vyvyan, who was soon to give up the living of Winterborne Monkton, the parish next to Came. Vyvyan told him that he had been at that moment walking to Came Rectory with a letter. Mrs Strangways, the patron of Monkton, had offered the living to Willie. This news brought huge delight to all the family, but especially to Barnes. It meant that, at last, his elder son was settled in the world, with a genteel profession and a moderate income of his own. Moreover, Barnes now knew that in his declining years, he would have a son on hand. So it proved. For the rest of Barnes's life, Willie was his neighbouring cleric. This proved especially fortunate because his son was very willing to act as his locum when he wanted to go off lecturing.

Though Willie was inducted as Rector of Monkton in October, he continued to live at home. Not until nearly two years later, in June 1865, did he move into his own Rectory, when he married Emily Le Cocq, daughter of a Jersey doctor. In the ensuing years, six children were born to the Barneses of Monkton, and though two died in infancy, there were still four to give their grandfather a noisy welcome whenever he walked over to Monkton. He integrated this walk into his parish rounds. He would begin by visiting the outlying cottages at Whitcombe, then call at Herringston House for tea with Mrs Williams, and afterwards take his supper at Monkton before walking home in the moonlight.

Delighting in his new duties, he now threw himself into innumerable parochial responsibilities. A choir was formed at Came and, with his daughters' help, a Sunday school. Then, on 6 November 1863, he opened a night school at the Rectory to teach the farm workers to read and write. With some financial help from the squire, Captain Damer, he also established an independent Church of England day school for the estate children under the elderly, untrained Miss Croft. Soon he became a regular visitor to her classroom. Nevertheless, raising the money to pay her was a continual problem, even though with fuel and furnished rooms provided, she received only £20 a year, lower even than the pay of many farm workers. There was always a struggle to find the money, but to employ a certificated teacher from one of the training colleges would have been even more expensive. Besides, Barnes had adopted a rather dismissive attitude to the colleges ever since his rejection for the post of principal at Winchester.

The school at Came was established because there was still no compulsory education for children in the 1860s. In the country, elementary education was provided chiefly by the various churches. So, when at last W. E. Forster's Education Act of 1870 made it compulsory for local authorities to provide free primary education for all, Barnes was by no means a supporter. He was jealous for the interests of the Church of England. In his opinion, Christian belief was the basis of all education, and schooling without religion was mere instruction. The trinity of the aristocracy, gentry and clergy were there to provide the poor with precisiely this kind of support. His views, therefore, were essentially feudal, with little understanding of just how far this social structure had already broken down in the great industrial centres of Victorian England.

Despite his many parish duties, he did not allow them to reduce his commitment to working-class education. He continued to travel the West Country, lecturing at various institutes and parish halls in towns and villages. But now he rarely, if ever, spoke about scientific subjects. This was probably because, like thousands of other thoughtful, pious people at this time, he had come to feel a profound unease at the direction of much scientific thought. As far back as 1844, when he had published his first book of poetry, he had lamented these new tendencies:

## The Happy Days When I Wer Young

In happy days when I wer young,
An' had noo ho, an' laugh'd an' zung,
The maid were merry by her cow,
An' men were merry wi' the plough;
But never talk'd, at hwome or out
O' doors, o' what's a-talk'd about
By many now, – that to despise
The laws o' God an' man is wise.

Vrom where wer all this venom brought,
To kill our hope an' taint our thought?[8]

('An had noo ho' – and had no care)

Nowhere in his writings does Barnes refer to Darwin's *The Origin of Species*, which came out in 1859, and he probably never read it. But he would have been aware of its content and it would have come as a shock, though not a surprise, for the geologists Lyell and Sedgwick had unwittingly prepared the way by demonstrating that the creation of the world must surely have occurred much earlier than the year 4004 BC, as calculated by Archbishop Ussher, and taken much longer than the biblical seven days. Nevertheless, the thesis of Darwin's book, that an evolution of species had been brought about by natural selection acting upon random mutation, seemed to many to be incompatible with the biblical doctrine of the creation of fixed and immutable species. And though a number of prominent churchmen, such as Charles Kingsley, found no contradiction between old beliefs and the new science, Barnes for one was having none of it. His innately conservative instincts rejected such views. Therefore, preferring the ancient pieties, he gave up science.

Instead he turned to his old loves, philology and poetry, and these were the chief topics of his lectures now. On 14 October 1862 he read his poems in Sherborne, and on 6 November he lectured in Devizes on 'The Western English Dialect'. This title was fast becoming the staple of his talks, because it still gave a veneer of instruction to these evenings, but also supplied a pretext for him to read his poems, which is what many of his listeners really came for. Audiences were enthusiastic. 600 people turned out to hear him at the YMCA in Bristol in 1864, and 230 packed in for a 'penny reading' in Somerton in 1868, with many turned away. Occasionally the audience was disappointing, as in Weymouth where 'the reader himself …[was] the only one in the room who appeared to enjoy the selection'[9] More typical was the adulation of Alfred Cockerell Taylor from Westbury, who wrote to say that he had walked nine miles to hear Barnes read at Warminster and would willingly do so again.[10] Few English poets at any time have elicited such love and veneration as Barnes received from these provincial audiences.

He was now something of a local institution. The awareness of his special contribution to Dorset life is revealed in the *Chronicle* review on 29 January 1863 of the third collection of his dialect poems. This paper, which for twelve years had refused to publish him, now discussed his work in reverential tones. Apparently, the editor was not prepared to trust this job to a local hack but got in someone of scholarship to do it. There were not too many people locally who could assert with confidence that Barnes had 'done [in philology] enough to place his name by the side of Horne Tooke and Max Muller, and that is more than any other British Philologist has achieved'. Moreover, the anonymous reviewer displayed a clear understanding that Barnes's philological work had provided a necessary refutation to those who had doubted whether anything written in dialect could ever be considered real poetry:

> The Dorset dialect has found no more fitting expositor than the reverend poet himself, whose linguistic attainments have enabled him to bestow a scholarly and philosophical attention on what might appear a very homely and unpromising subject… His poems are literally erudite as we assert, yet they are so popular that no-one ever suspected them of being learned.[11]

The word 'reverend' here is perhaps a trifle ambiguous, suggesting not only Barnes's clerical calling but also the degree of reverence in which he was held. He had become a sage.

Other, humbler, appreciations arrived regularly at the Rectory by post. Among these was a letter from a Dorset-born shoemaker who had been barely able to afford one of the books of verse but wrote to ask if a cheap collected edition could be made available. The poetry, he wrote:

> … brings back the familiar words of the loved ones that are gone, and I love you – I have tried for years to see you and hear you read, and I hope I shall yet; but if not, I hope I shall see you when earthly distinctions are passed; may you long live to write, and may you long live to read, and may the earth be always blessed with such lights.[12]

Occupied as he was with all these matters, Barnes's days at Came soon fell into into a gentle routine. After breakfast he would take a stroll round the garden before going up to his study-bedroom to answer the letters which had strewn the table. With obvious relief, he would eventually come down with the replies and drop them into the green postbox under the verandah, which was cleared each evening. Now he was free to take his stick, whistle up his little dog, Cara, and go off on his rounds visiting his parishioners. Afternoons were spent in his study, working at his sermons or his philology, before going downstairs for supper. Then he might relax in his favourite armchair to listen to his daughters play and sing.

Sometimes, on summer afternoons, the elderly poet would carry out his basket chair to sit in a favourite corner of the garden, beneath red hawthorn blossoms or golden laburnum collonades. Here among the tamarisks, syringa and lilac he would plant his seat and rest for an hour or so, dreaming with his eyes closed beside his favourite bush. It was one he had brought from South Street, in memory of Julia. She had tended it in life, and he had tucked the petals round her face when she lay in her coffin. It was a white rose.

# 21

# SIREN VOICES

## —— 1864-1870 ——

Following his move to Came, Barnes's impulse to write dialect poetry faded. He no longer felt the need to keep on with it. During those years in which he had battled his way in the world, recollections of Blackmore had provided refreshment and solace. But now he lived in Paradise he had no need for consolation. He was once more among the people he loved; the ploughmen, shepherds and cottage wives of the Came estate. It was as if he were in Bagber again.

Not uncommonly, when poetic energies flag these forces are transferred to prose. So it was with Barnes. Much of his leisure now was taken up with writing occasional pieces for magazines. These earned him a useful extra income which, though several of his adult children were at last independent, still came in handy. Happily, Victorian England supported quite a number of genteel publications addressed to the general reader and editors were willing to pay a modest rate for copy. Barnes was their man. His brain was still crowded with thoughts and his speculations on all sorts of topics served very well to fill up a column or two. Manuscripts in his arthritic scrawl were regularly addressed to: *Fraser's Magazine*, *The Reader*, *The Ladies' Treasury*, *MacMillan's Magazine* and *Chamber's Journal*. His articles were educational though rarely challenging, supplying the need of the middle class for general knowledge. Among other pieces, he wrote about: 'The Rise and Progress of Trial by Jury', 'Old Song-History and Tradition', 'A View of Christian Marriage', 'The Welsh Triads' (one of his hobby-horses was to point out the threeness of things), 'Plagiarism', 'The Origin of Mankind' and 'The Church in Ireland'.

There were other more scholarly pieces which appeared in such publications such as the *Philological Society Journal*, and the *Archaeological Journal*. These brought him prestige rather than money. He also supplied written evidence in 1869 to the 'Government Commisssion on the Employment of Children, Young Persons and Women in Agriculture'.

Everything now conspired to induce him to abandon his dialect poetry; one example was the advice of Alexander MacMillan. Having been persuaded to contribute one or two poems in standard English to *MacMillan's Magazine*, Barnes now received several letters from the publisher urging him to abandon the dialect and to write more English verses. On 21 October 1864, MacMillan wrote:

> I enclose a small cheque for your two admirable poems. I cannot help wishing that all your poems – or the greater part of them could be read in ordinary English speech. I personally don't dislike a dialect, and being used to the true basis of English the old Scottish tongue (perhaps you wouldn't admit this) (I) can always make a good shot at what any words mean, having Scotch character in them. But then you know it does not fall to the lot of the whole British public to have the blessing of a Scotch birth. For the sake of the more unfortunate can't you do something. Yours very truly A. MacMillan.[1]

This was all very flattering and he began to weaken. Another siren voice was heard in the New Year of 1866, when his old friend the Hon. Caroline Norton came to lunch at Came. Years before she had urged him to 'Cocknify' his verses, and she was not going to give up now. In the end, bowing to the pressure from such very distinguished people, he started to work on what he called 'translations' of some of his dialect poems. These did not come easily. Writing in the dialect had been completely natural to him. Switching to standard English was hard labour. This would not have been serious, except that the tedious work of 'translation' exhausted his imaginative energies and acted to repress his true poetic impulse.

The translation business accounts for the fact that there are many dual versions of Barnes's poems, dialect and standard English. The differences are revealing. Consideration of just one stanza of a poem will serve to illustrate the effects of translation. The dialect version reads:

## The Wind Up the Stream

The sheaded stream did run below
Tall elems, on the bank, in row,
That leafy ivy stems did clim'
In light a-shot vrom limb to limb:
An' winds did play, now brisk, now slack,
All up the stream, a dreven back
The runnen weaves; an' meake em seem
To be an upward-flowen stream:
As hope do zometimes meake us think
Our life do rise, the while do zink.[2]

('clim' – climb, but pronounced in the dialect to rhyme with 'limb')

The standard English translation runs:

## The Wind Up the Stream

The shaded river ran below
A ledge, with elms that stood in row,
By leafy ivy-stems intwin'd,
In light that shot from rind to rind;
And winds that play'd, now brisk, now slack,
Against the stream, were driving back
The running waves; and made them seem
To show an upward-flowing stream:
As man, while hope beguiles him, thinks
His life is rising, while it sinks.[3]

These two poems explore the same idea, that a phenomenon in nature, such as the wind blowing water upstream, mimics a recurrent feature of human experience, which is that at the very moment when our fortunes are fading, we may be deluded into hope by false omens. Yet the dialect version has a vividness and immediacy which the English one does not. The 'stream' in the first has been replaced by the less apposite 'river' in the second, purely to obtain another syllable to make the line scan. The 'stream' runs below the 'elems' in the one, and below the less relevant 'ledge' in the other, while the replacement of 'limb to limb' by 'rind to rind' seems to be a matter of desperate, and completely inappropriate, rhyming. The penultimate line of the English version gives the game away: 'As man, while hope beguiles him…' Barnes's English verses frequently resolve themselves into such Johnsonian generalities. By contrast the dialect version: 'As hope do zometimes meake us think…' is both natural and unforced. It has the rhythm of living speech. So, even within the space of a mere ten lines, the many changes needed to 'translate' the poem into standard English lead to a significant loss of precision and immediacy.

Not all of Barnes's readers shared MacMillan's opinions. One of his unknown admirers fully understood from the first the significance and originality of his use of dialect. In 1868, the same year in which Barnes published his English poems, a young Catholic convert, Gerard Manley Hopkins, resolved to become a Jesuit and priest, and burned his own poems with the intention of dedicating his life entirely to God, though eventually he began to write again. Years later he put his thoughts about the Dorset

POEMS

IN THE

DORSET DIALECT,

BY

WILLIAM BARNES.

" White Duncliffe is the traveller's mark."
*p.* 104.

LONDON :
JOHN RUSSELL SMITH,
36, SOHO SQUARE.
——
MDCCCLXX.

Title page to the 1870 edition of Barnes's poems. (Dorset County Museum)

poems in a letter to a friend, Robert Bridges, who had been disdainful about Barnes's use of dialect. In replying, Hopkins identified the value he found in it: that the dialect's 'lawful charm and use I take it to be this, that it sort of guarantees the spontaneousness of thought'. Of Barnes, he said, 'he is a perfect artist and of a most spontaneous inspiration; it is as if Dorset life and Dorset landscape had taken flesh and tongue in the man'. Later he wrote to Edmund Gosse, 'I am the only poet of this generation, except Barnes, who has steadily maintained a literary conscience'.[4]

Nevertheless, by 1868 Barnes had assembled enough 'translations' to fill a book and when bringing it out, he changed not only the language of his poems but also his publisher. For it was not his old friend and faithful supporter John Russell Smith, but Alexander MacMillan who issued his *Poems of Rural Life in Common English* in 1868. Barnes was hopeful that the book would at last make his reputation in the greater literary world. There was even talk of an edition uniform with that of Lord Tennyson. Yet Barnes had his doubts, and he put them in the 'Preface':

As I think that some people, beyond the bounds of Wessex, would allow me the pleasure of believing that they may have deemed the matter of my homely poems in our Dorset mother-speech to be worth their reading, I have written a few of like kind, in common English; not, however, without a misgiving that what I have done for a wider range of readers, may win the opinion of fewer.

His misgivings were justified. Whereas the 1879 collected edition of his dialect poems went into seven editions by 1905, his book of English poems was never reprinted in England.

Yet as his poetic output diminished, his reputation began to thrive, and he was even becoming known beyond the seas. In 1864 a Boston publisher issued an edition of the Dorset poems, and in 1869 another in Massachusetts brought out a volume of his poems in common English. Whether Barnes ever received any payment is doubtful. Even if he had, it was unlikely to have been substantial. He once admitted that he had rarely received more than £5 for any of his books. Nevertheless, to be thought worthy to be pirated was in itself flattering.

Even more satisfying was a letter he received from his old friend, Charles Tennant, dated 15 June 1870, inviting him to give a public reading of his poems at Tennant's home: 62 Russell Square. At last he was to have his London debut in front of an illustrious audience. Tennant wrote:

My Dear Mr Barnes, we have fixed Friday the 25th for the reading, and have sent out a good many cards. I enclose one to convince you that you are caught, and Mrs Tennant begs you to write the 'Hon. Mrs Norton' on the back, and send it to her, as she will be delighted to take the opportunity of meeting you, and we of making her acquaintance. We have asked Dawson Damer, and I am sure he will come if he can. Also Disraeli and other MPs on both sides.

The event duly took place and Barnes must have read some dialect poems because we know that his listeners were provided with printed words so that they might follow the sense. Yet it is very likely that his friends, especially Alexander MacMillan, would have persuaded him (always with his best interests in mind) to concentrate on reading his English poems. Indeed, the evening was probably something of a book launch for the collection of English poems that MacMillan had recently published. Lucy Baxter records that the occasion went off 'very successfully'. Following this, his society friends cooperated in giving him a jolly time in London for a few days. He had his likeness taken by a fashionable photographer, he sat with Tennyson and the Bishop of Gloucester at a dinner party, and was escorted to Lady Ashburton's to hear the singing of Titiens, Gardoni and others.

And after that… nothing. That was all there came of it; mere pleasantness in a fashionable drawing room. His poems did not take off like wildfire, nor was he lionised by the literary world. He was too old to be a lion. True, his dialect poems continued to be reprinted and enjoyed moderate sales. But his work never entered the general cultural consciousness, and he was not admitted to the national pantheon of poets; nor did he ever receive the due of one who had taken a language without a literature and shaped it into art.

# 22

# PILGRIMS

## —— 1862-1867 ——

In June 1862, while still packing up to remove to Came, Barnes received a parcel containing the current issue of *MacMillan's*, carrying an unsigned but flattering review of his recent book of poems. The author announced that Barnes was 'one of the few living poets in England', and stood out even among these, because he was indebted to no literary models.[1] Enclosed was a letter from Coventry Patmore, confessing that he himself was the writer of this and another favourable notice in the *North British Review*. At last Barnes had a champion in the press. There followed some correspondence between the two and an invitation for Patmore to visit Came. Replying, he hoped he might meet Barnes in London, but declined the invitation for the time being because he felt 'unable to venture from the bedside of [his] sick wife'.

Patmore was then a thirty-nine-year-old assistant librarian at the British Museum. In his spare time he wrote poetry, and he had already come to public notice with the appearance of *The Angel in the House*, a sequence of verses celebrating married love, two parts of which had been published in 1854 and 1856, and the penultimate, 'Faithful for Ever' in 1861. Though at odds with feminist views, and mocked by cynical critics, this sentimental poem seemed to confirm conventional notions of marriage, and therefore pleased many Victorian readers.[2] What they particularly liked was its representation of passionate love within the wedded state, depicting marriage as it ought to be.

Though its initial critical reception was mixed, the poem eventually became a huge success and Patmore a literary celebrity. Whereas Barnes might reckon to sell a few hundred copies of his books, within Patmore's lifetime, sales of *The Angel in the House* reached about a million. It sold as a sort of manual for marriage, and made a popular wedding present.[3] The Patmores themselves seemed to exemplify its philosophy. By the 1850s, Coventry and his wife, Emily, were at the centre of London literary life, entertaining such celebrities as Tennyson, Browning and Carlyle. Blessed with charming children, as well artistic and social success, they appeared to be the ideal Victorian couple. But Emily had long suffered from tuberculosis and was increasingly subject to periods of illness. In July, just a month after Patmore wrote to Barnes, she died, aged thirty-eight.

Meanwhile, at Came Rectory, *The Angel in the House* had become favourite reading for the rector and his daughters. Lucy remembered that their copy of the poem was 'covered with marks of admiration'. More formally, Barnes wrote an enthusiastic review of 'Faithful for Ever' for *Fraser's Magazine* in July 1863. On 15 August, Patmore and his ten-year-old daughter, Emily Honoria, arrived at Came for a week's stay. The Barneses were confronted with a tall, thin, moustachioed man of sudden enthusiasms and brooding silences, somewhat autocratic but deeply respectful of his host. He was accompanied by a curiously intense but lively girl who was much petted by Barnes's grown-up daughters.

At first, it seemed that the uxorious widowers had much in common. They were poets who admired each other's work. They were each fathers of six children. And they were both intensely pious Anglicans, seeking consolation from faith in their bereavement. Barnes, however, was more travelled in grief, having been a widower for eleven years. This consideration, as well as the fact that he was twenty-two years Patmore's senior, a poet of some forty years standing and a great linguistic scholar, induced his guest to treat him almost with reverence. For Patmore, the visit was a sort of pilgrimage.

In a black-bordered letter from the British Museum, he had confided to Barnes that his faith had been strengthened by his wife's death: 'It will be easier to draw nearer to the church now she is with Him, and it will be to draw near to her'.[4] Barnes should have been warned. For it transpired that Patmore wanted to discuss his mystical conception of marriage, which held that by death this union was transformed from the terrestrial to the celestial, and that the relation of husband to wife mirrored that of Christ to the human soul.[5] But Barnes was no mystic, and was never comfortable with this sort of talk. Patmore later complained to others, 'I wanted to discuss the mystery of the Incarnation and I found Barnes buried in a horrible kind of thing called TIW'.

Such considerations, however, were not allowed to spoil the visit. Both families behaved well. Nevertheless, there were aspects of Patmore's enthusiasms which might not have been expected in the author of 'Faithful for Ever'. Before the visit, he had written to say that he was a great walker and would not be content with 'little walks', but wished to visit the places made sacred by Barnes's poetry, especially the haunts of the 'Blackmore Maidens'. That he was rather vague about Dorset geography was not especially surprising, but his obvious interest in young girls was. Nevertheless, when the week ended, the Patmores went home to London accompanied by the kind wishes of their friends, and Lucy noted that the time was 'greatly enjoyed' by the family. It was only afterwards that divisions emerged.

This was because, in the following year, disturbing news came to the Rectory. Patmore, it seemed, had gone on his travels to Rome and had been converted to Catholicism.[6] There was more. While there, he had become enamoured of an English Catholic lady and, on returning to England, they had been married by Dr (later Cardinal) Manning, at the appropriately named Church of St Mary of the Angels, Bayswater.

In company with many of Patmore's admirers, Barnes must have felt betrayed. How far he had opened his heart to this man is not known. Nevertheless, he might have been forgiven for thinking that 'Faithful for Ever', should now be retitled 'Faithful for About Two Years'. Patmore's defection to Catholicism must have seemed a further breach of trust. Yet there was no quarrel; Barnes disliked contention. He simply dropped him. Patmore was never again invited to Came, nor did Barnes ever afterwards write to him or review his poetry. For his part though, Patmore retained a regard for Barnes for the rest of his life, and after the latter's death wrote an obituary in the *Fortnightly Review* in which he declared him to be 'An English Classic'. Patmore married three times in all.

He was only the first of a number of literary pilgrims to Dorset in these years. On 7 September 1863, Barnes's old friend, Prince Louis-Lucien Bonaparte arrived to consult him, and on the following day they drove down to Weymouth together in a splendid carriage. Though the Prince was a nephew of Napoleon, as far as possible he had avoided French politics. He preferred to study English dialects. What could be more natural then that he should wish to consult and to renew his friendship with the renowned Dorset philologist?

There is little record of the Prince's visit but, fortunately, later pilgrims to Came included two splendid diarists, both of whom have left lively and intimate accounts of Barnes when lecturing, talking with friends or simply at home. The first of these was a young Irish customs officer, then living at Lymington in Hampshire. William Allingham was already quite a well-known poet by that time, chiefly for 'The Fairies' ('Up the airy mountain…') which had come out in 1850. He called in at Came on 23 May 1864. The two men must have got on well because Barnes was subsequently invited to lecture at Lymington and to stay the night with him. Allingham's diary recounts:

Tuesday, November 1.-Rev. Wm. Barnes comes at my invitation to give a lecture at the Literary Institution. He duly arrives by train at 3, and I gladly welcome the good old poet. We walk about the Town and he shows much interest in the Furniture Broker's shops, old china, pictures, etc. – and bargains for a little oil painting. Aide arrives whom I have invited to meet Barnes. I take them for a walk to Buckland Rings, supposed ancient British Camp; then dinner at my lodging (which I hope went off tolerably), and we moved to the Lecture Room. Mr. Barnes lectured on 'West of England Speech', and read some of his own poems. What the audience liked best was 'A Bit o' Sly Coortin', which he gave at my particular request. It was evident that on the whole he seemed to them flat, in comparison with the paid Entertainers who occasionally come round. Aide came back to sup with us at my rooms, and then drove off to Lyndhurst, Barnes promising to visit him there. B. and I chatted till near 1.

> Wednesday, November 2. – Wm. Barnes; he praised my Stratford-on-Avon dialogue, suggested some
> points of dialect, but does not understand the Warwickshire. I saw him onto the train at 1.40. A man of
> simple manners and life, and a true poet. Though he is so much my elder, I was one of the first to make
> a stir about him, in talk and by the Press. The Brownings, Tennyson, Clough, Rossetti, etc. etc. – it was I
> who introduced Barnes's Dorset poems to each and all of them.[7]

On his way home, Allingham met 'old lawyer M' who had been at the lecture the previous night. He said it 'the damnedest stuff [he] ever heard'.

Undeterred, Allingham asked Barnes back again the following year. On the appointed afternoon, he left work and found Barnes sitting by his fire in Prospect Place. The subject of the lecture was 'House and House Life' – 'caves, tents, huts, etc. Wives (laughter), Praise of the good wife'. Clearly, Barnes was repeating material from his early writings, such as *Humilis Domus*. Allingham and his listeners could not make much of it: 'Odd lecture, rather puzzled everybody'.

After breakfast next day, Allingham read to his guest from The *Ancient Laws of Ireland* and *Gammer Gurton's Needle*, neither of which Barnes knew. The entertainment was merely to fill up the time before they were to embark on a crossing to the Isle of Wight, where Barnes had been invited to visit the Poet Laureate, Alfred Lord Tennyson. So off they marched down to the harbour, Barnes with 'his old-fashioned ways, his gaiters, his long-knitted purse which he ties up in a knot, broad-brimmed hat, homely speech'. In the event they were both very nearly drowned because their ferry 'fouled a collier' on the way.

> Wednesday , November 1 (1865).– We drive in a fly to Farringford, where T., Mrs T., Miss T. meet us in the
> hall. T. and B. at once on easy terms, having simple poetic minds and mutual goodwill. Talk of Ancient Britons,
> barrow roads, etc. I to upper room and dress, T. comes into me and we go down together. Dinner: stories of
> ghosts and dreams. To the drawing-room as usual, where T. has his port, B. no wine. T. says: 'modern fame is
> nothing: I'd rather have an acre of land. I shall go down, down! I am up now'. T. went upstairs by himself.[8]

After tea the proceedings became farcical with the entrance of the photographer, Julia Margaret Cameron, and her two sons. She was a friend and neighbour of Tennyson's. When the Laureate appeared she showed him:

> … a small firework toy called 'Pharaoh's Serpents', a kind of pastile, which, when lighted, twists about in
> a worm shape. Mrs C. said they were poisonous and forbade us to touch. T. In defiance put out his hand
> – 'Don't touch 'em!' shrieked Mrs. C. 'You sha'n't, Alfred'. But Alfred did. 'Wash your hands then!' But
> Alfred wouldn't and rubbed his moustache instead, enjoying Mrs. C.'s agonies. Then she said to him: 'Will
> you come tomorrow and be photographed?' He, very emphatically, 'No'.

For some reason, Mrs Cameron studiously ignored Barnes. Possibly this was because, from his homely appearance, she had concluded that he was a non-entity. Later she became quite malicious. She persisted in pointedly praising a 'great poet', by whom she meant the verse dramatist, Sir Henry Taylor. And she refused Tennyson's request that she should photograph Barnes, because 'she objected to the top of his head'. It is true that, as his hair receded, the shape of Barnes's forehead had become rather bulbous, and perhaps her objection genuinely derived from some sort of daft aesthetic. She had, however, already taken celebrated portraits of Tennyson, whose own forehead was not exactly inconspicuous. Probably her refusal was merely to disguise her jealousy. Be that as it may, a chance was lost, and posterity deprived of what might have been an interesting and useful portrait of the Dorset poet.

That evening, Tennyson took Barnes up to his top room for a chat, and the conversation strayed onto the contentious matter of religion:

> Darwinism – 'Man from ape – would that really make any difference? Huxley, Tyndall'.
> 'Time is nothing,' said T., 'are we not all part of Deity?' 'Pantheism?' hinted Barnes, who was not at ease in

this sort of speculation. 'Well!' says T., 'I think I believe in Pantheism, of a sort.' Barnes to bed, T. and I up ladder to the roof to look at Orion. Then to my room, where more talk. He likes Barnes, he says, 'but he is not accustomed to strong views theologic'.

There followed one last meeting between the three. Ever since he had first read *Persuasion*, Tennyson had wanted to see the Cobb at Lyme Regis, and in August 1867 he set out on a walking tour with Allingham to do so. First they took the train to Dorchester. Travelling second class, Tennyson busied himself smoking and talking to a 'cockney Clock-winder' who got out at every station to attend to the railway company's clocks. In Dorchester they booked rooms at the Antelope and walked around the town for a while. Allingham takes up the story:

> The twilight being fine I propose that we should visit William Barnes, whom T. knows and likes. I show the way to Came Vicarage, where I enjoyed hospitality from Saturday to Monday a year or two before. The cottage-parsonage lies in a hollow among trees about a mile from Dorchester, separated from the public road by a little grass-plot and shrubbery. We find the gate by starlight and reach the house door between 9 and 10 o'clock. The worthy old Poet-Vicar is truly delighted to see us, especially such a guest as T. (whose poetry, he used to say, has 'heart-tone' in it.)

> Barnes himself lets us in or comes out at once into the passage – 'Here's an honour!' Little Miss Barnes and Mrs. Shaw, a married daughter appear. B. says 'put out something! put out something!' with hospitable fervour, tho' we lack no bodily refreshment. Barnes himself, by the way, though not a teetotaller, is an abstemious man, very plain and inexpensive in his diet. We are pressed to stay but can't. Talk of Maiden Castle, Irish duns and raths. T. tells his story of his car-driver, 'The King of Connaught.' Then we go, with Barnes with us to near Dorchester, talking of British Antiquities, Wareham, Sun-worship, etc.[9]

A biographer of Barnes has suggested that there was another literary pilgrim to Came this year, one seeking advice on whether he could make a career as a writer.[10] Thomas Hardy was then twenty-seven, and had recently returned to Bockhampton in ill health from the London office of the architect Arthur Blomfield, where had been working as an assistant. Now, on the basis of only one published article, he was pondering the possibility of taking up writing as a profession. So he needed advice. To whom then, should he turn, but the only writer of prestige known to him personally, his erstwhile Latin mentor, William Barnes? At this time Hardy was pondering many questions. What were his prospects in the literary world? Should he write poetry or drama? How far should he employ the dialect? Surely, Barnes would know. What could have been easier then, than for him to walk over to Came one evening, to consult his old friend? He may indeed have called, but there is no evidence that he actually did so.[11]

Curiously, both writers were in contact with the publisher Alexander MacMillan at this date. As has been recounted, he had written a number of letters to Barnes attempting to persuade him to abandon dialect composition in favour of poems in 'common English'. Now, in 1868, Hardy sent MacMillan his first attempt at a novel, entitled *The Poor Man and the Lady*. MacMillan rejected it on the grounds that the depiction of upper-class life was unconvincing and too polemical, but enclosed with his letter was the written verdict of his reader. John Morley had pronounced the novel to be, 'a very curious and original performance', and added that 'the opening pictures of the Christmas Eve in the tranter's house are of really good quality'.[12] While MacMillan was urging Barnes to give up dialect writing, his own reader was praising its appearance in Hardy's first novel.

The text of *The Poor Man and the Lady* does not survive, but Morley's words suggest strongly that the passages to which he refers were those which Hardy later recycled to provide the opening chapters of *Under the Greenwood Tree*. And these are very Barnesian, for the Yuletide scenes at Tranter Dewy's cottage, with his family, friends and neighbours coming in, owe a great deal to such Barnes poems as 'Keepen Up O' Christmas' and 'Chris'mas Invitation':

Come down to-morrow night; an' mind,
Don't leave thy fiddle-bag behind;
We'll sheake a lag, an' drink a cup
O' eale, to keep wold Chris'mas up…

…An' ev'ry woone shall tell his teale,
An' ev'ry woone shall zing his zong,
An' ev'ry woone wull drink his eale
To love an' frien'ship all night long.[13]

Literary influence is difficult to prove but there is no doubt that the young Hardy was familiar with Barnes's poems, in which he would have discovered scenes, characters, motifs and dialogue which were later to reappear in a modified form in his own novels. Here he found accounts of haymakings, harvest homes and club walkings, like those described in *Far From the Madding Crowd* and *Tess of the D'Urbervilles*. Barnes's Blackmore maidens, moreover, chatting 'out o' door', anticipate Bathsheba and Lizzy Smallbury giggling over a valentine, while his shepherds and milkmaids 'O' the Farm' present prototypes of Gabriel Oak and Tess. Here too were tales of a homestead falling into hand, which he took up in *The Woodlanders*, and here was a cameo of a betrayed girl:

…blushen Jeane so shy an' meek,
That seldom let us hear her speak,
That wer a-courted an' undone
By Farmer Woodley's woldest son;
An' after she'd a-been vorzook,
Wer voun, a-drown'd in Longmead brook…[14]

This reads like a novel in little, a preliminary sketch for Tess.

Most important of all for its influence on Hardy was Barnes's demonstration that the Dorset dialect was fit for purpose as a literary medium. The lively dialogue of 'Don't Ceare' presents an ironical chorus of country voices much like that which Hardy later employed. It turns out, therefore, that Barnes's single-handed introduction of the Dorset dialect in literature was to have a future in Hardy's novels.

As time went on, Hardy's books became known as the 'Wessex' novels, because he employed the name of the sixth-century kingdom of Alfred, in Chapter 50 of *Far From the Madding Crowd*, to signify the south-west region of modern England.[15] Yet, as has been seen, even here he was anticipated by Barnes, who first used the term in 1868, six years before its appearance in Hardy.[16] In this matter, it seems that Hardy had not only forgotten where he had read the name, he had forgotten that he had done so. And this was because the works of Barnes were so familiar to him that they had become an unperceived omnipresence in his mind.

Whether or not Hardy, at this crucial moment in his career, actually did call on Barnes to seek advice remains a matter for speculation. Yet what might fairly be maintained is that of all the literary pilgrims who flocked to Came in the 1860s and '70s, Hardy was the most frequent, revisiting Barnes again and again, if only in recollection and creative imagination.

# 23

# PURE ENGLISH

## — 1862-1880 —

What so exasperated Coventry Patmore during his visit to Came was that all Barnes wanted to talk about was his new book on philology. He was absorbed with the subject, and continued to be so. For, in the early 1860s, when his poetic powers were dimishing fast, he began a great intellectual journey, undertaken entirely alone, which was to produce six books over the next two decades. His latest had a curious title, deriving from the name of the god from whom Barnes believed the Teutonic race had taken its name. It was called *Tiw; or, A View of the Roots and Stems of the English as a Teutonic Language.*[1] It became, according to Lucy, 'one of the author's pets among his literary children', which was not surprising because he believed that he had discovered nothing less than the origin of all language, the theory which was explained in his book.

The commonplace observation that clusters of English words of related meaning shared a similarity of form was the mainspring of his argument. For example, the word 'clang' indicates the sound produced by striking one hard body on another, as do similar words such as 'clunk' , 'clink' and 'clank'. Another of his examples was taken from the verb 'to mingle', which he defined as to be together, or to put together, with its related meanings of forming up, bending or wrapping up, and beating, blending, mincing or moistening into a mass. Drawing upon his knowledge of many dialects, he was able to list many related words such as 'mung' and 'mang', both of which mean to 'mix' or 'mash'. To these he could add: 'monger', which signifies a store owner who keeps together a collection of goods; a 'muggle', which is a confusion; 'muggy', which denotes mixed weather; 'munch', which means to chew together; and 'mag-pie', which is a bird of mingled colours.

Were these similiarities coincidental? Barnes thought not. In *Tiw*, he suggested that in primitive times language was limited to a few fundamental sounds or words which he calls 'roots'.[2] For example, the concept of mingling was indicated by the root, 'M$\star$NG', ($\star$ indicates a vowel). This was one of the forty-nine roots he identified in his book. And from this basic word stock, he believed that the whole English language had grown. Variations of form could be introduced by changing vowels and consonantal suffixes, and such changes allowed for modifications in meaning. New verbal requirements encouraged the growth of new forms which, in the course of time, sprouted, branched and rubbed together. Some of these 'stems' died and some flourished. But though they might be formed from the roots, the reverse was not true. Roots, he thought, were irreducible.

He outlined his theory in the 'Introduction':

> My view of the English, as a Teutonic tongue, is that the bulk of it was formed from about fifty primary roots, of such endings and beginnings as the sundry clippings that are still in use by the English speech. I have reached these roots through the English provincial dialects and other Teutonic speech-forms, and I deem them primary ones, inasmuch as, by the known course of Teutonic word-building and word-wear, our sundry forms of stem-words might have come from them, but could not have yielded them.[3]

There was a paradox here. After the publication of *The Origin of Species* in 1859, Barnes had turned away from science and taken refuge in his other love, philology. But the theory of language outlined in *Tiw* was not only original, it was evolutionary. It involved a progressive movement through time, brought about by a form of linguistic selection. Even if only subconsciously, he could not escape the Darwinian zeitgeist.

His theory was not only novel, it was universal. It accounted not just for the growth of the Anglo-Saxon language and Teutonic languages, but for all languages. Moreover, his metaphor of roots and stems was socially significant. Behind it was a vision of the primitive agricultural society, in which people lived close to the soil. The Teutonic root words, he felt, brought us nearer to fundamental human experiences, to simple actions, feelings and things, rather than the concepts and abstractions in which more developed societies deal. Moreover, these root words are 'purer', growing up, as they do, from the bottom of the 'well of English undefiled'.[4] They take their hold in the felt experience of folk communities, like that of the West Saxon kingdom. And he sensed that the lives of these people – and by implication those of Dorset labourers – were somehow less abstract and artificial, and more real than those of the Victorian middle classes. What is more, by deriving many of his examples of roots and stems from regional dialects, he felt their linguistic primacy: 'From this insight into the upbuilding of English I perceive that the provincial dialects are not jargons but true and good forms of Teutonic speech'. Once again, the Dorset dialect had come out on top.

Which is all very curious, if not entirely persuasive. One of the few readers who attempted to grasp his argument, his friend Charles Tennant, gently hinted at obvious difficulties when he wrote, 'Some of your distinctions between roots and stems seem to me to require a nice discernment'. And so they do. Yet Barnes himself was sure that he was on to something and continued for many years, while engaged in studying dialects, to collect more stem words from his original roots. And because he had convinced himself of the truth of his theory, he had no difficulty in finding further proof of it. But he also wanted to convince others. *Tiw* was not so much a thesis as a manifesto.

Little wonder then that, in some quarters, Barnes was getting the reputation of a crank, especially among the members of the Philological Society. This august body had been founded in 1842, and its members included Thomas Arnold of Rugby and Richard Chevenix Trench, Dean of Westminster. Though originally formed to 'investigate the Structure, the Affinity and the History of Languages', its members soon began to concentrate on aspects of English in particular. In 1861, Frederick James Furnivall was elected secretary and he, like Chevenix Trench, was a critic of the dominance of Latin and Romance elements in standard English. Therefore, sensing a fellow spirit down in Dorset, Furnivall wrote to Barnes to request a paper to be read to members. The reply he received was uncharacteristically grandiloquent for Barnes, though this may simply hint at his increasing confidence in the importance of his work: 'Yes, I will write you a paper on the Dorset or South Western English, with its Teutonic bearings. I want to give such a monograph to the world'.[5]

In total, he submitted four papers to the Society in 1863 and '64, but because he could not afford the return ticket to London they were read to members by Furnivall. They were: 'Our elder Brethren, the Frisians, their Language and Literature as illustrative of those of England'; 'Traces of a Primary Root f★ in the Indo-Teutonic Languages'; the 'Language of the Stone Age'; and 'Lost English Words'. Daringly, Barnes illustrated one of his papers with a dialect report of Queen Victoria's speech at the recent opening of Parliament. It read: 'We be a-bid by Her Majesty to tell you, that, vor-all the hwome war in North America [the Civil War] is a holden on, the common treade 'o the land, vor the last year, don't seem to be a vell-off'. This was, he said, a demonstration: 'to show that matter which is usually given in the language of hard words, as the poor call them, can be given them in their own homely speech, and therefore could be given them in plain English'.

This rendering of the Queen's speech seems to have offended members of the Philological Society, probably because they thought it both eccentric and disrespectful. On 4 June Furnivall reported:

> I read your papers last night at our meeting, but I am sorry to say that our members did not show much sympathy with them… A few of the shorter old words they liked, but all the old ones that have become strange to them, they did not want revived. The classical feeling was stronger than I had expected. The Stone Age they rebelled at. Your Tiw is not accepted.[6]

This failure was not surprising. After all, Barnes was a mere provincial scholar, having no colleagues with whom to discuss his ideas, and not even a university library to consult. Such situations, the members might have concluded, breed eccentrics. Yet Barnes had already successfully negotiated one agreement with them, which resulted in a book which was probably far more important than *Tiw*. It was a glossary. His 1844 collection of poems had included a list of local speech words, and he had appealed for more contributions. Nineteen years later, he had enough material to make a book. Nevertheless, he knew that such a production would have little commercial interest for any publisher, and he himself could not afford to print it. Fortunately, the Philological Society had been founded to promote just this sort of project, and in Furnivall he had an ally for his Saxonising views. So Barnes applied for help. Eventually, the Society agreed to publish his book, but only on certain conditions. Entries were to be put into alphabetical order – 'this is imperative'– and he was to substitute the usual linguistic terms for his own, for example, 'voicings' and 'clippings' were out – 'There being no reason to introduce such quaint and unhappy words'. 'What notion does "clippings" convey to one's mind?' he was asked. He did not reply.

In 1863, A. Asher & Co. of Berlin published for the Philological Society *A Grammar and Glossary of the Dorset Dialect*, by W. Barnes. B. D'.[7] Of the 103 pages, some sixty were devoted to the word list. Here were recorded, perhaps for the first time, many terms in which might be heard faint echoes of an earlier, pastoral world. The 'n' words, for example, include: 'nesh', meaning tender or soft, as in 'Do veel nesh'; and 'nesseltripe', the 'most weakly or last born of a brood of fowls, a fare of pigs, or a family of children'; a 'nitch', which was a load or burden of wood, hay or straw, or even drink; and a 'nunnywatch' or 'ninnywatch', an ancient term for a quandary or confusion. Lovingly, Barnes had collected these homely and often despised words. It was an act of linguistic conservation which he considered urgent, because he was well aware that within a few generations such words were likely to be forgotten.

As might have been expected, he discovered that many of his dialect words had an Anglo-Saxon origin. His linguistic origins were sometimes not much more than guesswork, or even wishful thinking. A number of his etymologies have since been challenged but, though he was sometimes wrong, it is remarkable how frequently he was right.[8] This is especially impressive because he was writing at a time when there was no easily available reference book to supply a biography of every English word. In 1863, not a single volume of what became known as the *Oxford English Dictionary* had yet been published.

This great enterprise had just started up a few years before Barnes's little glossary appeared, and the progenitors of the new dictionary were none other than the members of the Philological Society. Three of them, Herbert Coleridge, Frederick Furnivall and Richard Chevenix Trench, were by now convinced that contemporary dictionaries were not good enough in that they omitted great numbers of words. Accordingly, they persuaded the Society to set up an 'Unregistered Words Committee'. But when it was due to make its first report, on the evening of 5 November 1857 at the London Library, to the surprise of members, Dean Trench instead presented a paper on 'Some Deficiencies in our English Dictionaries'. The occasion was to have historic importance because it set in motion a sequence of events leading to the most ambitious publishing project in the English language. This was the preparation of what was first known as *The Society's Dictionary*, then *A New English Dictionary* and, finally, the *Oxford English Dictionary*, the expressed intention of the editors being to record the totality of the language, every meaning of every word that had ever been used.[9] No term was to be omitted because it was archaic, indecent, a dialect term, or for any other reason. Compiled 'On Historical Principles', each entry was to supply a complete biography of each word. Every nuance, shift and subtle turn of meaning was to be illustrated by quotations, chronologically presented, beginning with the earliest known examples. Of course, such a vast undertaking required far more readers than could be supplied by the Society from within its own ranks, and the answer was to appeal for volunteers, willing to read and record word usages from innumerable publications. The new dictionary was therefore a democratic project, in which the English-speaking people themselves would be invited to record the development of their own language. Fired up by Trench's advocacy, in the following year members passed a formal resolution to undertake the publication of the new dictionary.[10]

Barnes did not take up the invitation to become one of the army of readers for the new dictionary. This is understandable. In his first years at Came, with a new home and new profession, he was probably too busy to get involved. Besides, he may well have thought that he had already done enough to provide material for the dictionary project. Had he not recorded many dialect words and illustrated their usage in his poems? Had he not revived Anglo-Saxon terms, and suggested how new, purely English words might be shaped by combinations? And had he not already published his discoveries and suggestions in books and articles known to the editors of the dictionary? He had even supplied philological papers to the Society itself, and written a dialect glossary for it. Consequently, he may have been quietly confident that when the great book eventually appeared, his name would receive some prominence. After all, he was known to the editors.

And certainly, the *OED* archives contain a collection of extracts from other dictionaries, compiled either by Furnivall – who was editor from 1861-1878 – or somebody working for him, and these included material from Barnes's *Glossary*. So Furnivall must have referred to it to some extent, as well as the poems. But there are no records of correspondence with Barnes in the archives and his books of philology were passed over.[11]

When the first edition of the dictionary began to appear in parts, despite the professed aim of the editors to include all English words, many of Barnes's published terms did not feature at all. Excluded were his 'birdlore' (ornithology), 'sunprint' (photograph) and 'wortlore' (botany). This was probably because Furnivall and his colleagues took the view that these were neologisms dreamed up by a mere eccentric, but never actually spoken by anyone, and therefore not real English words at all. Yet, to take one example, 'birdlore', which word Barnes first published in 1830, became widely used, especially as the title of an American ornithological journal.[12]

The second edition of the *Oxford English Dictionary* (1989) has made some reparations, and there is quite a number of attributions to Barnes. But even this edition presents no more than a partial prospectus of his contributions to the language. Of the dialect words listed above, 'nesh' is included and quoted from the 1844 book of poems; 'nessletripe' does not appear; 'nitch' features, but not quite in Barnes's sense of a load or burden, and he himself is not credited; while neither 'nunnywatch' nor 'ninnywatch' appear at all.

The first part of the dictionary, A-ANT, was not issued until 1884 and even had he seen it, the aged Barnes would hardly have anticipated from this evidence that many of his beloved dialect words and Saxon compoundings would be omitted from subsequent volumes. Not that he lived to see any more published; the *OED* with supplement was not completed until 1933, long after his death. Nevertheless, in his declining years, he may have become conscious of the fact that he had been supplanted in the eyes of the editors as the final authority on West Country dialect. James Murray, who had succeeded Furnivall as editor in 1879, consulted not Barnes on this subject, but a personal friend, Frederick Elworthy from Wellington, who had written a paper on 'The Dialect of West Somerset' (1875).[13] Indeed, among the contributors thanked in the first edition of the dictionary are 'Mr. & Mrs. F.T. Elworthy and the Misses Elworthy'. Of Elworthy's paper to the Philological Society, 'An Outline of the Grammar of the Dialect of West Somerset' (1877), Murray remarked that it was 'the first grammar of an English dialect of any scientific value'.[14] Had he seen it, Barnes would have found the comment particularly hurtful.

Undeterred, though, by this neglect, he persisted in ploughing his lonely philological furrow. For the rest of his life he went on recording dialect words that he heard or that were sent to him. And it was his awareness that the Dorset speech was fast dying out that made him eager, perhaps too eager, in his etymologies to establish Anglo-Saxon origins for his dialect words. In the late 1860s and '70s, much of his spare time was given to the study of this ancient people, their language, history and customs. The subject became almost an obsession for him, if so mild a man might ever be suspected of harbouring one. Always on the lookout for Saxon connections, he was especially curious when on one evening, after he had given a reading of his dialect poems in a Somerset village, a stranger came up to him and said that he understood the poems perfectly because he had been familiar with similar speech in the south of Ireland.

Barnes was all attention. His new acquaintance revealed that he had lived for a time near Wexford, in the south-east of Ireland, near the ancient baronies of Forth and Bargy, where, according to a local historian, 'an Anglo-Saxon Colony' had been settled in the twelfth century. Apparently, the inhabitants of the baronies had developed a language quite different from that of the Irish around them, and some said that it was Flemish in origin. Barnes was having none of it. He had decided that this ancient dialect must be Saxon. Not that he had done any personal research; he had never been to Ireland, nor ever went there. But from his study of old documents he was certain of the Saxon link. Accordingly, he got to work re-editing a glossary of the Wexford speech, and predictably discovered that it had a great many links with the speech of the west of England, and with Anglo-Saxon.[15]

Nowhere, however, are his Saxonising opinions given sharper expression than in his next book, which came out in 1869. The opening of *Early England and the Saxon English* is composed largely of a rambling set of observations on such topics as their settlements, laws, clothes, customs and food. Then, suddenly Barnes forgets history and, almost arbitrarily, bursts out with his familiar linguistic manifesto:

> What we want for the pulpit, as well as for the book, and the platform, for the people, is a pure, homely, strong Saxon-English of English stems, such as would be understood by common English minds and touch English hearts.

It was the possessors of these common English minds, he argued, who still retained a pure and vigorous language:

> Luckily our tramways and railways were first made by working men who used the things under hand, English words of their own, as rail, sleeper, ballast, tram, truck, trolly, shunt, and siding; but when the railway was taken into the hands of more learned men, we had the permanent way for the full-settled way, and the terminus instead of the rail-end, or way-end, or outending.[16]

By now his imaginative identification of the Saxons with Dorset labourers was almost complete. Working in sympathy, his own prose now became heavily Saxonised; for example, describing that people as 'worksome', and their land as 'off-sundered'. And still persisting with his aim to reform modern English, here again he offered a list of Saxon words to replace foreign ones. 'Fore-elders' he suggested for ancestors; 'kindle' for ignite; 'upshot' for conclusion; 'inwit' for conscience; and 'neighbourhood' for vicinity. And, once again, he demonstrated how expressions formed from the Old English elements might be used to replace alien terms, for example, 'downcast' for abject; 'starkin' for asterisk; 'wordrich' for copious; and 'greatmindedness' for magnanimity. These neologisms – the term is disloyal but useful – he believed, were more homely, more direct and more comprehensible than the words they replaced. In the final analysis, *Early England* remains yet another Barnesian oddity. It is a badly constructed and obscurely phrased book, yet it is clearly the expression of a warm heart and a deep loyalty to the folk. It had no impact at all.

So the seasons came and went at Came, while the white-bearded rector filled page after page with his arthritic scrawl and went down in the evenings to slip them into the postbox. Even when nearing eighty, he was still busy with his philology. The sun rose high over his kitchen garden and still he bent over his desk, making lists of ancient words and probing their mysterious relationships. He expected, he said, neither 'prize or praise' for his books. He knew he was out of fashion and that hardly anyone would look into them. But he wanted, he said, to make one small trial, 'weak though it may be, towards the upholding of our own strong Anglo-Saxon speech, and the ready teaching of it to purely English minds by their own tongue'.

An *Outline in Speechcraft* came out in 1878 as a grammar not of written but of spoken English.[17] By now Barnes had devised a complete vocabulary of Saxonised linguistic terms, e.g. 'free breathings', 'thing mark-words', 'thing-sundriness' 'suchness', 'twin time-takings' and so on. The result is hardly a simplification, as is shown by his laborious account of comparative adjectives or 'Pitches of suchness' as he called them: 'The Suchnesses of Things are of sundry pitches, which are marked by sundry shapes or endings or bye-words of the mark-words', etc. The book has no 'Preface' but a 'Fore-say' and no 'Index' but a 'Clue to Matters Handled'. Much of it is devoted to rather laboured explanations of relatively simple matters, such as Saxon terms for gender differences between certain nouns; 'brother' and 'sister', for example – the 'spear-half' and 'spindle-half' of the race according to the Saxons. And though over the course of the book the Saxon prose becomes a little more comprehensible, it may be assumed that, for the majority of its few readers, it proved an impediment and an irritation.

Even then he was not finished with philology, for in 1880 he published *An Outline of Redecraft* ('rede' is defined as the craft or art of arguing).[18] This was was nothing less than a textbook of Aristotelian logic written in Saxon English. He wrote it just to prove that it could be done. The result is a learned perversity. He had reasoned that if it were possible to write a Saxon account of this most abstruse of all subjects, then there was no other academic discipline which would not allow of the same treatment. And Saxon English would make difficult subjects so much easier for 'homely men' to understand. Perhaps. What is more likely is that the reader would have found the resultant mix of logical complexity and antique terminology deliciously comic but completely unintelligible, as in his explanation of one form of syllogism: 'A man may sometimes want to find whether he can bring from a given head-thought-putting an upshot of a needed form, and so must seek a so-called middle term, middle step-end, or a step-end between the two ends of the first step or thought putting…'

There is a paradox here. From a lifelong determination to simplify the English language, in order to make it more comprehensible, Barnes ended by writing what to many would sound like gibberish. It is not only the difficulty of formal logic that causes the problem here, it is the language. In Saxonising it, Barnes makes it yet more difficult to understand, for the core of his belief was no longer true. What he called 'English', that is a language of purely Saxon vocabulary, would have been more incomprehensible to middle-class Victorians than the 'impure' 'Englandish' he so despised.

So were his labours simply a waste of time? His philological books are little read today, although his name crops up occasionally in linguisitic texts. And it seems that his general views on philology and etymology are regarded as oversimplifications.[19] Nevertheless, as a philogist he does have three claims to our consideration.

Firstly, his argument in *Tiw* that the English word-stock may derive from just a handful of basic 'roots' does seem to have something to be said for it. It is surely not a coincidence that 'gr' words such as 'grab', 'grapple', 'grasp', and 'grip' and 'grope', seem to share a basic notion of clutching. There are hundreds of examples of this sort of thing in English, and Barnes was right to draw attention to it and to suggest how it came about, whether or not his explanation is the correct one.

Secondly, there is the matter of plain English. It is at least arguable that Barnes's advocacy of a Saxon-based English vocabulary is well-advised, in that such English is not only 'purer' but better than that laced with foreign terms. And in his belief that old Saxon and dialect words were more in touch with actual human experience than the more alien, abstract terminology favoured by many educated people, he was an early advocate for the plain English movement. He would have approved of George Orwell's advice:

Never use a long word where a short one will do.

Never use a foreign phrase, a scientific word, or a jargon word if you can think of an everyday English equivalent.[20]

Lastly, he was an indefatigable recorder of the language of the south-western counties. He was to that dialect what Cecil Sharp was to folksong. What is more, he provided innumerable models of the usage of the dialect in his poetry. That we know today a good deal about speech and culture of the labouring peoples of Wessex during the 300 years between Elizabeth I and Victoria is, to a large extent, due to him.

What, then, was this old man really doing, year after year, puzzling over ancient English words? He was searching for home; peering back into the distant past to find his own folk. Not as they were in the impoverished times he knew as a boy, when his father trudged off along the lane each dawn to seek work with some distant farmer, and his poor mother was hard put to it to find food for the pot. No. He wanted to see that life as it once was, before enclosures, railways, and the mass exodus to the cities, when his people were independent and farmed their own land. To that far country, he took the only road still open to him – language. Starting out from the homely dialect of his childhood, and later making his way by long study and reflection, he fetched up at last among Anglo-Saxons. They were, he concluded, his true forbears.

Their world was much like his Blackmore home, but they were more free and independent than the peasant class of his own day. They knew nothing of evictions, enclosures, workhouses and class distinction:

> The people in these baronies live well, are industrious, cleanly, and of good morals; the poorest farmer eats meat twice a week, and the table of the wealthy farmer is daily covered with beef, mutton and fowl. The beverage is home-brewed ale and beer, of an excellent flavour and colour. The houses of the poorest are well-built and well-thatched; all have out-offices for cattle, fowls, carts or cars. The people are well clothed, are strong and laborious. The women do all manner of rustic work, ploughing excepted; they receive equal wages with the men. In this delightful spot the greatest harmony subsisists between the landlord and the farmer; it is common to meet the tenant at the landlord's table.[21]

Pure romanticism, of course. Such a society was only ever glimpsed by the light that never was. But Barnes wanted to believe in it. It was an abiding dream which found its expression in his philological textbooks. And in writing his philology, he had kept faith with his own people.

# 24

# HERMIT AND ENCHANTER

## —— 1874-1885 ——

It was at 7.15 a.m. on May Eve, 30 April 1874, when a young clergyman boarded the train at Chippenham Station in Wiltshire. He had in his pocket a letter from the Revd Henry Moule, the Vicar of Fordington near Dorchester.[1] It informed him that Moule's friend, William Barnes, would be happy to welcome him at his home. Later the traveller recorded his impressions of the day:

> … as I started on my journey… the unclouded sky shone with a splendid blue over the brilliant green elms and the rich warm golden brown of the oaks. The elms performed a solemn dance circling round each of the fine Church Towers of Somerset as we sped down into Dorset by the windings of the Frome and the elms of Castle Cary. And then the high downs began to rise and we seemed to breathe sweet salt air as soon as we saw the bold white chalk cliffs that look at the blue sea.[2]

This young man, so joyous and enthusiastic, was the Revd Francis Kilvert, and he had come to call on the man he regarded as 'the great idyllic poet of England'.

As arranged, Moule met him at Dorchester Station and, in order not to be too early at the Rectory, showed his guest round the town. They strolled along the famous sycamore and chestnut 'walks', stopping several times to get views of the huge prehistoric earthwork, Maiden Castle, on the horizon. Meanwhile, Moule chatted about his early days there. As with Barnes, his concern for the poor had sometimes got him into trouble. To the consternation of local notables, he had once written to Prince Albert himself to protest at the insanitary living conditions of the tenants of the Duchy of Cornwall in Fordington. Then, having offended the gentry, he proceeded to acquire a new set of enemies among the working people because he had helped to put an end to Dorchester races. For the next five years, he and his family had often been insulted in the street, and their property sometimes vandalised. But that, he said, was a long time ago, and nowadays he was treated with respect. Still busily talking, they reached the gates of Came Rectory, when Kilvert got his first glimpse of his host:

> The house lies a little back from the glaring white high road and stands on a lawn fringed with trees. It is thatched and a thatched verandah runs along its front. The thatched roof gives the Rectory house the appearance of a large lofty cottage. As we turned in at the iron gates from the high road and went down the gravel path the Poet was walking in the verandah. He welcomed us cordially and brought us into his drawing room on the right-hand side of the door. He is an old man, over seventy, rather bowed with age, but apparently hale and strong. 'Excuse my study gown', he said. He wore a grey loose gown girt round the waist with a black cord and tassel, black knee breeches, black silk stockings and gold buckled shoes.

Unlike Julia Cameron nine years before, Kilvert was deeply impressed by Barnes's appearance, with his 'apostolic head, bald and venerable, and a long white beard' which fell on his breast. The face was 'handsome and striking, keen yet benevolent', with 'finely pencilled eyebrows, still dark, and a beautiful benevolent loving look [that] lighted up his fine dark blue eyes'. Nor was it only his looks that impressed, but also the sheer charm of the man. He was, wrote Kilvert, 'half hermit, half enchanter'.

The three sat down to chat in the drawing room, the walls of which were hung from floor to ceiling with oil paintings. Kilvert told Barnes of the pleasure his poetry had given him, at which the poet smiled and thanked him with his characteristic old-world courtesy. The poems, he said, had been composed chiefly as a relaxation after his day's work as a schoolmaster. When writing them, 'all the dear scenes and well-remembered events and beloved faces of his youth [had] crowded upon his memory. "I saw them all distinctly before me", he said, "and all I had to do was to write them down"'. He had, though, sometimes changed the names of people and places.

By way of diversion, Moule was persuaded to play something. Accompanying himself on the little rosewood piano, he sang 'some verses of his own composition' concerning the death of his son, Horace, the previous autumn, while Barnes reclined on the ottoman, gravely stroking his white beard and keeping time with little claps.[3] To oblige his visitor, he read some of his dialect poems, including 'John Bloom in Lo'on', recounting his visit to the Crystal Palace, and then some of his more poignant pieces, which Kilvert preferred. Afterwards, they talked about Tennyson's two poems entitled the 'Northern Farmer', which were written in his own Lincolnshire dialect, and depicted a coarse, unloving miser. By contrast, Barnes explained, 'there was not a line [he had written] which was not inspired by the love for & kindly sympathy with the things and people described'. Ever after, Kilvert treasured his visit as, 'a happy and memorable day in my remembrance'.

Though now in his seventies, life was still full and satisfying to Barnes, what with his family and parish duties, his visitors, philology and antiquarian interests. For many years he kept up his lecturing programme to the working men's institutes, travelling over 10,000 miles in all, to deliver about 200 lectures as far afield as Bristol, Southampton and Salisbury.

His daughter Laura's life was not so fulfilling. Her dreams of becoming an artist had long since faded. Since 1852, she had been her father's housekeeper and, in devoting her life to him, had become a rather dowdy, provincial spinster, entirely dependent on his small income and clinging fiercely to her precarious gentility. One portrait survives, in which she is depicted playing a harp-like instrument. No doubt the photographer intended that she should appear spiritual, whereas she merely looks depressed. But though her father and siblings all took her for granted, she does not seem to have displayed any resentment at her situation.

Her sister, Isabel, also continued to live at the Rectory but her situation was very different. She was now an attractive, wealthy widow, dressing fashionably, keeping her own carriage with horse and groom and paying visits to London, Paris and Italy. It is perhaps surprising that she did not choose to set up in a house of her own, but life at Came was probably more convenient. After all, she had Laura to manage things for her. But it is doubtful if, when at home, Isabel continued indefinitely to act as one of her father's unpaid 'curates', walking through all weathers to call on his humble parishioners. She had a life elsewhere. This must have been so because, when almost forty-two, she contrived to meet and marry another rich man. Her husband-to-be was Thomas Dent Gardner, a senior partner in a City firm of solicitors. William Miles officiated at her wedding, which took place at Came in October 1882. Gardner then whisked her off to live amidst the splendour of suits of armour and oak panelling in his Gothic villa in the London suburb of Lee Green. Barnes's new son-in-law proved to be a great help to him in his last years. Gardner rewrote his will for him, became a trustee, helped to sort out the business of the Shaw estate and, even after Barnes died, continued to promote his work.[4]

Though Isabel remained childless, by 1882 the number of Barnes's grandchildren had increased to fourteen. At Monkton Rectory, William Miles had four surviving children; in Florence, Julia had three; and in the same city, Lucy and Tom Baxter had four. Meanwhile, in Wandsworth, Egbert the unfortunate, who had unsuccessfully tried to make a living as a heating engineer, was now the father of three children. Never in good health, however, he died there at the age of thirty in 1873. His wife, Jane, then became very poor and probably depended on parish relief until she too died at the age of forty-five in 1885. There is no record to show that Barnes attended the funerals of either his son or daughter-in-law.

As for helping Egbert's children, there seems to have been an understanding in the family that this was not a matter for Father. Nor could Laura have been expected to bring up the orphaned children at the Rectory. Other solutions had to be explored. Barnes was one of those who signed the successful petition which enabled his grandson, William Egbert Creasy Barnes, to board at the Christ's Hospital School at Westminster. And a tradition developed of Egbert's children paying an annual visit to the Rectory in summertime. They were there in 1882, though their mother did not

*Left:* Laura Barnes, the eldest daughter and a victim of circumstance. (Dorset County Museum)

*Below:* The Barnes family at Came Rectory. (Dorset County Museum)

accompany them, perhaps because she was not invited. But William Egbert Creasy, Laura Isabel and Alice Maude, aged fifteen, ten and six, arrived to meet their affluent 'Italian' relatives. How far these impoverished children smarted under the obviously greater affluence of their cousins can only be guessed at. Fortunately, their wealthy but childless Aunt Isabel, soon to be married to Gardner, now decided to take a practical interest in them. In later years, the Dunns and the Baxters stepped in and took Egbert's orphans to live in Italy.

Barnes kept a small household. In 1871 the census returns recorded that the occupants of the Rectory were Barnes; Laura; two young lady visitors from Ireland; Mary Hunt, the cook; Fanny Keats, the little housemaid; and the gardener, Herbert Crumpler. Ten years later, on 11 April 1881, the cast had changed but was no larger. There was Barnes, now aged eighty; Laura, aged fifty-three; Mary Cozens, the cook/domestic; Rosanna Shepherd, the maid; and Herbert Simmonds, the gardener. As always, Barnes was particularly courteous to his domestics and solicitous for their good. Rather than put a servant to more work, he would often bring down the empty coal scuttle himself. 'Oh, Mary,' he would ask, 'would you be so kind as to give me some more coals?' Sometimes he would offer to help Simmonds in the garden by trying out the new lawn-mowing machine. But he could never get on with it, and preferred the scythe with which he had loved to cut the grass at Chantry House years before.

In old age he enjoyed almost continuous good health, brought about, no doubt, by plain living, fresh air, abstention from tobacco and alcohol, and formidable daily walks through the parish. He paid no attention to the weather. If it rained he simply put an old sack round his shoulders and went on. After spending many hours among his books, he loved nothing better than to take his hat and stick, whistle up his little dog, Cara, and set off on his rounds to Whitcombe or Herringston:

## The Dog Wi' Me

Aye then, as I did struggle out
To your house, oh! how glad the dog,
Wi' lowzet nose, did nimbly jog
Along my path, an' hunt about:
An' his main pleasure were to run
Along by boughs, on timber'd brows;
An' ended where my own begun,
At your wold door, an' stwonen vloor.
An' there, wi time a-gliden by,
Wi' me so quick, wi' him so slow,
How he did look at me, an' blow,
Vrom time to time, a whinen sigh:
A-meanen, 'Come now, let us goo
Along the knolls wi rabbit holes;
I cant't think what you have to do
Wi' thease young feace, in this wold pleace'.[5]

Archaelogy now became a passion. These late Victorian years were perhaps the last during which an enthusiastic amateur might make a contribution to a field of knowledge. So, with a small but secure income, ample leisure and an aptitude for research, many a parson, like Barnes, had the opportunity to follow such scholarly inclinations. Among them were his friend, the Revd Osmond Fisher, sometime curate of All Saints, Dorchester, who became a respected geologist, and also his ex-pupil, the Revd Octavius Pickard-Cambridge, the world-renowned arachnologist.[6]

Barnes now devoted much of his attention to excavations in Dorset. Archaeology was closely allied to his linguistic studies, and had the added advantage of taking him out into the fresh air and providing him with like-minded people for company. In 1870 he attended the three-day meeting of the Somerset Archaeological Society at Wincanton, where he was a guest of Sir William Medlycott at Venn House. He wrote to his antiquarian friend Charles Warne to tell him of the visits to Cadbury Camp and the Barrows at Milbourne Wick. A paper of his was read for him on the derivation of the name 'Somerset'. He told Warne that he was embarrassed when one member asked him whether or not there were a similar society in Dorset, and he had to admit that there was not. Nevertheless, he told Warne, he would try to start one.

In 1871 the British Archaeological Association held their congress in Weymouth, when Barnes read a paper, 'The Origin of the Hundred and Tithing of English Law'. On the defensive about his stay with Sir William Medlycott, after a *Times* article had hinted that this event was just a jolly for members, he wrote to Warne to testify that none of them had received free lunches during the week. But the congress was justified, he said, in that it had 'brought out some good bits of history and knowledge'.

True to his resolve, in 1875 he became one of the first members of the newly formed Dorset Field Club and attended their meetings whenever he could. One of them examined the evidence from a cromlech which had recently been opened at Fuzbury, with skeletons but, curiously, no pottery, arms or coins. What were they to make of it? Members looked to Barnes to account for this unusual feature. He did. Sitting on the barrow, surrounded by them, he argued that those buried within could not possibly have been the Britons that Caesar knew, for the barrow showed no sign of metal implements. It was, therefore, much older. At least 1,000 years old. They were persuaded, and 'he was loudly cheered as he finished his remarks'.

Charles Warne died in 1873 and Caroline Norton in 1877. Refusing to be cast down by these losses, Barnes redoubled his interests in antiquarian matters, and these brought him a wide range of new friends, particularly fellow clergymen. Among them was Francis Close, the evangelical Dean of Carlisle, who had for years struggled to improve the condition of the poor in that town and had now come down to the south-west of England for his health.[7] Despite his indisposition, Close sometimes acted as Barnes's 'curate' when he was away lecturing and referred to Came as 'our church'. Their shared interest in archaeology also brought Barnes in contact with Samuel Wilberforce, Bishop of Oxford, that same 'Soapy Sam' who had debated Darwinism with Thomas Huxley. Predictably, Barnes's special interest was in the history of the Saxons, and among the many antiquarian studies he wrote is one on King Alfred, which appeared in *Somerset Worthies*, and a paper on the founding of Milton Abbey. He made a complete map of the great ancient roads of Dorset, and it was said that there was not a place in the county of which he could not give the history.

Meanwhile, following the publication of two editions of his poems in America, interest in his work was growing there. In 1869 came a letter from the poet Daniel Ricketson of New Bedford, Massachusetts, and later a complimentary copy of his book, *The Autumn Sheaf*. For the next fifteen years the two men kept up an occasional correspondence and, as in his talks with Conway, what most interested Barnes was establishing evidence of a cultural continuity between Dorset and New England, especially in common place names and dialect words.

One of his new American admirers, the writer Moncure Conway, telegrammed him on 28 October 1870 to say that he would call at 3.30 p.m. Welcomed with Barnes's habitual unfailing courtesy, he then spent the rest of the day with his host, talking about philology and folklore. He later wrote an account of his visit for *Harper's Magazine*, the reverential tones of which anticipate the attitude his readers would have considered appropriate in the depiction of an elderly, very English sage. Poetry, it hints, is a matter for the quaint old world, rather than the bustling life of modern Boston. Conway's emphasis, therefore, was on the picturesque. The Rectory was 'one of the loveliest country cottages that ever gave a poet a sacred solitude'; Barnes was dressed in 'an antique Dorset gentleman's dress', while his face was 'of the finest Saxon type, its natural strength filtered, so to say, and refined, through generations of pure and thoughtful life'. He had become a stereotype.[8]

Another American admirer was Amos Otis from Yarmouth, Massachusetts. In February 1874 he wrote to give him an account of the 'folk-games' in his state, which resembled those of the Dorset people. The 'quaker Dance', 'Thread the Needle' and 'Queen Anne', they agreed, were common to both countries. Then in 1886 came a letter from the office of the Secretary of the North-Western Literary Society, of Sioux City, Iowa:

Domestic staff at Came in the 1880s. Probably, from left to right: Rosanna Shepherd, housemaid; Mary Cozens, cook and housekeeper; Herbert Simmonds, gardener. (Dorset County Museum)

April 12th
DEAR SIR,

The members of this Society, desiring to convey to you in some manner an expression of their appreciation of your verses, and in recognition of your great learning, have, as a slight token of their esteem, unanimously elected you an honorary member of the Society.

Very respectfully yours,
BEN W. AUSTIN, Sec.

What lay behind this letter is a matter for speculation. Had some unknown emigrant picked up a copy of *Poems of Rural Life* on the Indian trail? Or taken to reading them aloud in bunkhouses and saloon bars? It seems unlikely, yet something like this must have happened to elicit such an approach. Whatever the truth of it, here was proof that these verses, written in a provincial dialect to be read by the labourers of Wessex, had far greater currency than their author might have thought. They could speak to other working people across the globe, such as those seeking a new life on homesteads far out on the prairies. Unfortunately, by the time that the letter came, Barnes was too ill to take much pleasure from it.

The study of such folklore was an inevitable accompaniment to that of dialect, and Barnes was soon involved in a book on the subject. A young friend of his, the barrister J.S. Udal, had helped him by supplying material for his glossary. Now Udal wanted his help. He was preparing a book on Dorset folklore and he asked Barnes to supply any material he had.[9] Eager to return past favours, Barnes obliged him. Both by virtue of his early years in the Vale and his lifelong observation of rural people, he had become an expert in the field, so that he was able to supply Udal with details of legends and superstitions from all round the county. He also provided a 'Fore-Say' to the book, reporting on such topics as local proverbs, mottos, symbols, charms, witchcraft, game rhymes, 'wort-lore' (the study of simples) and herblore. Written in the autumn of 1886, just a few months before he died, Barnes's 'Fore-Say' had one of the most delayed publications imaginable. Udal's book eventu-ally appeared in 1922, some thirty-six years after Barnes's contribution was written.

The appearance of a collected edition of his poems in 1879 brought about a modest revival of interest. Most influential among his new academic admirers was Francis Turner Palgrave, then a lecturer and soon to become the Professor of Poetry at Oxford. When compiling the first edition of his anthology, the *Golden Treasury*, Palgrave had made it a rule not to include any poets then alive, including Barnes. Nevertheless, Palgrave had become a profound and influential devotee. And though not able to visit the Rectory himself at that time, he sent his son Frank as a precursor.[10]

Other literary enthusiasts were closer at hand. On 22 July 1883, Hardy brought his friend, Edmund Gosse, over to the service at Came, and afterwards to meet Barnes. Hardy noted, 'Stayed for sermon. Barnes, knowing we should be on the watch for a prepared sermon, addressed it almost entirely to his flock, almost pointedly excluding us'.

Afterwards they walked to the Rectory and looked at his pictures.[11] Gosse was at that time a translator at the Board of Trade, and afterwards became a literary biographer and librarian to the House of Lords. In his mid-forties, Hardy was in process of moving back to Dorset permanently and was building a house for himself at Max Gate, near the Rectory, where he became an occasional caller. Relations between the poet and the successful novelist seem to have been affable but, at least on the part of Barnes, cautious. 'The last of the believers', as Llewelyn Powys later called him, was well aware that neither Hardy nor Gosse were orthodox in their religious views. Yet Gosse turned out to be a genuine enthusiast for Barnes's verse, and afterwards a trusted friend.

In 1882 the report of the Royal Comission into the state of agriculture had stimulated consider-able interest in the matter, and editors were on the lookout for authorities to write about it. By this time, both Barnes and Hardy had come to be regarded as experts on the 'rural problem' and editors were a little perplexed as to which of them was to be regarded as the authentic voice of Dorset. James Macaulay, the editor of *The Leisure Hour*, invited Barnes to contribute an article on 'Dorset Folk and Dorset', paying special attention to 'peculiarities of custom and character'. Hardy, mean-while, was commissioned by *Longman's* magazine to write a piece on 'The Dorsetshire Labourer'. Both articles appeared in 1883. The results were predictable. Barnes's articles were manifestly the work of an elderly man, consisting of collections of disparate and rather arbitrary ideas. He saw what he wanted to see, which was a vision of an arcadian past, though he admitted that, 'If I have painted a picture of Dorset life that is light, I have not given light where there is none; but I ought to say that there is darkness as well as light'. Hardy, by contrast, provided his readers with a careful analysis of recent changes in agriculture, such as the growing custom of labourers migrating from farm to farm on Lady Day, which practice he considered brought about 'a less intimate and kindly relation with the land'.[12]

In their conversations, both men tactfully avoided religion, politics and other contentious matters. But Hardy's ears were always cocked for Barnes's anecdotes. Rustic dialogues were then becoming a feature of his own novels, and Barnes had a ready supply of dialect stories. One concerned an old Blackmore farmer, incensed at seeing his neighbour's daughters going to their music lessons, which he described incredulously as, 'Going to spank the grand pianner at milking time'. There was also a story of a man whom Barnes had once helped to purchase a donkey and who, when he met the rector some time after, saluted him affectionately with the remark that, 'I do never see a donkey, sir, but what I do think o' you'. Hardy's rustics, his Robert Creedles and Abel Whittles, may well have taken their beginnings in such talk.

Barnes liked to have young people around him. In summertime, the garden at Came Rectory was alive with their cries. Some were his grandchildren, and some visitors come with their parents. The Revd Charles Powys of Montacute occasionally assisted him with his clerical duties when his large family might be invited to tea. Of the children who played in the garden, John Cowper Powys, who was twelve years old in 1884; Theodore, aged nine; and Llewelyn, a baby, were all to become famous as writers.[13] Another child who played there was John Meade Falkner, the author of *Moonfleet*. There were also the young women who were invited as guests of Barnes's daughters. Always susceptible to female charms, he adopted a rather arch, antique mannerism with them, leaving posies on their breakfast plates, writing little rhymes about them and giving them pet names.

One of Laura's friends left a record of Barnes's routine during her fortnight stay at the Rectory in August 1876:

First the morning prayers, when the priest-master read matins from a high lectern almost as if in church; the bright breakfast, at which he ate porridge and milk; and then the exact half-hour's walk round the garden. He wore a sort of tunic of brown fustian with a large worsted girdle, knee breeches, black stockings, shoes and buckles, and a felt hat that had peaked itself in front. The walk round the garden after breakfast was a delightful very short half-hour. He always went first to a leaden bath for bleaching old engravings, which stood in a corner under the trees, where one or two rare prints were undergoing restoration of some kind; and I think his last visit at night and his first in the morning were to these loves of his. Then round the grass plot and flower beds, talking of bird, leaf and flower; and of everything we talked he had something lovely to say.

He always spoke in pure English, with a beautiful simplicity and correctness, and never used an inappropriate term; indeed, it was one of his small daily troubles that people generally do not speak in truer terms, and specially that they use words of foreign origin or foreign words themselves, and he used to laugh in an amused, gentle way at many a popular misnomer. When the half-hour's walk was done, he went up to work in his 'den', which really did look something like a cave; a cave of books, all old, all rather ghostly-looking in their curious dusty bindings of calf and vellum. It was very touching to see him handle them; each one had been a sort of friend, teacher or helper to him, and he held them with a sort of reverent tenderness that was extremely pretty to see. A large piece of old tapestry hung on one side of the room, and this he prized very much; his writing table stood near one window, which overlooked the fields. Here he wrote, and here, as he put it, he had 'his visions'. The 'den', the garden, the whole place was so far removed in its loveliness from all thought of what we call the world that one hardly wonders to hear now that as largely sold as the 'Rural Poems' have been in America and in England, he never gained as much as £6 a year by them.

The interior of Came Church, Barnes's workplace for twenty-four years. (Private collection)

Barnes seated with a Bible. The photo is probably by Pouncy. (Dorset County Museum)

After the pleasant midday meal, he went back to his study and generally worked till tea time. After tea came the crowning hour of the day, as Lucy Baxter wrote:

'In the cool of the evening' we had chairs under the verandah, and sat nearly facing the west, seeing the sunset through the slender beeches. Here we sat and listened to him, or conversed together of a hundred things, from sunbeams to dewdrops, angels to men, he adding an ancient story to everything...

Walks with him were always full of interest. We were walking once round what to commonplace people would have been a very prosy field, but in his hands the field became poetry. He told me the English poetical names for all the grasses, pointing out why they were named so – as, for instance, the 'Shepherd's purse', which is like the shape of purses worn at the girdle in olden days.

He had a handsome presence and was a brave gentleman. He did many things in his gentlehood that a man of the world would never think of doing. I remember that he would not allow the gate to be shut when I left.[14]

Christmas at Came was a busy time. In the church lay the 400-year-old sculptured effigy of a certain Hugh Millar, whose bequest provided for meat and coals for the poor of the parish. Consequently, on Christmas Eve at the Rectory, there were innumerable comings and goings of people collecting their Millar money. In the evening the sextons and choristers of both Came and Whitcombe called in for supper in the kitchen, and when they were done, there would be a knock at the door and Barnes would come in to welcome them. Sitting at the table, he would listen delightedly to the old songs and carols, and laugh and clap and bang his stick on the floor. Finally, he would rise from his chair and say a word of Christian comfort to them, give a bow and leave. On Christmas day itself, there were sometimes three generations of all those of his family who were in England sitting at the dinner table.[15]

And still he walked his parish. In late January 1881, everything was covered with deep snow but he carried on with his duties as usual. By Sunday 6 February, the snow had gone and the bleak roads were now covered in mud. Yet, after breakfast, at half past eight, he started out to walk to Came Church to take a wedding there at nine o'clock. On the way he met someone who begged him to go to Whitcombe, two miles in the opposite direction, to offer Holy Communion to a dying woman. He married the couple at Came, reached Whitcombe at ten o'clock, and then walked back to Came to take the eleven o'clock service. Coming back to the Rectory, he snatched a hurried dinner and then trudged back to Came again to take a funeral service before evensong. So, at the age of eighty, on just one day he had walked six miles to and fro across the parish, performing two full services, a wedding and a funeral, and had given a dying person the last rites. He had help, of course. He could call on his son William in an emergency, and there were a number of other local clergy-men to come to his aid. Besides, he could not retire, even had he wanted to. Clergymen such as he depended on their profession both for their incomes and their homes. There was no respite.

# 25

# FALLING TO

— 1884-1886 —

After that walk home along the Wareham Road in the driving rain with Thomas Hardy, as described in Chapter One, Barnes became very unwell. He had caught a chill and was obliged to keep to his bed. Lucy Baxter is rather vague about his condition, describing it as a 'rheumatic illness', but the truth is that he was simply worn out. Having struggled on for years, trying to fulfil his duties as best he could, his great age and a life of constant exertion had finally taken their toll. To Laura fell the task of nursing him, with the aid of a Miss Benson who had come in to help.

In March 1884, Barnes was just able to conduct Holy Communion at Came Church, and a year later he was driven over to Whitcombe to hold what was to be his last service. From then on, he was mostly confined to his bed, though on better days he would manage to get up and sit in the verandah, or even stroll out into his garden to admire the oxslips. But he did not regain his strength, and his inability to fulfil his clerical duties became a serious problem. Hoping at first that he would soon recover, he depended on the help of friends, such as the Revds Spring Rice and W. Lock to take his services for him. At last, however, he had to agree to the appointment of a curate, the Revd Hayes.

Most of the time now he spent in bed, listening to the sounds of the household: murmuring voices; doors opening and closing; comings and goings; and the clicking of the gate. And slowly, for the first time in many years, some new verses began to frame themselves in his head. One day he called for Laura and dictated to her:

## The Geate A-Vallen To

In the zunsheen ov our zummers
Wi' the hay time now a-come,
How busy wer we out a-vield
Wi' view a-left at hwome,
When waggons rumbled out ov yard
Red-wheeled, wi' body blue,
As back behind 'em loudly slamm'd
The geate a-vallen to.

Drough daysheen ov how many years
The geate ha' now a-swung
Behind the veet o' vull-grown men
An' vootsteps ov the young.
Drough years o' days it swung to us
Behind each little shoe,
As we tripped lightly on avore
The geate a-vallen to.

In evenen time o'starry night
How mother zot at hwome,
An' kept her bleazen vire bright

Till father should ha' come,
An how she quickened up an' smiled
An' stirred her vire anew,
To hear the trampen ho'ses' steps
An' geate a-vallen to.

There's moonsheen now in nights o' fall
When leaves be brown vrom green,
When, to the slammen o' the geate,
Our Jenny's ears be keen,
When the wold dog do wag his tail,
An' Jean could tell to who,
As he do come in drough the geate,
The geate a-vallen to.

An' oft do come a saddened hour
When there must goo away
One well-beloved to our heart's core,
Vor long, perhaps vor aye:
An' oh! it is a touching thing
The loven heart must rue,
To hear behind his last farewell
The geate a-vallen to.[1]

When he finished, he said to her, 'Observe that word "Geate". That is how King Alfred would have pronounced it... Ah! If only the court had not been removed to London, then the speech of King Alfred would have been the court language of today...'

News had soon got about the parish that the rector was bedridden and the callers came. Musical friends dropped in to play and sing to the ailing man from the landing outside his bedroom door. Another visitor was Francis Turner Palgrave who, with his son, visited Barnes for the first and only time in October 1885:

Walked with Frank through twilight to Winterbourne Came: a pretty little thatched house among trees. I was allowed to go up to the great aged poet in the bedroom which – at eighty four and with now failing bodily strength – he is not likely to quit. Mr. Barnes had invited me when Frank visited him last Christmas, and truly glad was I and honoured did I feel, to accomplish it. A very finely cut face, expressive blue eyes, a long white beard, hands fine like a girl's – all was the absolute ideal of the true poet... He was dressed in red with white fur of some sort, and a darker red cap; Titian or Tintoret had no nobler, no more high born looking sitter among the doges of Venice. His welcome was equally cordial and simple; and, despite his bodily weakness, the soul, bright and energetic, seemed equally ready for death or for life. He talked of his visit to Tennyson; of his own work, saying he had taken Homer, and him only as his model in aiming at choosing the one proper epithet when describing: also his love for pure old English. I shall remember this most interesting half-hour all my life.[2]

On the 17th of that month, Barnes surprised everybody by coming downstairs for dinner, but he was soon wearied and had to go back to bed.

Yet all the time while he lay there, his life's work was nearing completion in Dorchester. Notice of it came, in the form of a packet, on 21 November, delivered by Mr Foster of the printing firm M. & E. Case. It contained the final, revised version of his *Glossary of the Dorset Dialect*. The first version had appeared twenty-two years before, but he had been adding to it ever since. And here, together with a grammar, were definitions of no fewer than 1,748 dialect words and phrases plucked from oblivion, words which were like old friends he had known all his life. Here they were; 'bucky', 'cag-mag', 'grintern' and the rest. Meeting them once more as he turned the pages, he could almost hear his mother's voice again. Had they been allowed to die, then her story and that of his own people would have been lost forever. When the book was placed into his hands, he said, 'I have done some little to preserve the speech of our forefathers, but I fear a time will come when it will be scarcely remembered, and none will be found who can speak it with the purity I have heard it spoken in my youth'.

That Christmas was the first in which he was unable to go downstairs to join his family at the table, so each went up in turn to the bedroom to receive his blessing. In January, Christopher Wordsworth, the Bishop of Salisbury, came to administer Holy Communion to him. Captain Damer, who had appointed him to the living twenty-four years before, also called. Alerted by her sister, Isabel came home from London and distracted him a little by singing to him. Mrs Emma Hardy came regularly. Another visitor, Edmund Gosse, wrote to tell Coventry Patmore:

> Hardy and I went on Monday last to Came Rectory where he lies bedridden. We found him in bed in his study, his face turned to the window, where the light came streaming in through flowering plants, his brown books on all sides of him save one, the wall behind him being hung with an old green tapestry. He had a scarlet bed gown on, a kind of soft biretta in dark red wool on his head, from which his long white hair escaped onto the pillow; his grey beard, grown very long on his breast; his complexion, which you recollect as deeply bronzed, has become blanched by keeping indoors, and is now waxily white where it is not waxily pink, the blue eyes, half shut, restless under languid lids… I wish I could paint for you the strange effect of this old, old man, lying in cardinal scarlet in his white bed, the only bright spot in the gloom of all those books…[3]

By the autumn his strength was failing. On the morning of 7 October 1886, he listened quietly to the prayers said over him, and sighed softly, 'Lighten our eyes O Lord, that we sleep not in death'. He soothed himself by repeating favourite couplets. The last he spoke was:

> Dry our eyes in weeping,
> Shut our eyes in sleeping.

Then he fell into a sleep so deep that no one was quite sure when it was that his breathing stopped.

# AFTERWARDS

The funeral on 11 October was a simple affair, with about 150 people present.[1] Of Barnes's children, only three were there: Laura, Isabel (Mrs Gardner) and William, along with his family from Winterborne Monkton. No members of the aristocracy attended and only a few of the gentry, though this may have been because there was no public notice given of the occasion. So it was word of mouth that brought Captain Williams over from Herringston House. Captain Dawson-Damer of Came House, the owner of the estate, was too ill to come, but telegraphed to say that his son would attend in his place. Mr Gregory, the Mayor of Dorchester, came on behalf of the town. The Church was represented by five local clergymen and the three churchwardens from Monkton and Whitcombe. Professor Francis Palgrave, the Oxford Professor of Poetry, arrived from Epsom. He was the sole witness from the academic world.

All the rest were working people. From all over the estate they came, Barnes's servants and parishioners. There were ploughmen, carters, shepherds, milkmaids, cottage wives and the children from the parish school, watched over by their teacher, Miss Foot.

Palgrave stood at the gate of the Rectory and watched as the simple elm coffin was carried out from the house. Upon it was an oak cross and 'many wreathes and crosses' of white flowers. Placed on a hand-bier, it was followed by the family on foot, along part of the the Wareham road and then down the path through the fields to Came Church. The procession was met by Barnes's curate, the Revd Hayes, reciting the 'sublime burial service of the Church of England' which Barnes himself had spoken over so many others. When the 'Office for the Dead' was concluded, and the coffin lowered into the grave, it was 'literally covered with beautiful wreathes and crosses sent by loving friends and parishioners'. Some mourners lingered afterwards while the children of Came dropped wild flowers into the grave. The funeral, reported the *Chronicle*, was like his life, 'quiet and unostentatious in character'.[2]

Thomas Hardy was too late to join the procession at the Rectory. He had just left Max Gate for the funeral when Barnes's coffin was pushed onto the road. But as he looked out on that dark day, something seemed to flash before his eyes. He knew what it was:

THE LAST SIGNAL
(OCT. 11, 1886)
A MEMORY OF WILLIAM BARNES

Silently I footed by an uphill road
That led from my abode to a spot yew-boughed;
Yellowly the sun sloped low to the westward,
And dark was the east with cloud.

Then, amid the shadow of the livid sad east,
Where the light was least, and a gate stood wide,
Something flashed the fire of the sun that was facing it,
Like a brief blaze on that side.

Looking hard and harder I knew what it meant –
The sudden shine sent from the livid east scene;

Barnes's gravestone at Winterborne Came, a Celtic cross. (Private collection)

It meant the west mirrored by the coffin of my friend there,
Turning to the road from his green,

To take his last journey forth – he who in his prime
Trudged so many a time from that gate athwart the land!
Thus a farewell to me he signalled on his grave-way,
As with a wave of his hand.

Winterborne Came Path.[3]

Having devoted thirty-four years of her life to looking after her father, at the time of his death Laura Barnes now found herself, at fifty-eight, without a home or income. The Rectory was required by the Church authorities for the new incumbent, and Barnes's stipend ceased with his demise. She had even lost what small status she had enjoyed as Miss Barnes, the rector's daughter.

So, just six weeks later, on 22 November she left the Rectory for the last time. It was, she noted, a 'very busy sad day', and the carriage was filled with remnants of familiar things. 'The good servants with tears and good wishes stood around'. 'Goodbye dear Came,' she wrote, 'our life with thee has been peace and happiness'.

Two days later, Henry Duke & Son, auctioneers, began the sale of Barnes's effects at the Rectory. The 1,000-plus books, and 120 paintings 'by or after' Sir Peter Lely, Backhuysen, Holbein, Serres, Wilson, Daniels, Westhall, Thorne and others, went under the hammer on Thursday 5 November, while furniture and 'the usual' kitchen equipment were auctioned the following day. The items for sale provide a glimpse into those long Victorian years. Here, the curious bystander might bid for the '6 3/4 Octave Cottage Pianoforte in Rosewood Case', or 'Butler's Zither', or Laura's 'Dital Harp (in case)'. Captain Williams made a number of purchases, as did Pouncy, the Dorchester photographer. Later on the first day, Thomas Hardy strolled down from Max Gate. He bought 'a small landscape with trees' for £1, and paid £1 3s for lot 237, a painting entitled 'The Three Marys' by Richard Wilson. He made a note on the back to record the purchase, and the picture hung on his wall for many years.[4]

The books tell their own tale. They are mostly what one would expect in the library of an unusually erudite country clergyman: sermons, history, theology, reproductions of paintings, and volumes of the *Spectator*, *Graphic*, and *Punch*. Barnes's literary taste was very conservative. Here are volumes of Shakespeare, Milton, Scott, Bryant and, perhaps surprisingly, Byron, but no sets of novels. No Fielding or Dickens (though there were some volumes of *All the Year Round*), both of whom he may have thought improper, and no George Eliot, whose private life definitely was. And no Jane Austen. Her social comedy was probably beyond him. The truth was that his literary sensibility had been formed long before the novel became popular. This was, perhaps, one of the reasons why there were none of Hardy's novels in his little library.

From the Rectory, Laura went for a time to Clewer, near Windsor, and later lived variously at Upwey near Weymouth, South Kensington, Aberdeen and Monkton Rectory, with her brother.[5] Her income must have been small because her one-fifth share of her father's estate cannot have amounted to much. Fortunately, Palgrave, with the support of Robert Browning and Matthew Arnold, petitioned that she should continue to receive his Civil List pension, and two years after his death she was awarded the reduced sum of £50 a year, 'as compensation for a lifetime of care and devotion'.[6] She may also have received some financial help from her rich sister, Isabel. Laura lived on for another thirty-two years, dying in Dorchester in 1918 at the age of eighty-eight. She was buried in Came churchyard, next to her father.

The Rectory was not left empty for long, but Barnes's immediate successors were distinctly less popular than he in the parish. The first of these was a rather mysterious figure who came and went swiftly. Hardy would have appreciated the irony of his name, the Revd Ernest Evill. He was succeeded by the Revd Herbert John Underhill Charlton MA, and he in turn by the Revd C. Homan. How these two were regarded by the local people was first revealed in August 1999, when some repairs were being carried out and floorboards were lifted on the Rectory landing. On the underside of one was a pencil inscription made by Victorian workmen:

> Mr Walter Geoffrey
> J.G. Palmer
> R House
> J H Geoffrey
> Laid this floor May 8th 1896

> (?) Charlton resigned this living after getting drunk (bad wine?) and worse come that was the Rev. Claud Homan he dont get drunk but he is interfearing with every bodys livings.

> So much for parsons like these all of them ought to get 6 months in a shit house head downwards. So help my (?)[7]

It was not only his parishioners at Came that felt the loss of Barnes. For many others in Dorset, he had seemed a fixture, an abiding presence. Hardy was one of these. According to his poem 'The Old Neighbour and the New', on an occasion when he had walked down to the Rectory to pay his respects and sat with Evill in the sitting room, he saw the old poet at every turn:

> Twas to greet the new rector I called here
> But in the arm-chair I see
> My old friend, for long years installed here,
> Who palely nods at me.[8]

In the obituary he wrote for the *Athenaeum*, he recorded that:

> … those who like the present writer knew him [Barnes] well and long, entertained for him a warm affection; while casual visitors from afar were speedily won to kindly regard by the simplicity of his character, his forbearance, and the charming spurts of youthful ardour which would burst out as rays even in his latest hours.[9]

In 1908 Hardy edited a selection of Barnes's poems.

Other obituaries included one by a former pupil of Barnes, the Revd Octavius Pickard Cambridge, who wrote an account of his work for the County Museum and the Dorset Natural History and Antiquarian Field Club, though he provided little detail. More informatively, on 14 October 1886, the *Chronicle* printed a notice of Barnes's death which provided an account of his life, extending over five columns, a degree of attention only normally devoted to obscure members of the Royal family and the aristocracy. This article incorporated other obituaries which had appeared in *The World* and the *Manchester Guardian*, in which the latter, in considering Barnes's long ministry as a priest, described him as 'no mean successor of George Herbert'. Of his predilection for dialect poetry, it observed that, 'It is a fallacy of certain half-trained critics that provincial dialects are essentially vulgar and beneath the attention of educated men. His rustics are real but they are not boors… [They] are charming figures'.

Shortly after Barnes's death, his children decided that a biography should be written. They had hoped that Thomas Hardy would undertake the task, but in the event it was Barnes's daughter, Lucy Baxter, who wrote it.[10] Her siblings provided her with their recollections, and Laura sent packets of documents to Florence to help with the work. *The Life of William Barnes: Poet and Philologist*, 'by his Daughter, Lucy Baxter ('Leader Scott') came out in 1887. Lucy was a published writer and had already translated and researched biographies for a friend. But, as might be expected, though charming and even moving at times, her biography is pervaded by a note of filial piety which reduces her father to just another rather dull Victorian worthy. For the book conveys little appreciation of just how forceful and uniquely gifted he was. This is partly because she did not know very much about

Detail of the
Barnes statue by
Roscoe Mullins in
Dorchester.

his early life and struggles. Nor is her account always accurate, for she had lived too far away from home for many years. Moreover, it seems that she had agreed that her conventional brother, the Revd William Miles Barnes, had the right to censor what she had written.

A more tangible memorial was also planned, eight weeks after Barnes's death. In the Dorchester Town Hall, on 2 December 1886, some ninety Dorset notables met at the invitation of Christopher Wordsworth, the nephew of the poet and Bishop of Salisbury, to discuss how they might honour the memory of Barnes. A number of ideas were put forward, such as a scholarship or a cheap edition of his poems, but in the end, the overwhelming view of those attending was that his memory would best be served by the erection of a statue.

So, on 4 February 1889, Roscoe Mullins's bronze figure, depicting Barnes as an old, bearded man, was unveiled by the bishop outside St Peter's Church, where he had once been the people's warden. And there he still stands, at the very centre of the town, where High West Street meets South Street, dressed in his curiously antique outfit of cassock, knee-breeches, stockings and buckled shoes. Self-absorbed, he seems to take little interest in contemporary Dorchester life swirling about him. On the plinth are inscribed lines from his poem: 'Culver Dell and the Squire', which seemed to the assembled notabilities a peculiarly apt commentary on their author:

But now I hope his kindly feace
Is gone to vind a better pleace;
But still, wi v'ok a-left behind
He'll always be a-kept in mind.

Barnes was easy to sentimentalise, and that is how the middle classes of Dorchester preferred to recollect him; as a wise, worthy, harmless old chap, who somehow had always been ancient. This was because, by 1889, few could remember him as anything else. Yet the statue lies. For the essence of Barnes is that of a young man with a warm heart, a cheerful nature and a luminous intellectual energy sufficient to overcome all the obstacles placed before him by a society ridden with class distinction. While he was never a man of the people, he was always a man for the people, and it was his profound affection for the labouring poor that inspired him to become one of the most original artists of his time. In one thing, however, the statue tells the truth. It is in its depiction of that grave, meditative face which suggests that he has travelled long roads to the farthest reaches of thought.

Barnes had predicted that those same people in Dorchester who had offered him a stone rather than bread would one day put up a statue of him. He was right.

# CODA

(One January afternoon in the 1880s, the Dorset dialect poet William Barnes, linguist, archaeologist and author of 'Linden Lea', walked through a storm to his home at Winterborne Came. As a result, he became ill, bedridden and died soon after.)

## Late Whispers

You turn your back on business in the town,
And start out for your rectory in the dark,
Pitching your ear to sighings from the down
Where ancient peoples leave their sovereign mark,
And earthworks still protect the startled lark.
Old Priest, this walk tonight will be your last,
Trudging through rain, pursued by voices past.

Now come the distant whispers from the tombs,
Something of Welsh but from a wilder school;
Telling of bogs and barrows, deep oak coombes,
Of tree and pen and crag and sacred pool,
Where blue-dyed kings set hooded hawks to rule,
And bards strum blood-strung harps with tales of woe,
While moon-mad priests secrete the mistletoe.

Listen! Imperial accents from the town:
The tongue of Tacitus on slave girls' lips;
Loquacious matrons ambling up and down,
Exchanging dreams of Roman shopping trips
On seas of cobalt blue, in Caesar's ships,
While veterans dice away the afternoon,
Recounting how the cohorts stormed Mai-Dun.

Calls from the mead-halls; clamorous cries that raise
Voices of warrior peoples, owning no alien yoke;
From antlered gables, winding Saxon ways,
Following forth to furrows and fold-folk;
Songs of the spinning wench; the jester's joke;
Thane thoughts; glee glads; Alfred's tongue;
The fallow fields of English speech when young.

But mos' you love the whomely Darzet talk
Of vriends and neighbours zot beside the Frome,
Gigglins o' zummer maidens on their walk
Along the river, wi' the May in bloom;
Chatty o' varmer's wives in stone-vlagged rooms;

Lippins vrom li'l varms, or zummer-leaze,
Or lwonesome parricks under elem trees.

You reach the final door, take to your bed,
And now once more those voices start to roam
From shelves of ancient speech-lore in your head,
And quarters in the past you still call 'home'.
But childrens' cries and one dead woman's tone
Catch at your heart for ever; echoing round
That plot of grass where linden trees abound.

AC

# NOTES

## Abbreviations used in the Notes

Ashdown: *William Barnes: My Hwomeward Road*, 2003
Baxter: *The Life of William Barnes*, 1887
DCC: *Dorset County Chronicle*
DCM: *Dorset County Museum*
DNB: *Dictionary of National Biography*
Dugdale: *William Barnes of Dorset*, 1953
GM: *The Gentleman's Magazine*
Hearl: *William Barnes the Schoolmaster*, 1966
B. Jones: *The Poems of William Barnes*, 2 Vols 1962
Millgate: *Thomas Hardy: A Biography*, 1982
Orel: *Thomas Hardy's Personal Writings*, 1967
PDNHAFC: *Proceedings of the Dorset Natural History and Antiquarian Field Club*
PDNHAS: *Proceedings of the Dorset Natural History and Archaeological Society*
PWBS: *Proceedings of the William Barnes Society*

## Epigraphs

The quotation from Sydney Smith is taken from Pearson, Hesketh, *The Smith of Smiths*, 1934, repr. 1984,
    p. 81.
Hopkins's observation is to be found in Abbot. C.C. (Ed.) *Further Letters of Gerard Manley Hopkins*, repr.
    in Geoffrey Grigson's anthology of Barnes. pp. 48-49.
E.M. Forster's comment is taken from his article: 'Homage to William Barnes', *New Statesman*, 9 December
    1939.

## Fore-Say

1. Baxter, p. 212.
2. *DCC*, 30 December 1841, and Jones, I, p. 162.
3. Hearl, p. 13.
4. Fowles, John, and Draper, Jo, *Thomas Hardy's England*, 1984.
5. Orel, p. 101.
6. Title of an article by Coventry Patmore: 'An English Classic, William Barnes', in the *Fortnightly Review*,
    November 1886, see Grigson, Geoffrey, *Selected Poems of William Barnes*, 1950, p. 45.

## 1  Going Home: The Wareham Road, 1880s

1. On p. 309, Baxter states that this walk took place on 26 January 1884, and adds that Hardy begged Barnes to
    take shelter from the driving rain in his house, Max Gate. But this is not possible because the building of Max
    Gate was only started eight weeks before. It is likely that the walk took place in January 1885 or even 1886.
    See Chedzoy, A., 'A Query: Barnes's Last Walk' in *The Hardy Society Journal*, Vol. 3, No. 3, Autumn 2007, p. 55
    and later correspondence.
2. An account of the Building of Max Gate is given by Millgate, pp. 249 and 257.

3. Hardy, Thomas, 'The Rev. William Barnes, B.D.', in the *Athenaeum*, 16 October 1886, repr. Orel, p. 100.

4. Hardy, Thomas, 'Some Romano-british Relics Found at Max Gate, Dorchester', in Orel, p. 192.

5. Ibid.

## 2  The Little Astrologer of Blackmore Vale, 1801-1818

1. Jones, I, p. 493.

2. Kerr, Barbara, *Bound to the Soil*, pp. 17-18.

3. Ibid.

4. Young, Robert, *Early Years*, pp. 15-16.

5. Ashdown, p. 23.

6. Baxter, p. 8.

7. Ashdown, pp. 66-69.

8. Kerr, p. 99.

9. Hobsbawm, E.J. and Rude, George, *Captain Swing*, p. 29.

10. Kerr, p. 90.

11. Jones, II, p. 643.

12. I have chosen to repeat the list of hill names as given by Thomas Hardy in *Tess of the D'Urbervilles*, Chap. II.

13. Baxter, p. 8.

14. Young, p. 15.

15. St John's College Cambridge, Barnes's Notebook 5, p. 7.

16. The whereabouts of the boys' school attended by Barnes has been a topic of recent debate. Austin and Jones, however, have shown fairly conclusively that it cannot have been located in what is now known as 'The Old School', with the iron lettering above the gate proclaiming 'The Foundation of God Standeth Sure'. This is because the school was not built until about 1835, long after Barnes had left the town. The school he attended was most likely to have been conducted in the three-storey building at the top of what is now called Lane Fox Terrace. This leads off Penny Street, which in those days was known as Tanyard Lane. See: Austin, Frances & Jones, Bernard, 'William Barnes and the Schools at Sturminster Newton' in *William Barnes of Dorset*, W.B. Soc. 2001, pp. 20-28.

17. Baxter, pp. 11-12.

18. Young, p.13.

19. Baxter, p. 10.

20. *DCC*, 21 July 1842, and Jones, Vol. 2, p. 210.

21. Young, p. 9.

22. Hearl, pp. 13-14.

23. Young, p. 10.

24. Ibid., pp.10-11.

25. Ibid., p. 8.

26. *DCC*, 24 September 1829.

27. *DCC*, 4 December 1856, and Jones, pp. 347-48.

28. *Hones Year Book* for 1832.

29. Ashdown, p. 34.

## 3  Love and Literature: Dorchester, 1818-1822

1. For details of early nineteenth-century Dorchester, I have borrowed unashamedly from *The Mayor of Casterbridge*, Chap. IV.

2. d'Arblay, Mme, (Fanny Burney), *Diary and Letters*, p. 294.

3. *The Mayor of Casterbridge*, Chap. IV.

4. MS Notes, DCM. Also Hearl, p. 17.

5. Baxter, p. 19.

6. Hearl, pp. 17-18.

7. Baxter, p. 14.

8. Lindgren, Charlotte, *The Love Poems and Letters of William Barnes and Julia Miles*, 1986, p. 29.

9. Jones, Vol. 1, pp. 25-35.

10. Ibid., p. 25.

11. Thomas Bewick (1753-1828), the celebrated wood engraver, was much admired by Barnes.

12. Baxter, p. 16. Unfortunately, neither these blocks, nor any pulls from them, seem to have survived. The DCM has a small collection of W.B.'s other blocks.

13. Dugdale, p. 48.

14. *Orra: A Lapland Tale*, Jones, Vol. 1., pp. 37-50.

15. Ibid., pp. 38-39.

16. Ibid., pp. 53-54.

## 4  Teaching Himself: Mere, 1823-1828

1. An illustration of the Market House appears in *Mere: A Wiltshire Country Town*, p. 46.

2. Hearl. An illustration of the interior of the Old Cross Loft appears in the plate facing p. 24.

3. Ibid., p. 22.

4. Lindgren, *The Love Poems and Letters*, p. 30.

5. Hearl, p. 24.

6. Lindgren, *The Love Poems and Letters*, p. 55.

7. Ibid., p. 79.

8. Ibid., p. 52.

9. Ibid., p. 66, and Jones, Vol. 1, p. 55.

10. Baxter, p. 24.

11. Lindgren, *The Love Poems and Letters*, p. 53.

12. Ibid., p. 82.

13. Jupe, R.J., 'Charles Card (1796-1875) Friend of William Barnes', *PWBS*, Vol. 2, 1989-1992, p. 94.

14. Lindgren, *The Love Poems and Letters*, p. 88.

15. Ibid., p. 94.

16. Baxter, p. 26.

## 5  The Universal Genius of Chantry House, 1827-1835

1. Baxter, pp. 31-32.

2. Dugdale, p. 94.

3. *Mere: A Wiltshire Country Town*, pp. 18-19.

4. Wallis, C.J., 'The Early Manhood of William Barnes, the Dorset Poet', *GM*, July 1888, pp. 23-40.

5. *Mere: A Wiltshire Country Town*, pp. 14-17.

6. Wallis, ibid.

7. For matters concerning Barnes's early career as a schoolmaster, I have drawn heavily on Hearl.

8. Hearl, p. 64.

9. Locke, John, 'Epistle to the Reader' in *An Essay Concerning Human Understanding*.

10. *The Etymological Glossary*, 1829, See Hearl, pp. 91-93.

11. *A Catechism of Government in General, and that of England in Particular*, 1833.

12. Ibid., pp. 6-7.

13. *A Few Words on the Advantage of a More Common Adoption of the Mathematics*, 1834.

14. *A Mathematical Investigation of the Principle of Hanging Doors, Gates, Swing Bridges, and Other Heavy Bodies,*
    1835.

15. Baxter, pp. 28-29.

16. Keen, L., *William Barnes: The Somerset Engravings*, pp. 12-13.

17. Wallis, ibid.

18 Keen, L. and Lindgren, C., *William Barnes: The Dorset Engravings*, passim.

## 6  Something to Say, 1827-1835

1. *DCC*, 29 November 1827.
2. Ibid., 6 December 1827.
3. The distinction between the English and Italian connotations of the word 'dilettante' was pointed out to the author in a letter from Mr Roger Gard.
4. *DCC*, 13 December 1827. There were eleven 'Linguiana' letters in all, between 6 December 1827 and 24 April 1828.
5. *DCC*, 3 April 1828. The psudonym 'Qui-Quondam' may be translated as the 'erstwhile or former one', suggesting someone in retirement.
6. Ibid., 5 February 1835, and in Jones, Vol. 2, p. 689.
7. *DCC*, 17 April 1828, and in Jones, Vol. 1, p. 60.
8. Ibid., 27 December 1827.
9. Ibid., 26 September 1833.
10. Ibid., 2 July 1829.
11. Ibid., 3 April 1828.
12. Ibid., 15 April 1830.
13. Ibid., 29 March 1834.
14. Ibid., 2 September 1830.
15. Ibid., 29 October 1829.

## 7  Tilling the Ground, 1830-1835

1. *DCC*, 19 November 1829.
2. Hammond, J.L. and Barbara, *The Village Labourer, 1760-1832*, 1912, p. 37.
3. Ibid., p. 39.
4. Hobsbawm, E.J., and Rude, George, *Captain Swing*, 1969, p. 27.
5. Ibid., p. 16.
6. Ibid., p. 51.
7. Kerr, Barbara, *Bound to the Soil*, 1968, pp. 98–99.
8. Ibid. p. 111.
9. Ibid. p. 91.
10. Hearl. pp. 83–84.
11. Kerr, p. 105.
12. Hobsbawm, E.J., and Rude, George, pp. 125–26.
13. *Mere: A Wiltshire Country Town*, 1975, p. 47.
14. Hobsbawm, E.J. and Rude, George, pp. 126–28.
15. Kerr, pp. 114–19.
16. Hearl, p. 84.
17. Ibid.
18. Kerr, p. 115.
19. For John Barnes's life, see Ashdown, pp. 37–49.
20. Boardman, J., Griffin, J., and Murray, O., *The Oxford History of the Classical World*, 1986, p. 617.
21. 'Rusticus Dolens or Inclosures of Common' appeared in the *DCC*, 2 January 1834. Jones reprints a later version entitled 'Eclogue: The Commons A–Took In', Vol. 1, p. 158. For convenience I have used Jones's text throughout when discussing the Dorset eclogues.
22. 'Rusticus Gaudens – The Allotment System', *DCC*, 9 January 1834, also Jones, Vol. 1, p. 93.
23. *The Times*, 1 April 1834.
24. Hearl, p. 111, notes that writers have 'expressed surprise at Barnes's silence after the Tolpuddle Martyrs conviction in March 1834'. He seems chiefly to have had in mind a piece by E.M. Forster, on 9 December 1939, which was reprinted in *Two Cheers for Democracy*. Forster wrote: 'He could live through the Labourer's Revolt of 1830 without its shadow falling across his verse'. In addition to confusing the dates, Forster betrays the fact that he did not really understand Barnes's situation at the time.
25. Thomas Hardy's poem 'The Curate's Kindness' recounts the story of one old pauper who positively looks forward to being separated from his wife.

26. *DCC*, 2 February 1834.

27. 'Rusticus Emigrans: Emigration', *DCC*, 11 November 1834, and Jones, Vol. 1, pp. 482-85.

28. *DCC*, 20 November 1834, and Jones, Vol. 1, pp. 182-85.

## 8  Foothold: Durngate Street, 1835-1837

1. Baxter, p. 41.

2. Jones, Vol. 2, p. 687.

3. The exact whereabouts of Barnes's Durngate Street school is unknown. It is likely that the building has been demolished.

4. 'Lady Day', 25 March, commemorated the Annunciation of the Virgin Mary and, until 1752, marked the beginning of the legal year, and hence the start of new contracts between farmers and their workers. On this day in the nineteenth century, workers would move their families and all their belongings to the farms of their new employers.

5. *DCC*, 28 March 1839, with the title 'Liady Day an' Ridden House', and in Jones, Vol. 1, pp. 73-74.

6. Hearl, pp. 117-18.

7. Advertisement in *Hanging Doors, Gates, and Swing Bridges*.

8. Hearl, pp. 115-16.

9. Wallis quoted in Hearl, p. 121.

10. *DCC*, 20 November 1856, and Jones, Vol. 1, pp. 233-34.

11. 'Linden Lea' is now looked upon as the unofficial Dorset anthem and, in the setting by Ralph Vaughan Williams, is sung on many Dorset occasions. There is a certain irony, therefore, in that, when writing it, Barnes was thinking of Chantry House in Wiltshire.

12. Dugdale, p. 101.

13. *Notes on Ancient Britain and the Britons*, pp. 3-5.

14. The poem 'Meary-Ann's Child' tells of a young mother left alone with a sick child who dies in the night. It may be that Julius died in this way. *DCC*, 4 August 1841, and Jones, Vol. 1, pp. 181-82.

15. *DCC*, 16 June 1859 and Jones, Vol. 1, pp. 470-71.

## 9  Almost a Gentleman, 1830-1844

1. Members of three generations of Nicholses were proprietors/editors of *GM*. These were John Nichols, 1745-1826; John Bowyer Nichols, 1779-1863; and John Gough Nichols, 1806-1873. Barnes was a corresponding friend of the first two, and perhaps the third, *DNB*.

2. Edward Cave, printer, 1691-1754, published the first issue of the *GM* in January, 1730, *DNB*.

3. The *GM* published four items by W.B. in 1830, four in 1831, six in 1832, six in 1833, one in 1834, one in 1835, two in 1837, two in 1838, two in 1839, three in 1840, four in 1841, one in 1842, one in 1843 and one in 1844.

4. W.B. must have been considerably out of pocket in contributing his first twenty-eight items to the *GM*, because Sir Rowland Hill's penny post was not introduced until 1840.

5. A partial account of such polymathic amateurs is given in Colloms, Barbara, *Victorian Country Parsons*, 1977.

6. For the story of the deciphering of the hieroglyphs, see Adkins, Lesley and Roy, *The Keys of Egypt*, 2001.

7. Baxter, p. 35.

8. *GM*, February 1832 and August 1832.

9. *GM*, November 1831.

10. *GM*, June 1833.

11. *An Outline of Speechcraft*, p. 89.

12. *The Mayor of Casterbridge*, XX.

13. *The Glossary of the Dorset Dialect*, 1886.

14. The dialect term 'ninnywatch' or 'nunnywatch' was completely meaningful. It signified a confused or baffled state.

## 10  Establishments: Norman's House, 1838-1847

1. Treves quoted in Hearl, op. cit. pp. 138-39.
2. Norman's House still stands. The ground floor has served as various shops.
3. Treves quoted in Dugdale, op. cit. p. 103.
4. J.B. Lock quoted in Baxter, op. cit. p. 43.
5. Baxter, pp. 49-50.
6. Ibid., pp. 65-67.
7. *A Corrective Concordance; or, Imposition Book*, probably 1839.
8. *An Investigation of the Laws of Case in Language*, 1840.
9. Hearl, op. cit. p. 157.
10. *An Arithmetical and Commercial Dictionary*, 1840.
11. *The Elements of English Grammar*, London, 1842. Printed by G. Clark.
12. Hearl, op. cit. pp. 213-14.
13. See: Lucking, J.H., *Railways of Dorset*, The Railway Correspondence and Travel Society, 1986, pp. 4-24.
14. Mary Anning (1799-1847) from Lyme Regis became famous as one of the first fossil collectors. See Fowles, John, *A Short History of Lyme Regis*, 1991, pp. 40-42.
15. Baxter, op. cit. pp. 89-90.
16. *DCC*, 17 March 1842, and Jones, Vol. 1, pp. 207-08.
17. Hearl, op. cit. pp. 201-02.
18. Ibid., p. 197.
19. Ibid., pp. 130-131.
20. Dugdale, op. cit. p. 121.
21. *DCC*, 21 May 1840, and Jones, Vol. 1, pp. 126-27.

## 11  Voices From Home, 1838-1846

1. Between 1838 and 1843, the *DCC* published at least 101 of Barnes's dialect poems. The records available, however, are not complete. See: Chedzoy, Alan, 'The First Publication of William Barnes's dialect poems in the DCC', *PDNHAS*, Vol. 129.208, pp. 178-80.
2. *DCC*, 6 December 1838, and Jones, Vol. 1, pp. 226-232, with the title of 'Eclogue: The Times'.
3. 'The Rev. William Barnes, B.D.' in the *Athenaeum*, 16 October 1886, Orel, p. 101.
4. *DCC*, 14 May 1840, and Jones, Vol. 1, p. 83.
5. *DCC*, 7 March 1839, and Jones Vol. 1, p. 86.
6. Orel, pp. 79-80.
7. *DCC*, 12 December 1842, and Jones, Vol. 1, pp. 143-44.
8. Urqhart, the Revd Frederick, in *DCC*, Jan, 1834.
9. *DCC*, 3 September 1840, and Jones, Vol. 1, pp. 198-99.
10. *DCC*, 25 March 1841, Jones, Vol. 1, p. 71.
11. Jones, Vol. 1, pp. 217-18.
12. *DCC*, 24 March 1842, and Jones, Vol. 1, pp. 166-67, with the revised title; 'What Dick an' I Did'.
13. *Poems of Rural Life, in the Dorset Dialect: with a Dissertation and Glossary*. By William Barnes. John Russell Smith, London; George Simonds, Dorchester, MDCCCXLIV.
14. *DCC*, 27 June 1839, and Jones, Vol. 1, pp. 115-6.
15. The 'Dissertation' to the above, pp. 36-37.
16. The cost of the second edition of the *Poems of Rural Life* was 10s.
17. In her recollections of rural life in the 1870s, some thirty years after the publication of the *Poems of Rural Life*, Flora Thompson observes that: 'Modern writers who speak of the booklessness of the poor at that time must mean books as possessions; there were always books to borrow'. *Larkrise to Candleford*, 1945, XXXI. The founding of the Dorchester working mens' institutes would also have helped to make Barnes's book more easily available.
18. *Sherborne and Yeovil Mercury*, January 1844.
19. *GM*, January 1844.
20. George Crabbe, 1754-1832.

21. Robert Bloomfield (1766-1823). See Goodridge, J. and Lucas, J., *Bloomfield, Selected Poems*, Trent, 1998. In his 'Introduction', John Lucas writes that Barnes 'must surely have known' the work of Bloomfield, pp. 35-6.

22. See: Brett, R.I., and Jones, A.R., the 'Preface' to the second edition of Wordsworth and Coleridge's *Lyrical Ballads* (1798), 1963, p. 241.

23. John Clare, 1793-1864. See Robinson, Eric, and Summerfield, Geoffrey, *Selected Poems And Prose of John Clare*, Oxford, 1967.

24. Abbot, Claude Colleer, *Further Letters of Gerard Manley Hopkins*, 1970, p. 371.

25. See: Chedzoy, A., *A Scandalous Woman: The Story of Caroline Norton*, 1992, pp, 190-92.

26. Jones, Vol. 2, p. 693.

27. *Poems, Partly of Rural Life (In National English)*, by William Barnes, London: J.R. Smith, 4 Old Compton Street, Soho Square. MDCCCXLVI. Dorchester: printed by George Simonds.

28. See: Millgate, Michael, *Thomas Hardy: A Biography*, Oxford, 1982, p. 26.

## 12  Wilderness, 1847-1850

1. William Barnes was ordained Deacon on 28 February 1847.

2. Luckings, J.H., *Railways of Dorset*, pp. 10-13, 1968.

3. Searby, Peter, *A History of Cambridge University*, Vol. III, (1750-1870), Cambridge, pp. 262-65 and 728.

4. Dugdale, op. cit. p. 126

5. Details of Barnes's chapel attendance when at St John's are taken from the Senior Dean's book (1843-52),
   St John's College Archives DS4.3.

6. Hearl, p. 228

7. Ibid.

8. Ibid., p. 234

9. Dugdale, op. cit. p. 234

10. The Buttery Book of St John's for the relevant years.

11. Searby, p. 144

12. The only estimate that I can find of the cost of taking a degree course at Cambridge in the mid-nineteenth century is by Swann, F., 'Hardy, Jude, Cambridge and the Moules', in the *Thomas Hardy Journal*, Autumn 2006, pp. 174-75. Swann's figures relate to undergraduates only, rather than the 10-year men on the BD course. He estimates that to take the undergraduate course in 1830 would cost about £200-250 per annum, though Barnes, of course, paid no fees. Nevertheless, if we include the cost of his frequent journeyings, Barnes's degree probably cost him between £600 and £750.

13. Baxter, p. 110

14. The 'Wilderness' block at St John's was demolished in 1869, along with the thirteenth-century chapel in which Barnes worshipped, to make way for a new chapel designed by Sir George Gilbert Scott.

15. Baxter, pp. 110-111

16. Dugdale, pp. 132-33

17. Hearl, pp. 249-50, and Dugdale, op. cit. p. 133

## 13  Anglo-Saxon Attitudes, 1846-1852

1. *DCC*, 21 February 1839, and Jones, Vol. 1, p. 80.

2. *Se Gefylsta (The Helper): An Anglo-Saxon Delectus*, Serving as A first Class-Book of the Language, By the Rev. W. Barnes, of St John's College, Cambridge, London, John Russell Smith, 4 Old Compton Square, MDCCCXLIX.

3. See: Crystal, David, *The Stories of English*, 2004, p. 292.

4. *Se Gefylsta*, pp. iv-v.

5. *Humilis Domus*, in the *Poole & Dorset Herald*, 12 April-24 May 1849.

6. Chief among those protesting at the plight of the Dorset poor was the Revd Lord Sidney Godolphin Osborne (1808-1889), Vicar of Durweston, who was almost certainly known to Barnes. Osborne wrote a series of letters on the subject, signed 'S.G.O.', and which appeared in *The Times* from the 1840s onwards.

7. Contrasted with Barnes's views are those of Marx and Engels, as they had appeared in *The Communist Manifesto* (1848), just a year before the publication of *Humilis Domus*. Whereas Barnes appears to welcome a return to feudalism, they applaud its evolution into a 'dynamic' capitalism, which they regard as the precursor of a socialist economy. According to Marx, great cities had 'rescued a considerable part of the population from the idiocy of rural life'. On the other hand, both Barnes and Marx denounced the injurious effect of repetitive factory work.
8. 'Dorsetshire 150 Years Ago', in the *Poole & Dorset Herald*, 25 Ocober 1849 until the end of the year.
9. Ibid., 10 October 1849.

## 14  Two Summers, 1851-1852

1. *DCC*, 16 December 1858, and Jones, Vol. 1, pp. 473-76
2. See: Jones, Irene, *Sir James Thornhill of Thornhill House Stallbridge*, Sturminster Newton, 1989.
3. *DCC*, 2 April 1840, and Jones, Bernard, Vol. 1, p. 93. This poem on the wall of the schoolroom was painted over at some time, and not discovered until 1954.
4. The cholera outbreaks in the 1850s were gallantly fought by Barnes's friend, the Revd Henry Moule, and the brewer, Sarah Eldridge. The story is told in David Edgar's play *Entertaining Strangers*.

## 15  Bereft, 1852-1853

1. John Pouncy (?-1894), like William Barnes, was born among working people and succeeded in pursuing a career in the arts. Beginning as a painter and decorator, with a shop in North Square, Dorchester, he later took up photography. By the mid-1850s, he had a successful studio and in, December 1854, offered to take portraits, the profits of which would go to families bereaved as a result of the Crimean War. For his achievements he was awarded the Silver Medal of the Royal Photographic Society, and took prizes for his work in Edinburgh, Berlin and Paris. One of his many sidelines was picture-framing, and it was probably he who encouraged Barnes in this pursuit. He was succeeded in the photographic business by his son, Walter.
2. Dugdale, pp. 146-47. In 1852, Barnes subsequently published a less personal version of this poem with the title 'Plorata veris Lachymis', with the first line changed to: 'O now, my true and dearest bride'. See Jones, Vol. 2, pp. 701-02.
3. *DCC*, 12 August 1858, and Jones, Vol. 1, pp. 333-34.
4. Working from memory, Lucy Baxter described Arden as a 'young surgeon'. She may have been mistaken, because there was a clergyman named George Arden living in Dorchester at this time.
5. Baxter, pp. 129-30.
6. Dugdale, p. 154. One painting, entitled 'The Three Marys', by Richard Wilson, was bought by Thomas Hardy for £1 3s at the sale of Barnes's collection of paintings on 25 November 1886. For many years it hung on the wall at Max Gate, and was recently purchased by the Thomas Hardy Society and rehung there on 19 December 2008.
7. Baxter. op. cit. p. 130.
8. Dugdale, op. cit. p. 154.
9. Jones, Vol. 1, pp. 343-44.
10. Baxter, p. 121.

## 16  The Language of Mankind, 1852-1854

1. Baxter, pp. 126-28.
2. See: the *Retrospective Review*, November 1852, pp. 44-58, and pp. 97-101, February 1853, pp. 105-09 and 201-05, and August 1853, pp. 408-18.
3. Baxter, pp. 135-36.
4. *A Philological Grammar*, By William Barnes, B.D., St John's College Cambridge, London, John Russell Smith, March 1854.
5. Baxter, p. 137.
6. *Philological Grammar*, pp. 258-59.

7. Ibid., pp. 6-7.
8. Ibid., p. 73.
9. Ibid., p. 51.
10. Ibid., p. 116. Barnes's insistence that a valid grammar should accord with 'the logical relation of things… in nature', reveals just how close he is to suggesting that our grammatical concepts are the necessary ways in which we structure the world. Despite this, there is no evidence that he had ever read Kant.
11. Hardy in Orel, pp. 78-80.
12. Hearl, p. 264.

## 17  Radical Shift, 1853-1859

1. Baxter, op.cit. pp. 153-54.
2. Ibid., pp. 153-58.
3. Charles Warne (1801-1887), archaeologist, lived in Dorset for many years. His *Illustrated map of Dorsetshire giving the sites of its numerous Celtic, Roman, Saxon and Danish Vestiges* came out in 1865. After he moved to London, it seems that Barnes acted as his eyes and ears in the county.
4. Tennant is referring to the Roman general, Lucius Quinctius Cincinatus, who retired to a simple life on his farm. In writing to Tennant to tell him that he had bought two fields in Blackmore, Barnes had evidently made some comparison between himself and the Roman soldier.
5. 'Picture Frames', in the *Art Journal*, 12 February, 1855, pp. 55-56.
6. Hearl, pp. 274-76.
7. Millgate, pp. 49-55.
8. *DCC*, 29 October 1857, and Jones, Vol. 1, p. 352.
9. Baxter, p. 163.
10. Hearl, p. 245.
11. *DCC*, 20 October 1857.
12. *DCC*, 15 October 1857.
13. *Notes on Ancient Britain and the Britons*, 1858.
14. Phillips, Fr. Andrew, *Views of Labour and Gold*, repr. 2003, p. 7.
15. *Views of Labour and Gold*, 1859.
16. Baxter, p. 179.
17. Hardy, Florence Emily, *The Life of Thomas Hardy*, 1962, p. 28.
18. Hardy, Thomas, Obituary of Lucy Baxter ('Leader Scott'), *DCC*, 27 November 1902.
19. At the same time that Barnes was applying to become the chaplain to the Forston Asylum, his fellow poet John Clare was an inmate at the Northampton General Asylum.

## 18  Performance, 1853-1859

1. It is curious that Barnes did not offer his poems to another local paper, such as the *Poole & East Dorset Herald* which had published *Humilis Domus*. Perhaps he felt that the dialect used was so locally based that only a west Dorset paper would do.
2. The actor William Charles Macready (1793-1873) retired to Sherborne, where he lived from 1850-1860 in Sherborne House, where he welcomed friends, such as Charles Dickens, at Christmas 1854. Barker, Katherine, *William Charles Macready: The Sherborne Literary institution and Charles Dickens*, Sherborne, 2007.
3. *DCC*, 23 October 1856. See Jones, op. cit. Vol. 1, p. 306.
4. In 1844, the year of the publication of the first collection of the *Poems of Rural Life*, no dialect poems appeared in the *DCC*. The figures for the following years are as follows: 1845 – none, 1846 – none, 1847 – none, 1848 – none, 1849 – none, 1850 – none, 1851 – none, 1852 – none, 1853 – none, 1854 – none, 1855 – none, 1856 – twelve, 1857 – forty-six, 1858 – fifty-one, 1859 – thirty-five, 1860 – none, 1861 – seventeen, 1862 – eleven, 1863 – none, 1864 – none.
5. *Hwomely Rhymes, A second collection of Poems in the Dorset Dialect*, by William Barnes, John Russell Smith, MDCCCLIX.

6. *DCC*, 18 December 1856. Jones, Vol. 1, p. 303.

7. *DCC*, 9 July 1857. Jones, ibid., p. 318.

8. *DCC*, 11 June 1856. Jones, ibid., p. 290.

9. *The Song of Solomon in the Dorset Dialect*. From the Authorised English Version. By the Rev. William Barnes, 1859. (250 copies printed by Geo. Barclay, 28 Castle Street, Leicester Square, under the auspices of HRH Prince Lucien Bonaparte.)

10. 'I awoke one day and found myself famous'. Remark by Lord Byron on the success of Childe Harold. See Moore, T., *Life of Byron*, p. 347.

11. For an account of Caroline Norton's relationship with Sidney Herbert, see Chedzoy, A., *A Scandalous Woman: the Story of Caroline Norton*, pp. 212-19.

12. Baxter, op. cit. p. 167.

13. Hardy, T., in Orel, p. 101.

14. *Times Literary Supplement*, 23 January 1903.

## 19  Deliverance, 1859-1862

1. See: Jones, op. cit. Vol. 1, p. 513.

2. See: Ashdown, op. cit. p. 147.

3. Treves, Sir Frederick, *Highways and Byways in Dorset* (1906) pp. 356-57.

4. Baxter, op. cit. pp. 180-81.

5. Ibid.

6. Ibid., pp. 187-88.

7. Ibid., p. 197.

8. Ibid., pp. 121-22.

9. Barnes, William, 'Preface' to *Poems of Rural Life in the Dorset Dialect*, Third Collection, 1862.

10. Hardy, Thomas, Obituary entitled 'The Rev. Willam Barnes B.D.', in Orel, op cit. p. 101.

11. *DCC*, 6 March 1862, also in Jones, op. cit. Vol. 1, pp. 378-79.

12. There is some doubt about the identity of the purchaser of 40 South Street. Hearl, op. cit. p. 307 says that Barnes accepted the first offer which was from a Mr Fitch, apparently to start a school there. Octavius Pickard Cambridge, however, in his obituary, 'In Memoriam: Rev. William Barnes B.d.' in the *PDNHAFC*, Vol. VIII, 1887, p. xvii, says that after Barnes left, a school was carried on there by a Mr de Winton.

## 20  In Paradiso, 1862-1870

1. Baxter, p. 199.

2. Chedzoy, A., 'Winterborne Came Rectory: The Home of William Barnes' in *PDNHAS*, Vol. 123, 2001, pp. 1-6.

3. Powys, Llewelyn, 'The Grave of William Barnes' in *Somerset and Dorset Essays*, 1935, p. 158. This is a beautiful and evocative piece of writing.

4. A copy of this skit is to be found in DCM, Scrapbook 3, p. 53

5. Baxter, pp. 199-200.

6. Ashdown, pp. 154-56, gives an account of W.B.'s stewardship of the Shaw estate.

7. See: Benzie, William, *Dr J.F. Furnivall: Victorian Scholar Adventurer*, 1983, W.B. to F.J.F., January 1863.

8. Jones, Vol. 1, pp. 171-72.

9. Hearl, p. 311.

10. DCM Scrapbook 3, p. 51.

11. *DCC*, 29 January 1863.

12. Baxter, p. 213.

## 21  Siren Voices, 1864-1870

1. Alexander MacMillan to W.B., DCM, Scrapbook 3, 21 October 1864.

2. Jones, Vol. 1, pp. 556-57.

3. Ibid., p. 823.
4. See: C.C. Abbot (Ed.), *The Letters of Gerard Manley Hopkins to Robert Bridges*, 1935, repr. in Grigson, pp. 47-49.

## 22 Pilgrims, 1862-1867

1. 'William Barnes, the Dorsetshire Poet', *MacMillan's Magazine*, June 1862. Anonymous article by Coventry Patmore.
2. For contemporary critism of 'The Angel in the House', see Anstruther, Ian, *Coventry Patmore's Angel*, 1992, pp. 74-82.
3. Ibid., p. 96. On the marriage of the Prince of Wales to Princess Alexandra of Denmark in 1863, one journalist wrote, 'We rejoice that "the Angel in the House" has come to dwell in the Royal Palace'.
4. William Barnes, DCM, Scrapbook 3.
5. See Patmore, Derek, *The Life and Times of Coventry Patmore*, 1949, p. 151-52 for an account of the poet's mystical views of marriage. These would not have accorded with those of another of Barnes's friends, the campaigner for women's rights, Mrs Caroline Norton; see Chedzoy, Alan, *A Scandalous Woman: The Story of Caroline Norton*, 1992.
6. Patmore's conversion to Catholicism was forseen by his first wife, Emily, who was strictly Protestant. She believed that it meant that they would not be reunited in heaven. In her last illness she said to Patmore, 'When I am gone, they will get you; and then I shall see you no more'. Anstruther, op. cit. p. 90.
7. See: Norwich, John Julius (Ed.), *William Allingham: A Diary, 1824-1889*, 1985, p. 109.
8. Ibid., pp. 126-27.
9. Ibid., pp. 156-57.
10. Dugdale, p. 191.
11. I have discovered no evidence in the Barnes literature to confirm Dugdale's suggestion that Hardy visited Barnes for advice in 1867. Michael Millgate, Hardy's foremost biographer, tells me that he is not aware of such a visit either, but that Hardy might have made it is undeniable, especially, Millgate adds, because both writers were on friendly terms with Horace Moule. On the whole, he thinks that such a visit is unlikely because Hardy would have felt 'too modest and insecure' to call on so admired a writer as Barnes.
12. Cox, R.G., *Thomas Hardy: The Critical Heritage*, 1970, pp. xiv-xv.
13. Jones, Vol. 1, p. 176.
14. Ibid., p. 162.
15. *Far From the Madding Crowd* first appeared in 1874. In the 'Preface' to the 1912 edition, Hardy records that it was in the chapters of that novel that he first 'ventured to adopt the word "Wessex" from the pages of English history'. He had intended the name to signify a 'partly-real, partly-dream country', but it became so popular that it has 'by degrees, solidified into a utilitarian region which people can go to, to take a house in, and write to the papers from'.
16. Six years earlier, in 1868, the 'Preface' to Barnes's *Poems of Rural Life in Common English*, began: 'As I think that some people beyond the bounds of *Wessex*, would allow me the pleasure of…' (my italics)

## 23 Pure English, 1862-1880

1. *Tiw or, A View of the Roots and Stems of the English as a Teutonic Tongue*, by William Barnes B.D., London, John Russell Smith, 1862.
2. Baxter, p. 189.
3. *Tiw*, p. 5.
4. *The Faerie Queene*, IV, ii. 32.
5. Benzie, William, *Dr F.J. Furnivall: Victorian Scholar Adventurer*, Oklahoma, 1983, p. 268.
6. Dugdale, p. 182.
7. *A Grammar and Glossary of the Dorset Dialect*, With the History, Outspreading, and Bearings of South-Western English, by W. Barnes, B.D. Philological Society, A. Asher & Co., Berlin, 1863.
8. Jacobs, Willis D., *William Barnes, Linguist*, New Mexico, 1952.

9. For convenience I have referred throughout to the Society's publication as the *OED*.

10. For the story of the inception of the *OED*, see Winchester, Simon, *The Meaning of Everything*, passim, Oxford, 2003.

11. I am grateful to Beverley Hunt of the *OED* for information from their archives.

12. Jacobs, ibid., pp. 71-72. He argues (passim) that Barnes was largely ignored by the editors of the *OED* who considered him to be an 'enthusiast'.

13. Elworthy, Frederick Thomas, *The Dialect of West Somerset*, 1875, and *The Grammar of the Dialect of West Somerset*, 1877-79, both published by the Philological Society.

14. The life of James Murray (1837-1915) bears remarkable similiarities to that of Barnes. Like Barnes, Murray was humbly born and provincial, being a linen-draper's son from a Teviotdale village near Hawick. Like Barnes, he was multi-talented but with a special bent for languages. As a child he gave Latin names to the family cows, and by fifteen had already taught himself Latin, French, Italian, German and Greek. Like Barnes, he became a schoolmaster and amateur archaeologist, and gave lectures at the local working men's mutual improvement institute. Like Barnes, he published a book on his local dialect, in this case a study of that of the southern counties of Scotland, which came out in 1873. In their later years, both men became the white-bearded fathers of many children. But their fortunes turned out different. While Murray succeeded to the editorship of the *OED*, was knighted, and received honours from many British and foreign universities, Barnes was granted little official recognition, save for his Civil List pension, and remained a relatively obscure and unprosperous scholar for his whole life.

15. See: *A Glossary With Some Pieces of Verse of the Old Dialect of the English Colony in the Baronies of Forth and Bargy, County of Wexford, Ireland*. Formerly collected by Jacob Poole, now edited… By William Barnes, B.D., London, J. Russell Smith, 1867.

16. *Early England and the Saxon English, with some Notes on the Father-Stock of the Saxon-English, The Frisians*, pp. 105-06 by William Barnes B.D., London, John Russell Smith, 1869.

17. *An Outline of Speech-Craft*, by William Barnes, B.D., London, C. Kegan-Paul & Co., 1878.

18. *An Outline of Rede-Craft (Logic) with English Wording*, by William Barnes, B.D., London, C. Kegan-Paul & Co., 1880.

19. Professor Crystal advises that although Barnes receives the occasional reference in historical surveys of linguistics, he is 'by no means mainstream', and it seems that his work is not widely read. Crystal adds, 'his general views on philology and etymology would today be regarded as something of an oversimplification'.

20. Orwell, George, 'Politics and the English Language', in *Inside the Whale and other Essays*, 1940, repr. 1968.

21. Forth and Bargy etc., op. cit. p. 123.

## 24 Hermit and Enchanter, 1874-1885

1. The Revd Henry Moule (1801-1880), friend of Barnes, was for many years Vicar of Fordington, the working-class area adjacent to Dorchester. He campaigned against the squalor of Mill Street, owned by the Duchy of Cornwall, wrote directly to Prince Albert with his evidence and published his findings. His popularity in the area was established when he stayed on to carry out relief work during a cholera outbreak in the town. He was the inventor of the earth closet, which he maintained was of superior merit to the water closet. He appeared in literature as the model of Angel Clare's benevolent father in *Tess of the D'Urbervilles*.

2. See: Plomer, William (Ed.), *Kilvert's Diary*, 1944, repr. 1977, pp. 255-60.

3. Horace Moule, the son of Henry, was a brilliant scholar, friend of Tolbort and Hardy, but committed suicide in 1873.

4. Ashdown, pp. 153-55.

5. Jones, Vol. 1, p. 567.

6. See: Colloms, Brenda, *Victorian Country Parsons*, 1977, for a general discussion of the subject and, Wilding, Richard, 'Osmond Fisher (1817-1914) Dorset Geologist and Pioneer Geophysicist', in *PDNHAS*, Vol. 110, 1988, pp. 17-22.

7. *DNB*.

8. *Harper's Magazine*, January 1874.

9. Udal, John Symonds, *Dorset Folk-Lore*, Dorchester, 1922, repr. 1989.

10. Palgrave, Gwenllian, *Francis Turner Palgrave, his Journals and Memories of his Life*, 1899, pp.185–86.

11. See: Hardy, Florence Emily, *The Life of Thomas Hardy 1840-1928*, 1962, repr. 1970, p. 161.

12. *Longman's Magazine*, 1883.

13. Hopkins, Kenneth, *The Powys Brothers*, 1967, repr. 1972, pp. 4-5. Llewelyn Powys recorded that his mother carried him to Came to receive Barnes's blessing.

14. Baxter, pp. 286-88.

15. Ibid., pp. 297-98.

## 25 Falling To, 1884-1886

1. Jones, Vol. 2, pp. 928–29.

2. Palgrave, Ibid.

3. Gosse is quoted in Dugdale, op. cit, p. 229.

## Afterwards

1. Like her sister Julia, Lucy Baxter was not present at their father's funeral because she was living in Italy, and she was therefore obliged to rely on the accounts of others. The description of the occasion given in her book was supplied by Francis Palgrave. Other information is taken from Palgrave, Gwenllian, *Francis Turner Palgrave, His Journals and Memories of his Life*, 1899, p. 202.

2. *DCC*, 14 October 1886.

3. See *The Collected Poems of Thomas Hardy*, 1965, p. 444.

4. 'Auctioneer's Book', Dorset History Centre.

5. Ashdown, pp. 185-87.

6. Dugdale, p. 228.

7. Chedzoy, A., 'Winterborne Came Rectory: The Home of William Barnes' in *PDNHAS*, Vol. 123, 2001, pp. 1-6.

8. Hardy, ibid., p. 639.

9. Orel, p. 106.

10. Ashdown, op. cit., pp. 136-38, and pp. 195-96. Of her projected biography, Lucy wrote to Laura, 'William shall have full powers to cut out what he likes, but not to alter it for I am responsible for the style and subject'.

# SELECT BIBLIOGRAPHY

(The place of publication is London, unless otherwise indicated.)

## WORKS BY BARNES

### Poetry

*Poetical Pieces*, Dorchester, 1820.
*Orra: A Lapland Tale*, Dorchester, 1822.
*Sabbath Lays: Six Sacred Songs*, Music by F.W. Smith, 1844.
*Poems of Rural Life in the Dorset Dialect, with a Dissertation and Glossary*, 1844 (second edition 1847, third
     edition 1862, fourth edition 1866).
*Poems Partly of Rural Life (In National English)*, 1846.
*The Song of Solomon in the Dorset Dialect*, 1859.
*Hwomely Rhymes: A Second Collection of Poems in the Dorset Dialect*, 1859 (second edition 1863).
*Poems of Rural Life in the Dorset Dialect, Third Collection*, second edition, 1869.
*Poems in the Dorset Dialect*, Boston, Massachussetts, 1864.
*Poems of Rural Life in Common English*, Boston, Massachussetts, 1869.
*A Selection of Unpublished Poems*, Winterborne Monkton, 1870.
*Poems of Rural Life in the Dorset Dialect* (repr. 1883, 1886, 1888, 1893, 1898, 1902, 1905).
*Ruth, A Short Drama from the Bible*, Dorchester, 1884.

### Prose

*Etymological Dictionary*, Shaftesbury, 1829.
*A Catechism of Government in General and that of England in Particular*, Shaftesbury, 1833.
*The Mnemonic Manual* (no known copy has survived), 1833.
*A Few Words on the Advantages of a More Common Adoption of the Mathematics as a Branch of Education, or
     Subject of Study*, 1834.
*A Mathematical Investigation of the Principle of Hanging Doors, Gates, Swing Bridges, and other heavy Bodies
     Swinging on Vertical Axes*, Dorchester, 1835.
*A Corrective Concordance or Imposition Book*, Dorchester, 1839.
*An Arithmetical and Commercial Dictionary*, 1840.
*An Investigation of the Laws of Case in Language, Exhibited in a System of Natural Cases*, 1840.
*The Elements of English Grammar, with a set of Questions and Exercises Dorchester*, 1842.
*The Elements of Linear Perspective and the Projection of Shadows*, 1842.
*Exercises in Practical Science*, Dorchester, 1844.
*Outlines of Geography and Ethnography for Youth*, Dorchester, 1847.
*Se Gefylsta (The Helper): An Anglo-Saxon Delectus. Serving as a First Class-book of the Language*, 1849.
*Humilis Domus: Some Thoughts on the Abodes, Life and Social Conditions of the Poor*, 1849.
*A Philological Grammar, Grounded upon English, and formed from a Comparison of More than Sixty Languages*,
     1854.
*Notes on Ancient Britain and the Britons*, 1858.
*Views of Labour and Gold*, 1859.
*TIW; or, a View of the Roots and Stems of the English as a Teutonic Tongue*, 1862.

*A Grammar and Glossary of the Dorset Dialect*, Berlin, 1863.
*A Glossary, With some Pieces of Verse, of the Old Dialect of the English Colony in the Baronies of Forth and Bargy*, 1867.
*Early England and the Saxon English*, 1869.
*An Outline of Speech-Craft*, 1878.
*An Outline of Rede-Craft (Logic) with English Wording*, 1880.
*A Guide to Dorchester and its Neighbourhoood*, 1881(?).
*A Glossary of the Dorset Dialect with Grammar of its Word Shapening and Wording*, Dorchester, 1886.
'Foresay' to *Dorsetshire Folklore* by John Symonds Udal, 1922.


(Barnes's occasional prose is uncollected but, as indicated here, it includes contributions to *Hone's Year Book*, the *Dorset County Chronicle*, *The Gentleman's Magazine*, *MacMillan's Magazine* and the *Leisure Hour*.)


## EDITIONS

Hardy, Thomas (Ed.), *Select Poems of William Barnes*, 1908.
Dugdale, Giles, *Poems Grave & Gay by William Barnes*, Dorchester, 1949.
Grigson, G. (Ed.), *Selected Poems of William Barnes*, 1950.
Jones, Bernard, *The Poems of William Barnes*, 2 Vols, Southern Illinois, 1962.
Chedzoy, Alan (Ed.), *Poems Grave & Gay by William Barnes*, Dorchester, 1978.
Wrigley, Chris, *William Barnes the Dorset Poet*, Wimborne, 1984.
Lindgren, Charlotte (Ed.), *The Love Poems and Letters of William Barnes and Julia Miles*, Dorchester, 1986.
Motion, Andrew (Ed.), *William Barnes: Selected Poems*, 1994.
*William Barnes Collected Prose Works*, 6 Vols, 'Introduction' by Richard Bradbury, Thoemmes Press, 1996.


## BIOGRAPHY

Ashdown, Douglas, *William Barnes: My Hwomeward Road*, privately published, Dorchester, 2003.
Baxter, Lucy, *The Life of William Barnes: Poet and Philologist*, 1887.
Chedzoy, Alan, *William Barnes: A Life of the Dorset Poet*, Wimborne, Dorset, 1985.
Dugdale, Giles, *William Barnes of Dorset*, 1953.
Hardy, Thomas, 'The Rev. Willam Barnes, B.D.' Obituary in the *Athenaeum*, 16 October 1886.
Hearl, Trevor, *William Barnes the Schoolmaster*, Dorchester, 1966.
Jones, Bernard, *William Barnes* (Dorset Worthies Series No. 1) 1997.
Levy, William Turner, *William Barnes: The Man and his Poems*, Dorchester, 1960.
Pickard Cambridge, Octavius, 'In Memoriam: William Barnes, B.D.', *PDNHAFC*, Vol. VIII, 1887.


## MONOGRAPHS

Bath, Francis R.L., *Flowers of William Barnes*, 1977.
Burton, T.L., *William Barnes's Dialect Poems: A Pronunciation Guide*, privately printed, 2008.
Gachelin, J.M., 'William Barnes and the Dorset Dialect', *Thomas Hardy Yearbook*, No. 15, Guernsey, 1988.
Jacobs, Willis J., *William Barnes Linguist*, New Mexico, 1952.
Keen, Lawrence, and Lindgren, Charlotte, *William Barnes: The Dorset Engravings*, DNH & AS, 1986.
Keen, Laurence, *William Barnes: The Somerset Engravings*, Somerset County Council, 1989.
Oliver, Vere L., *The Late Rev. William Barnes as Engraver*, PDNHAFC, 10 February 1925.


## CRITICISM

Austin, Frances and Jones, Bernard, *The Language and Craft of William Barnes, Poet and Philologist, (1801-1886)*, 2002.
Forster, E.M. 'William Barnes', the *New Statesman*, 1939, repr. in *Two Cheers for Democracy*, 1965.

Hardy, Thomas, 'An unsigned review of the Poems of Rural Life in the Dorset Dialect', in the *New Quarterly Magazine*, 1879; an obituary in the *Athenaeum*, 1886; and an 'Introduction' to his *Select Poems of William Barnes*, 1908, all reprinted in Orel.

Hopkins, G.M., *Further Letters of Gerard Manley Hopkins*, (Ed. Claude Colleer Abbot), 1970.

Larkin, Philip, *The Poetry of William Barnes*, 1962, Required Reading, 1983.

Powys, Llewelyn, 'The Grave of William Barnes', in *Somerset and Dorset Essays*, 1935.


## THE SOCIAL AND POLITICAL BACKGROUND

Anon. *Mere: A Wiltshire Country Town*, Blackmore Press, 1985.

Barker, Katherine, *William Charles Macready: The Sherborne Literary Institution and Charles Dickens*, Sherborne, 2007.

Fowles, John and Draper, Jo., *Thomas Hardy's England*, 1984.

Hammond, J.L. & Barbara, *The Village Labourer, 1760–1832*, 1912.

Hobsbawm, E.J. & Rude, George, *Captain Swing*, 1969.

Jones, Irene, *Sir James Thornhill of Thornhill House, Stallbridge*, Sturminster Newton, 1989.

Kerr, Barbara, *Bound to the Soil*, 1968.

Knott, Olive, and Rogers, Raymond, *Pictorial History of Sturminster Newton*, 1973.

Lucking, J.H., *Railways of Dorset*, The Railway Correspondence and Travel Society, 1968.

Marlow, Joyce, *The Tolpuddle Martyrs*, 1971.

Mountain, Penny (compiled and edited), *Stur: The Story of Sturminster Newton*, Wimborne, 2006.

Searby, Peter, *A History of Cambridge University*, Vol. III, 1750-1870, Cambridge, 1997.

Treves, Frederick, *Highways and Byways in Dorset*, 1906.

Woodward, E.L., *The Age of Reform: 1815-1870*, Oxford, 1946.


## RELATED LANGUAGE AND LITERATURE

Brett, R.L. and Jones, A.R. (Eds), *Wordsworth & Coleridge: Lyrical Ballads*, 1963.

Cox, R.G., *Thomas Hardy, The Critical Heritage*, 1970.

Crystal, David, *The Stories of English*, 2004.

Elliot, Ralph W.V., *Thomas Hardy's English*, 1984.

Goodridge, John, & Lucas, John (Eds), *Robert Bloomfield, Selected Poems*, Nottingham, 1998.

Lee, Guy, (Tr.), *Virgil, The Eclogues*, 1980.

Lucas, John (Ed.), *A Selection from the Poems of George Crabbe*, 1967.

Orel. Harold (Ed.), *Thomas Hardy's Personal Writings*, 1967.

Robinson, Eric & Summerfield, Geoffrey (Eds), *Selected Poems & Prose of John Clare*, Oxford, 1979.

Robinson, Eric & Summerfield, Geoffrey (Eds), *John Clare: The Shepherd's Calendar*, Oxford, 1973.

Taylor, Dennis, *Hardy's Literary Language and Victorian Philology*, Oxford, 1993.

Winchester, Simon, *The Meaning of Everything*, Oxford, 2003.


## MEMOIRS AND LIVES OF CONTEMPORARIES

Anstruther, Ian, *Coventry Patmore's Angel*, 1992.

Allingham, William, *A Diary, 1824-1889*, edited by John Julius Norwich, 1985.

Benzie, William, *Dr. F.J. Furnivall, Victorian Scholar and Adventurer*, Norman, Oklahoma, 1983.

Chedzoy, Alan, *A Scandalous Woman: The Story of Caroline Norton*, 1992.

Hardy, Florence Emily, *The Life of Thomas Hardy, 1840-1928*, 1970.

Millgate, Michael, *Thomas Hardy, A Biography*, 1982.

Palgrave, Gwenllian F., *Francis Turner Palgrave, His Journals and Memories of his Life*, 1899.

Patmore, Derek, *The Life and Times of Coventry Patmore*, 1949.

Thwaite, Ann, *Edmund Gosse: A Literary Landscape*, 1985.

Wilding, Richard, 'Osmond Fisher, Dorset Geologist and Pioneer Geophysicist' in *PDNHAS*, Vol. 110, 1988.

Young, Robert, *Early Years, Recollections of life in Sturminster Newton in the Early Nineteenth Century* (edited by Alan Chedzoy), Dorchester, 2008.

# INDEX

Other titles published by The History Press

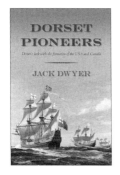

## Dorset Pioneers
JACK DWYER

Jack Dwyer reveals for the first time the intriguing link between a rural English county and the founders of seven US states, four Canadian provinces, a society doyen, an ambassador of the United States, a US Presidential candidate fundraiser and a Christchurch schoolma'am. For all those interested in Dorset and the history of the Americas, this book is a 'must have'.

978 0 7524 5346 0

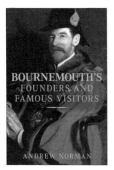

## Bournemouth's Founders and Famous Visitors
ANDREW NORMAN

Bournemouth was known as a health resort long before it became a holiday destination. W.H. Smith was one of the first patrons of the town's National Sanatorium for the treatment of chest diseases, including tuberculosis. From Tregonwell to Tolkien, this book celebrates the town's founders, and also its notable visitors during the last 200 years. Written by established local author Andrew Norman, this new title is ideal for anyone who wants to explore the tale of Bournemouth and its key figures.

978 0 7524 5088 9

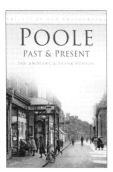

## Poole Past & Present
IAN ANDREWS & FRANK HENSON

This absorbing collection of photographs, containing many rare and unpublished images of Poole, illustrates the changes that have been seen in this picturesque seaside town as it has evolved over the years. Compiled by the authors of two previous books about the town, both long-term residents of Poole who have witnessed many of the changes for themselves, this volume will evoke feelings of nostalgia in all who know and love this area of Dorset.

978 0 7524 5286 9

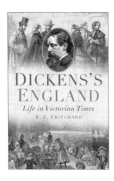

## Dickens's England: Life in Victorian Times
R.E. PRITCHARD

Dickens's England was a time of unprecedented energy and change which laid the foundations of our own modern society. Here, Dickens and his great contemporaries – John Ruskin, Henry Mayhew, Charles Darwin, Thomas Hardy – take us into the heart of what Elizabeth Barrett Browning called 'this live, throbbing age, that brawls, cheats, maddens, calculates, aspires'. This is the perfect book for anyone wanting to understand more about the world of our great novelist Charles Dickens.

978 0 7524 5380 4

Visit our website and discover thousands of other History Press books.

**www.thehistorypress.co.uk**